INFORMATION INDIA: 1993-94

CONCEPTS IN COMMUNICATION INFORMATICS & LIBRARIANSHIP (CICIL)

For a list of titles in this series,
see pp 390-392 at the end of this Book

About the Authors

S.P. Agrawal (*b.* 1929) was Director, National Social Science Documentation Centre, ICSSR, Government of India and Member Secretary, Indian Association of Social Science Institutions. He was also the Vice-Chairman of the Asia and Pacific Information Network in Social Sciences (APINESS). In 1988 he was awarded the degree of Doctor of Philosophy in Education (*Honoris Causa*) by International University Foundation. Presently, he is Member, IFLA Round Table on Research in Reading, International Committee for Social Science Information and Documentation, Board of Studies of National Archives of India and Hindi Advisory Committee, Ministry of Coal, Government of India. He is also Fellow of the Society of Ethnobotanists. Born and brought up in the cradle of freedom movement, which he joined at the tender age of twelve, he gained an insight into political problems and developed a sense of responsibility which bore fruit as an information scientist. He has written extensively on various aspects of Education, Indian Polity and Library and Information Science.

J.C. Aggarwal (*b.* 1928), former Deputy Director of Education/Executive Director of Delhi Bureau of Textbooks, Delhi Administration has a varied experience in the field of education. He has singly/jointly authored about 130 books on Education, Social Sciences and current problems,. In collaboration with S.P. Agrawal, he has written *Documentation Encyclopaedia of UNESCO and Education* (in two parts); *Women's Education in India; National Policy on Education, Agenda for India 2001*; and *Vocational of Education in India*; *Uttar Pradesh: Past, Present and Future; Modern History of Punjab; Modern History of Jammu & Kashmir*, etc.

His other recent publications include: *Year-book of Indian Education, 1991; World Overview; Ramamurti Report 1990 on National Policy on Education in India*; and *Survey of Educational Documents in the World since 1983*, etc.

CONCEPTS IN COMMUNICATION
INFORMATICS & LIBRARIANSHIP-67

GENERAL EDITOR: **S.P. AGRAWAL**

INFORMATION INDIA: 1993-94

Global View

S.P. AGRAWAL
former Member Secretary
Indian Association of Social Science Institutions, and
Director, National Social Science Documentation Centre,
ICSSR, Government of India

J.C. AGGARWAL
former Executive Director
Delhi Bureau of Textbooks, Delhi Administration
NEW DELHI

CONCEPT PUBLISHING COMPANY, NEW DELHI - 110059

ISBN 81-7022-537-X

First Published 1997

S.P. **Agrawal** (*b.* 1929)
J.C. **Aggarwal** (*b.* 1928)

Published and Printed by

Ashok Kumar Mittal

Concept Publishing Company

A/15-16, Commercial Block, Mohan Garden,
New Delhi - 110059 (India)

Phones: 5554042, 5504042

Fax: 091-11-5598898

GENERAL EDITOR'S INTRODUCTION

Information India was first brought out in 1989 under CICIL series which covers a wide range of disciplines—interrelated but at the same time including a very wide stretch of topics for investigation, research and study. It is of great consolation that previous editions of Information India placed in the hands of the discerning readers as also reviewers have been received well. In all humility, we assume that these annuals have fulfilled a long felt need.

The focus of the present volume is on India as it was in 1993. As many as 26 out of the total of 34 chapters, under suitable divisions, are devoted to various aspects of the country. The chapters are, by and large, a combination of descriptive accounts and vital statistics.

Information India is now accompanied by 3D companion volume—*Development/Digression Diary of India*.

S.P. AGRAWAL

PREFACE

In this compilation, it has been endeavoured to give all important facets of not only India but also the world as a whole.

A comparative study of the indicators of development with regard to 186 countries including populous and less populous countries, as also developed, developing and under-developed countries has been included.

Relating to India also, it has been attempted to provide almost all embracing facts and figures with regard to various sectors of development since 1947. A detailed account has been given about important aspects, as well as other topical areas which are of significance in any discussion on India.

As a matter of fact, the book includes a panoramic view of almost everything important that happened in India during the period under review.

It is observed that data collected by various national and international organisations from different sources and also used here, do not necessarily relate to the same year in a few cases.

S.P. AGRAWAL
J.C. AGGARWAL

CONTENTS

Part Two : India 1993-94

WORLD OVERVIEW

1

STATE OF THE NATIONS

1.1 Progress of Nations

United Nations Children's Fund (UNICEF), in its report called *The Progress of Nations* ranks all the world's countries in a series of tables showing progress in such areas as health care, nutrition, education, advances for women, and family planning. In little more than one generation, average real incomes have doubled, child death rates have been halved, malnutrition rates have been reduced by about 30 per cent, and life expectancy has increased by about a third. Since 1960, the proportion of couples using modern contraceptives has risen from less than 10 per cent to more than 50 per cent, and average family size is now falling almost everywhere. Such statistics hide great failures and great disparities, but by any realistic standards the progress made in the last 40 years has been remarkable.

Progress not by GNP Alone

The first table lists all countries according to the proportion of their children who die before reaching the age of five. Because child death rates reflect such things as incomes, education levels, health and family planning services, and the availability of clean water, they are a good measure of overall quality of life. The league table spans a huge range–from five deaths per 1000 births in Sweden to 320 per 1000 in Niger. The most successful nations in each region include Mauritius, Botswana, Sri Lanka, Cuba, Costa Rica, Chile and Colombia.

Richer nations do not always come out on top. Many poorer nations are much closer to meeting the basic needs of all their citizens than others that are considerably wealthier. For example, four of the poorest countries–Vietnam, China, Sri Lanka, and Honduras–have brought child deaths down to between 20 and 60 deaths per 1000 births; many other nations that are two or three times wealthier have far higher rates, including Turkey (91 deaths per 1000 births), Iraq (143), South Africa (72), and Brazil (67).

Family Size

Improvements in human well-being can be brought about very rapidly when there is sustained effort. Twenty nations, for example, have halved their child death rates in the last decade–including some large ones like Egypt and Mexico. Most remarkable is the pace of progress by some nations in promoting family planning. Seventeen nations have halved family size in only one generation. The number of children born to the average woman in Thailand, for example, has dropped from 6.4 to 2.3 since 1960.

Despite this, there is still a large unmet demand for family planning. An estimated 120 million women in the developing world do not want any more children but are not using any effective birth control. If family planning were adequate, then world population in the year 2025 would be about one billion less than is predicted.

Malnutrition

A new table is the world league table of child malnutrition. Despite well-publicized droughts and famines in Africa, malnutrition remains heavily concentrated in the densely populated areas of South Asia. In India and Bangladesh, for example, over 60 per cent of children are significantly underweight, compared with about 30 per cent in sub-Saharan Africa. The starving child misrepresents the problem, visible malnutrition affects only about 1 or 2 per cent of the world's children and is usually the result of exceptional circumstances. The deeper problem is the ordinary, unexceptional malnutrition which is invisible but which nonetheless stunts the mental and physical growth of one-third of the developing world's children.

Comparisons of malnutrition based on children's weight-for-age are often challenged on the grounds that 'some races are smaller than others', but young children in good nutritional health grow to the same pattern whether they live in slums in Bombay or apartments on Fifth Avenue. Conventional wisdom is also challenged by the finding that boys are not generally better nourished than girls. Male and female malnutrition rates are very similar for most countries.

As a result of a lack of iodine in their diet, an estimated six million people suffer from overt cretinism. Every year, another 120,000 infants are born as cretins because their mothers lacked iodine in pregnancy. The deficiency affects the mental and physical development of approximately 50 million school-age children in the developing world. The solution–iodizing all salt supplies–is relatively simple and cheap. Although few figures are available to measure progress, the UNICEF report divides countries with iodine problems into three categories: those doing nothing about it, those with plans to do something, and those with fully operational salt iodizing programmes. In the last category are the world's two most populous nations, India and China, which will both produce enough iodized salt for all their people by 1995.

Immunization

To rank nations according to their progress in health, the UNICEF report uses current immunization rates. In only ten years, the proportion of immunized children in the developing world has grown from under 20 per cent to almost 80 per cent. This achievement now saves an estimated three million young lives and prevents about 400,000 cases of polio each year. Specially, all countries by the percentage of their children who are immunized against measles–one of the most devastating childhood diseases in the developing world. Because measles immunization saves literally millions of lives a year and helps protect children against malnutrition, pneumonia, diarrheal disease and blindness, it is a good barometer of a nation's commitment to the task of bringing the most obvious and basic medical advances to the majority of its population. In total, almost 80 per cent of the world's children are now being vaccinated against measles. But it is again noticeable that several of the poorest developing countries have better records than richer nations. China, India, Egypt, the Philippines, Vietnam, Honduras, and Zimbabwe have all achieved higher immunization coverage than many developing nations with two or three times their income level–and higher than many nations in the industrialized world including France, Japan, and the United States. On the negative side, 19 countries have let immunization rates fall by more than 10 per cent since 1990.

New Goals

Success in the long struggle to reach 80 per cent immunization, a target set at the beginning of the 1980s by the World Health Organization and UNICEF, has led to the adoption of a range of new goals for the year 2000. These include a one-third reduction in child death rates, a halving of child malnutrition, 90 per cent immunization coverage, the eradication of polio, at least four years of schooling for 80 per cent of children, and universal availability of family planning services. These goals were accepted by the majority of the world's political leaders at the World Summit for Children in 1990. A total of 86 countries have since drawn up national plans to meet these targets and have begun putting them into effect with "varying degrees of commitment and vigour."

"The new goals amount to a programme to meet minimum human needs." Protecting children from malnutrition, ill health and illiteracy should be seen as a way of attacking one of poverty's most fundamental causes as well as some of its most distressing symptoms.

School Dropouts

The most difficult challenge, will be the goal of four years' schooling for the vast majority of the developing world's children. Fewer than half the children of South Asia, South America, and sub-Saharan Africa are now completing four years of primary school. The problem is not usually lack of schools. Over 90 per cent of children in the developing world now enrol in primary schools. But about half drop out before reaching grade five.

Progress for Women

Standard for measuring progress for women, is the maternal mortality rate (deaths of women from causes related to pregnancy and childbirth, per 100,000 births). The most striking point is that differences between countries are far greater than for any other measure used in the report. Several African countries, for example, have maternal mortality rates of close to 1000–meaning that a woman faces a one in 100 chance of dying in childbirth and a better than one in 20 chance of dying over the whole of her childbearing years. At the other end of the scale, Ireland has a maternal mortality rate of just two per 100,000 births.

Probably the biggest single contribution towards reducing the estimated 500,000 maternal deaths each year would be to make family planning services universally available. Smaller families and more widely spaced births are also strongly associated with improved health, nutrition, and education for both children and mothers. With all this at stake as well as concern over population growth, "failure to make family planning available to all couples may well come to be regarded as the 20th century's most costly mistake."

Performance Gaps

To compare the progress of nations while making allowance for different economic levels, the level of nutrition, education and child survival that each country could reasonably be expected to have achieved, given its level of economic progress (as measured by GNP per person) is to be calculated. The difference between this expected level and the actual level in each country is called the 'performance gap'

Looked at in this way, the world's outstanding achievers are Sri Lanka and Vietnam. Sri Lanka, with a per capita income of only US $ 500 a year, could be expected to have an under-five mortality rate of 118 per 1000; in fact its rate is only 21 per 1000–giving the country a performance gap of +97. Similarly, Vietnam's GNP of US$ 240 per person should give it an under-five mortality rate of 168 per 1000, whereas its actual level is only 52–a performance gap of + 116, the best in the world. Some countries, are clearly getting more social miles per economic gallon.

Industrialized Countries

Steady progress has been made over the last 20 years, except in the United States and the United Kingdom where children are judged worse off today than they were at the beginning of the 1970s. In the United States, the proportion of children living in poverty is twice as high as in any European country.

Ranking industrialized countries by such indicators as the suicide and murder rates among young people, the murder rate of young people in the United States, for example, is 15.3 per 100,000–seven times higher than in the worst European country. In total, nine out of ten murders of young people in the industrialized world happen in the United States.

Ranking industrialized nations according to how much they give in overseas aid, the league is comfortably headed by the three Scandinavian countries where government aid is well over US$ 200 per person per year. This contrasts with just under US$ 100 per person from the United Kingdom and Germany and less than US$ 50 per person from the United States.

Statistical Weakness

The figures used to measure national progress in all of these areas are inadequate. The figures for child survival, health and nutrition are often out of date or based on extrapolations and trends rather than detailed national surveys. Most nations can and do produce up-to-date quarterly statistics on the health and growth of their economies, "but very few produce even annual statistics on the health and growth of their children."

As a minimum, all nations should produce annual statistics to show what percentage of a nation's children are adequately nourished, or are immunized, or are enrolled in school, or have access to clean water and basic health care.

Aid for Basics

In its overview of progress towards meeting basic human needs, a less than all-out effort is being made to combat malnutrition, disease, and illiteracy. On average, the governments of developing countries have been devoting only about 10 per cent of their annual budgets to nutrition, water supply, primary health care, primary education, and family planning. Similarly, only about 10 per cent of all international aid for development is specifically devoted to these purposes.

A serious attempt to meet the minimum human needs of all has therefore not yet been made. If the task had been given any real priority over recent decades, then it would by now have been largely accomplished, and we would today be living in a world in which mass hunger, malnutrition, and preventable disease were things of the past.

"It is fair to assume, that it would also be a world with less conflict, slower population growth, and more manageable environmental problems."

Source : NGLS, *GO Between,* October 1993, Geneva.

2

UNITED NATIONS ORGANIZATION

2.1 Challenges for the UN

The United Nations, by undertaking a range of problems as wide as the globe itself, must be expected to experience failure as well as to achieve successes. The failures cannot be put to one side; they require continuing commitment. And successes cannot be regarded as permanent; every positive outcome is likely to require further effort.

The United Nations exists to carry out common world commitments. It is an indispensable mechanism for human betterment. But as it serves its Member States, it cannot be expected to protect them from hard decisions.

In this context, seven contradictions must be resolved. If the Member States can deal with these issues, the United Nations can turn towards greater global unity, justice and success. If these contradictions remain unresolved, we can expect to descend into ever-deepening troubles and ultimately, chaos.

Systemic Contradiction in World Affairs

After the Napoleonic Wars, the Congress of Vienna was convened. After World War I the Treaty of Versailles was signed. After Second World War the United Nations Charter was created at San Francisco. That vision was supplanted by the super-power struggle. The cold war bipolar system has now disappeared. No replacement has taken its place. And no world conference can be expected to set such a course at this time.

Thus, at a time of unprecedented global interaction, no new consensus for an international system has yet appeared.

Structural Contradiction

The United Nations is the world Organisation of sovereign States. But the time of fundamental and absolute sovereignty has passed. Commerce, communication and environmental facts transcend State borders and sometime are immune from State control.

In many cases States have voluntarily given aspects of their sovereignty to supra-national bodies or external multilateral groups. And internally, the sovereignty and cohesion of States have been created by ethnic, religious, social,

---

Excerpts from Gabrial Silver Memorial Lecture at Columbia University delivered by Boutros-Ghali, UN Secretary-General.

cultural or linguistic claims.

So the foundation-stone of international order and progress – the State – is being transformed. But no alternative to the State is in sight.

Psychological Contradiction

Modernization has swept away much of local, traditional and communal life. At the same time, impersonal forces of globalization are felt everywhere. This has created an overwhelming sense of insecurity. As a result, tribalism, nationalism, protectionism and fundamentalism increasingly appeal to the alienated individual.

This creates another contradiction. People need something to mediate between themselves and the outside world. But as they search for such support, they often are driven toward groups which look inward and which seek to defy the wider world of change.

Political-Military Contradiction

In the cold war era, every conflict was deemed important. Today, States see little reason for concern unless their own national security is threatened directly. They are deeply reluctant to use military force. They call upon diplomacy to resolve disputes.

But just as strength without diplomacy is self-defeating, diplomacy without strength is fruitless. It is clear that the international community cannot step in to try to solve every crisis. But if it turns its back too often, it will before long face a world of widening conflict and chaos.

Thus the political-military means of achieving security are at present not working in tandem. The world once saw international peace and security as a web of connected concerns. Today, it lacks consensus on what kind of conflict is significant to the maintenance of international peace and security.

Crisis and Contradiction of Development

Although the concept of development implies progress, it is now clear that it is not easy or automatic. While some States have been successful, more have remained stagnant, showing little or no progress at all. Worse stil, war and conflict have pushed many States backward on the path of development.

With the end of the cold war, the failure of centrally planned regions made it clear that market forces would be indispensable to economic prosperity. But the complexity of economic, social, political and environmental factors has not permitted a new consensus on development to arise. Old solutions have been revealed as inadequate, but new approaches have not won full acceptance.

The contradiction of development has several dimensions. A coherent and integrated approach is needed, but the capacity of governments to affect economic events has eroded. At a time when they are most needed, international institutions–the International Monetary Fund, World Bank and the General Agreement of Tariffs and Trade–affect smaller and smaller parts of the global picture. And while a more realistic understanding of the sources of growth has been achieved, the poorest people of the world are increasingly treated with indifference and disdain.

Contradiction in Communication

This is the age of information. Information is available instantly, in vast quantity, to every part of the globe. The sheer volume of material gives the media a crucial role. What they focus on, and what meaning they provide has vast significance to the course of world events.

Today those events are distorted in three ways: geographically, substantively and functionally. Where two conflicts are equally severe, the world learns more of one than the other when the national forces of the major media are involved there. When one upheaval is vastly more severe than a second, the first may be considered more significant if the reporting media feel their culture's interests are more profoundly affected. And political or military events which lend themselves to dramatic images are sure to be reported, while slow-moving changes to vastly greater significance over time, such as economic or social development, get little or no attention at all.

Thus the contradiction between information and knowledge distorts our understanding of world events.

Ways in which these Global Contradictions Affect, and can be Resolved through the United Nations

The United Nations is a world Organization. As such it provides a foundation for the new international system now needed.

The United Nations is the instrument of its Member States. Enlightened multilateralism is the guarantor, not the enemy, of the soverengnty and integrity of States.

As a voice for the poorest nations, the United Nations is critical to the cause of development. We now realise that non-economic factors–peace-building, democratisation, regional integration, human rights, the environment–are indispensable to development. Only the United Nations provides a global network and global forum for addressing these issues in all their complexity.

The United Nations invented peace-keeping to fill a critical need in the cold war years. Today it has begun to create the second generation of peace-keeping. In both quantitative and qualitative terms, comprehensive efforts such as have succeeded in Cambodia, will become increasingly necessary to help States elsewhere survive.

And the United Nations hears and responds to needs for assistance wherever they are felt. The United Nations should not pick and choose between suffering peoples. All deserve and should get equal treatment. For the first time in its history it now can be said that the United Nations is involved in more peace-keeping, development, humanitarian and social activities which do not appear in the press than in those which do.

Overwhelmingly the balance sheet–despite all current difficulties and uncertainties–is positive. The international community has at its disposal, in the form of the United Nations, a priceless instrument for the international cooperation.

. The United Nations Charter possesses a legitimacy, and a universality, which is unique. That legitimacy, and that universality, endow the United Nations with a very special moral authority.

The acts of the United Nations carry the authority of Nations, of the world, acting in concert. Its values are derived, not from the irreducible minimum of

2.2 PRINCIPAL UN ORGANS

INTERNATIONAL COURT OF JUSTICE

GENERAL ASSEMBLY

ECONOMIC AND SOCIAL COUNCIL

SECURITY COUNCIL

SECRETARIAT

* Main and other sessional committees
* Standing Committees and ad hoc bodies
* **UNRWA** United Nations Relief and Works Agency for Palestine Refugees in the Near East
* IAEA International Atomic Energy Agency
* **INSTRAW** International Research and Training Institute for the Advancement of Women
* UNCHS United Nations Centre for Human Settlements (Habitat)
* UNCTAD United Nations Conference on Trade and Development
* UNDP United Nations Development Programme
* UNEP United Nations Environment Programme
* UNFPA United Nations Population Fund
* UNHCR Office of the United Nations High Commissioner for Refugees
* UNICEF United Nations Children's Fund
* UNIFEM United Nations Development Fund for Women
* UNITAR United Nations Institute for Training and Research
* UNU United Nations University

* WFP World Food Programme
* ITC International Trade Centre UNCTAD/GATT

* FUNCTIONAL COMMISSIONS
  Commission for Social Development
  Commission on Human Rights
  Commission on Narcotic Drugs
  Commission on the Status of Women
  Population Commission
  Statistical Commission
* **REGIONAL COMMISSIONS**
  Economic Commission for Africa (ECA)
  Economic Commission for Europe (ECE)
  Economic Commission for Latin America and the Caribbean (ECLAC)
  Economic and Social Commission for Asia and the Pacific (ESCAP)
* **SESSIONAL AND STANDING COMMITTEES**
* **EXPERT, AD HOC AND RELATED BODIES**

* **ILO** International Labour Organisation
* **FAO** Food and Agriculture Organization of the United Nations
* **UNESCO** United Nations Educational, Scientific and Cultural Organization
* WHO World Health Organization
  World Bank Group
* **IBRD** International Bank for Reconstruction and Development (World Bank)
* **IDA** International Development Association
* **IFC** International Finance Corporation
* **IMF** International Monetary Fund
* **ICAO** International Civil Aviation Organization
* **UPU** Universal Postal Union
* **ITU** International Telecommunication Union
* **WMO** World Meteorological Organization
* **IMO** International Maritime Organization
* **WIPO** World Intellectual Property Organization
* **IFAD** International Fund for Agricultural Development
* **UNIDO** United Nations Industrial Development Organization
* **GATT** General Agreement on Tariffs and Trade
* United Nations programmes and organs (representative list only)
* Specialized agencies and other autonomous organzations within the system
* Other commissions, committees and ad hoc and related bodies

* Military Staff Committee
* Standing committees and ad hoc bodies
  Peace-keeping operations
* **UNTSO** United Nations Truce Supervision Organization June 1948 to present
* **UNMOGIP** United Nations Military Observer Group in India and Pakistan January 1949 in present
* **UNFICYP** United Nations Peace-keeping Force in Cyprus March 1964 to present
* **UNDOF** United Nations Disengagement Observer Force June 1974 to present
* **UNIFIL** United Nations Interim Force in Lebanon March 1978 to present
* **UNIKOM** United Nations Iraq-Kuwait Observation Mission April 1991 to present
* **UNAVEM II** United Nations Angola Verification Mission II June 1991 to present
* **ONUSAL** United Nations Observer Mission in El Salvador July 1991 to present
* **MINURSO** United Nations Mission for the Referendum in Western Sahara September 1991 to present
* **UNPROFOR** United Nations Protection Force March 1992 to present
* **UNTAC** United Nations Transitional Authority in Cambodia March 1992 to present
* **UNOSOM** United Nations Operation in Somalia April 1992 to present
* **ONUMOZ** United Nations Operation in Mozambique December 1992 to present

Source : UN Newsletter, August 21, 1993, New York

political consensus in the world, but from the values of our common humanity: the values of peace and security, economic and social equity, and democracy and human rights. Those are the values enshrined in the UN Charter.

The United Nations cannot, and should not, try to do everything. But with the right kind of understanding and support, it can, like Archimedes, move the world in the right direction with a relatively small use of strength.

My message is that the extraordinary opportunities of this moment in history require an extraordinary response. Member States must take on a new responsibility. They should see the United Nations as the projection of their will; not as something separate and apart. The political will and authority which accompany the passage of each United Nations resolution must flow into the implementation stage. The tasks of the world Organization must be seen through to their end. Mandate and missions must be backed by the financial and material means to do the job.

We are approaching the end of a century which has been described as the most bloody and hateful in history. We cannot escape a duty to move beyond this to a greater and more human vision.

Painfully, and with difficulty, the realization is drawning that, for millions of individual human beings across the world, in every country and of every background, the United Nations is more than an instrument of peace and cooperation among Nations: it is the repository of hope for humanity.

Source : UN Newsletter, February 26,1994.

2.3 MEMBERSHIP OF PRINCIPAL UN ORGANS IN 1994

General Assembly

The General Assembly is composed of all 184 United Nations Member States.

Security Council

The Security Council has 15 members. The charter designates five states as permanent members, and the General Assembly elects 10 other members for two-year terms. The term of office for each non-permanent member of the Council ends on 31 December of the year indicated in parentheses below.

The five permanent members of the security council are : China, France, Russian Federation, United Kingdom and United States.

The 10 non-permanent members of the Council in 1994 are : Argentina (1995), Brazil (1994), Czech Republic (1995), Djibouti (1994), New Zealand (1994), Nigeria (1995), Oman (1995), Pakistan (1994), Rwanda (1995) and Spain (1994).

Economic and Social Council

The Economic and Social Council has 54 members, elected for three-year terms by the General Assembly. The term of office for each member expires on 31 December of the year indicated in parentheses below. In 1994, the Council is composed of the following 54 states :

Angola (1994)
Australia (1994)
Bahamas (1995)
Bangladesh (1994)
Belarus (1994)
Belgium (1994)
Benin (1994)
Brazil (1994)
Bulgaria (1996)
Canada (1995)
Chile (1996)
China (1995)
Colombia (1994)
Costa Rica (1996)
Cuba (1995)
Denmark (1995)
Egypt (1996)
Ethiopia (1994)
France (1996)
Gabon (1995)
Germany (1996)
Ghana (1996)
Greece (1996)
India (1994)
Indonesia (1996)
Ireland (1996)
Italy (1994)
Japan (1996)
Kuwait (1994)
Libya (1995)
Magadascar (1994)
Mexico (1995)
Nigeria (1995)
Norway (1995)
Pakistan (1996)
Paraguay (1996)
Philippines (1994)
Poland (1994)
Portugal (1996)
Republic of Korea (1995)
Romania (1995)
Russian Federation (1995)
Senegal (1996)
Sri Lanka (1995)
Surinam (1994)
Switzerland (1994)
Ukraine (1995)
United Kingdom (1995)
United Republic of Tanzania (1996)
United States (1994)
Zimbabwe (1996)
Venezuela (1996)
Zaire (1995)

Trusteeship Council

The Trusteeship Council has five members. One member, the United States, administers Palau, one of the remaining four entities which constituted the original trust territory of the Pacific Islands, the only territory that still remained under the trusteeship system. On 22 December 1990, the Security Council terminated the trusteeship agreement for three of the four entities: The Federated States of Micronesia and the Marshall Islands (now United Nations Member States), which had drawn up compacts of free association with the United States, and the Northern Mariana Islands, which had agreed to a commonwealth convenant with the administering authority. Palau recently held a plebiscite to determine the nature of its future status with the administering authority. It remains a trust territory until the trusteeship agreement is terminated by the Security Council.

The non-administering members of the Trusteeship Council are the other four permanent members of the security council (China, France, Russian Federation, United Kingdom).

International Court of Justice

The International Court of Justice has 15 members, elected by both the General Assembly and the Security Council. Judges hold nine-year terms, which end on 5 February of the year indicated in parentheses below.

As of 6 February 1994, the compositon of the 15-member court will be as follows:

Roberto Ago, of Italy (1997) Andres Aguilar Mawdsley, of Venezuela (2000) Mohammed Bedjaoui, of Algeria (1997) Carl-August Fleischhauer, of Germany (2003) Gilbert Guillaume, of France (2000) Geza Herczegh, of Hungary (2003) Sir Robert Yewdall Jennings, of the United kingdom (2000) Abdul G. Koroma, of Sierra Leone (2003) Shigeru Oda, of Japan (2003) Raymond Ranjeva, of Madagascar (2000) Stephen M. Schwebel, of the United States (1997) Mohammed Shahabuddeen, of Guyana (1997) Jiuyong Shi, of China (2003) Nikolai K. Tarassov, of the Russian Federation (1997) and Christopher G. Weeramantry, of Sri Lanka (2000).

Source : UN Newsletter, January 8, 1994.

2.4 UNITED NATIONS EDUCATIONAL, SCIENTIFIC AND CULTURAL ORGANIZATION (UNESCO)

2.4.1 Programmes and Priorities

When the founding fathers of the United Nations Educational Scientific and Cultural Organization met in 1945, the world was recovering from two devastating wars. The old order lay in ruins, with many of its economic and political institutions shattered or in disarray. From these ashes arose the so-called Cold War era, characterized by ideological tension, the arms race and the fear of nuclear annihilation. Despite the darkness and destruction around them, the founding fathers who met in London had a vision of the dawn: they believed that conflicts could be prevented through the spread of knowledge and through international cooperation. This would be UNESCO's special mission.

'Since wars begin in the minds of men,' they wrote in UNESCO's Constitution, 'it is in the minds of men that the defences of peace must be constructed.' The organization had been set up, they went on to say, 'for the purpose of advancing, through the educational and scientific and cultural relations of the peoples of the world, the objectives of international peace and the common welfare of mankind for which the United Nations was established and which its Charter proclaims'.

In the more than four decades separating the postwar era from outs, these words have informed the work and ideals of the Organization in each of its chosen fields of competence: education, science, culture, communication.

The International Context

Today UNESCO is 47 years old, an age when institution–like individuals–must either respond with enthusiasm and resourcefulness to the challenges of the day or risk being pushed to the sidelines as something old and irrelevant. The world of the 1990s is subject to changes more powerful and rapid than at any time in recorded history. It bears little resemblance to the postwar era and little even to the recent past when the global order seemed defined in ideological terms of 'developed versus underdeveloped' or 'planned versus market' economies.

As of January 1993, UNESCO's membership stood at 170, an increase of fourteen countries in only four years, with more applications to come. This is the result of a shifting political environment in which popular aspirations have redefined the nation state, totalitarianism is in retreat, and the East-West conflict is no longer the predominant feature of the political landscape. There is a world-wide move towards such common values as respect for human rights and pluralist democracy as well as recognition of the need for ensuring a more equitable distribution of the fruits of economic progress and of the important role that private initiatives can play.

At the same time, population pressures have created enormous strains on both the physical and the social environment, so that existing institutions—especially in the poorer countries—are unable to meet demands for food, basic health care and education, housing, transportation or employment. Today's population of 5.3 billion could grow to 12 billion by the next century. Although a transition from high birth rates to low ones will not in itself promote development, it is equally true that without such a move, sustainable development and the alleviation of poverty are unlikely to be achieved.

Inseparable from population pressures and poverty is the question of environmental degradation. For the first time the world community of scientists and economists is trying to address systematically the impact of human activities on the planet's natural systems. Unchecked population growth, increasing poverty and uncontrolled development may lead us to destroy our own resource base. The life-styles of industrial societies, the clearing of forests to provide more firewood, timber and agricultural land, the burning of coal and other fossil fuels that contribute to the so-called 'green-house effect' and are destroying the ozone layer–all are implicated.

The United Nations Conference on Environment and Development (UNCED) that met in Brazil in June 1992, looked at the relationship between environmental degradation, poverty and development and has highlighted the extent of our global interdependence in terms of cause and effect on both economic and environmental policies. Climate change, conservation of marine and land resources, ozone depletion, deforestation, desertification, natural disasters and loss of biodiversity: it is clear that major reforms and international co-operation are crucial if we are to cope with these planetary issues and threats during the 1990s.

In the past there was a tendency to believe that development, like progress, was a linear process, and that the solution to the planet's ills and imbalances was a relatively simple matter of transferring capital or technology from one place to another. Now, however, we have come to appreciate that even if the right social, economic, political and especially cultural conditions are all present, the mix may not be adequate to sustain development. The mere acquisition of technology, for instance, without an understanding of its nature and purpose, is of little value; to be useful in a new context, it must be nurtured and maintained. That is why UNESCO places such a premium on knowledge, appropriate training and cultural awareness as the necessary paths to human development.

In his 'Agenda for Peace', the United Nations Secretary-General Butros Butros Ghali has emphasized the importance of 'peace-building' as the best investment in the future. By taking preventive measures now – to curb population growth, to overcome poverty and ignorance, to encourage sustainable development, to give access to, and to share, knowledge–we may avoid the much heavier costs incurred for 'peace-keeping' later. Nonetheless, building a better future is a long-term proposition: we must think and act boldly, yet with great patience, if we are to change the way people think.

New Opportunities

Times of trouble are also times of opportunity, however. UNESCO–with its special mandate that embraces all countries and all domains of knowledge–is in a unique position to foster new forms of international cooperation and commitment in facing these common challenges. Rich and poor alike must see that survival is a common interest requiring new solidarities and partnerships. We must learn to care, and to share, so that together we can find ways to make growth compatible with preservation of the environment.

UNESCO's mission is cultural and educational–to promote research and training; to assist in establishing and operating institutions dedicated to education, research and cultural development; to help countries to formulate national policies that will achieve these goals; to stimulate debate on important topics; to strengthen institutional capacity for research and training so that countries and regions can find their own paths to self-sufficiency rather than depend on imported expertise; to foster intercultural dialogue and cross-cultural understanding; to set international standards; to provide linkages and networking facilities that enhance the work of both individuals and institutions through resource-sharing and community partnerships.

UNESCO is not a funding agency. Its internal budget–based on dues and contributions from member countries–is about $ 222 million annually, less than that of a medium-sized university in an industrialized country. Given the scope of UNESCO's programmes, the numbers of projects deserving support, and the urgency of the need in so many corners of the developing world, this money is literally a drop in the ocean. What can be done and what is being done?

Less Means More

One answer is to set goals, to fix priorities and to stick by them. UNESCO has defined a limited set of priorities, and it has greatly reduced the scope and numbers of programmes and activities being undertaken.

The consolidation effort is house-wide, demanding new efficiency in administrative procedures as well as concentration and coherence in how activities are carried out. For example, in 1992-93, three groups have been targeted specifically as high priority beneficiaries of UNESCO's action: the least-developed countries of the world, African Member States, and women. In education, the natural and social sciences, culture and communication, UNESCO's sights are fixed primarily on these three groups.

At the same time, having systematically reduced the number of activities within each major programme area, UNESCO has also sought to broaden its approach to problem-solving. Multidisciplinary consultation and teamwork are encouraged: the different disciplinary 'sectors' of UNESCO pool resources and work together to design and implement their projects–whether for incorporating environmental education into school and university curricula, for giving women more control over decisions affecting their lives and well-being, or for strengthening institutions likely to promote the free flow of information and a more democratic exchange of ideas and experience. UNESCO strives for an integrated approach that cuts across disciplinary lines.

Building on Our Strengths: More and Better Partnerships

An an organization having a global reach and a multi-disciplinary mandate,

UNESCO enjoys a privileged position within the intellectual community. It has a long and rich experience in building institutional capacity and in developing networks to link individuals and institutions across the five continents. It can mobilize governments, agencies and centres of learning on behalf of development goals. And it can marshall the talents of outstanding individuals to serve humanity.

UNESCO's current programmes, as outlined here, show to what extent these existing linkages are providing the key to renewal and reform. Since the new directions result from the recommendations of UNESCO's own constituencies–Member States, inter-governmental bodies, international non-governmental organizations, regional representatives and field offices, Secretariat personnel, United Nations sister organizations, funding agencies and associated groups in the world intellectual and scientific communities–they are receiving broad support.

These partnerships will make greater demands on recipient institutions and countries. The decentralization of UNESCO's own operations will enhance the role of Member States' National Commissions and field units in carrying out research and implementing the programmes they themselves have said were important. At the same time, changing approaches to multilateral cooperation will lead national governments increasingly to call on UNESCO's advisory services for such 'upstream' assistance as sectoral surveys and project identification and evaluation.

UNESCO's forty-six field offices serve as conduits between the Secretariat in Paris, national authorities and the intellectual community. They seek active partnerships with United Nation's sister organizations and they are instrumental in advising countries on project design and fund-raising opportunities, while feeding back information to Headquarters on Member States' needs and aspirations. Through its field units the Organization can be more responsive and more efficient in fulfilling its mandate.

Fortunately, the funds available for development projects have increased in recent years as have the number of agencies and foundations involved in such support. UNESCO is exploring every avenue of cooperation, public and private. These initiatives have already borne fruit: they are expected to attract some $250 million in extra-budgetary funds for the 1992-93 biennium, compared with $230 million for 1990-91 and only $200 million for 1988-89.

The Programme Highlights

UNESCO's activities are divided into seven so-called 'major programme areas' which are themselves broken down into sub-sections.

There major programme area are, as follows : *(i) Education:* a commitment to improving access to basic education, especially for girls and women and in rural areas, as well as to the eradication of illiteracy; help in adapting educational systems to the demands of the 21st century by encouraging innovation and renewal in curriculum design, teaching methods and the formulation of educational policy, with particular emphasis on higher education; *(ii) Science :* Priority is given to environmental concerns and to understanding the relationship between environmental sciences and the management of natural resources; also important are the upgrading of university education and the promotion of research in basic and engineering sciences; (iii) *Culture:* emphasis on the cultural dimensions of development and on intercultural dialogue as a prerequisite for peace-building; special attention to protection of the cultural, physical and natural heritage; *(iv) Communication:* Strengthening the free flow of ideas by word and image and improving communication capacity in the developing countries; a greater role for women through improved training and access; *(v) Social Sciences and Development:* Improved training and research through networking, especially in the least-developed countries; strategies for integrating cultural and environmental factors into development and for coping with major social changes; population education and communication; a focus on philosophical and ethical issues related to science, technology and development; *(vi) Peace and human rights:* Priority to the preparation of teaching materials and conferences that foster international understanding, tolerance, and the consolidation of democratic process *(vii)* In addition to these programme areas, the UNESCO has also activities related to information services, libraries, archives, documentation systems and publications. Some of these activities provide support for UNESCO programmes in education, science, culture, communication, social sciences, peace and human rights.

(*Source: UNESCO: Programmes and Priorities,* 1992-93)

2.4.2 *Conventions, Agreements and Protocols Adopted by UNESCO General Conference since 1948*

TABLE 2.1: *Convention, Agreements and Protocols Adopted by UNESCO General Conference since 1948*

Name and Purpose	Date of Adoption	Number of States Parties
1	2	3
Agreement for Facilitating the International Circulation of **Visual and Auditory Materials of an Educational, Scientific and Cultural Character** (Beirut Agreement). (*Exempts this type of material from customs duties when it is imported into those states that have ratified the agreement, and ensures that it receives the same advantages as nationally produced material).*	10 December 1948	31
Agreement on the **Importation of Educational, Scientific and Cultural Materials,** with Protocol annexed. (*Has the same aims as the preceding agreement, but in this case for written works, and artworks of an educational, scientific and cultural nature).*	17 June 1950	84

(Contd.)

1	2	3
Universal **Copyright** Convention, with three Protocol annexed. (*Seeks to clearly define relations between States Parties to the Berne Convention on Copyright (1886), the Latin-American conventions, and those states who are not party to any of the established conventions in this domain*).	6 September 1952	92
Convention for the **Protection of Cultural Property in the Event of Armed Conflict,** with Protocol (The Hague Convention). *(The Contracting parties undertake in times of war to safeguard cultural property whether it be on their own territory of that of their adversary).*	14 May 1954	84
Convention concerning the **International Exchange of Publications.** *(Establishes a basis for the exchange of governmental and non-governmental publications such as books, and periodicals).*	3 December 1958	46
Convention concerning the **Exchange of Official Publications and Government Documents between States.** *(Idem for official journals and parliamentary annals).*	3 December 1958	50
Convention against **Discrimination in Education,** with a Protocol instituting a Conciliation and Good Offices Commission to be responsible for seeking the settlement of any disputes which may arise between States Parties to this Convention. *(Favorizes the adoption of measures to promote equal opportunities in this domain – between boys and girls, for example, or minority groups).*	14 December 1960	84
International Convention for the Protection of **Performers, Producers of Phonograms and Broadcasting Organizations** (The Rome Convention). *(Prompted by the arrival of records and radio, this convention sets out the rules to defend the rights of artists and performers as well as record producers and radio networks).*	26 October 1961	30

(Contd.)

1	2	3
Convention on the Means of Prohibiting and Preventing **the Illicit Import, Export and Transfer of Ownership of Cultural Property.** *(States parties undertake to regulate the transfer of ownership, and the import and export of cultural goods, and to recover and return stolen or illegally imported cultural property).*	14 November 1970	81
Convention on **Wetlands** of International Importance especially as **Waterfowl Habitat,** with Protocol. *(Promotes the rational exploitation of wetlands and protects waterfowl habitats).*	2 February 1971	80
Universal **Copyright** Convention as revised at Paris on 24 July 1971, with two annexed Protocols. *(Sets down a preferential copyright regime for developing countries).*	24 July 1971	57
Convention for the **Protection of Phonograms** against Unauthorized duplication of their Phonograms. *(Completes the Rome Convention for those states who have not joined this latter, to allow them to act against the illegal reproduction of records).*	29 October 1971	51
Convention concerning the **Protection of the World Cultural and Natural Heritage.** *(This convention requires each State Party to protect cultural and natural heritage of outstanding universal value located on its territory, and to help other states do the same).*	16 November 1972	137
Convention relating to the Distribution of **Programme-carrying Signals Transmitted by Satellite.** *(To prevent the pirating of radio programmes relayed by satellite).*	21 May 1974	18
Regional Convention on the **Recognition of Studies, Diplomas and Degrees in Higher Education in Latin America and the Caribbean.** *(Allows for the recognition, by a state in this region, of diplomas acquired in the other state there).*	19 July 1974	*16

(Contd.)

1	2	3
International Convention on the recognition of Studies, Diplomas and Degrees in Higher Education in the **Arab and European States bordering on the Mediterranean.** *(Idem).*	17 December 1976	*10
Idem for the **Arab States.**	22 December 1978	*14
Multilateral Convention for the Avoidance of **Double Taxation of Copyright Royalties,** and additional Protocol. *(Aims to prevent double taxation on royalties arising in one State party when their beneficiaries are resident in another State party).*	13 December 1979	6
Convention on the Recognition of Studies, Diplomas and Degrees concerning Higher Education in the **States belonging to the Europe Region.** *(The same as for the other regional conventions mentioned above).*	21 December 1979	*37
Regional Convention on the Recognition of Studies, Certificates, Diplomas, Degrees and other Academic Qualifications in Higher Eduation in the **African States.** *(As mentioned above).*	5 December 1981	*15
Idem for **Asia and the Pacific.**	16 December 1983	12
Convention on **Technical and Vocational Education.** *(Formulates directives to help states draw up programmes for this type of education).*	10 November 1989	8

* *These conventions concern specific regions only and as such have a limited number of States parties*

ADMITTING, BUT OFTEN ... NON-COMMITTING

Many countries vote in favour of a convention, but then fail to ratify it. French legal expert Pierre-Michel Eisemann explains why "this should not be viewed as bad faith or machiavellism".

Whether they are called "Declaration" or "Charter" the 33 Recommendations adopted by UNESCO's General Conference are alike in that, while they prescribe international standards or norms, they are not binding on Member States.

These rulings are not pointless, however, since each country is obliged by UNESCO's Constitution to submit them to its relevant bodies within a year or their adoption, and it is not rare that they influence national legislation.

On the other hand, the 21 Conventions adopted by UNESCO, or of which UNESCO is depositary, and their 11 Protocols may be legally binding, provided a State agrees to become a Party thereto.

Unlike a Recommendation, the legal nature of a Convention may persuade countries to obey it.

But strictly speaking, a country can do what it likes, since the international community does not have the means to draft the equivalent of national laws which, once voted by a parliament, become mandatory for all.

The simple adoption of a convention by UNESCO'S General Conference does not as such create an obligation. Out of respect for sovereignty, no country is held to a UNESCO-adopted convention, unless it expressly agrees to be.

Giving Consent

This consent is given in different ways sometimes through ratification by the Head of State, sometimes by approval or acceptance of a government. Each country has its own rules governing, notably, those instances which require parliamentary approval.

But, under no circumstances can a state which has not clearly manifested its intention of becoming a party to a convention, be held legally obligated by its terms. And, in any case, a convention can only take effect after a certain number of ratifications, approvals or acceptances have been received.

Except for the Multilateral Convention for the Avoidance of Double Txation on Copyright Royalties (1979), all UNESCO conventions have entered into force, although they bind a widely-varying number of countries. With the exception of the six regional conventions on the Recognition of Studies, Diplomas and Degrees in Higher Education, whose application is geographically limited, none of the other conventions open to UNESCO Member States (or other "guest" countries) has attracted all the nations entitled to adhere.

The Convention concerning the Protection of the World Cultural and Natural Heritage (1972) has the best score with 137 ratifications while, at the bottom of the list, the Convention of Technical and Vocational Education (1989) has only eight. The other instruments fall somewhere in between with an average 50 states parties each.

It may seem strange that a convention, on the day it is adopted, gets the required two-thirds vote at UNESCO's General Conference, but that then less than a third of Member States agree to become parties. This situation is, however, paradoxical only in appearance.

When a country votes at the General Congerence, it knows that the act is not a legal commitment to the convention. It can thus vote in favour of a convention while, at the same time, being totally opposed to its ratification.

This should not be viewed as bad faith or machiavellism. A state may simply be registering lack of objection to a convention which, after adoption, can be ratified by those states which so desire. In other words, a country may not want to commit itself but can agree to allow other states to do so.

In addition, a country may not choose to take an official postiion until after a comvention is adopted. National authorities may first consult several ministries and undertake a thorough examination of the consequences of adherence, weighing all of the contingent rights and obligations, before taking a decision.

In some cases, a state may not ratify because it sees no interest in the object of the convention. Others will object that the obligations are too heavy or compoiçated, or too difficult to put into effect.

The fact is that, although we are often tempted to believe the country, states attach great importance to their obligations under a convention and avoid becoming a party without due consideration.

Back Burner

On the other hand, it can also be said that many states which do not adhere to an international convention have not done so as a result of a long and carefully-weighed decision. In many cases, the choice of whether to ratify an instrument may simply be placed on a back burner by an overworked national administration and then "forgotten". In this case, the non-participation of a country reflects only a relative lack of interest, not rejection of the standards the convention seeks to set.

Since each state decides for itself, it is normal that even when multiateral covention have a universal dimension, the number of ratifications varies from one instrumentto another.

The broadest possible adherence to a convention is of course desirable, but this is not the only criterion of its practical importance.

Indeed, the very function of a convention is to present an ensemble of international standards and norms.

When these are written down, they can have an influence onthe behaviour of states, and guide even those countries which, for one reason or another, have not agreed to ratify the convention setting down these norms.

Source : UNESCO Sources No. 56, March 1994.

PROTECTING HUMANITY FROM ITSELF

The Human genome has the Potential to Change Humanity. Such a Vast and Perhaps Dangerous Field cannot be left Unchecked.

Should science be used for good or for evil, for human progress or for barbarity? Never before in human history has this dilemma been so acute.

We already know the huge potential of research into human genes, even if we don't yet have the details. The benefits to humanity could be countless. But it could also lead to amazing and very disturbing things like cloning–creating identical human beings.

These worries have sparked off a debate, mainly in Western countries, on what has become known as "bio-ethics". A number of national or even regional bodies have been set up to look at the questions posed, but UNESCO is the first international organisation to have set up truly international committee on the issue. It is chaired by Noelle Lenoir, a member of France's Constitutional Council, and includes well-known scientist, philosophers, jurists, sociologists and politicians.

The last UNESCO General Conference (1993) mandated this committee to prepare "*an international instrument on the protection of the human genome*". Texts of relevant international and national laws are already being compiled and studied, along with leval precedents and rulings, with the help of UN bodies, especially the World Health Organization.

A Wide Open Field

As yet there is no international document that really deals with the question. The nearest thing is a very general statement made last March by the UN Human Rights Commission, which stresses the need for international cooperation to ensure all human-kind benefits from the life sciences and to prevent any use of them for other than the gooa of humanlty.

Neither are there many regulation yet. Where they do exist, it is on a country by country basis. They are also widely different from one situation to the next. In Germany, for example, research is forbidden on human embryos except for therapeutic reasons, whilst the United Kingdom allows all research up until 14 days.

The legal void is worrying in view of the very dramatic research going on. As the UNESCO committee noted at its first meeting last September "*genetic research has implications for all aspects of people's lives*". Ethics, said the French writer Albert Camus, is "*introducing a bit of order into a chaotic world.*" And without laws, there is only anarchy or tyranny. How, for example, can details of a person's genetic make-up be kept confidential? And how can we prevent people being refused a job or insurance because they have a possible genetic predisposition to a disease?

Why are we thinking about a convention on human genetics and ignoring other aspects of bio-ethics? Well, too broad a convention could prove unwieldy. And then, genetic engineering has earthshaking ethical implications–it can change an emtire person. The memory of Nazi horrors still lingers to keep us on our guard. So the most crucial issues in bio-ethics will concern the human genome.

Drafting an international agreement on such a sensitive matter is very tricky. One possible solution would be a declaration by UNESCO or the UN General Assembly which would establish the basic principles, centred on respect for human rights and human dignity. But a declaration without a convention attached, means there would be no obligation to respect it.

The problems and pitfalls are huge. Enunciation of the broad principles must for example, take account of different cultures and traditions. What is acceptable in one country is out of the question in an other. Thus the scientific problem has heavy cultural, philosophical, political, religious and economic overtones.

A draft convention may clash with powerful commercial interests, since genetic treatment of diseases and genetic therapy represent an enormous new field of development worth tens of billions of dollars annually. We may fall into quarrels like the dispute over tariffs among members of GATT (General Agreement on Tariffs and Trade). Scientists who are already worry of talk about regulations, might also rebel against what they see as restrictions on their research.

Solid Foundations Needed

But can we really stand idly by, in the name of free research and free enterprise, in a field which is going to be so crucial for the future of all humanity?

A solid foundation of general principles seems especially important because laws on bio-ethics face a new and dramatic version of an old problems: even as they are being drawn up and passed, they may be already made irrelevant because of increasingly rapid scientific progress. This is very serious and has no real solution.

Perhaps a new balance should be sought between a convention's basic principles and the scientific restraints it seeks to impose. So when something new comes up not covered by the convention, the general principles could at least ensure such things as respect for human rights and human dignity as well as banning discrimination.

Whatever is finally decided, we should remember we are at the dawn of an astounding era whose implications are almost beyond imagination and which is likely to change both human beings and humanity.

Source : UNESCO Sources, No. 56, March 1994.

3

GENERAL AGREEMENT ON TARIFFS AND TRADE (GATT), 1994

3.1 Overview

At a ministerial conference in Marrakesh in Mid-April the final document on the eighth nogitiating round of GATT is due to be signed, which took 117 states more than seven years to be bargained out. It is planned to set up a new "World Trade Organization" (WTO) in 1995. This will end a provisional arrangment that since the Second World War has been the foundation for unanticipated dynamic development of world trade. With its liberal principles the system withstood all attempts to set up a "New World Economic Order" and in recent years, in line with changed development policy models has been enormously attractive to developing countries.

The question as to how the Ministerial Conference in Marrakesh will influence the future development of international economic relations has to be considered under three aspects against the background of past development of the international trading system.

— Will the system of international trade be more effective than hitherto in pursuing and asserting its liberal principles?
— Does the world trade system after Marrakesh correspond better than up to now to the changed world economic framework conditions?
— How far does the outcome of the GATT round concluded in December 1993 correspond to the interests of the developing countries?

Aims of GATT

The main aims of the agreement were to raise living standards, realize full employment, fully developing the world's resources and increasing production. Developing of the countries of the Third World, which was still mentioned in the charter for setting up the ITO, is not explicitly mentioned in the aims set out in the GATT treaty.

The General Agreement on Tariffs and Trade is to achieve its aims by securing a liberal world trade order by reducing and preventing protection in the international exchange of goods. In so doing it draws in the final analysis on the "classic" foreign trade theory according to which under certain assumptions nationally and internationally open markets lead to the production of individual goods in those places and in such a way that a maximum of production and therefore prosperity is achieved.

There is consensus that the prerequisites of the classic foreign trade theory-total competition on the national markets for production factors and goods, immobility of the production factors in the international sector-do not exist in reality. Liberal trade policy as reflected in GATT is based on the premise that open international markets, even under real conditions, still come closest to the optimal situation.

In line with the liberal basic philosophy, the most favoured-nation principle, non-discrimination, multilateralism and reciprocity are the decisive fundamentals of GATT.

GATT Trade Rounds and Developing Countries

Article XXVIII of GATT calls on the contracting parties regularly to hold negotiating rounds aimed essentially at reducing trade barriers.

The first rounds essentially limited themselves, in addition to successively expanding the GATT membership, to the classic themes of trade policy and reducing trade barriers. The fifth round (1961/62) was the first one to give wider consideration to the trading problems of the developing countries, although only in the traditional framework of tariff negotiations. The outcome of the liberalization negotiations-less than one per cent cut in tariffs on average—was meagre. It appeared that the rock bottom of protection regarded as indispensable had already been reached.

The sixth negotiating round—the Kennedy Round (1964/1967)—tried to take account of the trade demands of the developing countries articulated within the UNCTAD framework but stayed largely with the traditional negitiating themes. Most central demands of the developing countries—removal of trade barriers for tropical products and raw materials—failed, resisted mainly by the European Community.

The problems of the increasingly obstructive non-tariff barriers and monetary distortions remained unsolved.

Only the seventh negotiating round—the Tokyo Round (1973/1979)—was the one to take account of the changed role of the developing countries in world trade and the importance of non-tariff measures on the proliferating "new protectionism", essentially directed also against the new competitors in the Third World. The GATT protection system was to be worked over, agricultural and tropical products became special negotiating issues.

International Trade Policy

The eighth round—the Uruguay Round which ended in December 1993 was begun by the ministerial declaration of Punta del Este in September 1986 after long and controversial preliminaries. As in no previous round, the developing countries got involved already in the preliminary phase. This reflected their changed weight in world trade and within GATT, it reflected their new development concepts and their new interest in creating open markets.

The workload of the new GATT round was greater than that of any previous one. The 14 working groups dealt not only with traditional approaches of market opening by reducing tariffs and quantitative trade restrictions. The special agreements negotiated in the Tokyo Round were to be worked over, central elements of GATT such as the entire system of arbitration and protective clauses, anti-dumping regulations and export subsidies were to be newly negotiated. The Uruguay Round was to make the difficult sector—which had never been formally taken out of GATT—and the world trade with textiles and garments, which had been regulated since the early 60s in comprehensive quota agreements, most recently in the Multi Fibre Agreement. At the same time there were to be negotiations expanding GATT jurisdiction to three new sectors: Trade Related Intellectual Properties (TRIPs), Trade Related Investment Measures (TRIMs), and a General Agreement on Trade in Services (GATS).

The many individual issues were tied together as a package, which was also new it was to be negotiated and decided only as a whole. The aim of this procedure was to make it easier to balance out interests which differed widely and in part were very one-sided.

The preliminary negotiations to the Uruguay Round contained many and sometimes acrimonious controversies but on the whole one cannot speak of a North-South confrontation. In contrast to the criticism of the programme and interim results of the negotiations expressed particularly by NGO groups engaged in development policy during the negotiations and after their conclusion, the trade policy interests of the developing countries proved very varied. This also applies to the later courses of the real negotiations in sectors that initially remained controversial, such as TRIMs, TRIPs and GATS.

Especially the inclusion of services remained controversial in the preliminary negotiations, the developing countries fearing that because of their competitive weaknesses in the services sector they would be swamped by the vastly more powerful suppliers of services from industrial countries-banks, insurance companies, transport—if markets were opened. Hence they resisted a working programmes in which a link had been established between liberalization of trade in goods and trade in services. A diplomatic device—formally separate negotiations under a joint roof—solved the conflict and thereby enabled the Uruguay Round to start.

The long drawn out and crisis-shaken course of the negotiations is known. Already the ministerial conference in montreal in December 1988 which was to have not only drawn up an interim balance but also reap an "early harvest" gave no indication that the conflicts which had become visible in the preliminaries were soluble. In four sectors compromise formulas could only be found after months of additional talks. The ministerial conference in Brussels in December 1990, intended to be the final one, turned into a disaster.

It was not until 15 December 1993 that the negotiations could be concluded.

On the table was a 700-page document which, after the necessary ratifications, is to be signed in mid-April 1994 by the responsible ministers at a conference in Marrakesh in Morocco. At the moment it looks like the GATT agreement can go into force in 1995.

(*Source*: Benno Engeles, D+C 2/94)

3.2 THE FINAL ACT OF THE URUGUAY ROUND: A SUMMARY

The Final Act Embodying the Results of the Uruguay Round of Multilateral Trade Negotiations is 550 pages long and contains legal texts which spell out the results of the negotiations since the Round was launched in Punta del Este, Uruguay, in September 1986. In addition to the texts of the agreements, the Final Act also contains texts of Ministerial Decisions and Declarations which further clarify certain provisions of some of the agreements.

The following summarises all the components of the Final act. These summaries are intended to provide an informal guide to the agreements and have no legal status.

The Final Act covers all the negotiating areas cited in the Punta del Este Declaration with two important exceptions. The first is the results of the "market access negotiations" in which individual countries have made binding commitments to reduce or eliminate specific tariffs and non-tariff barriers to merchandise trade. These concessions are to be recorded in national schedules which will form an integral part of the Final Act. The second is the "initial commitments" on liberalization of trade in services. These commitments on liberalization are also to be recorded in national schedules.

Agreement Establishing the World Trade Organization

The agreement establishing the World Trade Organization (WTO) envisages a single institutional framework encompassing the GATT, as modified by the Uruguay Round, all agreements and arrangements concluded under its auspeces and the complete results of the Uruguay Round. Its structure will be headed by a Ministerial Conference meeting at least once every two years. A General Council will be established to oversee the operation of the agreement and ministerial decisions on a regular basis. This General Council will itself act as a Dispute Settlement Body and a Trade Policy Review Mechanism, which will concern themselves with the full range of trade issues covered by the WTO, and will also establish subsidiary bodies such as a Goods Council, a Services Council and a TRIPs Council. The WTO framework will ensure a "single undertaking approach" to the results of the Uruguay Round—thus, membership in the WTO will entail accepting all the results of the Round without exception.

General Agreement on Tariffs and Trade, 1994

Text on the interpretation of the following GATT Articles are included in the Final Act.

Understanding on the Interpretation of Article XII (State-trading Enterprises). Agreement increasing surveillance of their activities through stronger notification and review procedure.

Understanding on the Interpretation of Article II: 1(b) (Schedules of Concessions). Agreement to record in national schedules "other duties or charges" levied in addition to the recorded tariff and to bind them at the levels prevailing at the date established in the Uruguay Round Protocol.

Understanding on the Interpretation of Balance-of-Payments Provisions. Agreement that contracting parties imposing restrictions for balance-of-payments purposes should do so in the least trade-disruptive manner and should favour price-based measures, like import surcharges and import deposits, rather than quantitative restrictions. Agreement also on procedures for consultations by the GATT Balance-of-Payments Committee as well as for notification of BOP measures.

Understanding on the Interpretation of Article XXIV (Customs Unions and Free-Trade Areas). Agreement clarifying and reinforcing the criteria and procedures for the review of new or enlarged customs unions or free-trade areas and for the evaluation of their effects on third parties. The agreement also clarifies the procedure to be followed for achieving any necessary compensatory adjustment in the event of contracting parties forming a customs union seeking to increase a bound tariff. The obligations of contracting parties in regard to measures taken by regional or local governments or authorities within their territories are also clarified.

Understanding on the Interpretation of Article XXV (Waivers). Agreement of new procedures for the granting of waivers from GATT disciplines, to specify termination dates for any waivers to be granted in the future, and to fix expiry dates for existing waivers. The main provisions concerning the granting of waivers are, however, contained in the Agreement on the WTO.

Understanding on the Interpretation of Article XXVIII (Modification of GATT Schedules). Agreement on new procedures for the negotiation of compensation when tariff bindings are modified or withdrawn, including the creation of a new negotiating right for the country for which the product in question accounts for the highest proportion of its exports. This is intended to increase the ability of smaller and developing countries to participate in negotiations.

Understanding on the Interpretation of Article XXXV (Non-application of the General Agreement). Agreement to allow a contracting party or a newly acceding country to invoke Gatt's non-application provisions vis-a-vis the other party after having entered into tariff negotiations with each other. The WTO Agreement foresees that any invocation of the non-application provisions under that Agreement must extend to all the multilateral agreements.

Uruguay Round Protocol GATT, 1994

The results of the market access negotiations in which participants have made commitments to eliminate or reduce tariff rates and non-tariff measures applicable to trade in goods will be recorded in national schedules of concessions which will be annexed to the Uruguay Round Protocol that forms an integral part of the Final Act.

The Protocol has five appendices: Appendix I Section A: Agricultural Products—Tariff concessions on a Most-Favoured Nation basis, Section B: Agricultural Products—Tariff Quotas; Appendix II: Tariff Concessions on a Most-Favoured Nation Basis on Other Products; Appendix III: Preferential Tariff—Part II of Schedules (if applicable); Appendix IV: Concessions on Non-Tariff Measures-Part III of Schedules; and Appendix V: Agriculture Products: Commitments Limiting Subsidization—Part IV of Schedules (Section I: Domestic Support: Total AMS Commitments, Section II: Export Subsidies: Budgetary Outlay and Quantity Reduction Commitments and Section III: Commitments Limiting the Scope of Export Subsidies).

The schedule annexed to the Protocol relating to a Member shall become a Schedule to the Gatt 1994 relating to that Member on the day on which the Agreement Establishing the WTO enters into force for that Member.

For non-agricultural products the tariff reduction agreed upon by each Member shall be implemented in five equal rate reductions, except as may be otherwise specified in a Member's Schedule. The first such reduction shall be made effective on the date of entry into force of the Agreement Establishing the WTO. Each successive reduction shall be made effective on 1 January of each of the following years, and the final rate shall be made effective no later than the date four years after the date of entry into firce of the Agreement Establishing the WTO. However, participants may implement reduction in fewer stages or at earlier dates than those indicated in the Protocol, if they so wish.

For agricultural products, as defined in Article 2 of the Agreement on Agriculture, the staging of reductions shall be implemented as specified in the relevant parts of the schedules. Details are given in the section of this paper concerning the Agricultural Agreement.

A related Decision on Measures in Favour of Least-Developed Countries establishes, among other things, that these countries will not be required to undertake any commitments and concessions which are inconsistent with their individual development, financial and trade needs. Alongside other more specific provisions for flexible and favourable treatment, it also allows for the completion of their schedules of concessions and commitments in Market Access and in Services by April 1995 rather than 15 December 1993.

Agreement on Agriculture

The negotiations have resulted in four main portions of the Agreement; the Agreement on Agriculture itself; the concessions and commitments Members are to undertake on market access, domestic support and export subsidies; the Agreement on Sanitary and Phytosanitary Measures; and the Ministerial Decision concerning Least-Developed and net Food-importing Developing countries.

Overall, the results of the negotiations provide a framework for the long-term reform of agricultural trade and domestic policies over the years to come. It makes a decisive move towards the objective of increased market orientation in agricultural trade. The rules governing agricultural trade are strengthened which will lead to improved predictability and stability for importing and exporting countries alike.

The agricultural package also addresses many other issues of vital economic and political importance to many Members. These include provisions that encourage the use of less trade-distorting domestic support policies to maintain the rural economy, that allow actions to be taken to ease any adjustment burden, and also the introduction of tightly prescribed provisions that allow some flexibility in the implementation of commitments. Specific concerns of developing countries have been addressed including the concern of net-food importing countries and least-developed countries.

The agricultural package provides for commitments in the area of market access, domestic support and export competition. The text of the agricultural Agreement is mirrored in the GATT Schedules of legal commitments relating to individual countries (as noted in the section of this paper that describes the Uruguay Round Protocol).

In the area of *market access*, non-tariff border measures are replaced by tariffs that provide substantially the same leve of protection. Tariffs resulting from this "tariffication" process, as well as other tariffs on agricultural products, are to be reduced by an average 36 per cent in the case of developed countries and 24 per cent in the case of developing countries, with minimum reductions for each tariff line being required. Reductions are to be undertaken over six years in the case of developed countries and over ten years in the case of developing countries. Least-developed countries are not required to reduce their tariffs.

The tariffication package also provides for the maintenance of current access opportunities and the establishment of minimum access tariff quotas (at reduced-tariff rates) where current access is less than 3 per cent of domestic consumption. These minimum access tariff quotas are to be expanded to 5 per cent over the implementation period. In the case of "tariffied" products "special safeguard" provisions will allow additional duties to be applied in case shipments at prices denominated in domestic currencies below a certain reference level or in case of a surge of imports. The trigger in the safeguard for import surges depends on the "import penetration" currently existing in the market, i.e. where imports currently make up a large proportion of consumption, the import surge required to trigger the special safeguard action is lower.

In order to facilitate the implementation of tariffication in particularly sensitive situation, a "special treatment" clause was introduced into the Agreement on Agriculture. The special treatment allows, under certain carefully and strictly defined conditions, a country to maintain import restrictions up to the end of the implementation period. The conditions are (i) that imports of the primary agricultural products, and its worked and/or prepared product, the so-called designated products, were less than 3 per cent of domestic consumption during the period 1986-88; (ii) no export subsidies have been provided for these products since 1986; (iii) effective production restricting measures are applied to the primary agricultural product, and (iv) minimum access opportunities are provided. The minimum access opportunities represent four per cent of domestic consumption of the designated products in the first year of the implementation period and increase annually to reach 8 per cent in the sixth year. However, the final figure is lower if the designated products are tariffied before the end of the implementation period. For example, if the designated products are tariffied at the beginning of the third year of the implementation period the final minimum access opportunities are 6.4 per cent of domestic consumption of the designated products. Negotiations among trading partners on the possibility and terms of any continuation of special treatment beyond the implementation period must be completed by the end of the sixth year following the entry into force of the Agreement on Agriculture. In case of any continuation beyond the sixth year, additional commitments have to be taken.

A separate section in this context reflects the special and differential treatment applied to developing countries which is an integral element of all commitments taken in the Uruguay Round, including in all areas of the Agreement of Agriculture. The provisions apply to a primary agricultural product that is the predominant staple in the traditional diet of the developing countries which invokes this clause of the agreement.

Domestic support measures that have, at most, a minimal impact on trade ("green box" policies) are excluded from reduction commitments. Such policies include general government services, for example in the areas of research, disease control, infrastructure and food security. It also includes direct payments to producers, for example certain forms of "decoupled" (from production) income support, structural adjustment assistance, direct payments under environmental programmes and under regional assistance programmes.

In addition to the green box policies, other policies need not be included in the Total Aggregate Measurement of Support (Total AMS) reduction commitments. These policies are direct payments under production-limiting programmes, certain government assistance measures to encourage agricultural and rural development in developing countries and other support which makes up only a low proportion (5 per cent in the case of developed countries and 10 per cent in the case of developing countries) of the value of production of individual products or, in the case of non-product-specific support, the value of total agricultural production.

The Total AMS covers all support provided on either a product-specific or non-product-specific basis that does not qualify for exemption and is to be reduced by 20 per cent (13.3 per cent for developing countries with no reduction for least-developed countries) during the implementation period.

Members are required to reduce the value of mainly direct *export subsidies* to a level 36 per cent below the 1986-90 base period level over the six-year implementation period, and the quantity of subsidised exports by 21 per cent over the same period. In the case of developing countries, the reductions are two-thirds those of developed countries over a ten-year period (with no reductions applying to the least-developed countries) and subject to certain conditions, there are no commitments on subsidies to reduce the costs of marketing exports of agricultural products or internal transport and freight charges on export shipments. Where subsidised exports have increased since the 1986-90 base period, 1991-92 may be used, in certain circumstances, as the beginning point of reductions although the end-point remains that based on the 1986-90 base period level. The Agreement on Agriculture provides for some limited flexibility between years in terms of export subsidy reduction commitments and contains provisions aimed preventing the circumvention of the export subsidy commitments and sets out criteria for food aid donations and the use of export credits.

"Peace" provisions within the agreement include: an understanding that certain actions available under the Subsidies Agreement will not be applied with respect to green box policies and domestic support and export subsidies maintained in conformity with commitments; an understanding that "due restraint" will be used in the application of countervailing duty rights under the General Agreement; and setting out limits in terms of the applicability of nullification or impairment actions. These peace provisions will apply for a period of 9 years.

The agreement sets up a committee that will monitor the implementation of commitments, and also monitor the follow-up to the Decision on Measures Concerning the Possible Negative Effects of the Reform Programme on Least-Developed and Net Food-Importing Developing Countries.

The package is conceived as part of a continuing process with the long-term objective of securing substantial progressive reductions in support and protection. In this light, it calls for further negotiations in the fifth year of implementation which, along with an assessment of the first five years, would take into account non-trade concerns, special and differential treatment for developing countries, the objective to establish a fair and market-oriented agricultural trading system and other concerns and objectives noted in the preamble to the agreement.

Agreement on Sanitary and Phytosanitary Measures

This agreement concerns the application of sanitary and phytosanitary measures—in other words food safety and animal and plant health regulations. the agreement recognises that governments have the right to take sanitary and phytosanitary measures but that they should be applied only to the extent necessary to protect human, animal or plant life or health and should not arbitrarily or unjustifiably discriminate between Members where identical or similar conditions prevail.

In order to harmonize sanitary and phytosanitary measures on as wide a basis as possible. Members are encouraged to base their measures on international standards, guidelines and recommendations where they exist. However, Members may maintain or introduce measures which result in higher standards if there is scientific justification or as a consequence of consistent risk decisions based on an appropriate risk assessment. The Agreement spells out procedures and criteria for the assessment of risk and the determination of appropriate levels of sanitary or phytosanitary protection.

It is expected that Members would accept the sanitary or phytosanitary measures of others as equivalent if the exporting country demonstrates to the importing country that its measures achieve the importing country's appropriate level of health protection. The agreement includes provisions on control, inspection and approval procedures.

The agreement also contains requirements on transparency, including the publication of regulations, the establishment of national enquiry points and notification procedure. It would establish a Committee on Sanitary and Phytosanitary Measures which, among other things, would provides a forum for consultations, discuss matters with potential trade impacts, maintain contact with other relevant organizations and monitor the process of international harmonization.

The Decision on Measures Concerning the Possible Negative Effects of the Reform Programme on Least-Developed and Net Food-Importing Developing Countries

It is recognized that during the reform programme least-developed and net food-importing developing countries may experience negative effects with respect to supplies of food imports on reasonable terms and conditions. Therefore, a special Decision sets out objectives with regard to the provisions of food aid, the provision of basic foodstuffs in full grant form and aid for agricultural development. It also refers to the possibility of assitance from the international Monetary Fund and the World Bank with respect to the short-term financing of commercial food imports. The Committee of Agriculture, set up under the Agreement on Agriculture, will monitor the follow-up to the Decision.

Agreement on Textiles and Clothing

The object of this negotiation has been to secures the eventual integration of the textiles and clothing sector-where much of the trade is currently subject to bilateral quotas negotiated under the Multifibre Arrangement (MFA)-into the GATT on the basis of strengthened GATT rules and disciplines.

Integration of the sector into the GATT would take place as follows (on the assumption that the WTO enters into effects on 1 January 1995): first, on 1 January 1995; each party could integrate into the GATT products from the specific list in the Agreement which accounted for note less than 16 per cent of its total volume of imports in 1990. Integration means that trade in these products will be governed by the general rules of GATT.

At the beginning of Phase 2, on 1 January 1998, products which accounted for not less than 17 per cent of 1990 imports would be integrated. On 1 January 2002, products which accounted for not less than 18 per cent of 1990 imports would be integrated. All remaining products would be integrated at the end of the transition period on 1 January 2005. At each of the first three stages, products should be chosen from each of the following categories: tops and yarns, fabrics, made-up textile products, and clothing.

All MFA restrictions in place on 31 December 1994 would be carried over into the new agreement and maintained until such time as the restrictions are removed or the products integrated into GATT. For products remaining under restraint, as whatever stage, the agreement lays down a formula for increasing the existing growth rates. Thus, during Stage 1, and for each restriction previously under MFA bilateral agreements in force for 1994, annual growth should be not less than 16 per cent higher than the growth rate established for the previous MFA restriction. For Stage 2 (1998 to 2001 inclusive), annual growth rates should be 25 per cent higher than the Stage 1 rates. For Stage 3 (2002 to 2004 inclusive), annual growth rates should be 27 per cent higher than the Stage 2 rates.

While the agreement focuses largely on the phasing-out of MFA restrictions, it also recognizes that some members maintain non-MFA restrictions not justified under a GATT provision. These would also be brought into conformity with GATT within one year of the entry into force of the Agreement or phased out progressively during a period not exceeding the duration of the Agreement (that is, by 2005).

It also contains a specific transitional safeguard mechanism which could be applied products not yet integrated into the GATT at any stage. Action under the safeguard mechanism could be taken against individual exporting countries if it were demonstrated by the importing country that overall imports of a product were entering the country in such increased quantities as to cause serious damage—or to threaten it—tot he relevant domestic industry, and that there was a sharp and substantial increase of imports from the individual country concerned. Action under the safeguard mechanism could be taken either by mutual agreement, following consultations, or unilaterally but subject to review by the Textiles Monitoring Body. If taken, the level of restraints should be fixed at a level not lower than the actual level of exports or imports from the country concerned during the twelve-month period ending two months before the month in which a request for consultation was made. Safeguard restraints could remain in place for up to three years without extension or until the product is removed from the scope of the agreement (that is, integrated into the GATT), whichever comes first.

The agreement includes provisions to cope with possible circumvention of commitments through transshipment, re-routing, false declaration concerning country or place of origin and falsification of official documents.

The agreement also stipulates that, as part of the integration process, all members shall take such actions in the area of textiles and clothing as may be necessary to abide by GATT rules and disciplines so as to improve market access, ensure the application of policies relating to fair and equitable trading conditions, and avoid discrimination against imports when taking measures for general trade policy reasons.

In the context of a major review of the operation of the agreement to be conducted by the Council for Trade in Goods before the end of each stage of the integration process, the Council for Trade in Goods shall by consensus take such decisions as it deems appropriate to ensure that the balance of rights and obligations in this agreement is not upset. Moreover, the Dispute Settlement Body may authorise adjustments to the annual growth of quotas for the stage subsequent to the review with respect to Members it has found not to be complying with their obligations under this agreement.

A Textiles Monitoring Body (TMB) would be established to oversee the implementation of commitments and to prepare reports for the major reviews mentioned above. The agreement also has provisions for special treatment to certain categories of countries—for example, those which have not been MFA members since 1986, new entrants, small suppliers, and least-developed countries.

Agreement on Technical Barriers to Trade

This agreement will extend and clarify the Agreement on Technical Barriers to Trade reached in the Tokyo Round. It seeks to ensure that technical negotiations and standards, as well as testing and certification procedures, do not create unnecessary obstacles to trade. However, it recognizes that countries have the right to establish protection, at levels they consider appropriate, for example for human, animal or plant life or health or the environment, and should not be prevented from taking measures necessary to ensure those levels of protection are met. The agreement, therefore, encourages countries to use international standards where these are appropriate, but it does not require them to change their levels of protection as a result of standardization.

Innovative features of the revised agreement are that it covers processing and production methods related to the characteristics of the product itself. The coverage of conformity assessment procedures is enlarged and the disciplines made more precise. Notification provisions applying to local government and non-governmental bodies are elaborated in more detail than in the Tokyo Round agreement. A Code of Good Practice for the Preparation, Adoption and Application of Standards by standardizing bodies, which is open to acceptance by private sector bodies as well as the public sector, is included as an annex to the agreement.

Agreement on Trade-Related Investment Measures

The agreement recognizes that certain investment measures restrict and distort trade. It provides that no contracting party shall apply any TRIM inconsistent with Articles III (national treatment) and XI (prohibition of quantitative restrictions) of the GATT. To this end, an illustrative list of TRIMs agreed to be inconsistent with these articles is appended to the agreement. The list includes measures which require particular levels of local procurement by an enterprise ("local content requirements") or which restrict the volume or value of imports such an enterprise can purchase or use to an amount related to the level of products it exports ("trade balancing requirements").

The agreement requires mandatory notification of all non-conforming TRIMs and their elimination within two years for developed countries, within five years for developing countries and within seven years for least-developed countries. It establishes a Committee on TRIMs which will, among other things, monitor the implementation of these commitments. The agreement also provides for consideration, at a later date, of whether it should be complemented with provisions on investment and competition policy more broadly.

Agreement on Implementation of Article VI (Anti-Dumping)

Article VI of the GATT provides for the right of contracting parties to apply anti-dumping measures, i.e. measures against imports of a product at an export price below its "normal value" (usually the price of the product in the domestic market of the exporting country) if such dumped imports cause injury to a domestic industry in the territory of the importing contracting party. More detailed rules governing the application of such measures are currently provided in an Anti-Dumping Agreement concluded at the end of the Tokyo Round. Negotiations in the Uruguay Round have resulted in a revision of this Agreement which addresses many areas in which the current Agreement lacks precision and detail.

In particular, the revised Agreement provides for greater clarity and more detailed rules in relation to the method of determining that a product is dumped, the criteria to be taken into account in a determination that dumped imports cause injury to a domestic industry, the procedures to be followed in initiating and conducting anti-dumping investigations, and the implementation and duration of anti-dumping measures. In addition, the new agreement clarifies the role of dispute settlement panels in disputes relating to anti-dumping actions taken by domestic authorities.

On the methodology for determining that a product is exported as a dumped price, the new Agreement adds relatively specific provisions on such issues as criteria for allocating costs when the export price is compared with a "constructed" normal value and rules to ensure that a fair comparison is made between the export price and the normal value of a product so as not to arbitrarily create or inflate margins of dumping.

The agreement strengthens the requirement for the importing country to establish a clear casual relationship between dumped imports and injury to the domestic industry. The examination of the dumped imports on the industry concerned must include an evaluation of all relevant economic factors bearing on the state of the industry concerned. The agreement conforms the existing interpretation of the term "domestic industry". Subject to a few exceptions, "domestic industry" refers to the domestic producers as a whole of the like products or to those of them whose collective output of the products constitutes a major proportion of the total domestic production of those products.

Clear-cut procedures have been established on how anti-dumping cases are to be initiated and how such investigations are to be conducted. Conditions for ensuring that all interested parties are given an opportunity to present evidence are set out. Provisions on the application of provisional measures, the use of price undertakings in anti-dumping cases, and on the duration of anti-dumping measures have been strengthened. Thus, a significant improvement over the existing Agreement consists of the addition of a new provision under which anti-dumping measures shall expire five years after the date of imposition, unless a determination is made that, in the event of termination of the measures, dumping and injury would be likely to continue or recur.

A new provision requires the immediate termination of an anti-dumping investigation in cases where the authorities determine that the margin of dumping is de *minimis* (which is defined as less than 2 per cent, expressed as a percentage of the export price of the product) or that the volume of dumped imports is negligible (generally when the volume of dumped imports from an individual country accounts for less than 3 per cent of the imports of the product in question into the importing country).

The agreement calls for prompt and detailed notification of all preliminary or final anti-dumping actions to a Committee on Anti-Dumping practices. The agreement will afford parties the opportunity of consulting on any matter relating to the operation of the agreement or the furtherance of its objectives, and to request the establishment of panels to examine disputes.

Agreement on Implementation on Article VII (Customs Valuation)

The Decide on Customs Valuation would give customs administrations the right to request further information of importers where they have reason to doubt the accuracy of the declared value of imported goods. If the administration maintains a reasonable doubt, despite any additional information, it may be deemed that the customs value of the imported goods cannot be determined on the basis of the declared value, and customs would need to establish the value taking into account the provisions of the Agreement. In addition, two accompanying texts further clarify certain of the agreement's provisions relevant to developing countries and relating to minimum values and importations by sole agents, sole distributors and sole concessionaires.

Agreement on Preshipment Inspection

Preshipment inspection (PSI) is the practice of employing specialized private companies to check shipment details—essentially price, quantity, quality—of goods ordered overseas. used by governments of developing countries, the purpose is to safeguard national financial interests (prevention of capital flight and commercial fraud as well as customs duty evasion, for instance) and to compensate for inadequacies in administrative infrastructures.

The agreement recognizes that GATT principle and obligations apply to the activities of preshipment inspection agencies mandated by governments. The obligations placed on PSI-user governments include non-discrimination, transparency, protection of confidential business information, avoidance of unreasonable delay, the use of specific guidelines for conducting price verification and the avoidance of conflicts of interest by the PSI agencies.

The obligations of exporting Members towards PSI users include non-discrimination in the application of domestic laws and regulations, prompt publication of such laws and regulations and the provision of technical assistance where requested.

The agreement establishes an independence review procedure administered jointly by an organization representing PSI agencies and an organization representing exporters—to resolve disputes between an exporter and a PSI agency.

Agreement Rules of Origin

The agreement aims at long-term harmonization of rules of origin, other than rules of origin relating to the granting of tariff preferences, and to ensure that such rules do not themselves create unnecessary obstacles to trade.

The agreement sets up a harmonization programme, to be initiated as soon as possible after the completion of the Uruguay Round and to be completed within three years of initiation. It would be based upon a set of principles, including making rules of origin objective, understandable and predictable. The work would be conducted by a Committee on Rules of Origin in the GATT and a technical committee under the auspices of the Customs Cooperation Council in Brussels.

Until the completion of the harmonization programme, contracting parties would be expected to ensure that their rules of origin are transparent; that they do not have restricting, distorting or disruptive effects on international trade; that they are administered in a consistent, uniform, impartial and reasonable manner, and that they are based on a positive standard (in other words, they should state what does confer origin rather than what does not).

An annex to the agreement sets out a "common declaration" with respect to the operation of rules of origin on goods which qualify for preferential treatment.

Agreement on Import Licensing Procedures

The revised agreement strengthens the disciplines on the users of import licensing systems—which, in any event, are much less widely used now than in the past-and increases transparency and predictability. For example, the agreement requires parties to publish sufficient information for traders to know the basis on which licences are granted. It contains strengthened rules for the notification of the institution of import licensing procedures or changes therein. It also offers guidance on the assessment of applications.

With respect to automatic licensing procedures, the revised agreement sets out criteria under which they are assumed not to have trade restrictive effects. With respect to non-automatic licensing procedures, their administrative burden for importers and exporters should be limited to what is absolutely necessary to administer the measures to which they apply. The revised agreement also sets a maximum of 60 days for applications to be considered.

Agreement on Subsidies and Countervailing Measures

The Agreementon Subsidies and Countervailing Measures is intended to build on the Agreement on Interpretation and Application of Articles VI, XVI and XXIII which was negotiated in the Tokyo Round.

Unlike its predecessor, the agreement contains a definition of subsidy and introduces the concept of a "specific" subsidy—for the most part, a subsidy available only to an enterprise or industry or group of enterprises or industries within the jurisdiction of the authority granting the subsidy. Only specific subsidies would be subject to the disciplines set out in the agreement.

The agreement establishes three categories of subsidies. First, it deems the following subsidies to be "prohibited": those contingent, in law or in fact, whether solely or as one of several other conditions, upon export performance; and those contingent, whether solely or as one of several other conditions, upon the use of domestic over imported goods. Prohibited subsidies are subject to new dispute settlement procedures. The main features include an expedited timetable for action by the Dispute Settlement body, and if it is found that the subsidy is indeed prohibited, it must be immediately withdrawn. If this is not done within the specified time period, the complaining member is authorized to take countermeasures.

The second category is "actionable" subsidies. The agreement stipulates that no member should cause, through the use of subsidies, adverse effects to the interests of other signatories, i.e. injury to domestic industry of another signatory, nullification or impairment of benefits accruing directly or indirectly to other signatories under the General Agreement (in particular the benefits of bound tariff concessions), and serious prejudice to the interests of another member, "Serious prejudice" shall be presumed to exist for certain subsidies including when the total *ad volerem* subsidization of a product exceeds 5 per cent. In such a situation, the burden of proof is on the subsidizing member to show that the subsidies in question do not cause serious prejudice to the complaining member. Members affected by actionable subsidies may refer the matter to the Dispute Settlement body. In the event that it is determined that such adverse effects exist, the subsidizing member must withdraw the subsidy or remove the adverse effects.

The third category involves non-actionable subsidies, which could either be non-specific subsidies, or specific subsidies involving assistance to industrial research and pre-competitive development activity, assistance to disadvantaged regions, or certain type of assistance for adapting existing facilities to new environmental requirements imposed by law and/or regulations. Where another member believes that an otherwise non-actionable subsidy is resulting in serious adverse effects to a domestic industry, it may seek a determination and recommendation on the matter.

One part of the agreement concerns the use of countervailing measures on subsidized imported goods. It sets out disciplines on the initiation of countervailing cases, investigations by national authorities and rules of evidence to ensure that all intrested parties can present information and argument. Certain disciplines on the calculation of the amount of a subsidy are outlined as is the basis for the determination of injury to the domestic industry. The agreement would require that all relevant economic factors to taken into account in assessing the state of the industry and that a casual link be established between the subsidized imports and the alleged injury. Countervailing investigations shall be terminated immediately in cases where the amount of a subsidy is *de minimis* (the subsidy is less than 1 per cent *ad volerem*) or where the volume of subsidized imports, actual or potential, or the injury is negligible. Except under exceptional circumstances, investigations shall be concluded within one year after their initiation and in no case more than 18 months. All countervailing duties have to be terminated within 5 years of their imposition unless the authorities determine on the basis of a review that the expiry of the duty would be likely to lead to continuation or recurrence of subsidization and injury.

The agreement recognizes that subsidies may play an important role in economic development programmes of developing countries, and in the transformation of centrally-planned economies to market economies. Least-developed countries and developing countries that have less than $ 1,000 per capita GNP are thus exempted from disciplines on prohibited export subsidies, and have a time-bound exemption from other prohibited subsidies. For other developing countries, the export subsidy prohibition would take effect 8 years after the entry into force of the agreement establishing the WTO, and they have a time-bound (though fewer years than for poorer developing countries) exemption from the other prohibited subsidies. Countervailing investigation of a product originating from a developing country member would be terminated if the overall level of subsidies does not exceed 2 per cent (and from certain developing countries 3 per cent) of the value of the product, or if the volume of the subsidized imports represents less than 4 per cent of the total imports for the like product in the importing signatory. For countries in the process of transformation from a centrally planned into a market economy, prohibited subsidies shall be phased out within a period of seven years from the date of entry into force of the agreement.

In anticipation of the negotiation of special rules in the *civil aircraft* sector, under the subsidies agreement, civil aircraft products are not subject to the presumption that *ad valorem* subsidization in excess of 5 per cent causes serious prejudice to the interests of other Members. In addition, the Agreement provides that where repayment of financing in the civil aircraft sector is dependent on the level of sales of a product and sales fall below expectations, this does not in itself give rise to such presumption of serious prejudice.

Agreement on Safeguards

Article XIX of the General Agreement allows a member to take a "safeguard" action to protect a specific domestic industry from an unforeseen increase of imports of any product which is causing, or which is likely to cause, serious injury to the industry.

The agreement breaks major ground in establishing a prohibition against so-called "grey area" measures, and in setting a "sunset clause" on all safeguard actions. The agreement stipulates that a member shall not seek, take or maintain any voluntary export restraints, orderly marketing arrangements or any other similar measures on the export or the import side. Any such measure in effect at the time of entry into force of the agreement would be brought into conformity with this agreement, or would have to be phased out within four years after the entry into force of the agreement establishing the WTO. An exception could be made for one specific measure for each importing member, subject to mutual agreement with the directly concerned member, where the phase-out date would be 31 December 1999.

All existing safeguard measures taken under Article XIX of the General Agreement 1947 shall be terminated not later than eight years after the date on which they were first applied or five years after the date of entry into force of the agreement establishing the WTO, whichever comes later.

The agreement sets out requirements for safeguard investigation which include public notice for hearings and other appropriate means for interested parties to present evidence, including on whether a measure would be in the public interest. In the event of critical circumstances, a provisional safeguard measure may be imposed based upon a preliminary determination of serious injury. The duration of such a provisional measure would not exceed 200 days.

The agreement sets out the criteria for "serious injury" and the factors which must be considered in determining the impact of imports. The safeguard measures should be applied only to the extent necessary to prevent or remedy serious injury and to facilitates adjustment. Where quantitative restrictions are imposed, they normally should not reduce the quantities of imports below the annual average for the last three representative years for which statistics are available, unless clear justification is given that a different level is necessary to prevent or remedy serious injury.

In principle, safeguard measures have to be applied irrespective of source. In cases in which a quota is allocated among supplying countries, the member applying restriction may seek agreement with others. Members having a substantial interest in supplying the product concerned. Normally, allocation of shares would be on the basis of proportion of total quantity or value of the imported product over a previous representative period. However, it would be possible for the importing country to depart from this approach if it could demonstrate, in consultations under the auspices of the Safeguards Committee, that imports from certain contracting parties had increased disproportionately in relation to the total increase and that such a departure would be justified and equitable to all suppliers. The duration of the safeguard measure in this case cannot exceed four years.

The agreement lays down time limits for all safeguard measures. Generally, the duration of a measures should not exceed four years though this could be extended up to a maximum of eight years, subject to confirmation of continued necessity by the competent national authorities and if there is evidence that the industry is adjusting. Any measure imposed for a period greater than one year should be progressively liberalized during its lifetime. No safeguard measure could be applied again to a product that had been subject to such action for a period equal to the duration of the previous measure, subject to a non-application period of at least two years. A safeguard measure with a duration of 180 days or less may be applied again to the import of a product if at least one year had elapsed since the date of introduction of the measure on the product, and if such a measure had not been applied on the same product more than twice in the five-year period immediately preceding the date of introduction of the measure.

The agreement envisages consultations on compensation for safeguard measures. Where consultations are not successful, the affected members may withdraw equivalent concessions or other obligations under GATT 1994. However, such action is not allowed for the first three years of the safeguard measure if it conforms to the provisions of the agreement, and is taken as a result of an absolute increase in imports.

Safeguard measures would not be applicable to a product from a developing country member, if the share of the developing country member in the imports of the product concerned does not exceed 3 per cent, and that developing country members with less than 3 per cent import share collectively account for no more than 9 per cent of total imports of the product concerned. A developing country member has the right to extend the period of application of a safeguard measure for a period of up to two years beyond the normal maximum. It can also apply a safeguard measure again to a product that had been subject to such an action after a period equal to half of the duration of the previous measure, subject to a non-application period of at least two years.

The agreement would establish a Safeguard Committee which would oversee the operation of its provisions and, in particular, be responsible for surveillance of its commitments.

General Agreement on Trade in Services

The Services Agreement which forms part of the Final Act rests on three pillars. The first is a Framework Agreement containing basic obligations which apply to all member countries. The second concerns national schedules of commitments containing specific further national commitments which will be the subject of a continuing process of liberalization. The third is a number of annexes addressing the special situations of individual services sectors.

Part I of the basic agreement defines its scope-specifically, services supplied from the territory of one party to the territory of another; services supplied in the territory of one party to the consumers of any other (for example, tourism); services provided through the presence of service providing entities of one party in the territory of any other (for example, banking); and services provided by nationals of one party in the territory of any other (for example, construction projects or consultancies).

Part II sets out general obligations and disciplines. A basic most-favoured-nationa (m.f.n.) obligation states that each party "shall accord immediately and unconditionally to services and service providers of any other Party, treatment no less favourable than that it accords to like services and service providers of any other country". However, it is recognized that m.f.n. treatment may not be possible for every service activity and, therefore, it is envisaged that parties may indicate specific m.f.n. exemptions. Conditions for such exemptions are included as an annex and provide for reviews after five years and a normal limitation of 10 years on their duration.

Transparency requirements include publication of all relevant laws and regulations. Provisions to facilitate the increased participation of developing countries in world services trade envisage negotiated commitments on access to technology, improvements in access to distribution channels and information networks and the liberalization of market access in sectors and modes of supply of export interest. The provisions covering economic integration are analogous to those in Article XXIV of GATT, requiring arrangements to have "substantial sectoral coverage" between the parties.

Since domestic regulations, not border measures, provide the most significant influence on services trade, provisions spell out that all such measures of general application should be administered in a reasonable, objective and impartial manner. There would be a requirement that parties establish the means for prompt reviews of administrative decisions relating to the supply of services.

The agreement contains obligations with respect to recognition requirements (educational back ground, for instance) for the purpose of securing authorizations, licenses or certification in the services area. It encourages recognition requirements achieved through harmonization and internationally-agreed criteria. Further provisions state that parties are required to ensure that monopolies and exclusive service providers do not abuse their positions.

Restrictive business practices should be subject to consultations between parties with a view to their elimination.

While parties are normally obliged not to restrict international transfers and payments for current transactions relating to commitments under the arrangement, there are provisions allowing limited restrictions in the event of balance-of-payments difficulties. However, where such restrictions are imposed they would be subject to conditions; including that they are non-discriminatory, that they avoid unnecessary commercial damage to other parties and that they are of a temporary nature.

The agreement contains both general exceptions and security exceptions provisions which are similar to Articles XX and XXI of the GATT. It also envisages negotiations to the develop disciplines on trade-distorting subsidies in the services area.

Part III contains provisins on market access and national treatment which would not be general obligations but would be commitments made in national schedules. Thus, in the case of market access, each party "shall accord services and service providers of other Parties treatment no less favourable than that provided for under the terms, limitations and conditions agreed and specified in its schedule". The intention of the market-acess provision is to progressively eliminate the following type of measures: limitations on numbers of service providers, on the total value of service transactions or on the total number of service providers, on the total value of service transactions or on the total number of service operations or people employed. Equally, restrictions on the kind of legal entity or joint venture through which a service is provided or any foreign capital limitations relating to maximum levels of foreign participation are to be progressively eliminated.

The national-treatment provision contains the obligation to treat foreign service suppliers and domestic service suppliers in the same manner. However, it does provide the possibility of different treatment being accorded the service providers of other parties to that accorded to domestic service providers. However, in such cases the conditions of competition should not, as a result, be modified in favour of the domestic service providers.

Part IV of the agreement establishes the basis for progressive liberalization in the services are through successive rounds of negotiations and the development of national schedules. It also permits, after a period of three years, parties to withdraw or modify commitments made in their schedules. Where commitments are modified or withdrawn, negotiations should be undertaken with interested parties to agree on compensatory adjustments. Where agreement cannot be reached, compensation would be decided by arbitration.

Part V of the agreement contains institutional provisions, including consultation and dispute settlement and the establishment of a Council of Services. The responsibilities of the Council are set out in a Ministerial Decision.

The first of the annexes to the agreement concerns the movement of labour. It permits parties to negotiate specific commitments applying to the movement of people providing services under the agreement. It requires that people covered by a specific commitment shall be allowed to provide the service in accordance with the terms of the commitment. Nevertheless, the agreement would not apply to measures affecting employment, citizenship, residence or employment on a permanent basis.

The annex on financial services (largely banking and insurance) lays down the right of parties, notwithstanding other provisions, to take prudential measures, including for the protection of investors, deposit holders and policy holders, and to ensure the integrity and stability of the financial system. However, a further understanding on financial services would allow those participants who choose to do so to undertake commitments on financial services through a different method. With respect to market access, the understanding contains more detailed obligations on, among other things, monopoly rights, cross-border trade (certain insurance and reinsurance policy writing as well as financial data processing and transfer), the right to establish or expand a commercial presence, and the temporary entry of personnel. The provisions on national treatment refer explicity to access to payments and clearing systems operated by public entities and to official funding and refinancing facilities. They also relate to membership of, or participation in, self-regulatory bodies, securities or futures exchanges and clearing agencies.

The annex on telecommunications relates to measures which affect access to and use of public telecommunications services and networks. In particular, it requires that such access be accorded to another party, on reasonable and non-discriminatory terms, to permit the supply of a service included in its schedule. Conditions attached to the use of public-networks should be no more than is necessary to safeguard to public service responsibilities of their operators, to protect the technical integrity of the network and to ensure that foreign service suppliers do not supply services unless permitted to do so through a specific commitment. The annex also encourages technical cooperation to assist developing countries in the strenthening of their own domestic telecommunications sectors.

The annex on air-transport services excludes from the agreement's coverage traffic rights and directly related activities which might affect the negotiation of traffic rights. Nevertheless, the annex, in its current form, also states that the agreement should apply to aircraft repair and maintenance services, the marketing of air-transport services and computer-reservation services. The operation of the annex would be reviewed at least every five years.

In the final days of the services negotiations, three Decisions were taken-on Financial Services, Professional Services and the Movement of Natural Persons. The Decision of Financial Services confirmed that commitments in this sector would be implemented on an MFN basis, and permits Members to revise and finalize their schedules of commitments and their MFN exemptions six months after the entry into force of the Agreement. Contrary to some media reports, the audio-visual and maritime sectors have not been removed from the scope of the GATS.

Agreement on Trade-Related Aspects of Intellectual Property Rights, including Trade in Counterfeit Goods

The agreement recognizes that widely varying standards in the protection and enforcement of intellectual property rights and the lack of multilateral framework of principles, rules and disciplines dealing with international trade in counterfeit goods have been a growing source of tension in international economic relations. Rules and disciplines were needed to cope with these tensions. To that end, the agreement addresses the applicability of basic GATT principles and those of relevant international intellectual property agreements; the provision of adequate intellectual property rights; the provision of effective enforcement measures for those rights; multilateral dispute settlement; and transitional arrangements.

Part I of the agreement sets out general provisions and basic principles, notably a national-treatment commitment under which the nationals of other parties must be given treatment no less favourable than that accorded to a party's own nationals with regard to the protection of intellectual property. It also contains a most-favoured-nation clause, a novelty in an international intellectual property agreement, under which any advantage a party gives to the nationals of another country must be extended immediately and unconditionally to the nationals of all other parties, even if such treatment is more favourable than that which it gives to its own nationals.

Part II addresses each intellectual property right in succession. With respect to copyright, parties are required to comply with the substantive provisions of the Bene Convention for the protection of literary and artistic works, in its latest version (Paris 1971), though they will not be obliged to protect moral rights as stipulated in Article 6b is of that Convention. It ensures that computer programs will be protected as literary works under the Berne Convention and lays down on what basis data bases should be protected by copyright. Important additions to existing international rules in the area of copyright and related rights are the provisions on rental rights. The draft requires authors of computer programmes and producers of sound recordings to be given the right to authorize or prohibit the commercial rental of their works to the public. A similar exclusive right applies to films where commercial rental has led to widespread copying which is materially impairing the right of reproduction. The draft also requires performers to be given protection from unauthorized recording and broadcast of five performances (bootlegging). The protection for performers and producers of sound recording would be for no less than 50 years. Broadcasting organizations would have control over the use that can be made of broadcast signals without their authorization. This right would last for at least 20 years.

With respect to trade marks and service marks, the agreement defines what types of signs must be eligible for protection as a trade mark or service mark and what the minimum rights conferred on their owners must be. Marks that have become wellknown in a particular country shall enjoy additional protection. In addition, the agreement lays down a number of obligations with regard to the use of trademarks and service marks, their term of protection, and their licensing or assignment. For example, requirements that foreign marks be used in conjunction with local marks would, as a general rule, be prohibited.

In respect of geographical indications, the agreement lays down that all parties must provide means to prevent the use of any indication which misleads the consumer as to the origin of goods, and any use which would constitute an act of unfair competition. A higher level of protection is provided for geographical indications for wines and spirits, which are protected even where there is no danger of the public's being misled as to the true origin. Exceptions are allowed for names that have already become generic terms, but any country using such an exception must be willing to .negotiate with a view to protecting the geographical indications in question. Furthermore, provision is made for further negotiations to establish a multilateral system of notification and registration of geographical indications for wines.

Industrial designs are also protected under the agreement for a period of 10 years. Owners of protected designs would be able to prevent the manufacture, sale or importation of articles bearing or embodying a design which is a copy of the protected design.

As regards patents, there is a general obligation to comply with the substantive provisions of the Paris Convention (1967). In addition, the agreement requires that 20-year patent protection be available for all inventions, whether of products or processes, in almost all fields of technology. Inventions may be excluded from patentability if their commercial exploitation is prohibited for reasons of public order or morality; otherwise, the permitted exclusions are for diagnostic; therapeutic and surgical methods, and for plants and (other than microorganisms) animals and essentially biological processes for the production of plants or animals (other than microbilogical processes). Plant varieties, however, must be protectable either by patents or by a *sui generis* system (such as the breeder's rights provided in a UPOV Convention). Detailed conditions are laid down for compulsory licensing or governmental use of patents without the authorization of the patent owner. Rights conferred in respect of patents for processes must extend to the products directly obtained by the process; under certain conditions alleged infringers may be ordered by a court to prove that they have not used the patented process.

With respect to the protection of layout designs of integrated circuits, the agreement requires parties to provide protection on the basis of the Washington Treaty on Intellectual Property in Respect of Integrated Circuits which was opened for signature in May 1989, but with a number of additions; protection must be available for a minimum period of 10 years; the rights must extend to articles incorporating infringing layout designs; innocent infringers must be allowed to use or sell stock in hand or ordered before learning of the infringement against a suitable royalty: and compulsory licensing and government use is only allowed under a number of strict conditions.

Trade secrets and know-how which have commercial value must be protected against breach of confidence and other acts contrary to honest commercial practices. Test data submitted to governments in order to obtain marketing approval for pharmaceutical or agricultural chemicals must also be protected against unfair commercial use.

The final section in this part of the agreement concerns anti-competitive practices in contractual licences. It provides for consultations between governments where there is reason to believe that licensing practices or conditions pertaining to intellectual property rights constitute an abuse of these rights and have an adverse effect on competition. Remedies against such abuses must be consistent with the other provisions of the agreement.

Part III of the agreement sets out the obligations of member governments to provide procedures and remedies under their domestic law to ensure that intellectual property right can be effectively enforced, by foreign right holders as well as by their own nationals. Procedures should permit effective action against infringement of intellectual property rights but should be fair and equitable, not unnecessarily complicated or costly, and should not entail unreasonable time-limits or unwarranted delays. They should allow for judicial review of final administrative decisions. There is no obligation to put in place a judicial system distinct from that for the enforcement of laws in general, nor to give priority to the enforcement of intellectual property rights in the allocation of resources or staff.

The civil and administrative procedures and remedies spelled out in the text include provisions on evidence of proof, injunctions, damages and other remedies which would include the right of judicial authorities to order the disposal or destruction of infringing goods. Judicial authorities must also have the authority to order prompt and effective provisional measures, in particular where any delay is likely to cause irreparable harm to the right holder, or where evidence is likely to be destroyed. Further provisions relate to measures to be taken at the border for the suspension by customs authorities of release, into domestic circulation, of counterfeit and pirated goods. Finally, parties should provide for criminal procedures and penalties at least in cases of wilful trade mark counterfeiting or copyright piracy on a commercial scale. Remedies should include imprisonment and fines sufficient to act as a deterrent.

The agreement would establish a Council for Trade-Related Aspects of Intellectual Property Rights to monitor the operation of the agreement and governments' compliance with it. Dispute settlement would take place under the integrated GATT dispute-settlement procedures as revised in the Uruguay Round.

With respect to the implementation of the agreement, it envisages a one-year transition period for developed countries to bring their legislation and practices into conformity. Developing countries and countries in the process of transformation from a centrally-planned into a market economy would have a five-year transition period, and least-developed countries 11 years. Developing countries which do not at present provide product patent protection in an area of technology would have up to 10 years to introduce such protection. However, in the case of pharmaceutical and agricultural chemical products, they must accept the filling of patent applications from the beginning of the transitional period. Though the patent need not be granted until the end of this period, the novelty of the invention is preserved as of the date of filing the application. If authorization for the marketing of the relevant pharmaceutical or agricultural chemical is obtained during the transitional period, the developing country concerned must offer an exclusive marketing right for the product for five years, or until a product patent is granted, whichever is shorter.

Subject to certain exceptions, the general rule is that the obligations in the agreement would apply to existing intellectual property rights as well as to new ones.

Understanding on Rules and Procedures Governing the Settlement of Disputes

The dispute settlement system of the GATT is generally considered to be one of the cornerstones of the multilateral trade order. The system has already been strengthened and streamlined as a result of reforms agreed following the Mid-Term Review Ministerial Meeting held in Montreal in December 1988. Disputes currently being dealt with by the Council are subject to these new rules, which include greater automatically in decisions on the establishment, terms of reference and composition of panels, such that these decisions are no longer dependent upon the consent of the parties to a dispute. The Uruguay Round Understanding on Rules and Procedures Governing the Settlement of Disputes (DSU) will further strengthen the existing system significantly, extending the greater automatically agreed in the Mid-Term Review to the adoption of the panels' and a new Appellate Body's findings. Moreover, the DSU will establish an integrated system permitting WTO Members to base their claims on any of the multilateral trade agreements included in the Annexes to the Agreement establishing the WTO. For this purpose, a Dispute Settlement Body (DSB) will exercise the authority of the General Council and the Councils and committees of the covered agreements.

The DSU emphasizes the importance of consultations in securing dispute resolution, requiring a Member to enter into consultations within 30 days of a request for consultations from another Member. If after 60 days from the request for consultations there is no settlement, the complaining party may request the establishment of a panel. Where consultations are denied, the complaining party may move directly to request a panel. The parties may voluntarily agree to follow alternative means of dispute settlement, including good offices, concilliation, mediation and arbitration.

Where a dispute is not settled through consultations, the DSU requires the establishment of panel, at the latest, at the meeting of the DSB following that at which a request is made, unless the DSB decides by consensus against establishment. The DSU also sets out specific rules and deadlines for deciding the terms of reference and composition of panels. Standard terms of reference will apply unless the parties agree to special terms within 20 days of the panel's establishment. And where the parties do not agree on the composition of the panel within the same 20 days, this can be decided by the Director-General. Panels normally consist of three persons of appropriate background and experience from countries not party to the dispute. The Secretariat will maintain a list of experts satisfying the criteria.

Panel procedures are set out in detail in the DSU. It is envisaged that a panel will normally complete its work within six months or, in cases of urgency, within three months. Panel reports may be considered by the DSB for adoption 20 days after they are issued to Members. Within 60 days of their issuance, they will be adopted, unless the DSB decides by consensus not to adopt the report or one of the parties notifies the DSB of its intention to appeal.

The concept of appellate review is an important new feature of the DSU. An Appellate Body will be established, composed of seven members, three of whom will serve on any one case. An appeal will be limited to issues of law covered in the panel report and legal interpretations developed by the panel. Appellate proceedings shall not exceed 60 days from the date a party formally notifies its decision to appeal. The resulting report shall be adopted by the DSB and unconditionally accepted by the parties within 30 days following its issuance to Members, unless the DSB decides by consensus against its adoption.

Once the panel report or the Appellate Body reports adopted, the party concerned will have to notify its intentions with respect to implementation of adopted recommendations. If it is impracticable to comply immediately, the party concerned shall be given a reasonable period of time, the latter to be decided either by agreement of the parties and approval by the DSB within 45 days of adoption of the report or through arbitration within 90 days of adoption. In any event, the DSB will keep the implementation under regular surveillance until the issue is resolved.

Further provisions set-out rules for compensation or the suspension of concessions in the event of non-implementation. Within a specified time-frame, parties can enter into negotiations to agree on mutually acceptable compensation. Where this has not been agreed, a party to the dispute may request authorization of the DSB to suspend concessions or other obligations to the other party concerned. The DSB will grant such authorization within 30 days of the expiry of the agreed time-frame for implementation. Disagreements over the proposed level of suspension may be referred to arbitration. In principle, concessions should be suspended in the same sector as that in issues in the pane case. If this is not practicable or effective, the suspension can be made in a different sector of the same agreement. In turn, if this is not effective or practicable and if the circumstances are serious enough, the suspension of concessions may be made under another agreement.

One of the central provisions of, DSU reaffirms that Members shall not themselves make determinations of violations or suspend concessions, but shall make use of the dispute settlement rules and procedures of the DSU.

The DSU contains a number of provisions taking into account the specific interests of the developing and the least-developed countries. It also provides some special rules for the resolution of disputes which do not involve a violation of obligations under a covered agreement but where a Member believes nevertheless that benefits are being nullified or impaired. Special decisions to be adopted by Ministers in 1994 foresee that the Montreal Dispute Settlement Rules which would otherwise have expired at the time of the April 1994 meeting are extended until the entry into force of the WTO. Another decision foresees that the new rules and procedures will be reviewed within four years after the entry into force of the WTO.

Decision on Achieving Greater Coherence in Global Economic Policy-Making

This Decision will set out concepts and proposals with respect to achieving greater coherence in global economic policy-making. Among other things, the text notes that greater exchange rate stability based on more orderly underlying economic and financial conditions should contribute to "the expansion of trade, sustainable growth and development, and the timely correction of external imbalances". It recognizes that while difficulties whose origins lie outside the trade field cannot be redressed through measures taken in the trade field alone, there are nevertheless interlinkages between the different aspects of economic policy. Therefore, WTO is called upon to develop its cooperation with the international organizations responsible for monetary and financial matters. In particular, the Director-General of WTO is called upon to review, with his opposit numbers in the World Bank and the International Monetary Fund, the implications of WTO's future responsibilities for its cooperation with the Bretton Woods institutions.

Trade Policy Review Mechanism

An agreement confirms the Trade Policy Review Mechanism, introduced at the time of the Mid-term Review, and encourages greater transparency in national trade policy-making. A further Ministerial decision reforms the notification requirements and procedures generally.

Source: GATT Focus, December 1993, Geneva.

3.3 GATT MEMBERS AND GATT OFFICERS

GATT Members

GATT membership has risen to 119 with the accession of *St. Kitts and Nevis* (24 March), *Guinea-Bissau* (17 March) and the *United Arab Emirates* (8 March).

They became members following separate notifications to Mr. Peter Sutherland, GATT Director-General, under the terms of Article XXVI: 5(c) of the General Agreement.

GATT Officers (1994)

At the close of the forty-ninth session of the Contracting Parties, the following officers were elected for the period until the end of the fiftieth session.

Chairman of the Contracting Parties	Ambassador Andrds Szepesi Permanent Representative of Hungary to GATT
Vice-Chairman of the Contracting Parties	Ambassador K. Kesavapany Permanent Rep. of Singapore to the UN Office at Geneva
	Ambassador Christer Manhusen Permanent Representative of Sweden to GATT
	Ambassador Alexis Reyn Permanent Representative of Belgium to the UN Office at Geneva
Chairman of the Committee on Trade and Development	Ambassador Ernesto Tironi Barrios Permanent Representative of Chile to the UN Office at Geneva.

Source: GATT Newsletter, Jan.-Feb. and March-April, 1994, Geneva.

4

CHILD WELFARE AND DEVELOPMENT

4.1 The State of the World's Children

Through the lens of history, rather than of news, what is now happening in the developing world may come to be seen as the beginning of a final offensive against some of the oldest and most common enemies of the world's children.

Those enemies include five diseases that today kill over 8 million children a year and the malnutrition which holds back the mental and physical development of one child in three in the developing world. Also in retreat are some of the most common causes of childhood disability, the viruses and the micronutrient deficiencies which every year leave hundreds of thousands of children permanently deaf, blind, mentally retarded, or paralysed.

Although profoundly affecting millions of lives, these tragedies, and the progress now being made against them, are largely neglected by the media. In part, this is because these problems are seen as normal rather than exceptional. But primarily it is because their consequences fall almost exclusively on the children of the poorest and least influential people on earth.

The limited good news of recent years is therefore largely an untold story in the midst of the many well-publicized disasters. Measles, for example, which still kills more children every year than all the world's wars and famines put together, is being forced to relinquish its grip. Deaths from this most devastating of childhood diseases have been brought down from more than 2.5 million a year in 1980 to just over 1 million a year today. Simultaneously, the number of non-fatal cases of measles, a major cause of disability and malnutrition in children, has fallen from approximately 75 million a year to about 25 million.

Similar successes have been recorded, by dint of large-scale but little-recognized efforts in the developing world, against several other major problems facing the children of poor communities. In 10 years, infant deaths from neonatal tetanus have been cut from more than 1 million a year to just over half a million. At the same time, the toll of dehydration caused by diarrhoeal disease has been cut from 4 million deaths a year to less than 3 million.

Polio, which has disabled so many millions of children over the years, is also now in retreat. Since 1980, new cases of paralysis have fallen from approximately half a million a year to an estimated 140,000 in 1992. In several regions of the developing world the virus itself is close to being eradicated. As an overall measure of this achievement, it is now estimated that there are more than 3 million children living normal lives who would have been paralysed by polio had it not been for the increase in immunization coverage in the last decade.

At the end of the 1980s, the internationally agreed target of 80 per cent immunization against the major vaccine-preventable diseases of childhood was reached by almost half of the developing countries. Nearly all reached a covorage level of 70 per cent or more. By 1995, there is a reasonable chance that severai other internationally agreed goals will also have been largely achieved.

Iodine deficiency, which causes 120,000 children a year to be bom as cretins and is the world's major cause of preventable mental retardation, could soon be brought to an end.

Vitamin A deficiency, which blinds an estimated 250,000 children a year and is a major cause of ill health and early death among the world's underfives, could be almost eliminated.

Deaths from neonatal tetanus, preventable by the immunization of pregnant women, should soon become a rarity.

Proper treatment of diarrhoeal disease, including oral rehydration therapy (ORT), should be known to 80 per cent of the developing world's families: the result would be the prevention of a further 1.5 million child deaths each year.

Polio should be eradicated from most countries of the world by 1995.

Meanwhile, progress is also being made towards the universal ratification of the Convention on the Rights of the Child, now ratified by 150 nations of which 28 have so far reported on the steps they have taken towards its full implementation.

The bad news, though more widely travelled, cannot be ignored. Problems of the most acute kind–extremes of deprivation and exploitation, and the inhuman abuse of children in war, in the workplace, on the street, and in the home–continue to afflict many millions of young people in both developing and industrialized countries. But even here, there are the first tentative signs of a new ethic emerging which might one day offer children better protection from the worst evils of the adult world.

PPE Spiral

The PPE problem (i.e., the issues of poverty, population growth, and environment) is itself part of an even broader challenge. For it is becoming clear that the world has only a limited time in which to focus its attention and capacities on managing what will undoubtedly be the most complex and difficult transition in all of human history–the transition to a new path of progress characterized by the universal meeting of minimum human needs, by the stabilization and possible reduction of population levels, and by environmentally sustainable patterns of progress in all nations. It is also evident that this multifaceted challenge will demand all of the technological ingenuity, managerial capacity, and political auity that national societies and the international community can command. Negotiating this great transition must therefore replace the military and ideological preoccupations of the past, and become the new central organizing principle of the post-cold war-world.

The path pioneered by a small group of nations over the last five centuries has brought to the rest of the world many benefits amid much pain. It has also pushed the tolerance of the biosphere close to breaking-point. Overwhelmingly, global environmental pressures arise from the already industrialized nations.

Such a state of affairs cannot long continue, both because the industrialized world's levels of consumption and pollution are in themselves unjust and unsustainable, and because the other four-fifths of the world cannot reasonably be expected to restrain or modify the course of its own development in order to protect the biosphere while the industrialized nations continue to monopolized the earth's capacity to provide and to absorb.

This challenge, which many are unwilling to think about today, will become more and more unavoidable as the 21st century begins.

For the industrialized world, the most difficult challenge will undoubtedly be the redefining of its own concepts of growth and progress. But if the great transition is to be made, then it is clear that the industrialized nations will also have to play a major part in resolving the PPE problem in the developing world.

In the face of all the immediate political and economic issues that command the attention of press, public, and politicians in all countries, it might be expected that the problems faced by the poorest people in the poorest countries would continue to occupy a lowly place on the international agenda. But sooner or later this too will have to change. For it will simply not be possible to negotiate the transitions that lie ahead without addressing the PPE problem in the poorest communities of theworld. Within a very few years, failure to cope with the combined impact of the worst aspects of poverty, rapid population growth, and environmental decline will almost certainly translate itself into increasing social division, economic disruption, political unrest, and the gradual dwindling of the present opportunity for progress towards democracy and international stability. From the consequences of such a failure, no country–north or south, rich or poor–would be immune.

Action Now

Pursuing today's low-cost opportunities to protect the health, nutrition, and education of women and children in the developing world is one of the most immediately available and affordable ways of weakening the grip of poverty, population growth, and environmental deterioration.

In particular, the PPE problem will not be resolved without a sustained national and international effort to overcome the very worst aspects of poverty in the remaining years of this century. For poverty is the root of the population and environment crisis in the developing world, and it is also the most accessible point at which to break into the powerful synergisms which form the downward spiral of PPE problems.

What is now required is a determined effort to protect millions of children from the very worst effects of the poverty into which they are born. Today's knowledge and outreach capacity make it possible, for the first time, to protect the mental and physical development of almost all the world's children. It has therefore become possible to interrupt one of the major processes by which poverty is perpetuated from one generation to the next.

An adequate response to the PPE problem must therefore include, among many other actions in many other fields, at least four basic kinds of investment in the lives of the world's poorest communities. They are :

* The prevention of common diseases and disabilities, and a steep

reduction in both severe and moderate malnutrition;

* Rapid progress towards at least a primary education for all children, and especially for all girls;
* An unprecedented worldwide effort to improve the lives of women in poor communities–their health and education, their status and choices, their rights and opportunities. This is an important issue of principle; it is also the most important practical step that could be taken towards weakening the hold of the PPE problem; and
* The making available of family planning information and services to all who need them.

In sum, the central message of this year's report is that making further investments in the well-being of women and children–investments which are at risk of being neglected in the face of newer and seemingly more dramatic problems–is not only one of the most important humanitarian goals that the world could set for itself, but also one of the most incisive and cost-effective contributions that could be made towards coping with the broader problems of poverty, population growth, and environmental deterioration.

The cost of making such an investment in the 1990s would amount to not much more than one-tenth of 1 per cent of the world's annual economic product.

It is a rare bargain. And one that the world cannot afford to miss.

Source : *The State of the World's Children* 1994, UNICEF.

4.2 CHILD ABUSE AND THE CONVENTION ON THE RIGHTS OF THE CHILD

The stories (of child abuse) pour forth in an avalanche of horror.

From Bosnia, young girls raped, gang-raped, raped again, mutilated, murdered. From Angola, Cambodia, Afghanistan, Mozambique, children literally torn to shreds by land-mines or, at best, dismembered, consigned to live entire lives as amputees. From Brazil, a paramilitary massacre of street children while they sleep in the quiet shadows of a church. From Thailand, young girls, very young girls, girls who are still pre-pubescent, stolen from their Myanmar villages to be locked in brothels, servicing ten, fifteen, twenty, thirty male sexual predators every 24 hours. From Somalia, Sudan, Rwanda, child, refugees on the run, tears and terror intermingled, frantically fleeing civil war, cut down in their light by mortars, bullets, machetes.

These incidents are merely examples that can be multiplied in the hundreds of thousands, perhaps millions, without ever the world calling a halt.

It is not that the crimes against children go unnoticed. The media give them regular, sometimes massive coverage. Whenever there's particularly grotesque episode, as in the case of a tiny girl injured in a Sarajevo shelling while waiting for transport to an outside hospital, there's a concomitant media frenzy.

It is not that there are not a sufficient number of advocates. In every part of the globe, there are non-governmental organizations (NGOs) working every waking hour of the day to document the injustices heaped upon children. They miss almost nothing. They make their case with unanswerable force.

It is not that there aren't powerful voices within the United Nations system. I won't apologize for special pleading by describing UNICEF as *primus inter pares* in that role. But one should never forget the work of the Human Rights Commission, the Centre for Human Rights, or the experts who report on every conceivable aspect of the abuse of children.

Yet withal, we appear to be moving backwards. If anything, the growing public awareness clashes directly with the growing international reality of violence against children. Something truly awful is happening: by design, by wilful premeditation, by conduct unbecoming in a civilized society, we are actually choosing children as targets. It would seem–and the evidence suggests that there's an aggravated moral disintegration under way, that we are assaulting children more mercilessly than ever.

The huge question is: will it change, and if so, when? And the answer is, that if there is any real hope, it must lie in the Convention on the Rights of the Child.

The Convention has transformed the struggle around the human rights of children. Every time a country ratifies, new momentum is created. By virtue of public pressure, by virtue of international monitoring, it's simply not possible for a State to ratify and then wash its hands of implementation. A government may get away with it for a while; it will not get away with it forever.

It's fashionable to scoff at these tools of international law. More often than not they don't work. But that isn't true of the Convention on the Rights of the Child. For three reasons, it's different.

First, the rights are indivisible. This is the only international covenant where political, civil, economic, social and cultural rights have identical and equal status.

Second, many of the social and economic rights are already being implemented–health, education, and nutrition, for example. By virtue of the quantifiable goals established by the World Summit for Children, and the National Programmes of Action which, country by country, give expression to those goals, these social and economic rights are not abstractions. They are real. And the fact that they are real can be sustained because the Convention acts as a legal imperative–indeed, as a kind of legislative foundation–for the policies of the countries which have ratified.

Third, and most important, the things we cannot quantify–the physical, emotional and psychological damage done by the sex trade, bonded labour, the streets, violence, armed conflict–are explicitly dealt with. It is the triumph of the Convention on the Rights of the Child that nothing is left out. Its clauses provide uncompromising protection against economic exploitation and sexual exploitation and torture and war and homelessness and every other evil to which the lives of children, in this perverse and brutal world, are subject.

What exactly does that mean? Does it mean that there is an obvious way to stop the carnage? The answer is no. Does it mean that when a country violates international law, it can be hauled up before a court somewhere and forced to comply? The answer is no. Nor does it mean, unfortunately, that there is some form of penalty imposed on countries guilty of practising or tolerating destructive malice against their children.

What, then, is the point of the Convention?

The answer is straightforward! the Convention provides a standard, a benchmark against which the behaviour of nations can be tenaciously and perpetually measured. To be sure, nothing will change overnight. We have never been able to fashion a regimen of international law which holds countries irrevocably accountable. But we can apply such unrelenting pressure that, over time, policies will change and sanity will prevail.

How much time? It matters not so long as we keep hammering away. And that's the beauty of the Convention. There it is – principled, unambiguous, a sacred text for the Rights of the Child. We can nail country policies to the mast; we can nail country policies to the mast; we can label countries as pariahs in the domain of human rights; we can take a given clause of the Convention and rhetorically ram it down the throat of some offending State, or exquisitely employ it to make a persuasive legal argument. One day – not so far off, I judge–rather than using 'democratization' or a 'market economy' as conditions for aid or trade, we will be able to demand respect for the rights of children as the quid pro quo of stable international relationships.

I give it ten years, may be twenty, and there will come a time when we no longer count the scars and the bodies. Look at Viet Nam: it is reforming its juvenile justice system because of the Convention. Look at Barbados: it passed legislation prohibiting the execution of minors because of the Convention. Look at Namibia: it's written portions of the Convention into its Constitution. Look at Bangladesh: it made schooling compulsory for girls, in part because of the Convention.

Yes, human beings being what we are, it will take time, a long time. But with the appropriate combination of rage and persuation, we'll transform the condition of children throughout the world.

Source: Stephen Lewis, *The Progress of Nations,* 1994.

4.3 HUMAN DEVELOPMENT REPORT, 1993 AND CHILD

"Street children are one of the most obvious signs of urban development. Happy, children sick and often homeless children with little chance of a basic education are a sharp reminder of the human potential the world is wasting.

India probably has the greatest number of street children.

New Delhi, Bombay and Calcutta have around 1,00,000 street children each, and Bangalore 45,000. There, as elsewhere, they must work to survive – collecting rags, shinging shoes, selling newspapers, scavenging on rubbish dumps. Many also turn to crime. India's juvenile crime rate is 3.1 per 1,000 people.

Thirty years ago, the population of Brazil was 55 per cent rural. Now it is 75 per cent urban. Around three-quarters of street children in Brazil are thought to be migrants.

Many street children do have homes and parents, the report notes, but they may visit them only rarely. They are forced to earn their livelihood on the streets and driven from the squalor of one or two crowded rooms in the shanty towns.

In Manila, in the Philippines, three million people live in slums, about half of them children. Fewer than a quarter of families have piped water, and two-thirds have no sanitary facilities. Manila has about 75,000 street children.

Street children are also a growing problem in Africa. There too, migration from the countryside is swelling the urban slums. Mathare valley in Nairobi is the largest slum community in Kenya, with around 200,000 people. The majority are migrants and a high proportion are children. Four years ago, Nairobi had about 16,000 street children, today there are thought to be 25,000.

Source: *Human Development Report, 1993,* UNDP, New York.

5

ECONOMIC AND SOCIAL DEVELOPMENT COMPARATIVE COUNTRY PROFILE

A wide range of economic and social statistics are given in tables in this chapter. These tables provide a comparative study of various facets of life in 186 countries, the data derived by the United Nations Children Fund (UNICEF) from the following international agencies among others assume a special significance (i) United Nations Education Scientific and Cultural Organisation (UNESCO), Food and Agricultural Organisation (FAO), International Monetary Fund (IMF), United Nations Statistical Office, World Bank, United Nations Population Division, Organisation for Cooperation and Development (OECD), World Health Organisation (WHO) and US Bureau of the Census.

Official government data received by the responsible United Nations agency have been used whenever possible. In many cases where there are no reliable official figures, estimates made by the responsible United Nations agency have been used. Where such internationally standardized estimates do not exist, the tables draw on other sources, particularly data received from the appropriate UNICEF field office. Where possible only comprehensive or representative national data have been used.

Data for life expectancy, crude birth and dealth rates, infant mortality rates, etc. are part of the regular work on estimates and projections undertaken by the United Nations Population Division. These and other internationally produced estimates are revised periodically, which explains why some of the data will differ from those found in earlier UNICEF publications. In particular, the Under-Five Mortality Rate (U5MR) estimates have been revised using new data and a methodology first applied on a small number of countries in the last report.

Following symbols have been used in the tables.

— Data not available.

* Indicates data that refer to years of periods other than those specified in the column heading, differ from the standard definition, or refer to only part of a country.

TABLE 5.1: Basic Data

	Under 5 mortality rate		Infant mortality rate (under 1)		Total population (millions)	Annual no. of births (thou-sands)	Annual no. of under-5 deaths (thou-sands)	GNP per capita (US$)	Life expect-ancy at birth (years)	Total adult literacy rate	% of age-group enrolled in primary school (gross)	% share of household income 1980-1991 lowest	highest
	1960	1992	1960	1992	1992	1992	1992	1991	1992	1990	1986-91	40%	20%
1	2	3	4	5	6	7	8	9	10	11	12	13	14
1 Niger	320	**320**	191	191	8.3	428	137	3.0	46	28	29	—	—
2 Angola	345	**292**	208	170	9.9	514	150	610x	46	42	96	—	—
3 Mozambique	331	**287**	190	167	14.9	683	196	80	47	33	58	—	—
4 Afghanistan	360	**257**	215	165	19.1	1031	265	280x	43	29	24	—	—
5 Siera Leone	385	**249**	219	144	4.4	213	53	210	43	21	48	—	—
6 Guinea-Bissau	336	**239**	200	141	1.0	43	10	180	43	37	59	—	—
7 Guina	337	**230**	203	135	6.1	313	72	460	44	24	37	—	—
8 Malawi	365	**226**	206	143	10.4	567	128	230	44	—	71	—	—
9 Rwanda	191	**222**	115	131	7.5	396	88	270	46	50	69	23	39
10 Mali	400	**220**	233	122	9.8	504	111	280	46	32	24	—	—
11 Liberia	288	**217**	192	146	2.8	132	29	450x	55	40	40x	—	—
12 Somalia	294	**211**	175	125	9.7	469	99	150x	47	24	15x	—	—
13 Chad	325	**209**	195	123	5.8	258	54	210	47	30	57	—	—

(Contd.)

TABLE 5.1 *Contd.*

1	2	3	4	5	6	7	8	9	10	11	12	13	14
14 Eritrea	294	**208**	175	123	3.3	140	29	120	47	—	—	—	—
15 Ethiopia	294	**208**	175	123	53.0	2627	547	120	47	24x	38	21	41
16 Mauritania	321	**206**	191	118	2.1	100	21	510	48	34	51	40	—
17 Zambia	220	**202**	135	113	8.6	403	81	420x	45	73	93	11x	61x
18 Bhutan	324	**201**	203	131	1.6	65	13	180	48	38	26	—	—
19 Nigeria	204	**191**	122	114	115.7	5259	1004	340	52	51	72	—	—
20 Zaire	286	**188**	167	121	39.9	1912	359	230x	52	72	78	—	—
21 Uganda	218	**185**	129	111	18.7	960	178	170	42	48	76	21	42
22 Cambodia	217	**184**	148	117	8.8	349	64	200x	51	35	—	—	—
23 Burundi	255	**179**	151	108	5.8	271	48	210	48	50	72	—	—
24 Central African Rep.	294	**179**	174	105	3.2	142	25	390	47	38	67	—	—
25 Yemen	378	**177**	214	107	12.5	611	108	520	52	39	73	—	—
26 Tanzania U. Rep. of	249	**176**	147	111	27.8	1351	238	100	51	—	63	8	63
27 Ghana	215	**170**	128	103	16.0	67'	114	400	56	60	75	18	44
28 Madagascar	364	**168**	219	110	12.8	589	99	210	55	80	92	—	—
29 Sudan	292	**166**	170	100	26.7	1128	187	420x	52	27	49	—	—
30 Gabon	287	**158**	171	95	1.2	53	8	3780	53	61	—	—	—
31 Lesotho	204	**156**	138	108	1.8	64	10	580	60	—	107	11	61
32 Burkina Faso	318	**150**	183	101	9.5	449	67	290	48	18	36	—	—
33 Benin	310	**147**	184	88	4.9	243	36	380	46	23	61	—	—
34 Senegal	303	**145**	174	90	7.7	334	48	720	49	38	58	—	—
35 Lao Peo. Dem. Rep.	233	**145**	155	98	4.5	205	30	220	51	84x	104	—	—

(Contd.)

TABLE 5.1 *Contd.*

1	2	3	4	5	6	7	8	9	10	11	12	13	14
36 Pakistan	221	**137**	137	95	124.8	5117	701	400	59	35	37	21	40
37 Togo	264	**137**	155	86	3.8	169	23	410	55	43	103	—	—
38 Haiti	270	**133**	182	87	6.8	240	32	370	56	53	84	6x	48x
39 Nepal	279	**128**	186	90	20.6	778	100	180	53	26	86	22	40
40 Bangladesh	247	**127**	151	97	119.3	4623	587	220	53	35	73	23	39
41 Cote d'Ivoire	300	**124**	165	91	12.9	650	81	690	52	54	75x	19	42
42 India	236	**124**	144	83	879.5	25900	3212	330	60	48	97	21	41
43 Bolivia	252	**118**	152	80	7.5	261	31	650	61	78	82	23x	58x
44 Cameroon	264	**117**	156	74	12.2	499	58	850	56	54	101	—	—
45 Myanmar	237	**113**	158	83	43.7	1431	162	220x	57	81	127	—	—
46 Indonesia	216	**111**	127	71	191.2	5146	571	610	62	82	117	21	42
47 Congo	220	**110**	143	82	2.4	107	12	1120	52	57	—	—	—
48 Libyan Arab Jamahiriya	269	**104**	160	70	4.9	206	21	5310x	63	64	—	—	—
49 Turkmenistan	—	**91**	—	72	3.9	140	13	1700	66	—	—	23	—
50 Turkey	217	**87**	161	70	58.4	1653	144	1780	57	81	110	11x	56x
51 Zimbabwe	181	**86**	109	60	10.5	434	37	650	56	67	117	—	—
52 Tajikistan	—	**85**	—	65	5.7	239	19	1050	69	—	—	23	—
53 Iraq	171	**80**	117	64	19.3	753	60	1500x	66	60	96	—	—
54 Mongolia	185	**80**	128	61	2.3	79	6	780x	63	—	98	—	—
55 Namibia	206	**79**	129	62	1.5	66	5	1460	58	—	94	—	—
56 Papua New Guinea	248	**77**	165	53	4.1	136	11	830	56	52	71	—	—

(Contd.)

TABLE 5.1 *Contd.*

1	2	3	4	5	6	7	8	9	10	11	12	13	14
57 Guatemala	205	**76**	137	55	9.7	380	29	930	64	55	77	8	63
58 Nicaragua	209	**76**	140	54	4.0	163	12	460	66	—	98	12x	58x
59 Kenya	202	**74**	120	51	25.2	1111	82	340	59	69	94	9	61
60 Algeria	243	**72**	148	60	26.3	901	65	1980	66	57	95	—	—
61 South Africa	126	**70**	89	53	39.8	1253	88	2560	63	76x	—	—	—
62 Uzbekistan	—	**68**	—	56	21.5	736	50	1350	69	—	—	22	—
63 Brazil	181	**65**	118	54	154.1	3626	236	2940	66	81	108x	7	51
64 Peru	236	**65**	143	46	22.5	658	43	1070	64	85	126	14	51
65 El Salvador	210	**63**	130	47	5.4	182	11	1080	66	73	78	8x	66x
66 Morocco	215	**61**	133	50	26.3	854	52	1030	63	50	68	17	46
67 Kyrgyzstan	—	**60**	—	49	4.5	135	8	1550	66	—	—	21	—
68 Philippines	102	**60**	73	46	65.2	1992	120	730	65	90	111	17	48
69 Ecuador	180	**59**	115	47	11.1	332	20	1000	66	86	118	—	—
70 Botswana	170	**58**	117	45	1.3	51	3	2530	61	74	110	6	66
71 Honduras	203	**58**	137	45	5.5	205	12	580	66	73	108	9	64
72 Iran, Islamic Rep. of	233	**58**	145	44	61.6	2473	143	2170	67	54	112	—	—
73 Egypt	258	**55**	169	43	54.8	1732	95	610	61	48	98	21x	41x
74 Azerbeijan	—	**53**	—	37	7.3	189	10	1570	71	—	—	—	—
75 Dominican Rep.	152	**50**	104	42	7.5	214	11	940	67	83	95	12	56
76 Kazakhstan	—	**50**	—	43	17.0	351	18	2470	69	—	—	—	—
77 Viet Nam	219	**49**	147	37	69.5	2039	100	240x	64	88	102x	—	—
78 Lebanon	91	**44**	68	35	2.8	78	3	2150x	68	80	100x	—	—
79 China	209	**43**	140	35	1188.0	25057	1077	370	71	73	135	17	42
80 Saudi Arabia	292	**40**	170	35	15.9	474	23	7820	69	62	78	—	—

(*Contd.*)

TABLE 5.1 *Contd.*

1	2	3	4	5	6	7	8	9	10	11	12	13	14
81 Syrian Arab Rep.	201	**40**	136	34	13.3	569	23	1:160	67	65	109	—	—
82 Tunisia	244	**38**	163	32	8.4	230	9	1500	68	65	116	16	46
83 Moldova	—	**36**	—	31	4.4	69	2	2170	68	—	—	23	—
84 Albania	151	**34**	112	28	3.3	76	3	790x	73	—	98	—	—
85 Armenia	—	**34**	—	29	3.5	79	3	2150	72	—	—	22	—
86 Paraguay	90	**34**	66	28	4.5	151	5	1270	67	90	107	—	—
87 Korea, Dem. Peo. Rep.	120	**33**	85	25	22.6	553	18	970x	71	—	106	—	—
88 Mexico	141	**33**	98	28	88.2	2491	82	3030	70	88	112	12	56
89 Thailand	146	**33**	101	27	56.1	1176	39	1570	69	93	85	16	51
90 Russian Federation	—	**32**	—	28	148.3	1809	58	3220	69	—	—	—	—
91 Oman	300	**31**	180	24	1.6	67	2	6120	69	—	103	—	—
92 Jordan	148	**30**	103	25	4.3	171	5	1050	68	80	104x	—	—
93 Georgia	—	**29**	—	25	5.5	84	2	1640	73	—	—	21	—
94 Romania	82	**28**	69	23	23.3	363	10	1390	70	—	91	—	—
95 Latvia	—	**26**	—	22	2.7	37	1	3410	71	—	—	—	—
96 Ukraine	—	**25**	—	21	51.9	633	16	2340	70	—	—	21	—
97 Argentina	68	**24**	57	22	33.1	673	16	2790	71	95	111	14x	51x
98 Estonia	—	**24**	—	20	1.6	22	1	3830	71	100x	—	20	—
99 Mauritius	84	**24**	62	20	1.1	20	0	2410	70	—	106	12x	46x
100 Venezuela	70	**24**	53	20	20.2	531	13	2730x	70	88	92	14	50
101 Belarus	—	**23**	—	20	10.3	136	3	3110	71	—	—	22	—
102 Trinadad & Tobgo	73	**22**	61	19	1.3	30	1	3670	71	95x	95	13x	50x
103 U. Arab Emirates	240	**22**	160	18	1.7	35	1	19860x	71	—	116	—	—

(*Contd.*)

TABLE 5.1 *Contd.*

1	2	3	4	5	6	7	8	9	10	11	12	13	14
104 Uruguay	47	**22**	41	20	3.1	54	1	2840	72	96	106	18x	44x
105 Yugoslavia	113	**22**	92	19	23.9	338	7	3060x	72	93	95	16	44
106 Colombia	132	**20**	82	17	33.4	809	16	1260	69	87	110	13	53
107 Lithuania	—	**20**	—	17	3.8	56	1	2710	73	98x	—	—	—
108 Panama	104	**20**	67	18	2.5	63	1	2130	73	88	107	8	60
109 Bulgaria	70	**20**	49	16	9.0	111	2	1840	72	—	96	—	—
110 Sri Lanka	130	**19**	90	15	17.7	371	7	500	71	88	107	13	56
111 Malaysia	105	**19**	73	14	18.8	545	10	2620	71	78	93	13	54
112 Chile	138	**18**	107	15	13.6	309	6	2160	72	93	98	11	63
113 Kuwait	128	**17**	89	14	2.0	54	1	16150x	75	73	100	—	—
114 Poland	70	**16**	62	14	38.4	550	9	1719	72	—	98	23	36
115 Hungary	57	**16**	51	15	10.5	127	2	2720	70	99x	94	26	34
116 Costa Rica	112	**16**	80	14	3.2	85	1	1850	76	93	102	13	51
117 Jamaica	76	**14**	58	12	2.5	55	1	1380	73	98	105	16	48
118 Slovakia	—	**14**	—	12	5.4	79	1	—	72	—	—	—	—
119 Portugal	112	**13**	81	11	9.9	114	2	593	75	85	119	—	—
120 Czech Republic	—	**12**	—	11	10.4	135	2	—	72	—	—	—	—
121 Cuba	50	**11**	39	10	10.8	190	2	1170x	76	94	103	—	—
122 Israel	39	**11**	32	9	5.1	110	1	11950	76	92x	93	18	40
123 Belgium	35	**11**	31	9	10.0	122	1	18950	76	—	102	22	36
124 USA	30	**10**	26	9	255.2	4078	42	22240	76	—	105	16	42
125 New Zealand	26	**10**	22	8	3.5	60	1	12350	76	—	106	16	45
126 Italy	50	**10**	44	8	57.8	478	6	18520	77	97	97	19	41
127 Spain	57	**9**	46	8	39.1	422	4	12450	77	95	109	19	40

(Contd.)

Table 5.1 *Contd.*

1	2	3	4	5	6	7	8	9	10	11	12	13	14
128 Greece	64	**9**	53	8	10.2	106	1	6340	77	93	100	—	—
129 Korea, Rep. of	124	**9**	88	8	44.2	723	7	6330	71	96	107	20x	42x
130 Austria	43	**9**	37	7	7.8	91	1	20140	76	—	103	—	—
131 France	34	**9**	29	7	57.2	773	7	20380	77	—	111	18	41
132 United Kingdom	27	**9**	23	7	57.7	801	7	16550	76	—	107	17	40
133 Australia	24	**9**	20	7	17.6	265	2	17050	77	—	105	16	42
134 Switzerland	27	**9**	22	7	6.8	86	1	33610	78	—	—	17	45
135 Germany	40	**8**	34	7	80.3	912	8	23650	76	—	105	20	39
136 Canada	33	**8**	28	7	27.4	391	3	20440	77	—	105	18	40
137 Denmark	25	**8**	22	7	5.2	64	1	23700	76	—	98	17	39
138 Norway	23	**8**	19	6	4.3	63	0	24220	77	—	99	19	37
139 Netherlands	22	**7**	18	6	15.2	207	2	18780	77	—	117	20	38
140 Sweden	20	**7**	16	6	8.7	120	1	25110	78	—	107	21	37
141 Hong Kong	52	**7**	38	6	5.8	75	1	13430	78	—	105	16	47
142 Singapore	40	**7**	31	6	2.8	44	0	14210	74	83x	110	15	49
143 Finland	28	**7**	22	6	5.0	64	0	23980	76	—	99	18	38
144 Japan	40	**6**	31	4	124.5	1390	8	26930	79	—	101	22	38
145 Ireland	36	**6**	31	5	3.5	50	0	11120	75	—	100	—	—

Note: Countries listed in descending order of their under-five mortality rates (shown in bold types).

TABLE 5.2: Demographic Data

	Population (millions) 1992		Population annual growth rate (%)		Crude death rate		Crude birth rate		Life expectancy		Total fertility rate	% of population urbanized	Average annual growth rate of urban population (%)	
	under 16	under 5	1985-90	1980-82	1960	1992	1960	1992	1960	1992	1992	1992	1965-80	1980-92
1	2	3	4	5	6	7	8	9	10	11	12	13	14	15
1 Niger	41	1.7	2.8	3.3	29	19	53	51	35	46	7.1	21	7.2	7.2
2 Angola	4.9	2.0	2.0	2.9	31	19	49	51	33	46	7.2	30	5.5	5.9
3 Mozambique	7.0	2.7	2.5	1.7	26	18	47	45	37	47	6.5	30	9.5	8.7
4 Afghanistan	8.2	3.5	1.9	1.4	30	22	52	52	33	43	6.9	19	5.3	3.1
5 Sierra Leone	2.0	0.8	2.0	2.5	33	22	48	48	32	43	6.5	34	5.1	5.2
6 Guinea-Bissau	2.0	0.8	2.0	2.5	33	22	40	48	34	43	6.5	34	5.1	5.2
7 Guinea	3.0	1.2	1.6	2.6	31	20	53	51	34	44	7.0	27	4.9	5.7
8 Malawi	5.3	2.1	3.0	4.3	28	21	54	55	38	44	7.6	13	7.1	6.9
9 Rwanda	3.9	1.6	3.2	3.1	22	18	50	52	42	46	8.5	6	6.8	4.8
10 Mali	4.8	1.9	2.2	3.0	29	19	52	51	36	46	71	25	4.8	5.6
11 Liberia	1.3	0.5	3.0	3.2	25	14	50	47	41	55	6.8	48	6.1	5.8
12 Somalia	4.6	1.8	3.1	2.6	28	19	50	50	36	47	7.0	25	4.0	3.6
13 Chad	2.7	1.0	2.0	2.2	30	18	46	44	35	47	5.9	34	7.5	6.5
14 Eritrea	1.6	0.6	—	—	—	16	—	42	—	47	5.8	—	—	—

(Contd.)

TABLE 5.2 *Contd.*

1	2	3	4	5	6	7	8	9	10	11	12	13	14	15
15 Ethiopia	25.6	10.3	2.4	2.6	28	19	51	49	36	47	7.0	13	4.5	4.3
16 Mauritania	1.0	0.4	2.3	2.7	28	18	48	46	35	48	6.5	50	10.1	7.2
17 Zambia	4.4	1.7	3.1	3.4	22	18	50	47	42	45	6.4	42	6.6	3.9
18 Bhutan	0.7	0.3	1.9	2.2	28	17	42	40	37	48	5.9	6	4.2	5.4
19 Nigeria	57.3	22.1	3.2	3.2	24	14	52	45	40	52	6.5	37	6.3	5.8
20 Zaire	19.9	7.8	2.9	3.3	23	15	47	48	41	52	6.7	29	3.5	3.2
21 Uganda	9.5	3.8	3.3	2.9	21	21	50	51	43	42	7.3	12	5.3	5.4
22 Cambodia	3.8	1.4	0.4	2.5	21	14	45	39	42	51	4.5	12	0.0	3.9
23 Burundi	2.8	1.1	1.7	2.9	23	17	46	46	41	48	6.8	6	6.1	5.2
24 Central African Rep.	1.5	0.6	2.1	2.6	26	18	43	45	39	47	6.2	48	4.5	4.6
25 Yemen	6.5	2.5	2.3	3.5	28	14	53	49	35	52	7.2	31	6.3	7.1
26 Tanzania U. Rep. of	13.8	5.5	3.0	3.4	23	15	51	48	41	51	6.8	22	9.9	6.9
27 Ghana	7.6	2.9	2.1	3.3	19	12	48	42	45	56	6.0	35	3.3	4.3
28 Madagascar	6.1	2.4	2.5	3.2	24	13	48	45	41	55	6.6	25	5.1	5.9
29 Sudan	12.6	4.7	2.8	3.0	25	14	47	42	39	52	6.1	23	5.6	4.3
30 Gabon	0.4	0.2	3.3	3.6	24	16	31	42	41	53	5.3	48	6.7	6.0
31 Lesotho	0.8	0.3	2.2	2.6	24	10	43	35	43	60	4.7	21	7.1	6.5
32 Burkina Faso	4.4	1.7	2.3	2.6	28	18	49	47	36	48	6.5	17	5.5	8.5
33 Banin	2.4	1.0	2.4	2.9	33	18	47	49	35	46	7.1	40	8.3	4.9
34 Senegal	3.7	1.4	2.8	2.8	27	16	50	43	37	49	6.1	41	3.4	3.9
35 Lao Peo Dem. Rep.	2.1	0.8	1.8	28	23	15	45	45	40	51	6.7	20	5.1	6.1

(Contd.)

TABLE 5.2 *Contd.*

1	2	3	4	5	6	7	8	9	10	11	12	13	14	15
36 Pakistan	57.3	21.7	2.7	3.2	23	11	49	41	43	59	6.2	33	3.8	4.6
37 Togo	1.8	0.8	3.2	3.0	26	13	48	45	39	55	6.6	30	7.9	5.2
38 Haiti	2.9	1.0	1.7	1.9	23	12	42	35	42	56	4.8	30	3.7	3.9
39 Nepal	9.4	3.4	2.4	2.7	26	13	46	38	38	53	5.5	12	6.6	7.8
40 Bangladesh	51.5	18.2	2.8	2.5	22	14	47	39	40	53	48	18	6.7	6.3
41 Cote D'Ivoire	6.6	2.6	4.0	3.8	25	15	53	50	39	52	7.4	42	6.7	5.4
42 India	330.8	112.1	2.2	2.0	21	10	43	29	44	60	3.9	26	3.6	3.1
43 Bolivia	3.2	1.1	2.5	2.5	22	10	46	35	43	61	4.6	52	3.2	3.9
44 Cameroon	5.7	2.1	2.6	2.9	24	12	44	41	39	56	5.7	42	6.9	5.4
45 Myanmar	17.4	6.2	2.2	2.1	21	11	42	33	44	57	4.2	25	3.1	2.6
46 Indonesia	70.5	23.1	2.3	2.0	23	9	44	27	41	62	3.1	30	4.6	4.6
47 Congo	1.1	0.4	2.7	2.9	23	15	45	45	42	52	6.3	42	3.4	4.2
48 Libyan Arab Jamahiriya	2.3	0.9	4.2	3.9	19	8	49	42	47	63	6.4	84	10.4	5.5
49 Turkmenistan	1.7	0.6	—	—	—	8	—	36	—	66	4.5	—	—	—
50 Turkey	21.6	7.6	2.4	2.3	18	7	45	28	50	67	3.5	64	4.0	5.5
51 Zimbabwe	5.0	1.9	3.1	3.3	20	11	53	41	45	56	5.4	30	6.0	5.8
52 Tajikistan	2.7	1.0	—	—	—	6	—	41	—	69	5.3	32	—	—
53 Iraq	8.9	3.3	3.3	3.3	20	7	49	39	48	66	5.7	73	5.0	4.2
54 Mongolia	1.0	0.4	2.8	2.7	18	8	43	34	47	63	4.7	59	4.2	3.8
55 Namibia	0.7	0.3	2.7	3.0	22	11	45	43	42	59	6.0	29	4.8	5.1
56 Papua New Guinea	1.7	0.6	2.4	2.3	23	11	44	34	41	56	4.9	17	8.6	4.3

(*Contd.*)

TABLE 5.2 *Contd.*

1	2	3	4	5	6	7	8	9	10	11	12	13	14	15
57 Guatemala	4.6	1.7	2.8	2.9	19	8	49	39	46	63	5.4	40	3.4	3.5
58 Nicaragua	2.0	0.7	3.1	2.9	19	7	51	41	47	66	5.1	61	4.6	4.0
59 Kenya	12.8	4.7	3.6	3.5	22	10	53	44	45	59	6.3	25	7.7	7.3
60 Algeria	11.9	3.9	3.0	2.8	20	7	51	34	47	66	4.9	53	4.0	4.6
61 South Africa	16.1	5.5	2.7	2.5	17	9	42	31	49	63	4.1	50	2.8	2.8
62 Uzbekistan	9.4	3.3	—	—	—	6	—	34	—	69	2.3	41	—	—
63 Brazil	55.2	17.3	2.4	2.0	13	7	43	24	55	66	2.8	77	4.3	3.2
64 Peru	8.8	2.9	2.7	2.2	19	8	47	29	48	64	3.6	71	4.2	3.0
65 El Salvadore	2.4	0.8	2.7	1.5	16	7	48	34	50	66	4.1	45	3.2	2.2
66 Morocco	11.1	3.9	2.5	2.6	21	8	50	33	47	63	4.4	47	4.2	3.7
67 Kyrgyzstan	1.8	0.6	—	—	—	8	—	30	—	66	3.9	38	—	—
68 Philippines	27.0	9.2	2.8	2.4	15	7	45	31	53	65	4.0	44	3.9	3.8
69 Ecuador	4.5	1.5	3.0	2.6	15	7	46	30	53	66	3.7	58	4.6	4.3
70 Botswana	0.6	0.2	3.3	3.1	20	10	52	39	46	61	5.1	28	12.5	8.2
71 Honduras	2.5	0.9	3.1	3.3	19	7	51	37	46	66	5.0	45	5.4	5.3
72 Iran, Islamic Rep. of	29.7	11.1	3.1	3.8	21	7	47	40	50	67	6.0	58	4.9	5.1
73 Egypt	22.5	7.7	2.2	2.5	21	9	45	32	46	61	4.2	44	2.7	2.5
74 Azerbaijan	2.6	0.9	—	—	—	6	—	26	—	71	3.2	5.4	—	—
75 Dominican Rep.	2.9	1.0	2.7	2.3	16	6	50	29	52	67	3.4	62	5.1	4.0
76 Kazakhstan	5.6	1.9	—	—	—	8	—	21	—	69	2.7	57	—	—
77 Viet Nam	27.9	9.3	2.3	2.2	23	9	41	29	44	64	3.9	20	3.3	2.6
78 Lebanon	1.0	0.4	1.4	0.5	14	7	43	27	60	68	3.1	85	4.1	1.8
79 China	343.8	119.1	2.1	1.5	19	7	37	21	47	71	2.2	28	2.6	4.4

(Contd.)

TABLE 5.2 *Contd.*

1	2	3	4	5	6	7	8	9	10	11	12	13	14	15
80 Saudi Arabia	7.1	2.6	4.5	4.4	23	5	49	36	44	69	6.4	79	8.1	5.8
81 Syrian Arab Rep.	6.7	2.5	3.3	3.5	18	6	47	43	50	67	6.2	51	4.3	4.3
82 Tunisia	3.3	1.1	2.1	2.3	19	7	47	27	48	68	3.5	57	3.8	3.4
83 Moldova	1.4	0.4	—	—	—	10	—	16	—	68	2.5	47	—	—
84 Albania	1.1	0.4	2.4	1.8	10	5	41	23	62	73	2.7	36	2.9	2.4
85 Armenia	1.1	0.3	—	—	—	7	—	23	—	72	3.0	68	—	—
86 Paraguay	1.9	0.7	2.9	3.0	9	6	43	33	64	67	4.4	49	3.8	4.3
87 Korea, Dem. Peo. Rep.	6.9	2.5	2.6	l.8	13	5	42	24	54	71	2.4	60	4.1	2.3
88 Mexico	34.7	11.6	30	2.3	13	6	45	28	57	70	3.2	74	4.2	3.2
89 Thailand	18.5	5.6	2.8	1.5	15	6	44	21	52	69	2.3	24	4.7	4.2
90 Russian Federation	36.1	11.5	—	—	—	12	—	12	—	69	1.8	74	—	—
91 Oman	0.8	0.3	3.7	4.2	28	5	51	41	40	69	6.8	12	7.6	8.0
92 Jordan	2.0	0.7	2.7	3.2	23	6	50	35	47	68	5.7	70	4.4	4.5
93 Romania	5.7	1.8	1.0	0.4	9	11	20	16	65	70	2.1	55	2.8	1.3
95 Latvia	0.6	0.2	0.7	0.5	10	12	16	14	70	71	2.0	72	1.6	0.9
96 Ukraine	11.6	3.6	—	—	—	13	—	12	—	70	1.8	67	—	—
97 Argentina	10.3	3.2	1.6	1.3	9	9	24	20	65	71	2.8	87	2.1	1.7
98 Estonia	0.4	0.1	0.9	0.6	11	12	16	14	69	71	2.1	72	1.7	0.8
99 Mauritius	0.3	0.1	1.7	1.1	10	7	44	18	59	70	2.0	41	2.6	0.7
100 Venezuela	7.8	2.5	3.4	2.5	10	5	45	26	60	70	3.2	91	4.6	3.2
101 Belarus	2.5	0.8	—	—	—	11	—	13	—	71	1.9	66	—	—
102 Trinadad & Tobago	0.5	0.1	1.3	1.3	9	6	38	24	63	71	2 8	66	1.2	1.6

(*Contd.*)

TABLE 5.2 *Contd.*

1	2	3	4	5	6	7	8	9	10	11	12	13	14	15
103 U. Arab Emirates	0.5	0.2	13.0	4.2	19	4	46	21	53	71	4.5	82	15.6	5.3
104 Uruguay	0.8	0.3	0.5	0.6	10	10	22	17	68	72	2.3	89	0.9	1.0
105 Yugoslavia (former)	5.7	1.7	0.9	0.6	10	9	23	14	63	72	1.9	58	3.4	2.6
106 Colombia	12.2	3.8	2.4	1.9	12	6	45	24	57	69	2.7	71	3.6	2.8
107 Lithuania	0.9	0.3	1.0	0.8	8	10	21	15	69	73	2.0	70	3.0	1.9
108 Panama	0.9	0.3	2.6	2.1	10	5	41	25	61	73	2.9	54	3.3	2.7
109 Bulgaria	1.9	0.5	0.5	0.1	9	12	18	13	68	72	18	69	2.4	1.1
110 Sri Lanka	6.0	1.8	1.9	1.5	9	6	36	21	62	71	2.5	22	2.4	1.6
111 Malaysia	7.5	2.6	2.5	2.6	15	5	44	29	54	71	3.7	45	4.4	4.7
112 Chile	4.4	1.5	1.7	1.7	13	6	37	23	57	72	2.7	85	2.6	2.1
113 Kuwait	0.8	0.3	7.1	3.0	10	2	44	28	60	75	3.7	96	8.1	3.4
114 Poland	10.1	2.9	0.8	0.6	8	10	24	14	67	72	2.1	63	1.8	1.3
115 Hungary	2.2	0.6	0.4	-0.2	10	14	16	12	68	70	1.3	66	1.9	1.0
116 Costa Rica	1.2	0.4	2.9	2.8	10	4	47	27	62	76	3.2	48	3.7	3.7
117 Jamaica	0.8	0.3	1.3	1.2	9	6	39	22	63	73	2.4	54	2.7	2.4
118 Slovakia	1.4	0.4	—	—	—	10	—	15	—	72	2.0	—	—	—
119 Portugal	2.1	0.6	0.5	0.1	11	10	24	12	63	75	15	35	18	15
120 Czech Republic	2.3	0.7	—	—	—	11	—	13	—	72	19	—	—	—
121 Cuba	2.6	0.9	1.5	0.9	9	7	31	17	64	76	1.9	75	2.6	1.7
122 Israel	1.6	0.5	2.8	2.3	6	7	27	21	69	76	2.9	92	3.4	2.7
123 Belgium	1.9	0.6	0.3	0.1	12	11	17	12	70	76	1.6	96	0.4	0.2
124 USA	58.8	19.2	1.1	1.0	9	9	23	16	70	76	2.1	76	1.2	1.2
125 New Zealand	0.8	0.3	1.1	0.9	9	8	26	17	71	75	2.1	84	1.5	0.9

(Contd.)

TABLE 5.2 *Contd.*

1	2	3	4	5	6		7	8	9	10	11	12	13	14
126 Italy	10.3	2.9	0.5	0.2	10	10	18	10	69	77	1.3	70	1.0	0.6
127 Spain	7.9	2.1	1.1	0.3	9	9	21	11	69	77	1.4	79	2.2	1.1
128 Greece	2.0	0.5	0.8	0.5	8	10	19	10	69	77	1.5	63	2.1	1.3
129 Korea, Rep. of	11.7	3.4	1.9	1.2	14	6	43	16	54	71	1.8	74	5.7	3.5
130 Austria	1.4	0.4	0.3	0.3	12	11	18	12	69	76	1.5	59	0.8	0.9
131 France	12.3	3.8	0.7	0.5	12	10	18	14	70	77	0.8	73	1.3	0.4
132 United Kingdom	11.8	3.9	0.2	0.2	12	11	17	14	71	76	1.9	89	0.4	0.2
133 Australia	4.1	1.3	1.7	1.5	9	8	22	15	71	77	1.9	85	1.9	1.4
134 Switzerland	1.2	0.4	0.5	0.6	10	10	18	13	71	78	1.6	63	1.0	1.4
135 Germany	14.5	4.6	0.2	0.2	12	11	17	11	70	76	1.5	85	0.6	0.5
136 Canada	6.1	1.9	1.3	1.1	8	8	26	14	71	77	1.8	78	1.6	1.3
137 Denmark	0.9	0.3	0.5	0.1	9	12	17	12	72	76	1.7	85	1.0	0.2
138 Norway	0.9	0.3	0.6	0.4	9	11	18	15	73	77	2.0	76	2.0	1.0
140 Sweden	1.7	0.6	0.5	0.3	10	11	15	14	73	78	2.1	84	1.0	0.5
141 Hong Kong	1.3	0.4	2.1	1.2	7	6	35	13	66	78	1.4	95	2.5	1.4
142 Singapore	0.7	0.2	1.7	1.1	8	6	38	16	64	74	1.7	100	1.7	1.1
143 Finland	1.0	0.3	0.3	0.4	9	10	19	13	68	76	1.8	60	2.4	0.4
144 Japan	23.7	6.8	1.1	0.5	8	7	18	11	68	79	1.7	77	1.9	0.7
145 Ireland	1.0	0.3	11	0.2	12	9	21	15	70	75	2.1	58	2.0	0.5

Note: Countries listed in descending order of their 1992 under-five mortality rates (table 5.1).

TABLE 5.3: Economic Data

	GNP per capita (US$)	GNP per capita average annual growth rate (%)		rate of inflation	% of population below absolute poverty level 1960-89		% of central government expenditure allocation to (1986-92)			ODA inflow in million US$)	ODA inflow at a % of recipient GNP	Debt service at a % of exports of goods & service	
	1991	1965-80	1980-81	1980-81	urban	rural	health	education	defence	1991	1991	1970	1991
	1	2	3	4	5	6	7	8	9	10	11	12	13
1 Niger	300	-2.5	-4.1	2	—	35x	—	—	—	418	18	4	30
2 Angola	610x	—	61x	—	—	—	6x	15x	34x	250	—	—	4
3 Mozambique	80	—	-1.1	38	50	67	5x	10x	35x	1022	79	—	11
4 Afghanistan	280x	0.6	—	—	18x	36x	—	—	—	521	—	—	—
5 Sierra Leone	210	0.7-1.6	59	—	65x	10	13	10	108	12	11	4x	—
6 Guinea-Bissau	180	-2.7	1.1	56	—	—	1	3	4	123	68	—	26x
7 Guinea	460	1.3	—	—	—	—	—	11x	29x	331	12	—	14
8 Malawai	230	3.2	0.1	15	25	85	7	9	5	494	24	8	16x
9 Rwanda	270	1.6	-2.4	4	30	90x	5x	26x	—	328	17	1	14
10 Mali	280	21x	-0.1	4	27x	48x	2	9	8	408	17	1	3
11 Liberia	450x	0.5	5.2x	—	—	23x	5	11	9	143	—	8	—
12 Somalia	150x	-0.1	-1.8x	50x	40x	70x	1x	2x	38x	282	—	2	8x
13 Chad	210	-1.9	3.8	1	30x	56x	8x	8x	—	269	22	4	4

(Contd.)

TABLE 5.3 *Contd.*

	1	2	3	4	5	6	7	8	9	10	11	12	13
14 Eritrea	120	—	—	—	—	—	—	—	—	—	—	—	—
15 Ethopia	120	0.4	-1.6	2	60	65	3	11	—	951	15	11	23
16 Mauritania	510	-0.1	-1.8	9	—	—	4x	23x	—	208	20	3	12
17 Zambia	420x	-1.2	-2.9x	42x	25	—	7	9	—	587	—	6	12x
18 Bhutan	180	—	6.8	8	—	—	5	11	—	55	21	—	7x
19 Nigeria	340	4.2	-2.3	18	—	—	1	3	3	293	1	4	24
20 Zaire	230x	-1.3	-1.6	61x	—	80x	4x	6x	14x	505	—	4	6x
21 Uganda	170	-2.2	3.3	107x	—	—	2x	15x	26x	566	20	3	42
22 Cambodia	200x	—	—	—	—	—	—	—	—	62	4	—	—
23 Burundi	210	2.4	1.3	4	55x	85x	4x	16x	16x	249	21	2	30
24 Central African Rep.	390	0.8	-1.4	5	—	91	—	—	—	225	19	5	5
25 Yemen	520	—	—	—	—	—	5	21	21	—	—	—	8
26 Tanzania U. Rep. of	100	0.8	-0.8	26	—	—	6x	8x	16x	1038	41	5	19x
27 Ghana	400	-0.8	-0.3	40	59	37	9	26	3	603	10	6	15
28 Madagascar	210	-0.4	02.5	17	50x	50x	7	17	8	358	14	4	24
29 Sudan	420x	0.8	-2.4	34x	—	85x	—	—	—	836	—	11	4
30 Gabon	3780	5.6	-4.2	2	—	—	—	—	—	142	3	6	6x
31 Lesotho	580	6.8	-0.5	14	50x	55x	11	22	6	125	12	5	5
32 Burkina Faso	290	1.7	1.2	4	—	—	5	14	18	379	14	7	8x
33 Benin	380	-0.3	-0.9	2	—	—	6x	31x	17x	270	15	2	7
34 Senegal	720	-0.5	0.1	6	—	—	—	—	—	769	14	3	14x
35 Lao Peo. Dem. Rep.	220	—	1.2	—	—	—	—	—	—	161	17	—	8x

(Contd.)

TABLE 5.3 *Contd.*

		1	2	3	4	5	6	7	8	9	10	11	12	13
36	Pakistan	400	1.8	3.2	7	32x	29x	1	2x	28x	1133	3	24	22x
37	Togo	410	1.7	-1.3	4	42x	—	5	20	11	201	13	3	5
38	Haiti	370	0.9	-2.4	7	65	80	—	—	—	197	8	69	5
39	Nepal	180	—	2.1	9	55x	61x	5	11	6	403	12	3	12
40	Bangladesh	220	0.3	1.9	9	86x	86x	5x	11x	10x	2142	9	—	19
41	Cote d'Ivoire	690	2.8	-4.6	4	30	26	4x	—	—	597	7	7	14
42	India	330	1.5	3.2	8	29	33	2	2	17	1657	1	22	27
43	Bolivia	650	1.7	-2.0	263	—	—	3	19	13	540	11	11	24
44	Cameroon	850	2.4	-1.0	5	15x	40x	3	12	7	507	5	3	13x
45	Myanmar	220x	1.6	—	—	40x	40x	7	16	22	167	—	12	—
46	Indonesia	610	5.2	3.9	9	20	16	23	9	8	1733	2	7	21
47	Congo	1120	2.7	-0.2	0	—	—	—	—	—	134	5	12	19
48	Libyan Arab Jamahiriya	5310x	0.0	-9.2x	0x	—	—	—	—	—	9	—	—	—
49	Turmkenistan	1700	—	0.7	—	—	—	—	—	—	—	—	—	—
50	Turkey	1780	3.6	2.9	45	—	—	3	18	10	1640	2	22	29
51	Zimbabwe	650	1.7	-0.2	13	—	—	8x	—	17x	376	6	2	23
52	Tajikistan	1050	—	-0.1	—	—	—	—	—	—	—	—	—	—
53	Iraq	1500x	—	—	—	—	—	—	—	—	417	—	—	—
54	Mongolia	780x	—	—	-1x	—	—	—	—	—	18	—	—	—
55	Namibia	1460	—	-1.2	13	—	—	10	22	7	79	8	—	—
56	Papua New Guinea	830	—	-0.6	5	10x	75x	9	15	5	381	12	1	14

(*Contd.*)

TABLE 5.3 *Contd.*

	1	2	3	4	5	6	7	8	9	10	11	12	13
57 Guatemala	930	3.0	-1.8	16	17	51	10	20	13	189	2	7	15
58 Nicaragua	460	-0.7	04.4	584	21x	19x	11x	9x	50	680	39	11	111
59 Kenya	340	3.1	0.3	9	10x	55x	5	20	10	884	10	6	22x
60 Algeria	1980	4.2	-0.7	10	20x	—	—	—	—	351	1	4	69
61 South Africa	2560	3.2	0.7	14	—	—	—	—	—	—	—	—	—
62 Uzbekistan	1350	—	0.8	—	—	—	—	—	—	—	—	—	—
63 Brazil	2940	6.3	0.5	328	9	34	7	3	4	196	0	13	22
64 Peru	1070	0.8	-2.4	287	46	83	6	21	18	339	1	12	18
65 El Salvador	1080	1.5	-0.3	17	20	32	8	14	21	—	—	4	—
66 Morocco	1030	2.7	1.6	7	28x	45x	3	17	15	1203	5	9	32
67 Kyrgyzstan	1550	—	2.1	—	—	—	—	—	—	4	0	—	—
68 Philippines	730	3.2	-1.2	15	52	64	4	16	11	1231	3	8	19
69 Ecuador	1000	5.4	-0.6	38	40	65	11	18	13	208	2	9	27
70 Botswana	2530	9.9	5.6	13	40	55	5	21	13	131	4	1	3
71 Honduras	580	1.1	-0.5	7	31	70	—	—	7x	332	11	3	25
72 Iran, Islamic Rep. of	2170	2.9	-1.3	14	—	—	8	21	10	81	0	—	1
73 Egypt	610	2.8	1.9	13	34	34	3	13	13	4638	14	38	16
74 Azerbaijan	1670	—	0.4	—	—	—	—	—	—	—	—	—	—
75 Dominican Rep.	940	3.8	-0.2	25	45x	43x	14	10	5	95	1	4	9
76 Kazakhstan	2470	—	0.9	—	—	—	—	—	—	—	—	—	—
77 Viet Nam	240x	—	—	—	—	—	—	—	—	218	—	—	—
78 Lebanon	2150x	—	—	—	—	—	—	—	—	138	—	—	—

(Contd.)

TABLE 5.3 *Contd.*

		1	2	3	4	5	6	7	8	9	10	11	12	13
79	China	370	4.1	7.8	6	—	13	—	—	8x	2166	2	—	10
80	Saudi Arabia	7820	4.0x	-3.4	-2	—	—	—	—	—	43	0	—	—
81	Syrian Arab Rep.	1160	5.1	-1.4	14	—	—	2	7	32	219	2	11	27x
82	Tunisia	1500	4.7	1.1	7	20x	15x	6	17	6	312	3	20	21
83	Moldova	2170	—	1.8	—	—	—	—	—	—	—	—	—	—
84	Albania	790x	—	—	—	—	—	—	—	—	303	—	—	—
85	Armenia	2150	—	2.1	—	—	—	—	—	—	—	—	—	—
86	Paraguay	1270	4.1	-0.8	25	19x	50x	4	13	13	111	2	12	16x
87	Korea, Dem. Peo. Rep.	970x	—	—	—	—	—	—	—	—	8	—	—	—
88	Mexico	3030	3.6	-0.5	67	—	—	2	14	2	183	0	24	22
89	Thailand	1570	4.4	5.9	4	10	25	7	20	17	738	1	3	5
90	Russian Federation	3220	—	1.3	—	—	—	—	—	—	—	—	—	—
91	Oman	6120	9.0	4.4	-3	—	—	5	11	35	15	0	—	13x
92	Jordan	1050	5.8x	-1.7	2	14x	17x	5	15	21	668	17	4	22
93	Georgia	1640	—	2.2	—	—	—	—	—	—	—	—	—	—
94	Romania	1390	—	0.0	6	—	—	9	10	10	—	—	—	1
95	Latvia	3410	—	2.8	—	—	—	—	—	—	—	—	—	—
96	Ukraine	2340	—	2.3	—	—	—	—	—	—	—	—	—	—
97	Argentina	2790	1.7	-1.5	417	—	—	3	10	10	255	0	22	37
98	Estonia	3830	—	2.1	—	—	—	—	—	—	—	—	—	—
99	Mauritius	2410	3.7	6.1	8	12x	12x	9	15	2	95	4	3	6
100	Venezuela	2730x	2.3	-1.3	21	—	—	10	20	6x	81	0	—	13

(*Contd.*)

TABLE 5.3 *Contd.*

		1	2	3	4	5	6	7	8	9	10	11	12	13
101	Belarus	3110	—	3.3	—	—	—	—	—	—	—	—	—	—
102	Trinidad & Tobago	3670	3.1	-5.2	7	—	39x	—	—	—	9	0	5	15x
103	U. Arab Emirates	19860x	—	-5.8	1x	—	—	7	15	44	6	0	—	—
104	Uruguay	2840	2.5	-0.4	64	22	—	4	7	9	59	1	22	27
105	Yugoslavia (former)	3060x	5.2	-1.4	123	—	—	—	—	53	130	—	10	14
106	Colombia	1260	3.7	1.2	25	32	70	—	—	—	143	0	12	32
107	Lithuania	2710	—	2.5	—	—	—	—	—	—	—	—	—	—
108	Panama	2130	2.8	-1.8	2	21x	30x	21	17	5	112	2	8	3
109	Bulgaria	1840	—	1.7	8	—	—	5	6	6	—	—	—	21
110	Sri Lanka	500	2.8	2.5	11	—	—	5	8	9	651	8	11	11
111	Malaysia	2520	4.7	2.9	2	13	38	5	19	12	459	1	4	7
112	Chile	2160	0.0	1.6	21	12	20	6	10	8	12	0	19	24
113	Kuwait	16150x	0.6x	-2.2x	-3x	—	—	7	14	20	—	—	—	—
114	Poland	1790	—	0.6	63	—	—	—	—	—	—	—	—	5
115	Hungary	2720	5.1	0.7	10	—	—	8x	3x	4x	—	—	—	30
116	Costa Rica	1850	3.3	0.7	23	8	20	32	19	2	193	3	10	15
117	Jamaica	1380	-0.1	0.0	20	—	80	7x	11x	8x	197	6	3	24
118	Slovakia	—	—	—	—	—	—	—	—	—	—	—	—	—
119	Portugal	5930	4.6	3.1	17	—	—	—	—	6x	—	—	7	22
120	Czech Republic	—	—	—	—	—	—	—	—	—	—	—	—	—
121	Cuba	1170x	—	—	—	—	—	23x	10x	—	42	—	—	—
122	Israel	11950	3.7	1.7	89	—	—	4	10	22	1365	2	3	—
123	Belgium	18950	3.6	2.0	4	—	—	12x	2x	5x	—	—	—	—

(*Contd.*)

TABLE 5.3 *Contd.*

		1	2	3	4	5	6	7	8	9	10	11	12	13
124	USA	22240	1.8	1.7	4	—	—	14	2	22	—	—	—	—
125	New Zealand	12350	1.7	0.7	10	—	—	12	12	4	—	—	—	—
126	Italy	18520	3.2	2.2	10	—	—	11x	8x	4x	—	—	—	—
127	Spain	12450	4.1	2.8	9	—	—	14	6	5	—	—	—	—
128	Greece	6340	4.8	1.1	18	—	—	—	—	—	36	0	9	—
129	Korea, Rep. of	6330	7.3	8.7	6	18x	11x	1	16	22	64	0	20	6x
130	Austria	20140	4.0	2.1	4	—	—	13	9	2	—	—	—	—
131	France	20380	3.7	1.8	6	—	—	15x	7x	7x	—	—	—	—
132	United Kingdom	16550	2.0	2.6	6	—	—	13	3	11	—	—	—	—
133	Australia	17050	2.2	1.6	7	—	—	13	7	9	—	—	—	—
134	Switzerland	33610	1.5	1.6	4	—	—	13	3	10	—	—	—	—
135	Germany	23650	3.0x	2.2	3	—	—	19x	1x	8x	—	—	—	—
136	Canada	20440	3.3	2.0	4	—	—	5	3	7	—	—	—	—
137	Denmark	23700	2.2	2.2	5	—	—	1x	9x	5x	—	—	—	—
138	Norway	24220	3.6	2.3	5	—	—	10	9	8	—	—	—	—
139	Netherlands	18780	2.7	1.5	2	—	—	12	11	5	—	—	—	—
140	Sweden	25110	2.0	1.7	7	—	—	1	9	6	—	—	—	—
141	Hong Kong	13430	6.2	5.6	8	—	—	—	17x	—	34	0	—	—
142	Singapore	14210	8.3	5.3	2	—	—	5	20	24	-18	—	1	—
143	Finland	23980	3.6	2.5	7	—	—	11	15	5	—	—	—	—
144	Japan	26930	5.1	3.6	2	—	—	—	—	—	—	—	—	—
145	Ireland	11120	2.8	3.3	6	—	—	13	12	3	—	—	—	—

Note: Countries listed in descending order of their under-five mortality rates (table 1).

TABLE 5.4: Educational Data

	Adult Literacy rate 1970 male	Adult Literacy rate 1970 female	Adult Literacy rate 1990 male	Adult Literacy rate 1990 female	Population 1990 radio	Population 1990 television	Primary school enrolment ratio 1960 (gross) male	Primary school enrolment ratio 1960 (gross) female	Primary school enrolment ratio 1986-91 (gross) male	Primary school enrolment ratio 1986-91 (gross) female	Primary school enrolment ratio 1986-91 (net) male	Primary school enrolment ratio 1986-91 (net) female	% of grade 1 enrolment reaching final primary school 1988	Secondary enrolment ratio 1986-91 (gross) male	Secondary enrolment ratio 1986-91 (gross) female
	1	2	3	4	5	6	7	8	9	10	11	12	13	14	15
1 Niger	6	2	40	17	60	5	8	3	37	21	31	19	75	9	4
2 Angola	16	7	56	29	54	6	30	14	98	91	—	—	—	—	—
3 Mozambique	29	14	45	21	42	3	71	43	68	48	45	37	39	9	5
4 Afghanistan	13	2	44	14	105	8	14	2	31	16	25	13	63	11	5
5 Siera Leone	18	8	31	11	223	10	30	15	56	39	—	—	—	21	12
6 Guinea-Bissau	13	6	50	24	39	—	35	15	76	42	58	32	8	9	4
7 Guinea	21	7	35	13	42	7	27	9	50	24	34	17	44	15	5
8 Malawi	42	18	—	—	238	—	50	26	77	64	55	52	47	6	3
9 Rwanda	43	21	64	37	62	—	65	29	69	68	65	65	36	9	6
10 Mali	11	4	41	24	43	1	13	5	30	17	24	14	40	9	4
11 Liberia	27	8	50	29	225	18	40	13	51x	28x	—	—	—	31x	12x
12 Somalia	5	1	36	14	43	14	6	2	20x	10x	14x	8x	37	12x	7x
13 Chad	20	2	42	18	238	1	29	4	79	35	52	23	71	12	3
14 Eritrea	—	—	—	—	—	—	—	—	—	—	—	—	—	—	—

(Contd.)

TABLE 5.4 *Contd.*

	1	2	3	4	5	6	7	8	9	10	11	12	13	14	15
15 Ethiopia	8	—	33x	16x	191	2	9	3	46	30	32	24	44	17	12
16 Mauritania	—	—	47	21	144	23	12	3	60	42	—	—	68	22	10
17 Zambia	66	37	81	65	77	30	61	40	99	91	81	79	64	25	14
18 Bhutan	—	—	51	25	16	—	5	—	31	20	—	—	26	7	2
19 Nigeria	35	14	62	40	172	32	54	31	82	63	—	—	52	22	17
20 Zaire	61	22	84	61	103	1	89	32	89	67	67	53	73	32	16
21 Uganda	52	30	62	35	101	10	39	18	76	63	57	50	76x	16	8
22 Cambodia	—	23	48	22	113	9	—	—	—	—	—	—	50x	—	—
23 Burundi	29	10	61	40	58	1	33	10	79	64	55	46	83	6	4
24 Central African Rep.	26	6	52	25	66	4	50	11	83	51	66	43	48	17	6
25 Yemen	14	3	53	26	—	—	—	—	111	43	—	—	53	47	10
26 Tanzania U. Rep. of	48	18	—	—	24	2	33	16	64	63	46	47	73	5	4
27 Ghana	43	18	70	51	266	15	58	31	82	67	—	—	87	48	31
28 Madagascar	56	43	88	73	200	20	74	57	94	90	64	63	32	20	18
29 Sudan	28	6	43	12	250	71	29	11	58x	41x	—	—	76	23x	17x
30 Gabon	43	22	74	49	141	37	—	—	—	—	—	—	44	—	—
31 Lesotho	49	74	—	—	70	6	73	109	99	115	64	76	50	21	31
32 Burkina Faso	13	3	28	9	26	5	12	5	45	28	36	23	64	9	5
33 Benin	23	8	32	16	90	5	39	15	87	44	69	36	40	16	6
34 Senegal	18	5	52	25	113	36	37	18	67	49	55	41	85	21	11
35 Lao Peo. Dem. Rep.	37	28	92x	76x	126	7	43	20	116	91	—	—	38x	31	21

(Contd.)

TABLE 5.4 *Contd.*

	1	2	3	4	5	6	7	8	9	10	11	12	13	14	15
36 Pakistan	30	11	47	21	87	17	39	11	47	26	—	—	51	29	13
37 Togo	27	7	56	31	211	6	64	25	126	80	85	58	46	33	10
38 Haiti	26x	17x	59	47	46	5	50	39	86	81	44	44	9	20	19
39 Nepal	23	3	38	13	34	2	19	3	112	57	84	43	—	42	17
40 Bangladesh	36	12	47	22	42	5	80	31	78	68	69	61	46	23	12
41 Cote d'Ivoire	26	10	67	40	142	61	62	22	88x	62x	—	—	73	27	12
42 India	47	20	62	34	79	32	83	44	109	83	—	—	53	54	33
43 Bolivia	68	46	85	71	599	163	70	43	87	78	83	75	50	37	31
44 Cameroon	47	19	67	43	139	29	77	37	108	93	80	69	68	31	21
45 Myanmar	85	57	89	72	82	2	60	53	106	100	—	—	—	25	23
46 Indonesia	66	42	88	75	147	60	78	58	119	114	100	96	79	49	41
47 Congo	59	19	70	44	110	6	—	—	—	—	—	—	62	37	14
48 Libyan Arab Jamahiriya	60	13	75	50	224	99	—	—	—	—	—	—	—	—	—
49 Turkmenistan	—	—	—	—	—	—	—	—	—	—	—	—	—	—	—
50 Turkey	69	34	90	71	161	175	90	58	114	105	—	—	97	66	42
51 Zimbabwe	63	47	74	60	85	31	82	65	118	116	—	—	75	54	46
52 Tajikistan	—	—	—	—	—	—	—	—	—	—	—	—	—	—	—
53 Iraq	50	18	70	49	205	69	94	36	104	87	90	78	58	58	37
54 Mongolia	87	74	—	—	132	41	80	80	96	100	—	—	—	87	96
55 Namibia	—	—	—	—	135	17	—	—	89	99	—	—	—	30	38
56 Papua New Guinea	39	24	65	38	72	2	24	15	77	65	79	67	61	15	10

(*Contd.*)

TABLE 5.4 *Contd.*

	1	2	3	4	5	6	7	8	9	10	11	12	13	14	15
57 Guatemala	51	37	63	47	65	52	48	39	82	79	—	—	36	20x	17x
58 Nicaragua	58	57	—	—	249	62	57	59	94	101	74	77	29	31	44
59 Kenya	44	19	80	59	125	9	62	29	96	92	92x	89x	62	27	19
60 Algeria	39	11	70	46	233	74	55	37	103	88	94	83	90	66	53
61 South Africa	—	—	78x	75x	326	105	—	—	—	—	—	—	—	—	—
62 Uzbekistan	—	—	—	—	—	—	—	—	—	—	—	—	—	—	—
63 Brazil	69	63	83	80	379	213	58	56	101x	97x	—	—	22	31x	36x
64 Peru	81	60	91	79	253	97	98	74	125x	120x	—	—	70x	66x	60x
65 El Salvadore	61	53	76	70	—	—	59	56	77	78	69	71	27	26	25
66 Morocco	34	10	61	38	209	74	69	28	81	55	66	45	63	42	30
67 Kyrgyzstan	—	—	—	—	—	—	—	—	—	—	—	—	—	—	—
68 Philippines	84	81	90	89	13	48	98	93	111	110	100	98	71	72	75
69 Ecuador	75	68	88	84	315	83	82	75	118	117	—	—	63	55	57
70 Botswana	37	44	84	65	115	15	38	43	107	112	88	93	95	44	47
71 Honduras	55	50	75	71	385	72	68	67	108	109	89	94	43x	29x	30x
72 Iran, Islamic Rep. of	40	17	64	43	247	70	59	28	119	106	99	90	91	63	47
73 Egypt	50	20	63	34	324	109	79	52	105	90	—	—	95	92	71
74 Azerbaijan	—	—	—	—	—	—	—	—	—	—	—	—	—	—	—
75 Dominican Rep.	69	65	85	82	170	84	75	74	95	96	73	73	33	44x	57x
76 Kazakhstan	—	—	—	—	—	—	—	—	—	—	—	—	—	—	—
77 Viet Nam	—	—	92	84	108	39	103	74	105x	99x	—	—	57x	43x	40x
78 Lebanon	79x	58x	88	73	840	330	112	105	105x	95x	—	—	—	57x	56x
79 China	—	—	84	62	184	31	131	90	140	129	100	100	81	53	41

(Contd.)

TABLE 5.4 *Contd.*

	1	2	3	4	5	6	7	8	9	10	11	12	13	14	15
80 Saudi Arabia	15	2	73	48	318	283	32	3	83	72	69	56	90	55	41
81 Syrian Arab Rep.	60	20	78	51	251	59	89	39	114	102	100	93	85	60	43
82 Tunisia	44	17	74	56	196	80	88	43	122	109	100	91	79	50	40
83 Moldova	—	—	—	—	—	—	—	—	—	—	—	—	—	—	—
84 Albania	—	—	—	—	176	86	102	86	98	98	—	—	91	85	74
85 Armenia	—	—	—	—	—	—	—	—	—	—	—	—	—	—	—
86 Paraguay	85x	75x	92	88	171	59	106	94	109	106	95	94	57	29	31
87 Korea, Dem. Peo. Rep.	—	—	—	—	119	15	—	—	110	103	—	—	—	—	—
88 Mexico	78	69	90	85	243	139	80	75	113	110	—	—	70	52	53
89 Thailand	86	72	96	90	185	112	97	88	86	85	—	—	59	33	32
90 Russian Federation	—	—	—	—	—	—	—	—	—	—	—	—	—	—	—
91 Oman	—	—	—	—	646	766	—	—	108	99	87	82	91	59	48
92 Jordan	64	29	89	70	254	81	—	—	105x	102x	94x	91x	95	79x	73x
93 Georgia	—	—	—	—	—	—	—	—	—	—	—	—	—	—	—
94 Romania	96	91	—	—	198	194	101	95	86	96	—	—	94	93	90
95 Latvia	—	—	—	—	—	—	—	—	—	—	—	—	—	—	—
96 Ukraine	—	—	—	—	794	327	—	—	—	—	—	—	—	—	—
97 Argentina	94	92	95	95	681	222	99	99	107	114	—	—	—	69	78
98 Estonia	—	—	100x	100x	—	—	—	—	—	—	—	—	—	—	—
99 Mauritius	77	59	—	—	356	215	96	90	102	104	92	94	99	53	53
100 Venezuela	79	71	87	90	436	167	98	99	94	94	60	62	70	30	41
101 Belarus	—	—	—	—	306	268	—	—	—	—	—	—	—	—	—

(*Contd.*)

TABLE 5.4 *Contd.*

	1	2	3	4	5	6	7	8	9	10	11	12	13	14	15
102 Trinadad & Tobago	95	89	97x	93x	468	302	111	108	95	95	90	90	89	79	82
103 U. Arab Emirates	24	7	—	—	324	110	—	—	117	114	100	100	96	63	62
104 Uruguay	93x	93x	97	96	603	233	117	117	107	106	—	—	93	61x	62x
105 Yugoslavia (former)	92	76	97	88	246	198	—	—	95	95	80	79	—	80	79
106 Colombia	79	76	97	86	170	115	74	74	109	111	—	—	56	48	57
107 Lithuania	—	—	99x	98x	—	—	—	—	—	—	—	—	—	—	—
108 Panama	81	81	88	88	223	165	89	86	109	105	91	92	79	57	62
109 Bulgaria	94	89	—	—	438	250	94	92	97	95	85	84	62	72	75
110 Sri Lanka	85	69	93	84	197	35	107	95	108	105	100	100	94	72	77
111 Malaysia	71	48	86	70	429	148	108	79	93	93	—	—	96	55	58
112 Chile	90	88	93	93	342	205	87	86	99	97	—	—	77	71	77
113 Kuwait	65	42	77	67	343	285	132	99	101	99	84	86	90	93	87
114 Poland	98	97	—	—	429	293	110	107	99	98	97	97	92	80	84
115 Hungary	98	98	99x	99x	595	410	103	100	94	94	90	91	94	78	79
116 Costa Rica	88	87	93	93	259	149	94	92	102	101	87	87	77	41	43
117 Jamaica	96	97	96	99	411	130	78	79	104	105	98	100	85	57	63
118 Slovakia	—	—	—	—	—	—	—	—	—	—	—	—	—	—	—
119 Portugal	78	65	89	81	218	177	132	129	121	117	99	100	—	58	59
120 Czech Republic	—	—	—	—	—	—	—	—	—	—	—	—	—	—	—
121 Cuba	86	87	95	93	345	207	109	110	105	100	96	95	88	84	94
122 Israel	93	83	95x	89x	471	266	99	97	92	95	—	—	78	79	86
123 Belgium	99	99	—	—	778	452	111	108	102	103	98	99	78	103	104
124 USA	99	99	—	—	2123	815	—	—	105	104	99	99	90	92	91

(Contd.)

TABLE 5.4 *Contd.*

	1	2	3	4	5	6	7	8	9	10	11	12	13	14	15
125 New Zealand	—	—	—	—	829	442	110	106	106	105	100	100	95	88	91
126 Italy	95	93	98	96	797	442	112	109	96	96	—	—	100	78	78
127 Spain	93	87	97	93	306	396	106	116	109	108	100	100	94	102	112
128 Greece	93	76	96	89	423	196	104	101	100	101	96	97	100	101	97
129 Korea, Rep.	94	81	99	94	1006	210	108	94	106	109	100	100	100	89	86
130 Austria	—	—	—	—	624	481	106	104	103	102	93	93	97	82	85
131 France	99	98	—	—	896	406	144	143	112	110	100	100	96	93	100
132 United Kingdom	—	—	—	—	1146	435	92	92	106	107	100	100	—	82	85
133 Australia	—	—	—	—	1280	486	103	103	105	105	97	97	99	82	85
134 Switzerland	—	—	—	—	155	20	118	118	—	—	—	—	—	—	—
135 Germany	—	—	—	—	—	—	—	—	105	105	89	90	—	99	96
136 Canada	—	—	—	—	1026	641	108	105	106	104	96	97	96	106	107
137 Denmark	—	—	—	—	1030	535	103	103	97	98	—	—	99	108	110
138 Norway	—	—	—	—	798	425	100	100	99	99	99	98	100	98	102
139 Netherlands	—	—	—	—	906	495	105	104	115	118	100	100	94	104	101
140 Sweden	—	—	—	—	888	474	95	96	106	107	100	100	100	89	93
141 Hong Kong	—	—	—	—	649	274	88	72	105	104	95x	95x	98	71	75
142 Singapore	92	55	92x	74x	643	376	120	101	111	109	100	100	100	68	71
143 Finland	—	—	—	—	998	497	100	95	100	99	—	—	100	104	124
144 Japan	99	99	—	—	907	620	103	102	101	101	100	100	100	94	97
145 Ireland	—	—	—	—	583	276	107	112	100	101	87	89	97	93	102

Note: Countries listed in descending order of their under-five mortality rates (table 4).

TABLE 5.5: Health Data

	% of population with access to safe water 1988-91			% of population with access to adequate sanitation 1988-91			% of population with access to health services 1985-94			% fully immunized 1990-92 1 year old children				Pregnant women	ORT use rate 1987-92
	total	urban	rural	total	urban	rural	total	urban	rural	TB	DPT	polio	measles	tetanus	
	1	2	3	4	5	6	7	8	9	10	11	12	13	14	15
1 Niger	53	98	45	14	71	4	41	99	30	40	21	21	28	45	17
2 Angola	41	71	20	19	25	15	30x	—	—	27	12	13	26	8	48
3 Mozambique	22	44	17	20	61	11	39	100	30	64	53	53	60	32	30
4 Afghanistan	23	40	19	—	13	—	29	80	17	48	27	27	37	9	26
5 Siera Leone	37	33	37	58	92	49	38	90	20	89	72	72	65	80	60
6 Guinea-Bissau	41	56	35	31	27	32	—	—	—	100	66	65	60	35	6
7 Guinea	53	87	56	21	84	5	75	100	55	65	52	52	50	70	65
8 Malawi	56x	97x	50x	84	100	81	80	—	—	99	86	84	82	66	14
9 Rwanda	66	75	62	58	77	56	80	—	—	94	85	85	81	88	26
10 Mali	41	53	38	24	81	10	35	—	—	70	34	34	41	8	41
11 Liberia	50	93	22	—	—	—	39	50	30	78	28	28	61	20	15
12 Somalia	37	50	29	18	44	5	27x	50x	15x	31x	18x	18x	30x	5x	78
13 Chad	57	25	70	—	—	—	30	—	—	43	17	17	41	5	15
14 Eritrea	—	—	—	—	—	—	—	—	—	—	—	—	—	—	—

(Contd.)

TABLE 5.5 *Contd.*

	1	2	3	4	5	6	7	8	9	10	11	12	13	14	15
15 Ethiopia	25	91	19	19	97	7	46	—	—	21	13	13	10	7	68
16 Mauritania	66	67	65	—	34	—	45	72	33	73	34	34	39	40	54
17 Zambia	53	70	28	37	75	12	75x	100x	50x	83	57	59	56	20	90
18 Bhutan	34	60	30	13	50	7	65	—	—	81	79	77	82	43	85
19 Nigeria	36	81	30	35	40	30	66	85	62	50	31	30	36	25	80
20 Zaire	39	68	24	23	46	11	26	40	17	65x	32x	31x	31x	29x	45
21 Uganda	33	60	30	32	63	28	61x	90x	57x	98	72	72	70	16	30
22 Cambodia	36	65	33	14	81	8	53	80	50	50	32	32	33	22	6
23 Burundi	57	99	54	49	71	47	80	100	79	91	80	80	70	56	49
24 Central African Rep.	24	19	26	46	45	46	45	—	—	94	77	77	62	87	24
25 Yemen	36	61	30	65	87	60	38	81	32	77	62	62	64	13	6
26 Tanzania U. Rep. of	49	65	45	64	74	62	76x	99x	72x	99	84	83	82	15	83
27 Ghana	52	93	35	42	64	32	60	92	45	57	34	36	40	9	44
28 Madagascar	23	55	9	3	12	3	65	65	65	46	32	32	27	2	29
29 Sudan	48	55	43	75	89	65	51	90	40	75	67	67	66	14	28
30 Gabon	68	90	50	—	—	—	90x	—	—	96	78	78	76	86	25
31 Lesotho	47	59	45	22	14	23	80	—	—	59	58	58	80	40	78
32 Burkina Faso	68	44	72	10	35	5	49x	51x	48x	66	39	39	41	26	15
33 Benin	51	66	46	34	42	31	18	—	—	84	73	73	70	83	45
34 Senegal	48	84	26	55	85	36	40	—	—	65	47	47	43	26	27
35 Lao Peo. Dem. Rep.	36	54	33	21	97	8	67	—	—	39	23	25	55	19	30

(Contd.)

TABLE 5.5 *Contd.*

	1	2	3	4	5	6	7	8	9	10	11	12	13	14	15
36 Pakistan	56	80	45	24	55	10	55	99	35	91	78	78	76	47	34
37 Togo	60	77	53	23	56	10	61	—	—	64	53	47	29	81	33
38 Haiti	39	55	33	24	55	16	50	—	—	45	24	27	24	5	20
39 Nepal	42	67	39	6	52	3	—	—	—	82	72	72	64	18	16
40 Bangladesh	84	82	81	31	63	26	45	—	—	89	63	63	59	80	24
41 Cote d'Ivoire	76	70	81	60	59	62	30x	61x	11x	47	47	47	51	35	16
42 India	85	87	85	16	53	2	—	—	—	96	89	89	85	77	37
43 Bolivia	52	77	27	26	40	13	63	90	36	86	77	84	80	52	63
44 Cameroon	48	100	27	74	100	64	41	44	39	52	37	37	37	7	84
45 Myanmar	32	37	—	36	39	35	48	—	—	80	73	73	71	72	19
46 Indonesia	51	68	43	44	64	36	80	—	—	95	91	91	89	60	44
47 Congo	38	92	2	—	—	—	83	97	70	88	74	74	64	60	67
48 Libyan Arab Jamahiriya	97	100	80	98	100	85	—	—	—	91	62	62	59	16	80
49 Turkmenistan	—	—	—	—	—	—	—	—	—	97	84	91	76	—	—
50 Turkey	78x	95x	63x	—	—	—	—	—	—	65	76	76	72	22	—
51 Zimbabwe	84	95	80	40	95	22	85	96	80	79	73	73	72	60	77
52 Tajikistan	—	—	—	—	—	—	—	—	—	—	92	—	—	—	—
53 Iraq	77	93	41	—	96	—	93	97	78	79	63	64	68	45	70
54 Mongolia	80	100	58	74	100	47	95	—	—	85	84	84	86	—	65
55 Namibia	52	98	35	14	24	11	72	92	60	90	65	65	63	52	—
56 Papua New Guinea	33	94	20	—	57	—	96	—	—	67	61	61	66	52	46

(*Contd.*)

TABLE 5.5 *Contd.*

	1	2	3	4	5	6	7	8	9	10	11	12	13	14	15
57 Guatemala	62	92	43	60	72	52	34	47	25	56	65	69	58	18	24
58 Nicaragua	54	76	21	—	78	—	83	100	60	79	73	86	72	12	40
59 Kenya	49	74	43	43	69	35	77	—	40	93	85	85	81	37	69
60 Algeria	68x	85x	55x	57	80	40	88	100	80	97	89	89	82	27	27
61 South Africa	—	—	—	—	—	—	—	—	—	85	67	69	63	—	—
62 Uzbekistan	—	—	—	—	—	—	—	—	—	97	63	85	84	—	—
63 Brazil	87	95	61	72	84	32	—	—	—	87	69	62	93	21	63
64 Peru	56	77	10	57	77	20	75x	—	—	82	80	81	80	27	31
65 El Salvador	47	85	19	58	86	36	56	80	40	71	65	65	62	26	45
66 Morocco	56	100	18	—	100	—	70	100	50	93	87	81	81	80	13
67 Kyrgyzstan	—	—	—	—	—	—	—	—	—	96	88	91	94	—	—
68 Philippines	82	85	79	69	78	62	75	77	74	94	92	92	90	52	25
69 Ecuador	55	63	43	48	56	38	88	—	—	99	83	83	66	5	70
70 Botswana	90	100	88	88	100	85	89x	100x	85x	71	82	82	65	45	64
71 Honduras	77	98	63	61	98	43	66	80	56	91	93	95	89	16	70
72 Iran, Islamic Rep. of	89	100	75	71	100	35	80	95	65	92	87	87	84	87	85
73 Egypt	90	95	86	50	80	26	—	—	—	92	89	89	89	70	34
74 Azerbaijan	—	—	—	—	—	—	—	—	—	53	69	70	50	—	—
75 Dominican Rep.	67	82	45	87	95	75	80	—	—	48	48	63	75	24	35
76 Kazakhstan	—	—	—	—	—	—	—	—	—	90	85	87	90	—	—
77 Viet Nam	24	39	21	17	34	13	91	100	80	91	88	89	90	42	52
78 Lebanon	92	95	85	—	—	—	95	98	85	4	85	85	51	—	45

(Contd.)

TABLE 5.5 *Contd.*

	1	2	3	4	5	6	7	8	9	10	11	12	13	14	15
79 China	72	87	68	79	68	81	90	100	88	94	94	95	94	3	22
80 Saudi Arabia	95	100	74	86	100	30	97	100	88	97	96	96	90	62	45
81 Syrian Arab Rep.	74	90	58	83	84	82	83	92	68	93	89	89	84	63	95
82 Tunisia	99	100	99	96	98	94	90x	100x	80x	80	95	95	87	44	22
83 Moldova	—	—	—	—	—	—	—	—	—	96	89	93	92	—	—
84 Albania	—	—	—	—	—	—	—	—	—	94	94	96	87	—	—
85 Armenia	—	—	—	—	—	—	—	—	—	—	—	—	—	—	—
86 Paraguay	35	50	24	62	56	67	61	—	—	99	85	87	86	54	52
87 Korea, Dem. Peo. Rep.	—	—	—	—	—	—	—	—	—	99	90	98	96	97	72
88 Mexico	76	81	68	50	70	17	78	80	60	95	91	92	91	42	63
89 Thailand	77	87	72	74	80	72	90	90	90	99	85	84	74	72	65
90 Russian Federation	—	—	—	—	—	—	—	—	—	88	73	69	83	—	—
91 Oman	84	91	77	71	75	40	95	100	95	97	97	97	97	97	19
92 Jordan	99	100	97	100	100	100	97	98	95	—	98	97	91	32	77
93 Georgia	—	—	—	—	—	—	—	—	—	63	45	45	58	—	—
94 Romania	—	—	—	—	—	—	—	—	—	99	97	90	92	—	—
95 Latvia	—	—	—	—	—	—	—	—	—	94	87	92	95	—	—
96 Ukraine	—	—	—	—	—	—	—	—	—	93	88	89	90	—	—
97 Argentina	65	73	17	69	75	35	71	80	21	99	78	83	89	—	70
98 Estonia	—	—	—	—	—	—	—	—	—	96	70	71	75	—	—
99 Mauritius	96	100	92	94	92	96	100	100	100	87	91	91	87	77	7
100 Venezuela	89	89	89	92	97	70	—	—	—	82	66	72	61	—	80

(*Contd.*)

TABLE 5.5 *Contd.*

	1	2	3	4	5	6	7	8	9	10	11	12	13	14	15
101 Belarus	—	—	—	—	—	—	—	—	—	94	90	90	94	—	—
102 Trinidad & Tobago	97	99	91	79	99	98	99	—	—	—	82	81	93	—	70
103 U. Arab Emirates	95	—	—	77	93	22	99	—	—	98	86	86	85	—	81
104 Uruguay	75	85	5	61	60	65	82	—	—	99	93	93	93	13	96
105 Yugoslavia (former)	—	—	—	—	—	—	—	—	—	81	79	81	76	—	—
106 Colombia	86	87	82	64	84	18	60	—	—	86	77	84	74	40	40
107 Lithuania	—	—	—	—	—	—	—	—	—	94	78	88	89	—	—
108 Panama	83	100	66	84	100	68	80x	95x	64x	98	82	83	71	27	55
109 Bulgaria	—	—	—	—	—	—	—	—	—	100	99	99	97	—	—
110 Sri Lanka	60	80	55	50	68	45	93x	—	—	89	86	86	79	67	76
111 Malaysia	78	96	66	81	—	—	—	—	—	99	90	90	79	83	47
112 Chile	86	100	—	83	100	20	97	—	—	99	91	91	90	—	10
113 Kuwait	—	100	—	—	100	—	100	—	—	3	92	92	93	22	10
114 Poland	—	—	—	—	—	—	—	—	—	94	98	98	94	—	—
115 Hungary	—	—	—	—	—	—	—	—	—	99	100	98	100	—	—
116 Costa Rica	93	100	86	97	100	94	80x	100x	63x	92	90	90	84	68	78
117 Jamaica	100	100	100	89	100	80	90	—	—	85	84	74	63	50	10
118 Slovakia	—	—	—	—	—	—	—	—	—	91	99	99	96	—	—
119 Portugal	—	—	—	—	—	—	—	—	—	89	95	95	96	—	—
120 Czech Republic	—	—	—	—	—	—	—	—	—	98	99	99	97	—	—
121 Cuba	98	100	91	92	100	68	98	99	96	98	91	93	98	98	80
122 Israel	—	—	—	—	—	—	—	—	—	—	85x	89x	88x	—	—
123 Belgium	—	—	—	—	—	—	—	—	—	—	87	99	75	—	—

(*Contd.*)

TABLE 5.5 *Contd.*

	1	2	3	4	5	6	7	8	9	10	11	12	13	14	15
124 USA	—	—	—	—	—	—	—	—	—	—	58	74	77	—	—
125 New Zealand	97	100	82	—	—	—	—	—	—	20	81	68	82	—	—
126 Italy	—	—	—	—	—	—	—	—	—	6	95	85	50	—	—
127 Spain	—	—	—	—	—	—	—	—	—	—	93	94	97	—	—
128 Greece	—	—	—	—	—	—	—	—	—	56	54	96	76	—	—
129 Korea, Rep. of	97	97	96	100	100	100	100	100	100	76	80	79	96	—	—
130 Austria	—	—	—	—	—	—	—	—	—	97	90	90	60	—	—
131 France	—	—	—	—	—	—	—	—	—	80	95	85	71	—	—
132 United Kingdom	—	—	—	—	—	—	—	—	—	75	90	95	89	—	—
133 Australia	—	—	—	—	—	—	—	—	—	—	95	72	86	—	—
134 Switzerland	—	—	—	—	—	—	—	—	—	—	89	95	83	—	—
135 Germany	—	—	—	—	—	—	—	—	—	84	95	95	80	—	—
136 Canada	—	—	—	—	—	—	—	—	—	85x	85x	70x	85x	—	—
137 Denmark	—	—	—	—	—	—	—	—	—	—	99	99	86	—	—
138 Norway	—	—	—	—	—	—	—	—	—	95	91	86	90	—	—
139 Netherlands	—	—	—	—	—	—	—	—	—	—	97	97	94	—	—
140 Sweden	—	—	—	—	—	—	—	—	—	14	99	99	95	—	—
141 Hong Kong	100	100	96	88	90	50	99x	—	—	94	90	90	42	—	—
142 Singapore	100	100	—	99	99	—	100	100	—	99	85	85	90	—	—
143 Finland	—	—	—	—	—	—	—	—	—	99	95	97	97	—	—
144 Japan	97	100	85	—	85	—	—	—	—	85	87	90	66	—	—
145 Ireland	—	—	—	—	—	—	—	—	—	—	65	81	78	—	—

Note: Countries listed in descending order of their 1992 under-five mortality rates (table 5.1).

TABLE 5.6: Nutrition Data

		% of infants with low birth weight 1990	% of children (1988-92) who are: exclu-sively (0-3 month)	breast-fed with comple-mentary food (6-9 months)	still breast fedding (20-23) months)	severe	% of children (1980-82) suffering from: Under-weight (0-4 years moderate & serve severe	wasting (12-23 months mode-rate & serve	stunting (24-59 months) mode-rate & serve	Total goitre rate (6-11 years) (%) 1990-92	Daily percapita calorie suppy as • % of require-ments 1988-90	% share of total household consumption 1980-85: all food	cereal
		1	2	3	4	5	6	7	8	9	10	11	12
1	Niger	15	—	—	—	49	—	23x	38x	9	95	—	—
2	Angola	19	3	83	53	—	—	—	—	7	80	—	—
3	Mozambique	20	—	—	—	—	—	—	—	20	77	—	—
4	Afghanistan	20	—	—	—	—	—	—	—	20	72	—	—
5	Sierra Leone	17	—	94	41	29	—	18	39	7	83	56	22
6	Guinea-Bissau	20	—	—	—	23x	—	—	—	19	97	—	—
7	Guinea	21	—	—	—	—	—	—	—	19	97	—	—
8	Malawi	20	3	89	—	27	8	11	62	13	88	30	9
9	Rwanda	17	90	75	—	29x	6x	9x	58x	49	82	29	10
10	Mali	17	8	45	44	31x	9x	16	34x	29	96	57	22
11	Liberia	—	15	56	26	20x	—	—	—	6	98	—	—

(Contd.)

TABLE 5.6 *Contd.*

		1	2	3	4	5	6	7	8	9	10	11	12
12	Somalia	16	—	—	—	—	—	—	—	7	81	—	—
13	Chad	—	—	—	—	—	—	—	—	15	73	—	—
14	Eritrea	—	—	—	—	—	—	—	—	—	—	—	—
15	Ethiopia	16	74	—	35	48x	16x	12x	63x	22	73	49	24
16	Mauritania	11	12	39	—	48	—	18	65	—	106	—	—
17	Zambia	13	13	88	34	25	6	10	47	51x	87	36	8
18	Bhutan	—	—	—	—	38	—	4x	56x	25	128	—	—
19	Nigeria	16	2	52	43	36	12	16	54	10	93	48	18
20	Zaire	15	—	—	—	—	—	—	—	9	96	—	—
21	Uganda	—	70	67	39	23x	5x	4x	51x	7	93	—	—
22	Cambodia	—	—	—	—	—	—	—	—	15	96	—	—
23	Burundi	—	89	66	73	38x	10x	10	60x	42	84	—	—
24	Central African Rep.	15	—	—	—	—	—	—	—	63	82	—	—
25	Yemen	19	15	51	—	30	4	17	49	32	—	—	—
26	Tanzania U. Rep. of	14	32	59	57	29	7	10	58	37	95	64	32
27	Ghana	17	2	57	52	27	6	15	39	10	93	50	—
28	Madagascar	10	—	—	—	33x	8x	17	56x	24	95	59	26
29	Sudan	15	14	45	44	35x	7x	13x	32x	20	87	60	—
30	Gabon	—	—	—	—	—	—	—	—	5	104	—	—

(Contd.)

TABLE 5.6 *Contd.*

		1	2	3	4	5	6	7	8	9	10	11	12
31	Lesotho	11	—	—	—	16	2	7	23	16	93	—	—
32	Burkina Faso	21x	3	35	—	—	—	—	—	16	94	—	—
33	Benin	—	—	—	—	—	—	—	—	24	104	37	12
34	Senegal	11	7	68	37	22	2	8	30	12	98	49	15
35	Lao Peo. Dem. Rep.	18	—	—	—	37	—	20	44	25	111	—	—
36	Pakistan	25	25	29	52	40	14	11	60	32	99	37	12
37	Togo	20	10	86	68	24x	6x	10	37x	22	99	—	—
38	Haiti	15	—	—	—	37x	3x	17x	51x	4x	89	—	—
39	Nepal	—	—	—	—	—	—	—	—	44	100	57	38
40	Bangladesh	50	—	—	—	66	27	28	65	11	88	59	36
41	Cote d'Ivoire	14x	—	—	—	12	2	17	20	6	111	39	13
42	India	33	—	—	—	63x	27x	—	65x	9	101	52	18
43	Bolivia	12	59	57	30	13x	3x	2	51x	21	84	33	—
44	Cameroon	13	7	77	35	14	3	7	32	26	95	24	7
45	Myanmar	16	—	—	—	32x	9x	—	—	18	114	—	—
46	Indonesia	14	53	76	62	40	—	—	—	28	121	48	21
47	Congo	16	43	—	27	24	—	13	33	8	103	37	16
48	Libyan Arab Jamahiriya	—	—	—	—	—	—	—	—	6	140	—	—
49	Turkmenistan	—	—	—	—	—	—	—	—	20	—	—	—

(Contd.)

TABLE 5.6 *Contd.*

		1	2	3	4	5	6	7	8	9	10	11	12
50	Turkey	8	—	—	—	—	—	—	—	36	127	40	9
51	Zimbabwe	14	11	94	26	12	2	2	31	42	94	40	9
52	Tajikistan	—	—	—	—	—	—	—	—	6	140	—	—
53	Iraq	15	—	—	—	12	2	—	—	7	128	—	—
54	Mongolia	10	—	—	—	12x	—	2x	29x	7	97	—	—
55	Namibia	12	22	65	23	26	6	13	29	35	—	—	—
56	Papua New Guinea	23	—	—	—	35	—	—	—	30	114	—	—
57	Guatemala	14	—	—	44	34x	8x	3	68x	20	103	36	10
58	Nicaragua	15	—	—	—	11	1	0	22	4	99	—	—
59	Kenya	16	24	87	46	14x	3x	5x	32x	7	89	38	16
60	Algeria	9	—	—	—	9	—	7	18	9	123	—	—
61	South Africa	—	—	—	—	—	—	—	—	2	128	34	—
62	Uzbekistan	—	—	—	—	—	—	—	—	18	—	—	—
63	Brazil	11	4	27	13	7	1	3	16	14x	114	35	9
64	Peru	11	40	62	36	11	2	3	46	36	87	35	8
65	El Salvadore	11	—	—	—	15	—	3	36	25	102	33	12
66	Morocco	9	48	48	18	16x	4z	6	34x	20	125	38	12
67	Kyrgyzstan	—	—	—	—	—	—	—	—	20	—	—	—
68	Philippines	15	—	—	—	34	5	14	45	15	104	51	21

(*Contd.*)

TABLE 5.6 *Contd.*

	1	2	3	4	5	6	7	8	9	10	11	12
69 Ecuador	11	31	31	23	17	0	4	39	10	105	30	—
70 Botswana	8	41	82	23	15x	—	—	—	8	97	25	12
71 Honduras	9	—	—	—	21	4	2x	34x	9	98	39	—
72 Iran, Islamic Rep. of	9	—	—	—	—	—	—	—	30	125	37	10
73 Egypt	10	38	52	—	10	3	4	32	5	132	49	10
74 Azerbaijan	—	—	—	—	—	—	—	—	20	—	—	—
75 Dominican Rep.	16	10	23	7	10	2	1	22	—	102	46	13
76 Kazakhstan	—	—	—	—	—	—	—	—	20	—	—	—
77 Viet Nam	17	—	—	—	42	14	12x	49x	20	103	—	—
78 Lebanon	10	—	—	—	—	—	—	—	15	127	—	—
79 China	9	—	—	—	21x	3x	8x	41x	9	112	61	—
80 Saudi Arabia	7	—	—	—	—	—	—	—	—	121	—	—
81 Syrian Arab Rep.	11	—	—	—	—	—	—	—	73	126	—	—
82 Tunisia	8	21	53	25	10x	2x	4	23x	4	131	37	7
83 Moldova	—	—	—	—	—	—	—	—	—	—	—	—
84 Albania	7	—	—	—	—	—	—	—	41	107	—	—
85 Armenia	—	—	—	—	—	—	—	—	10	—	—	—
86 Paraguay	8	7	61	8	4	1	0	17	49	116	30	6
87 Korea, Dem. Peo. Rep.	—	—	—	—	—	—	—	—	—	121	—	—

(*Contd.*)

TABLE 5.6 *Contd.*

		1	2	3	4	5	6	7	8	9	10	11	12
113	Kuwait	7	—	—	—	6	—	2	14	—	—	—	—
114	Poland	—	—	—	—	—	—	—	—	10	131	29	4
115	Hungary	9	—	—	—	—	—	—	—	—	137	25	3
116	Costa Rica	6	—	—	—	6	—	3	8	3	121	33	8
117	Jamaica	11	—	—	—	7	1	6	7	—	114	36	14
118	Slovakia	—	—	—	—	—	—	—	—	—	—	—	—
119	Portugal	5	—	—	—	—	—	—	—	15	136	34	8
120	Czech Republic	—	—	—	—	—	—	—	—	—	—	—	—
121	Cuba	8	—	—	—	—	—	1x	—	10	135	—	—
122	Israel	7	—	—	—	—	—	—	—	—	125	21	—
123	Belgium	6	—	—	—	—	—	—	—	5	149	15	2
124	USA	7	—	—	—	—	—	—	—	—	138	10	2
125	New Zealand	6	—	—	—	—	—	—	—	—	131	12	2
126	Italy	5	—	—	—	—	—	—	—	20	139	19	2
127	Spain	4	—	—	—	—	—	—	—	10	141	24	3
128	Greece	6	—	—	—	—	—	—	—	10	151	30	3
129	Korea, Rep. of	9	—	—	—	—	—	—	—	—	120	35	14
130	Austria	6	—	—	—	—	—	—	—	—	133	16	2
131	France	5	—	—	—	—	—	—	—	5	143	16	2
132	United Kingdom	7	—	—	—	—	—	—	—	—	130	12	2
133	Australia	6	—	—	—	—	—	—	—	—	124	13	2
134	Switzerland	5	—	—	—	—	—	—	—	—	130	17	—
135	Germany	—	—	—	—	—	—	—	—	10	—	12	2

(*Contd.*)

TABLE 5.6 *Contd.*

		1	2	3	4	5	6	7	8	9	10	11	12
136	Canada	6	—	—	—	—	—	—	—	—	122	11	2
137	Denmark	6	—	—	—	—	—	—	—	5	135	13	2
138	Norway	4	—	—	—	—	—	—	—	—	120	15	2
139	Netherlands	—	—	—	—	—	—	—	—	3	114	13	2
140	Sweden	5	—	—	—	—	—	—	—	—	111	13	2
141	Hong Kong	8	—	—	—	—	—	—	—	—	125	12	1
142	Singapore	7	—	—	—	14x	—	—	—	—	136	19	—
143	Finland	4	—	—	—	—	—	—	—	—	113	16	3
144	Japan	6	—	—	—	—	—	—	—	—	125	17	4
145	Ireland	4	—	—	—	—	—	—	—	—	157	22	4

TABLE 5.7: Women Data

	Life expectancy females as a % of males	Adult literacy rate females as a % of males 1990	Enrolment ratios females as a % of males 1988-91		Contraceptive prevalence (%) 1980-81	Pregnant woman immunized against tetanus 1980-81	% of births attended by trained health personnel 1983-92	Mental mortality rate 1980-91
			primary school	secondary school				
	1	2	3	4	5	6	7	8
1 Niger	107	43	57	44	4	45	15	700
2 Angola	107	52	93	—	1x	8	15	—
3 Mozambique	107	47	71	56	4	32	25	300
4 Afghanistan	102	32	52	45	2x	9	9	640
5 Siera Leone	108	35	70	57	4	80	25	450
6 Guinea-Bissau	108	48	55	44	1x	35	27	700x
7 Guinea	102	37	48	33	1x	70	25	800
8 Malawi	103	—	83	50	13	66	55	400
9 Rwanda	107	58	99	67	21	88	29	210
10 Mali	107	59	57	44	5	8	32	2000
11 Liberia	105	58	55x	39x	6	20	58	—
12 Somalia	107	39	50x	58x	1	5x	2	1100
13 Chad	107	43	44	25	1x	5	15	960
14 Eritrea	—	—	—	—	—	—	—	—

(Contd.)

TABLE 5.7 *Contd.*

	1	2	3	4	5	6	7	8
15 Ethiopia	107	48x	65	71	2	7	14	560x
16 Mauritania	107	45	70	45	4	40	40	—
17 Zambia	103	80	92	56	15	20	51	150
18 Bhutan	103	49	65	29	2	43	7	1310
19 Nigeria	107	65	77	77	6	25	37	800
20 Zaire	106	73	75	50	1x	29x	—	800
21 Uganda	105	56	83	50	5	16	38	300
22 Cambodia	106	46	—	—	—	22	47	500
23 Burundi	107	66	81	67	9	56	19	—
24 Central African Rep.	110	48	61	35	—	87	66	600
25 Yemen	101	49	39	21	7	13	16	—
26 Tanzania U. Rep. of	106	—	98	80	10	15	53	340x
27 Ghana	107	73	82	65	13	9	40	1000
28 Madagascar	106	83	96	90	17	2	58	570
29 Sudan	105	28	71x	74x	9	14	69	550
30 Gabon	106	66	—	—	—	86	80	190
31 Lesotho	109	—	116	148	5x	40	40	—
32 Burkina Faso	107	32	62	56	8	26	42	810
33 Benin	107	50	51	38	9	83	45	160
34 Senegal	104	48	73	52	11	26	41	600
35 Lao Peo. Dem. Rep.	106	83x	78	68	—	19	—	300
36 Pakistan	100	45	55	45	12	42	35	500
37 Togo	107	55	63	30	34	81	54	420

(Contd.)

TABLE 5.7 *Contd.*

	1	2	3	4	5	6	7	8
38 Haiti	106	80	94	95	10	5	20	340
39 Nepal	98	34	51	40	14	18	6	830
40 Bangladesh	99	47	87	52	31	80	5	600
41 Cote d'Ivoire	106	60	70	44	3	35	50	—
42 India	101	55	76	61	43	77	33	460
43 Bolivia	108	84	90	84	30	52	55	600
44 Cameroon	106	64	86	68	13	7	64	430
45 Myanmar	106	81	94	92	13	72	57	460
46 Indonesia	106	85	96	84	48	60	32	450
47 Congo	110	63	—	38x	—	60	—	900
48 Libyan Arab Jamahiriya	106	67	—	—	—	16	76	70x
49 Turkmenistan	—	—	—	—	—	—	—	—
50 Turkey	108	79	92	64	63	22	77	150
51 Zimbabwe	105	81	98	85	43	60	70	—
52 Tajikistan	—	—	—	—	—	—	—	—
53 Iraq	105	70	84	64	18	45	50	120
54 Mongolia	104	—	104	110	—	—	99	140
55 Namibia	104	—	11	127	26	52	68	370x
56 Papua New Guinea	103	58	84	67	4	52	20	900
57 Guatemala	108	75	85	85x	23	18	51	200
58 Nicaragua	106	—	107	142	27	12	73	—

(*Contd.*)

TABLE 5.7 *Contd.*

	1	2	3	4	5	6	7	8
59 Kenya	107	74	96	70	27	37	50	170x
60 Algeria	104	66	85	80	51	27	15	140x
61 South Africa	110	96x	—	—	48	—	—	84x
62 Uzbekistan	—	—	—	—	—	—	—	—
63 Brazil	109	96	96x	116x	66	21	95	200
64 Peru	106	87	96x	91x	59	27	52	300
65 El Salvadore	108	92	101	100	47	26	66	—
66 Morocco	106	62	68	71	42	80	26	300x
67 Kyrgyzstan	—	—	—	—	—	—	—	—
68 Philippines	106	99	99	104	36	45	55	100
69 Ecuador	107	95	99	104	53	5	34	170
70 Botswana	110	77	105	107	33	46	78	250
71 Honduras	107	95	101	103x	41	16	81	220
72 Iran, Islamic Rep. of	102	67	89	75	23x	87	70	120
73 Egypt	104	54	86	77	47	70	41	270
74 Azerbaijan	—	—	—	—	—	—	—	—
75 Dominican Rep.	107	96	101	130x	56	24	92	—
76 Kazakhstan	—	—	—	—	—	—	—	—
77 Viet Nam	107	91	94x	93x	53	42	95	120
78 Lebanon	106	83	90x	98x	55x	—	45	—
79 China	105	74	92	77	83	3	94	95
80 Saudi Arabia	104	66	87	75	—	62	90	41

(*Contd.*)

TABLE 5.7 *Contd.*

		1	2	3	4	5	6	7	8
81	Syrian Arab Rep.	106	65	89	72	52	63	61	140
82	Tunisia	103	76	89	80	50	44	69	70
83	Moldova	—	—	—	—	—	—	—	—
84	Albania	109	—	100	87	—	—	99	—
85	Armenia	—	—	—	—	—	—	—	—
86	Paraguay	07	96	97	107	48	54	66	300
87	Korea, Dem. Peo. Rep.	109	—	94	—	—	97	100	41
88	Mexico	110	94	97	102	53	42	77	110
89	Thailand	108	94	99	97	66	72	71	50
90	Russian Federation	—	—	—	—	—	—	—	—
91	Oman	106	—	92	81	9	97	80	—
92	Jordan	106	79	97x	92x	35	32	87	48x
93	Georgia	—	—	—	—	—	—	—	—
94	Romania	109	—	112	97	58x	—	100	72
95	Latvia	—	—	—	—	—	—	—	—
96	Ukraine	—	—	—	—	—	—	—	—
97	Argentina	110	100	107	113	74	—	87	140
98	Estonia	114	100x	—	—	—	—	—	—
99	Mauritius	110	89x	102	100	75	77	85	99
100	Venezuela	109	103	100	137	49x	—	69	—
101	Belarus	—	—	—	—	—	—	—	—
102	Trinidad & Tobago	107	96x	101	104	53	—	98	110

(Contd.)

TABLE 5.7 *Contd.*

		1	2	3	4	5	6	7	8
103	U. Arab Emirates	106	66x	97	114	—	—	99	—
104	Uruguay	109	99	99	102x	—	13	96	35
105	Yugoslavia (former)	109	91	100	99	55x	—	86	27
106	Colombia	109	99	102	119	66	40	94	200
107	Lithuania	113	99	—	—	—	—	—	—
108	Panama	106	100	96	109	58	27	96	60
109	Bulgaria	109	—	98	104	76x	—	100	9
110	Sri Lanka	106	90	97	107	62	67	94	80
111	Malaysia	106	81	100	105	51	83	87	59
112	Chile	110	100	98	108	43x	—	98	67
113	Kuwait	106	87	98	94	—	22	99	6
114	Poland	113	—	99	105	75x	—	100	11
115	Hungary	112	100x	100	101	73	—	99	15
116	Costa Rica	106	100	99	105	70	68	93	36
117	Jamaica	106	101	101	111	55	50	82	120
118	Slovakia	—	—	—	—	—	—	—	—
119	Portugal	110	91	97	102	66x	—	90	10
120	Czech Republic	—	—	—	—	—	—	—	—
121	Cuba	105	98	95	112	70	98	90	39
122	Israel	105	94x	103	109	—	—	99	3
123	Belgium	109	—	101	101	81	—	100	3
124	USA	109	—	99	99	74	—	99	8
125	New Zealand	108	—	99	103	70x	—	99	13

(Contd.)

TABLE 5.7 *Contd.*

		1	2	3	4	5	6	7	8
126	Italy	109	98	100	100	78x	—	—	4
127	Spain	108	96	99	110	59	—	96	4
128	Greece	107	91	101	96	—	—	97	5
129	Korea, Rep. of	109	95	103	97	77	—	89	26
130	Austria	109	—	99	104	71	—	—	8
131	France	111	—	98	108	79x	—	94	9
132	United Kingdom	—	101	104	104	72	—	100	8
133	Australia	109	—	100	104	67x	—	99	3
134	Switzerland	109	—	—	—	71	—	99	5
135	Germany	109	—	100	97	—	—	99	5
136	Canada	109	—	98	101	73	—	99	5
137	Denmark	108	—	101	102	63x	—	100	3
138	Norway	109	—	100	104	71x	—	—	3
139	Netherlands	108	—	103	97	76	—	100	10
140	Sweden	108	—	101	104	78	—	100	5
141	Hong Kong	107	—	99	106	81	—	100	6
142	Singapore	108	80x	98	104	74	—	100	10
143	Finland	111	—	99	98	119	80x	100	11
144	Japan	108	—	100	103	64	—	100	11
145	Ireland	108	—	101	110	—	—	—	2

Note: Countries listed in descending order of their under-five mortality rates (table 5.1).

TABLE 5.8: Basic Data on less Populous Countries

		Under 5 mortality rate		Infant mortality rate (under 1)		Total population (thousands)	Annual no. of births (thousands)	Annual no. of under-5 deaths (thousands)	GNP per capita (US$)	Life expectancy of birth (years	Total adult literacy rate	% of age-group enrolled in primary school (gross)	% of children immunized against measles
		1969	1992	1969	1992	1992	1992	1992	1991	1992	1985-90	1985-91	1991-92
		1	2	3	4	5	6	7	8	9	10	11	12
1	Gambia	375	220	213	133	908	40.3	8.8	360	45	27	64	83
2	Equatorial Guinea	316	182	188	118	369	16.2	3.0	330	48	50x	134x	66
3	Djibouti	289	158	186	113	467	21.9	3.5	1210	49	12	47	83
4	Comorus	248	130	165	90	585	28.7	3.7	500	55	48x	75	32
5	Swaziland	223	107	157	74	792	29.6	3.2	1050	58	67	104	85
6	Marshall Islands	—	92	—	63	49	1.4	0.1	*	—	91	95	86
7	Sao Tome and Principe	—	85	—	65	124	4.5	0.4	400	68	57x	—	61
8	Vanuatu	—	85	—	65	157	6.0	0.5	1150	65	64	103	74
9	Kirbati	—	81	—	60	74	2.4	0.2	720	56	93	91	77
10	Maldives	258	78	158	56	227	8.8	0.7	460	63	91	87	98
11	Guyana	126	65	100	49	808	20.7	1.3	430	65	96x	115	76
12	Cape Verde	164	60	110	44	384	13.8	0.8	750	68	37x	116	82

(Contd.)

TABLE 5.8 *Contd.*

		1	2	3	4	5	6	7	8	9	10	11	12
13	Samoa	—	58	—	45	158	5.2	0.3	960	66	98	100	91
14	Tuvalu	—	56	—	40	12	—	0.0	650	—	99	101	63
15	Belize	—	52	—	41	198	7.2	0.4	2010	69	93	90	72
16	Saint Kitts and Nevis	—	42	—	34	42	0.8	0.0	3960	71	90	—	99
17	Suriname	96	35	70	28	438	11.4	0.4	3630	70	95	132	84
18	Grenada	—	35	—	29	91	2.2	0.1	2180	71	96x	88x	73
19	Palau	—	35	—	25	16	0.5	0.0	790	—	98	103	94
20	Solomon Islands	185	34	120	27	342	12.9	0.4	560	70	62	93	74
21	Qatar	239	33	145	27	453	10.4	0.3	14770	70	76	97	79
22	British Virgin Islands	—	33x	—	27x	17	0.3	0.0x	8500	75	98x	—	99
23	Turks and Caicos Islands	—	31x	—	25x	13	0.2	0.0x	780	—	98x	—	59
24	Bahamas	68	29	51	24	264	5.2	0.2	11750	72	—	—	93
25	Fiji	97	29	71	24	739	17.6	0.5	1930	71	87	123	91
26	Micronesia, Fed. State of	—	29	—	25	109	3.7	0.4	*	71	81	100	88
27	Cook Islands	—	28	—	26	17	0.4	0.0	1550	—	99	98	87
28	Antigua and Barbuda	—	25	—	20	66	1.1	90	4430	95	74	100	100
29	Saint Vincent/ Grenadines	—	25	—	20	109	2.4	0.1	1730	71	82	95x	100
30	Tonga	—	25	—	21	97	2.9	0.1	1280	68	99	98	90
31	Dominica	—	22	—	18	72	1.5	0.0	2440	73	94x	—	98
32	Saint Lucia	—	21	—	17	137	3.8	0.1	2490	72	82x	95x	97

(Contd.)

TABLE 5.8 *Contd.*

		1	2	3	4	5	6	7	8	9	10	11	12
33	Seychelles	—	20	—	16	72	1.6	0.0	5110	71	88	102x	92
34	Bahrain	208	16	130	13	533	14.1	0.2	7130	71	77x	101	87
35	Montserrat	—	15	—	12	11	0.2	0.0	3330	75	97x	100x	100
36	Barbados	90	12	74	10	259	4.1	0.0	6630	76	98	114	90
37	Malta	42	11	37	9	359	5.5	0.1	7280	76	86	109	80
38	Cyprus	36	11	30	9	716	12.3	0.1	8640	77	94	103	74
39	luxembourg	41	11	33	9	378	4.7	0.1	31780	75	—	93	80
40	Brunei Darussalam	87	10	63	8	270	6.5	0.1	20760	74	78x	—	99
41	Iceland	22	7	17	6	260	4.5	0.0	23170	78	—	101	99

*Range $1500-$3499.

TABLE 5.9: Country Grouping

	1	2	3	4
SUB-SAHARAN AFRICA	Angola	Eritrea	Malawi	Sierra Leone
	Benin	Ethiopia	Mali	Somalia
	Botswana	Gabon	Mauritania	South Africa
	Burkina Faso	Ghana	Mauritius	Tanzania, Rep. of
	Burundi	Guinea	Mozambique	Togo
	Cameroon	Guinea-Bissau	Namibia	Uganda
	Central African Rep.	Kenya	Niger	Zaire
	Chad	Lesotho	Nigeria	Zambia
	Congo	Liberia	Rwanda	Zimbabwe
	Cote d'Ivoire	Madagascar	Senegal	
MIDDLE EAST AND NORTH AFRICA	Algeria	Kuwait	Saudi Arabia	United Arab Emirates
	Egypt	Lebanon	Sudan	Yemen
	Iran, Islamic Rep. of	Libyan Arab Jamahiriya	Syrian Arab Rep.	
	Iraq	Morocco	Tunisia	
	Jorden	Oman	Turkey	
SOUTH ASIA	Afghanistan	Bhutan	Nepal	Sri Lanka
	Bangladesh	India	Pakistan	

(Contd.)

TABLE 5.9 *Contd.*

	1	2	3	4
EAST ASIA AND PACIFIC	Cambodia	Korea, Dem. Peo. Rep.	Mongolia	Singapore
	China	Korea, Rep. of	Myanmar	Thailand
	Hong Kong	Lao Peo, Dem. Rep.	Papua New Guinea	Viet Nam
	Indonesia	Malaysia	Philippines	
LATIN AMERICA AND CARIBBEAN	Argentina	Cuba	Honduras	Peru
	Bolivia	Dominican Rep.	Jamaica	Trinidad and Tobago
	Brazil	Ecuador	Mexico	Uruguay
	Chile	El Salvador	Nicaragua	Venezuela
	Colombia	Guatemala	Panama	
	Costa Rica	Haiti	Paraguay	
FORMER USSR	Armenia	Georgia	Lithuania	Turkmenistan
	Azerbaijan	Kazakhstan	Moldova	Ukraine
	Belarus	Kyrgyzstan	Russian Federation	Uzbekistan
	Estonia	Latvia	Tajikistan	
INDUSTRIALIZED COUNTRIES	Albania	Finland	Japan	Spain
	Australia	France	Netherlands	Sweden
	Austria	Germany	New Zealand	Switzerland

(Contd.)

TABLE 5.9 *Contd.*

	1	2	3	4
	Belgium	Greece	Norway	United Kingdom
	Bulgaria	Hungary	Poland	USA
	Canada	Ireland	Portugal	Yugoslavia (former)
	Czech Republic	Israel	Romania	
	Denmark	Italy	Slovakia	
DEVELOPING COUNTRIES	Afghanistan	Egypt	Liberia	Rwanda
	Algeria	El Salvador	Libyan Arab Jamahiriya	Saudi Arabia
	Angola	Eritrea	Madagascar	Senegal
	Argentina	Ethiopia	Malawi	Sierra Leone
	Bangladesh	Gabon	Malaysia	Singapore
	Benin	Ghana	Mali	Somalia
	Bhutan	Guatemala	Mauritania	South Africa
	Bolivia	Guinea	Mauritius	Sri Lanka
	Botswana	Guinea-Bissau	Mexico	Sudan
	Brazil	Haiti	Mongolia	Syrian Arab Rep.
	Burkina Faso	honduras	Morocco	Tanzania, U. Rep. of
	Burundi	Hong Kong	Mozambique	Thailand
	Cambodia	India	Myanmar	Togo
	Cameroon	Indonesia	Namibia	Trinidad and Tobago
	Central African Rep.	Iran, Islamic Rep. of	Nepal	Tunisia
	Chad	Iraq	Nicaragua	Turkey

(*Contd.*)

TABLE 5.9 *Contd.*

	1	2	3	4
	Chile	Jamaica	Niger	Uganda
	China	Jordan	Nigeria	United Arab Emirates
	Colombia	Kenya	Oman	Uruguay
	Congo	Korea, Dem. Peo. Rep.	Pakistan	Venezuela
	Costa Rica	Korea, Rep. of	Panama	Viet Nam
	Cote d'Ivoire	Kuwait	Papua New Guinea	Yemen
	Cuba	Lao Peo Dem. Rep.	Paraguay	Zaire
	Dominican Rep. of	Lebanon	Peru	Zambia
	Ecuador	Lesotho	Philippines	Zimbabwe
LEAST DEVELOPED COUNTRIES	Afghanistan	Chad	Malawi	Somalia
	Bangladesh	Ethiopia	Mali	Sudan
	Benin	Guinea	Mauritania	Tanzania, U. Rep. of
	Bhutan	Guinea-Bissau	Mozambique	Togo
	Botswana	Haiti	Myanmar	Uganda
	Burkina Faso	Lao Peo. Dem. Rep.	Nepal	Yemen
	Burundi	Lesotho	Niger	Zaire
	Cambodia	Liberia	Rwanda	Zambia
	Central African Rep.	Madagascar	Sierra Leone	

6

ECONOMY : GLOBAL PERSPECTIVE

6.1 ECONOMIC SURVEY, 1993

With no signs of accelerated output in developed countries overall,the resumption of growth remains the overriding issue in world economy in 1993. (*World Economic Survey,* 1993, United Nations, New York, 1993, June 24).

Despite faster growth in a number of developing countries and in particular China, world output is forecast to grow by only 1.5 per cent this year and 3 per cent in 1994 from 0.6 per cent in 1992. Russia and other economies in transition are expected to experience a further 10 per cent fall in output this year after a near 17 per cent decline in 1992, while growth in Africa and Latin America will show only modest improvements, despite some hopeful signs of recovery in the latter.

Developed countries can provide only a weak pole of growth for the rest of the world, the survey says. While a hesitant recovery appears to be under way in the United States, Canada and the United Kingdom, Japan's output will barely rise–to a projected 1.5 per cent from 1.3 per cent in 1992–and in France and Italy output growth is forecast to slow, and to actually decline in Germany by some 0.5 per cent.

Even in the three or four industrial countries where growth has resumed,continuing unemployment has made consumers reluctant to spend. In many countries at least one in 10 workers was unemployed in 1992 and this situation is not expected to cease this year. Even where credit is cheap, there have been few takers, the survey notes, further constraining demand. Despite mounting social problems, fears over renewed inflation continue to make governments fiscally cautious–neglect has been replaced with only tentative activism, in sustaining economic growth, the survey observes.

Mixed Fortunes for Developing Countries

Overall, developing countries are registering strong growth, a significant development which represents a major boost in the growth of per capita income, this year's survey says. It argues that the acceleration of growth, under way since last year and which is forecast to continue in 1994, has begun to improve living standards of the large majority of the population in the countries enjoying growth of 5 per cent or more a year. These countries now include more than half the population of the developing world, the survey observes. But strongly warning against any complacency, it points out that 500 million people live in countries where output stagnated or declined.

For many developing countries, hesitant recovery in industrial countries has meant continuing poor demand for their exports and a further fall in the price of their vital raw material exports in particular, many of which are already at historic lows. For Africa and Latin America, as well as for oil-producers–oil prices are predicted to be an unchanged $ 18 a barrel on average this year–this presents a major constraint on growth prospects. At 3 per cent, Africa's expected growth this year will merely stem the fall in per capita output under way for many years. A similar level of growth expected for Latin America will mean that only limited inroads can be made in reducing the 40 per cent of the region's population now living in extreme poverty, despite efforts in a number of countries to focus more resources on poverty eradication.

China's Unique Style

In contrast, Asia is expected to show continued strong growth, of some 5.5-6 per cent, with China registering a staggering 11 per cent after a growth of close to 13 per cent in 1992. A special study in this year's survey shows the unique style of China's recent economic success. Growth has been predominantly in the non-state sector. This sector's share of industrial output has risen form 25 per cent in 1980 to 46 per cent in 1991. But while China has actively sought to subject all production to market forces, this has been without significant privatization of state assets. While accumulation of wealth seems to be a major motivation of entrepreneurs, there was no necessary link of entrepreneurship to private ownership, Collectively-owned enterprises were the largest source of the growth of entrepreneurial activities in China in the 1980s.

Rather than undertaking the large-scale privatization of public assets now under way in Russia and Eastern Europe, as well as Africa, China has concentrated on providing managers with wage and other incentives, coupled with price and market reforms, which has enabled the non-state sector to compete with the state sector. Autonomy for individual enterprises has varied widely across regions, but rural collective enterprises have seen rapid income growth, often supported and encouraged by local government.

There is a danger of a overheating of the economy, pointing to the rapid growth in money supply, inadequate growth in government revenues, and inflation in urban areas. It also argues for more clearly-defined property rights and other aspects of the legal framework, the removal of domestic market barriers, and warns of the problem of frequent government interventions in collective enterprises which have hindered their efficient operation.

Economies in Transition Face Social Turmoil

China's experience contrasts sharply with the difficulties of economic transition now being experienced in Russia and a number of other countries of the former Soviet Union and Eastern Europe. While Hungary and Poland should see a resumption of growth this year most other economies will suffer a further sharp fall in output, with zero growth overall again expected in 1994. There will be no relief for incomes, which have plunged sharply since 1989. With open unemployment, previoulsy unknown, continuing to gorw, and a strong risk that inflation will soar in some countries, social strees will remian acute and represents a potent threat to the process of economic transition. Crime rates have jumped, while easier travel has facilitated an mounting problem of drug trafficking and drug-related crimes and there has been a alarming increase in deaths from murder, alcohol abuse and suicide.

Western assistance has exceeded $170 bn in commitments since 1990, but slow disbursements have meant actual amounts received have been far less than expected. Western advice has also been on many occasions poorly conceived and haphazard, the survey says. The world economy stands to lose in the long run if Western external assistance to Russia and other countries in economic transition is not better coordinated and targeted, the survey warns. Western assistance will also be made less effective if devloped countries do not open their markets to exports from these economies, it argues. Despite new trade agreements with the European Community and others, exporters continue to complain of market restrictions.

Growth in Financial Flows

Net transfers were $51.9 bn in 1992, compared with $47.3 bn in 1991, which followed four consecutive years of net outflows. West Asia–at $27.2 bn–again showed a significant net transfer, though down on 1991 when foreign assets were cashed and funds borrowed in order to finance the Gulf war. Other Asian economies also registered another year of strong positive inflows. For Latin America there was a remarkable turnround, from a $7.2 bn outflow in 1991 to a $6.9 bn inflow since the start of the international debt crisis in 1982.

Africa was the only major developing-country region not to share in the increased financial transfers, the survey says. While there was a net inflow of $10 bn for the countries of sub-Saharan Africa, excluding Nigeria, substantial payments by north Africa and Nigeria meant a net outflow of $1.6 bn in 1992 for the continent as a whole. If the region's terms of trade losses are factored in, Africa suffered a significant outflow of resources in 1992.

Much of the growth in financial flows to developing countries is attributable to increased private flows, to which Africa has very limited access. There is a disquieting trend in official resource flows on which Africa and low-in-come countries depend for the bulk of their financial inflows. Of particular concern, it says, is a decline in commitments by multilateral institutions. In 1992, commitments by the UN were $3.62 bn, against $3.98 bn in 1991. Overall, multilateral commitments totalled $38.7 bn in 1992 against $39.8 bn in 1991.

The decline reflects the general pressure on aid budgets resulting from public spending cutbacks in developed countries. Japan is one of the few major donors expected to significantly increase its Official Development Assistance (ODA) over the next five years. But the world's aid needs cannot be met by Japan alone, the survey warns. The political and economic role of ODA needs to be rethought and the image and effectiveness for international assistance is to be rebuilt, the survey argues.

Rising World Dependence on OPEC Oil

A special look at world energy trends points to a growing world dependence on oil supplies from the Organization of Petroleum Exporting Countries (OPEC), and in particular from the Persian Gulf. OPEC now produces 40 per cent of the world's output, up from 30 per cent in 1985. It possesses 77 per cent of the world's proven reserves of one trillion barrels. The Persian Gulf alone contains two-thirds of those reserves and will be the most significant source of incremental supply in the future, the survey says. OPEC production could rise to over 31 million barrels a day by 2000 from 24.4 million in 1992, though very large investments will be required to achieve this expansion in capacity. This seems to be one factor behind a reintegration of the international oil industry. Major international Oil companies are being offered joint ventures and partnerships with nationalized industries in some OPEC countries, while OPEC producers are expanding downstream to the consumer end of the market.

Hunger Amid Plenty

There is continuing prevalence of famine and hunger in the world with the generally adequate level of food stocks at the global level. World stocks of food are adequate to meet any conceivable shortfall in any country or region through imports. But warfare has become the most important determinant of famine, it argues, pointing to the experience of Somalia as one of many recent tragic examples.

And hunger is intimately related to poverty. Policies that simply involve the distribution of food and do not include health care, sanitation, education and other components of a broader approach are not likely to have a lasting impact on hunger.

There has been success in countering the severe drought in southern Africa in 1992 in which shows that there is no necessary link between local food availability and famine. Despite production losses of up to 70 per cent, a massive response by the international community and regional governments, coordinated through the UN and the southern African development community, succeeded in averting a large-scale famine.

Source : UN Newsletter, July 2, 1993.

6.2 EUROPEAN ROUND TABLE (ERT) SURVEY ON DEVELOPING COUNTRIES

A move towards less restrictive regulations and a stronger private sector is creating significant gains in efficiency and, ultimately, competitiveness and wealth. New opportunities and challenges of a strategic nature are emerging, to which the European industry must respond.

A sample study of countries like Argentina, India, Mexico, Thailand, the Philippines and Pakistan found that "these countries have implemented sets of particularly well focussed and oten quite radical measures."

In 1990, the size of markets, in all the developing countries together, amounted to more than $4 trillion, a sum equal to about two-thrids of the Gross National Product of the European Community. What matters more than the actual size is the market dynamics and trend: The grówth rates in developing countries being twice that of the Europeran community (5 to 6 per cent compared to 2.52 to 3 per cent in 1993-97). In the most dynamic region of the developing world–Asia–the economic growth is expected to be three times as high as in the EC. Until the end of the decade, if there is a centre of gravity for global economic growth, it is farther away from Europe than ever before.

The study of replies to a set of questionnaire sent to developing countries by ERT shows: first, attitudes changed as early as the 1970s, the aversion to, and distress of foreign direct investment (FDI) in numerous developing countries gradually began to be superseded by a desire to attract new investors.

Secondly, the policy approach was one of the selective attraction using investment incentives or interfering directly with investors' allocatioin decisions, often according to an interventionist industrial policy. Some host countries entered into a "negative sum game," competing with subsidies (tax holidays etc.). Thirdly, since the mid-1980s the most countries are competing for new investments by liberalising and de-regulating their economies (competition on rules).

Markets in the developing world are no longer single economic and social units, separated in various ways from the rest of the world. The globalisation of competition and demand has merged home and foreign markets including those of increasing number of developing countries. The change is taking place while the Soviet Union and communist ideologies are collapsing.

The failure of State capitalism and interventionism in the extreme having become evident some of the concepts for a mixed economy are now being questioned as well. The breakdown of the communist ideology stopped the competition between different economic systems, while widening both the scope and intensity of the new competition on rules within the generally accepted free market economy.

As regards spectacular changes in the developing countries in extent, nature and speed, certain political leaders, often under extremely difficult economic conditions, have been pushing this process forward 'with courage and determination, thereby involving private intrepreneurship–which include foreign direct investors–more and more in designing development policies."

The medium and longer term results are gains for all concerned–local private investors, foreign direcct investors and the economy as a whole. Statistics show that the impact is in the form of a significantly higher flow of FDI. The most important impact, is on investment efficiency.

Improvements in the investment conditions are still possible.

Europeans have to do their own homework on liberalisation better; they need to support opening markets abroad and to remain competitive and credible.

Europeans also need to both comprehend the situation better (intellectually), and at the same time to understand the people and their difficulties better. Optimal FDI, successful and sustainable over the long term, presupposes this comprehension and understanding more than anything else.

The E.R.T. survey covered the following countries: Argentina, Bangladesh, Brazil, Columbia, Ecuador, Egypt, Ghana, Guatemala, India, Indonesia, Iran, Kenya, Korea, Malaysia, Mexico, Pakistan, the Philippines, Saudi Arabia, Sri Lanka, Taiwan, Thailand, Tunisia, Turkey, Vietnam, Zaire and Zimbabwe.

Source : Hindustan Times, June 14, 1993.

6.3 ECONOMIC GROWTH IN ASIA AND THE PACIFIC REGION

The developing economies of the Asian and Pacific region will continue their pace, growing at 7 per cent in 1994 and 7.2 per cent in 1995.

General trend of policy changes in the region has been to promote outward-looking export-oriented industries, reduce protectionism, increase economic efficiency and encourage competition. Such policies continue to be stressed in the newly industrializing economies (NIEs), Southeast Asia and China.

Trade barriers have been progressively reduced in China, and the former centrally planned economies of Lao PDR and Viet Nam have undertaken a series of policy reforms designed to promote industry, increase trade and stimulate competition.

Economic growth in the NIEs is expected to increase over the next two years. In Korea, both domestic consumption and investment should pick up as the internal political situation stabilizes and gross domestic product (GDP) should rise to 6.7 per cent in 1994 and 6.9 per cent in 1995.

The future for Hong Kong is closely linked to the performance of China's economy. It China continues to grow at rates of around 10 per cent and the world economy begins to recover, Hong Kong's growth prospects remain bright, with GDP projected to increase to 5.7 per cent in 1994 and 5.9 per cent in 1995.

In Singapore, with GDP growth of 9.9 per cent in 1993, the sudden expansion in manufacturing experienced last year is expected to abate, although overall growth will remain high. GDP should rise to 7 per cent in 1994 and fall to 6 per cent in 1995.

With GDP growth at 13.4 per cent last year, China was not only one of the fastest-growing economies in Asia but in the world. The growth rate in 1993 was high, mainly due to the rapid expansion of the industrial sector.

A less satisfactory feature of China's economic performance was that inflation increased to 14.5 per cent in 1993 from 8.6 per cent in 1992. However, inflation is expected to ease in the immediate future. For 1994 and 1995, China's economy is forecast to grow by 10 per cent and 9 per cent, respectively.

Sustained high growth performance of Southeast Asia attests to the continuing policy reforms and generally sound and prudent economic policies followed by these countries. Further liberalization and an outward-looking orientation were maintained to ensure that competitiveness in world markets remained strong.

Over the next two years, the performance of all the economies in Southeast Asia is expected to improve and, with the world economy beginning to recover, the growth and trade prospects for the region are bright.

For example, Indonesia is expected to have GDP growth of 6.7 per cent in 1994, improving to 7 per cent in 1995. The Malaysian economy is forecast to grow by 8.6 per cent in 1994 before moderating to 8.4 per cent in 1995. With improved power supply and higher investment spending, the Philippine economy should expand by 4 per cent in 1994 and 5.5 per cent in 1995.

GDP growth inThailand is expected to reach 8.2 per cent in 1994 and 8.5 per cent in 1995. GDP growth for Vietnam is projected to increase to 9 per cent in 1994 and 10 per cent 1995. Lao PDR should increase its growth momentum, especially in the agriculture sector. GDP growth for Cambodia is also expected to reach more than 7 per cent over the next two years.

All the countries of South Asia have, in the last few years, undertaken wide-ranging reform programs that have led to the dismantling of many rigid controls and the removal or relaxation of restrictive policies.

The liberalization measures have begun to attract the attention of foreign investors and both trade and growth prospects for the sub-region look hopeful. The enormous potential of an economy the size of India is likely to have a major impact on the future of development in Asia if this potential is fully tapped.

The performance of South Asia over the next two years is expected to improve. With Pakistan's economy recovering and GDP growth in India expected to improve, the ovrerall growth of GDP for the subregion is expected to reach 5.6 per cent by 1995.

In India, foreign investment, including portfolio investment, is likely to rise, leading to further expansion in industrial growth and exports. As such, GDP growth is expected to be 4.8 per cent in 1994 and 5.5 per cent in 1995. Pakistan's economy is likely to recover, showing GDP growth of 5.5 per cent in 1994 and 6.5 per cent in 1995.

Source: Asian Development Outlook 1994 as reported in D+C 4/94.

6.4 ECONOMIC SCENARIO IN AFRICA

6.4.1 Africa Agenda

UN Secretary-General Boutros Boutros-Ghali and the General Assembly have both restated Africa's urgent need for debt relief and higher levels of resource flows to back its courageous economic and political reforms. Responding to Mr.Boutros-Ghali's first review of the UN New Agenda for the Development of Africa in the 1990s (NADAF), a 23 December General Assembly resolution called for "full and tangible" international support for NADAF, adopted in 1991 to reverse Africa's decline. It stressed the crucial need for increased financial flows to support African economic reforms, and urged that special attention be paid to poverty eradication and the social impact of structural adjustment programmes. However, a proposal by the Secretary-General to establish a $50-75 mn facility to help Africa diversify its commodity-dependent economies was deferred. Instead, donors proposed another round of "intensive consultations" now set to begin in April 1994.

The Secretary-General's report makes clear the urgency of active measures for Africa. Economic growth rates stagnated or turned negative 1991-93, per capita incomes fell further, financial inflows fell sharply, the debt burden grew steadily heavier and terms of trade worsened. In contrast, NADAF estimates that recovery in Africa requires 6 per cent annual growth in the 1990s, supported by rising inflows of aid and other financial resources. Mali's UN Ambassador Nouhoum Samassekou voiced widespread concern that the New Agenda may "suffer the same sad fate that befell UNPAAERD (the 1986-90 UN Programme of Action for African Economic Recovery and Development)".

Other African delegates expressed sharp disappointment at the divergence from NADAF goals. africans have "spared no effort in shouldering responsibility" for their economic and social development, said Egypt's Permanent Representative to the UN Nabil Elaraby. Speaking on 4 November on behalf of the Organization of African Unity (OAU), he told the General Assembly that "the efforts of the international community thus far have not risen to the level of commitments outlined in the New Agenda or the aspirations of African countries".

"While Africa strives to put its own political and economic house in order, the international community must not remain idle or indifferent," Mr. Boutros-Ghali told a 2 December meeting of the Panel of High-Level Personalities on African Development.

The UN system had itself failed to launch any large-scale measures to implement NADAF, declared Mr.Rene Valery Mongbe, Benin's Permanent Representative to the UN, reminding the General Assembly that African development was one of the five highest priorities for the UN in the 1990s. But Namibia's Ambassador to the UN Tunguru Huaraka was confident that NADAF "can be a vehicle for ensuring that Africa is at the focus of attention" in the UN system throughout the 1990s.

Debt Cancellation

The December resolution reminded international creditors of the agreed need for a 4 per cent real annual rise in aid flows to Africa, and for measures in support of capital formation. It also urged African countries to continue their efforts to improve the investment climate. The resolution implicitly reaffirmed Africa's need for debt-relief and debt cancellation. But the urgent call for an international conference on Africa's external indebtedness contained in Algeria's draft resolution was diluted in a final text that mentioned continuing "serious consideration" of such a conference.

While recognizing the "persistent efforts" at political and economic reform in Africa, the General Assembly also stressed good governance and the "crucial importance of adequate social services" in a human-centred development process. It also insisted that "full participation of the people, especially women" was essential to sustainable growth and development.

NADAF sets out an agreed framework for action by Africa, creditor countries and the UN system with a clear set of targets aimed at promoting sustainable development. It describes adequate resource flows as a 'critical element in Africa's economic recovery", and calls for an increase of official development assistance (ODA) to Africa from $20 bn in 1990 to $30 bn in 1992, and by 4 per cent in real terms each succeeding year until 1999.

"Such resources still have not materialized," Mr. Mongbe said in the General Assembly. In fact, (ODA) fell to $18.3 bn in 1991 and plunged to $12.1 bn in 1992.

"It is unlikely that the level of ODA to Africa will grow substantially during the 1990s," Africa will have a harder time attracting foreign investment, given the competition from the new countries of the former Soviet Union and from Eastern Europe.

With the Secretary-General reporting only 2.1 per cent average annual growth of Africa's gross domestic product (GDP) in 1990-92, clearly exceeded by average population growth of 3 per cent a year, prospects of attaining the NADAF goal of 6 per cent average annual growth of GDP during the 1990s are receding rapidly. An undesirable reminder of Africa's vulnerabililty was the drought that hit the eastern, southern and central regions of Africa, resulting in a decline in their per capita GDP of 2 per cent in 1992.

Africa lost $5.6 bn from continuing decline in commodity prices in 1991 alone. With early signs of a possible end to the 20-year downtrend in prices remaining uncertain, commodity analysts believe by markets will remain volatile.

It is crucial for African countries to be able to increase their capacity to process primary commodities locally as well as to produce and export a broadened range of commodities. Addressing the General Assembly, Ambassador Ernst Sucharipa of Austria and Ambassador Paul Noterdaeme of Belgium agreed that Europe should facilitate better access for African products.

Africa's massive debt grew even larger during the first year of NADAF. The Secretary-General reported that the stock of debt was equivalent to 93 per cent of the continent's 1992 GDP, and servicing it consumed 32 per cent of that year's export earnings.

Net Exporters of Capital

"The heavy and unbearable external debt burden of African countries has led to the paradoxical situation that such countries have become net exporters of capital to developed countries and multilateral financial institutions" commented Mr. Luis Fernando Jaramillo, Colombia's representative to the UN and, at the time, chairman of the Group of 77.

Help Needed

Many African countries were carrying out difficult economic adjustment programmes requiring both "courage and political conviction," said Mr. Boutros-Ghali in his speech to the Panel of High-Level Personalities. However, "structural adjustment is not popular on the streets of Africa," he warned, adding that "political will alone cannot guarantee results".

He said the fruits of these efforts had yet to ripen, "but the hardships they have brought are already very apparent. Dislocation, unemployment and declining living standards are only a few of the immediate difficulties that many countries are now experiencing. Governments must be encouraged to stay the course. Greater care must also be taken to help governments address the dire human consequences of such reforms".

The importance of improved regional cooperation and integration, a major goal of NADAF, was highlighted by the Secretary-General and the High-Level Panel. "Regional markets can provide export alternatives for local producers," Mr. Boutros-Ghali said, adding that regional projects could help to rationalize "the use of resources and talent". Regional alliances would also enable African countries to "negotiate on more favourable terms with their international counterparts".

Regional Cooperation

National adjustment programmes should also be harmonized at regional level, said Mr. Layashi Yaker, Executive Secretary of the Economic Commission for Africa, in a paper to the High-Level Panel. Orthodox structural adjustment programmes, he argued, mandate currency devaluations, fiscal policies and changes in interest rates at the national level that can work against regional integration.

Key objectives for socio-economic transition identified in the Secretary-General's report include reduction of poverty and provision of vital services, improved education and technical training, support for agriculture and environmental protection promotion of women's rights and opportunities, mobilization of domestic savings and foreign investment, more efficient and accountable political and administrative structures, and greater popular participation in decision-making.

"Development is a political undertaking as well as an economic undertaking," Mr. Boutros-Ghali said in his address to the Panel of High-Level Personalities. "Political reform, economic adjustment, regional intergration and the promotion of economic justice require a strong political commitment if they are to succeed".

Taking up the Secretary-General's assertion that "peace, stability and security are prerequisites for development," OAU Executive Secretary Ibrahima Sy told the General Assembly that his organization "has geared its efforts to the settlement of conflicts in Africa". The OAU's Mechanism for Conflict Prevention, Management and Resolution was working to restore peace in Rwanda, Somalia, Liberia, Mozambique and Burundi and to avert new violent conflicts, he said.

Source: Times Wall, *Africa Recovery,* December 1993–March 1984.

Excerpts from Secretary-General's Speech to the 2 December, 1993 Meeting of the High-Level Panel on African Development.

> "The recent history of Africa has very clearly demonstrated that peace, stability, and security, are prerequisites for development. Time and time again, all across Africa, hopeful steps towards development have faltered because of unrest and instability".
>
> "...it is clear that peace cannot long be preserved where economic injustice is systematically perpetuated, or where the opportunity for economic advancement is continually denied".
>
> It is clear that peace will be fragile if political institutions are not accountable, if political participation is not widespread, or if human rights are not respected".
>
> "...regional cooperation and integration [is] one of the key areas for the future development of Africa. Regional markets can provide export alternatives for local producers. Regional projects can help to rationalize the use of resources and talent. Through regional alliances, African countries can give themselves the means to negotiate on more avourable terms with their international counterparts".
>
> "Africans have demonstrated that they do not lack courage or commitment in addressing the problems of development. Many African countries are implementing difficult economic adjustment programmes... Structural adjustment is not popular on the streets of Africa. The fruits of these efforts have yet to ripen, but the hardships they have brought are already very apparent. Disloction, unemployment, and declining living standards are only a few of the immediate difficulties that many countries

are now experiencing".

"Regional cooperation has been most effective when it has been broad based. Economic cooperation is helped by political cooperation. Political cooperation is boosted by economic partnership....Regional cooperation should include not only trade, but political, social, and cultural cooperation well".

"In the face of such challenges, reform has required both courage and political conviction. Governments must be encouraged to stay the course. Greater care must also be taken to help governments address the dire human consequences of such reforms".

"The international community must do its part, by addressing the issues that impede Africa's ability to compete on fair terms. Critical questions such as access to markets, debt relief, technology transfer, and the reorientation of bilateral assistance must be addressed by the international community as a whole".

"While Africa strives to put her own political and economic house in order, the international community must not remain idle or indifferent... The international community must show its support for Africa's reforms by its actions, as well as by its words".

"Political instability discourages support for development. Political conflict destroys the foundations of development".

6.4.2 World Bank Adjustment

Report on Africa

Adjustment is working in Africa. Moving away from an aggregate picture of Africa which suggests unrelenting economic crisis, countries which undertook the most comprehensive reform programmes were rewarded by the fastest turnaround in growth rates. Those that refromed less or not all experienced slower improvements or further deterioration. These findings remain true even after allowing for the impact of external factors such as aid flows and trade losses.

For a continent which many observers argue is already suffering from "adjustment fatigue", a lot more still needs to be done. "The good news is that some African countries have improved their policies and reaped the gains in higher rates of growth," the Bank's Vice-President for Africa Edward Jaycox said during the March launch of the report in Washington. "The bad news is that they still have a long way to go in implementing the policies needed for growth sufficient to reduce poverty at a reasonable rate". The report is already fuelling controversy in some quarters, particularly in Africa where structural adjustment policies are often condemned for exacerbating poverty.

Out of 26 sub-Saharan countries closely studied, the Bank says six–Burkina Faso, The Gambia, Ghana, Nigeria, Tanzania, and Zimbabwe–have improved policies the most and reaped the returns. But in one of its more disturbing conclusions, the Bank observes that "current growth rates among the best African performers are still too low to reduce poverty much in the next two or three decades."

Challenging much recent criticism, the report argues that adjustment in general has not had a high social cost and in fact is probably helping to reduce poverty. But the report admits that the evidence on this issue remains inconclusive because of inadequate data. In any case, adjustment is only "the tip of the iceberg of development efforts in Africa," according to Mr. Jaycox. "It is not a substitute for strong public investment programmes, capacity-building and better public sector management."

Billed as the most comprehensive effort to date on "one of the most controversial aspects of the Bank's involvement in Africa," the report largely restricts its detailed analysis to the relationship between reform and economic growth. For the Bank, the foundation for growth consists of reining in budget deficits, flexible exchange rates, controlling inflation, freeing agriculture from price controls and taxes, reducing trade barriers and reforming the public and financial sectors. In ranking countries by their policy performance, however, the Bank concentrates on just three areas—fiscal, monetary and exchange rate policy. The six countries which went furthest in putting appropriate measures into practice in what the Bank calls the "adjustment period" from 1987-91, experienced a median improvement of 1.8 percentage points in the growth rate of per capita gross domestic product (GDP) and an improvement in GDP per capita of 1.1 per cent. The nine moderate adjusters also saw a median improvement of 1.5 percentage points in average per capita growth rates between the two periods, though average per capita growth remained negative. But for countries where policies deteriorated, there was a median fall in growth rates of 2.6 percentage points.

The differences in performance between countries with improving and deteriorating policies was true for most indicators. Countries which made the most radical changes in policies experienced the largest upturns in growth of exports and industrial production and, where agricultural reforms were undertaken, for farm output as well. However, the Bank observes, less satisfactory progress has been made in the crucial areas of public sector and financial reform.

Reforms are helping to bring only very modest levels of growth–0.4 per cent per captia during 1987-91 for all 15 countries where policies improved. Secondly, countries have found it difficult to stick with the reform process in all its necessary rigour, with 11 out of 26 countries demonstrating a deterioration in policies and one of its six best performers–Nigeria–recently abandoning the measures are most crucial for growth.

Major Findings

Trade: The Bank stresses that export promotion and greater integration into the world's trading system is the way forward to faster growth in Africa. Governments should consider an "exporters first" rule when considering policy reforms, the Bank argues.

The so-called "adding-up" problem is limited to only a few of Africa's exports, the Bank argues–cocoa, coffee, sisal, tea and tobacco, with only the first suggesting a serious chance of a decline in revenue resulting from increased production. However, its own data shows that these commodities account for over half of Africa's agricultural export revenues; and there is no comparable analysis of possible 'adding-up' problems for other exports, such as oil.

While its advocacy of export promotion remains undiminished, the Bank appears to have modified its embrace of full import liberalization. Driven by the need to preserve government revenue, rather than any acceptance of the need to protect infant industries, the report urges caution in reducing tariffs. "African governments are correct to put revenue consideration ahead of any push to achieve a low (10 per cent) uniform tariff rate," the report says. "Even very high tariffs, if imposed only for a clearly limited transition period, can be consistent with the long-term objectives of adjustment,"

Agriculture: With the overwhelming majority of Africa's poor living in rural areas, one of the most gratifying findings of the Bank study, according to Mr. Jaycox, is that countries that have liberalized their pricing and marketing of agricultural products and reduced taxation of farmers have seen a marked resurgence in production. Countries that decreased taxes the most experienced a difference in average agricultural growth between the two periods of 2 percentage points. Those that lowered taxation less or that actually increased it recorded a downturn in rates of production. Similarly, increase in real producer prices for export crops led to a jump in production, whereas declining real prices led to a fall-off in output, the study finds. However, the Bank's six best policy performers, as a group, experienced a downturn in the rate of agricultural growth, largely as a result of sharp falls in The Gambia and Zimbabwe.

The response of the private sector to removal of price controls has "sometimes been disappointing". The Bank emphasizes that policy reforms have to be complemented by investment in rural infrastructure.

Industry: The Bank finds no "systematic evidence" that Africa is being "deindustrialized" by adjustment and trade liberalization. Instead, it says, countries that improved policies most saw a sharp turnaround in industrial output–The Gambia was the only exception. Countries with a small improvement in policies also saw a noticeable gain, though even countries where policies deteriorated experienced an upturn in output.

Much of the evidence remains circumstantial, but it cites Ghana as evidence that adjustment is leading to a more vibrant industrial sector, not less. With policies enforcing closures among usually large, often state-owned producers deemed inefficient, at the same time as they are providing incentives for more competitive, usually small, private companies, the longterm trend is still unclear. However, in Ghana almost two-thirds of the increase in manufacturing employment since 1987 is attributable to new firms entering the market. How sustainable these new producers–often little more than single households–will prove to be is the "big question". Increased technological capability may be a "prerequisite for further fast-paced industrial growth," which raises the issue of both access to overseas "know how" and investment in local education and technical training systems.

Source: Roy Laishley, Africa Recovery, December 1993-March 1994.

6.4.3 Tokyo Declaration on African Development

Against a background of troubling economic indicators for Africa, positive visions of commitment at continental and national level and of strengthened international support were evident at Tokyo International Conference on African Development (TICAD). Over 400 high-level participants, including five African heads of state, unanimously adopted a Tokyo Declaration which spelied out a strategy combining good governance and private sector development with supportive international measures in a framework for African economic recovery.

Summary of the Tokyo Declaration on African Development

Political and Economic Reforms

* Africa to continue political and economic reforms, especially as regards democratization, quality of government, human and social development and economic liberalization. Development partners to provide priority support for reforms and capacity building.
* Structural adjustment programmes to improve access of the poor to income-earning opportunities and social services; give increased priority to poverty alleviation and to investment in human capital through nutrition, health and education programmes.
* Rapid population growth to be addressed within the socio-economic development process.

Economic Development through Activities of the Private Sector

* African countries to foster private sector and to encourage entrepreneurship.
* Improved financial systems needed to stimulate savings and foreign investment and stem capital flight.
* Development partners to facilitate market access for African products and assist in upgrading and diversifying African exports.

Regional Cooperation and Integration

* Africa's move toward regional integration and cooperation to continue in the context of the Abjua Treaty, with support from development partners.

Emergency Relief and Development

* African countries responsible for disaster prevention and management, addressing root causes of manmade and natural disasters and ensuring food security. Development partners pledge to provide humanitarian assistance for disaster-stricken communities.

Asian Experience and African Development

* Asian successes demonstrate the value of commitment by leaders and people to economic prosperity, long-term development and functional government administration.
* Achievements in East Asia have enhanced opportunities for South-South cooperation with Africa.

International Cooperation

* Solidarity between Africa and the international community.
* Promotion of the role of African women, and a larger role for local

NGOs.

* Donor countries to make all efforts to enhance development assistance. Assistance oriented to priorities set by African countries, with the expectation that it is efficiently utilized.
* African debt to be urgently addressed in the context of debt relief and flows of new financial resources.
* Protection of African natural environment.
* A stronger response to the AIDS pandemic.

6.5 ECONOMIC SCENARIO OF LATIN AMERICA AND THE CARIBBEAN

Overview

In 1993, the phase of moderate growth in most of the Latin American and Caribbean economies continued, with relative price stability and support from a massive inflow of external captial.

The region's economic performance remained heavily influenced by two conflicting factors. First, the cumulative effect of the adjustment policies and reforms adopted in previous years, which have been gradually changing the bases on which economies function. Second, the slow, uncertain evolution of the international economy, whose adverse consequences included the limited growth of global demand and the deterioration of commmodity prices, but which also brought about a drop in international interest rates which benefited the countries of the region.

Preliminary ECLAC estimates indicate that the region's gross domestic product increased by 3.2 per cent in 1993, while per capita GDP rose for the third consecutive year, this time by 1.3 per cent. Although the region's aggregate performance was similar to that for 1992, it was heavily influenced by economic recovery in Brazil. If we exclude Brazil, the output of the rest of the region's economies grew by only 2.6 per cent, compared to nearly 5 per cent in the preceding biennium.

This decline in the region's performance (excluding Brazil) took different forms, however. It was caused both by the emergence or exacerbation of some recessionary situations and by a widespread slow-down, which in some cases occurred in a context of rapid growth and in others caused a drop in per capita GDP.

Venezuela's economy, for instance, was plunged into a recession; its outputfell by 1 per cent after having risen by almost 7 per cent the previous year. Nicaragua's economy slipped back into a recession, contracting by nearly 1 per cent after its modest recovery of 1992. The level of economic activity in Haiti and Trinidad and Tobago also continued to drop, although for different reasons.

Half the countries of the region on which information is available have experienced a slow-down in their economic growth. Argentina, Chile, Cosia Rica and Panama have moderated their high growth rates of the previous year, although at around 6 per cent they are still among the region's highest. Growth has also slowed to annual rates of around 4 per cent in Belize, Guatemala, Guyana and honduras, around 2 per cent in the Dominican Republic and Uruguay-down from 7 per cent-and under 2 per cent in Ecuador.

Mexico's output grew by less than 1 per cent in 1993, completing a three-year slow-down of growth.

Only a few countries have improved on their previous year's performance. For two of these, the improvement was due to a recovery of economic activity: in Brazil, a 4.5 per cent increase and in Peru, a major recovery (6.5 per cent) after a recessionary phase. Countries whose growth picked up include Colombia (from 3.6 per cent to 4.5 per cent), El Salvador (from 4.7 per cent to 5 per cent) and Paraguay (from 1.7 per cent to 3.7 per cent).

Generally speaking, the growth slow-down has coincided with a slow-down or levelling out of export volumes. In the few cases in which growth picked up, exports also grew. Price stabilization continued to strengthen in the greater part of the region. Brazil was an exceptionto this trend, with three-digit inflation soaring even higher, although at the end of the year the authorities, after adopting a package of fiscal adjustment measures, proposed to parliament the bases for a programme of gradual stabilization. By contrast, the average increase in the other countries' consumer prices, which had dropped from 49 per cent to 22 per cent the previous year, fell to 19 per cent in 1993. Moreover, countries with an annual inflation rate of under 15 per cent became the majority in 1993.

These countries maintained strict antiinflation programmes which in some cases brought the inflation rate down to a single digit. Three years after its latest bout of hyper-inflation, Argentina brought its annual rate of consumer price increases down to under 8 per cent. Mexico's stabilization was consolidated, with annual inflation down from 12 per cent to under 9 per cent. Bolivia and Costa Rica also managed to reduce their inflation to under 10 per cent, while the Dominican Republic reduced its rate from 7 per cent to 3 per cent and Barbados and Panama brought their rates even lower.

Other economies where inflation has been moderate for years resisted further substantial reductions in their annual rate of price increases: Colombia, from 25 per cent to 21 per cent, and Chile, from under 13 per cent to 12 per cent. However, few countries in this group (Haiti, Paraguay and Trinidad and Tobago) saw inflation rise agian.

Another group of countries remain in situations of controlled instability. This has enabled them to avoid inflationary spirals and, in some cases, to reduce their high inflation rates. In 1993, Ecuador cut its annual rate of price increases form 60 per cent to 32 per cent, Peru from 57 per cent to 41 per cent, Uruguay from 59 per cent to 52 per cent and Jamaica from 40 per cent to 25 per cent. In Nicaragua, on the other hand, inflation picked up again, from 4 per cent last year to 28 per cent, while in Venezuela the annual rate of price increases rose from 32 per cent to 44 per cent.

In general, the consolidation of fiscal adjustment processes has helped promote stabilization. In 1993, roughly half of the 19 countries on which information is available improved their fiscal management, either by reducing the deficit or by increasing the public account surplus. The fact that the credit expansion brought about by the inflow external financing has not had a particularly inflationary impact, especially in countries where stabilization is a recent phenomenon, also has to do with the increased demand for real monetary balances, which has outstripped the growth of output, and with the channelling of a large part of this increase in demand to imports.

To sum up, in the three cases of recession (Nicaragua, Venezuela and

Trinidad and Tobago), inflation has speeded up; the recovery of activity in Brazil has taken place in a highly inflationary context, while that in Peru has coincided with a reduction in the rate of price increases; in a few countries (Bolivia, Colombia and Honduras), there has been a simultaneous slow-down of inflation and an acceleration of growth; and in most countries where inflation has been reduced, growth has also slowed, although in some cases growth rates none the less remain satisfactory.

It is striking that despite the sluggishness of world trade and of the industrialized countries' imports, the volume of Latin American and Caribbean exports has grown by almost 9 per cent. This is attributable in part to the vigorous growth of intra-Latin American trade and, in many cases, to the successful diversification of export structures in previous years.

This export effort was eroded by the drop in export prices, with the result that the value of Latin American and Caribbean external merchandise sales increased, as in the previous year, at a rate of close to 5 per cent, totalling US$ 133 billion. At the same time, the region's terms of trade deteriorated even further, this by 5 per cent, resulting in a cumulative drop of 18 per cent over the past triennium and continuing the virtually uninterrupted deterioration in these terms since 1984.

The value of Latin American and Caribbean merchandise imports increased by 8 per cent, to almost US$ 148 billion, after rising at an average annual rate of 18 per cent over the previous triennuium. The increase remained relatively widespread, although some countries reduced their purchases and the variation in the regional aggregate was particularly influenced by the growth of Brazil's imports (an increase of US$ 4.8 billion) and the continued growth of Colombia's (US$ 2.7 billion).

The merchandise trade deficit grew from US$10 billion the previous year to US$ 14.7 billion and was distributed more widely among the countries of the region. In fact, only three countries (Brazil, with a US$ 13.5 billion surplus, Ecuador and Venezuela) still have a positive balance in their merchandise trade. Among deficit countries, Mexico's negative balance stayed close to US$ 20 billion.

Net payments of profits and interest held steady at US$ 29 billion, since the effect of the drop in nominal interest rates was offset by higher profit remittances.

In these circumstances, the region's already considerable import capacity was maintained in 1993 thanks to the modest increase in the value of exports, since captial inflows were down form the high level of the previous year and net profit and interest payments remained stable. This result and the smaller accumulation of reserves enabled imports to continue to grow, albeit at a more moderate pace than during the import boom of the preceding triennium, despite the fact that in most cases imports were also stimulated by the erosion of the real exhange rate, in a stable context of abundant exteranal financing and relatively liberal trade regimes.

The current-account deficit of the region's balance of payments continued to grow in 1993, this time to nearly US$ 43 billion or 3.4 per cent of regional output, owing to the deterioration of the trade balance.

The growing current-account deficit continued to be easily financed through the net flow of capital into the region, attracted largely by the differentials between dollar returns on Latin American investments and those prevailing on international financial markets. The net capital inflow into the Latin American and Caribbean countries totalled almost US$ 55 billion in 1993, compared to almost US$ 62 billion the previous year and over US$ 39 billion in 1991. Net inflows to remained fairly widespread and the lower figure was the result of reduced flows to some of the main recipients: Brazil (which received US$ 5.4 billion less than the previous year), Argentina (US$ 2.9 billion less) and Venezuela (US$ 1 billion less). The main recipient, Mexico, continued to attract around US$ 25 billion, while Colombia, whose net inflows had been minimal, this year received US$ 1.5 billion. Capital entering Latin America and the Caribbean continued to come essentially from private, non-banking sources and consisted of various types of investments. The most dynamic instrument was the placement of government or private sector bonds, which brought in US$ 19.3 billion, almost doubling the already large amount invested the previous year. Levels of foreign direct investment remained very high. Time deposits in local banks and trade credits, which continued to grow in response to the influx of imports, remained important sources of funds. The boom on the region's main equity markets also attracted foreign investors, and some Latin American firms maintained their access to international stock markets through special instruments.

As the net capital inflow continued to be far greater than the current-account deficit, the international reserves of most countries of the region increased for the fifth year in a row, although to a lesser extent than in the previous biennium.

The reduction in net capital inflows. in circumstances in which net payments of profits and interest remained almost constant, meant that the net transfer of financial resources to the region fell from almost US$ 33 billion in 1992 to less than US$ 26 billion in1993.

The region's external debt increased by 4 per cent, reaching US$ 487 billion. This expansion was due partly to new bond placements on the international market, an increase in short-term credit operations and, to a far lesser extent, some disbursements of official loans. The only factors which helped to shrink the debt were some debt-reduction operations.

In 1993, the indicators of the region's external debt burden continued to abate. The coefficient representing interest owed as a percentage of exports dropped for the seventh year running, this time to 18 per cent. The decline was due mainly to the increase in exports of goods and services. For the region as a whole, the debt-export ratio decreased slightly, to 293 per cent, owing to the improvement of this ratio in the non-oil-exporting countries. None the less, only seven countries had a coefficient lower than the threshold of 200 per cent.

The downward trend inflation, coupled with acceptable, though declining, growth rates in most countries is not just the outcome of an economic policy aimed at restricting the growth of internal demand in order to stabilize prices. Because the credit expansion is the result largely of an inflow of external capital, monetary and foreign-exchange policies have little margin for achieving this goal on their own. Measures to sterilize the gowth of the monetary base resulting from the accumulation of reserves contribute to this goal, but only to a limited extent.

In many countries, the fact that a disproportionate share of the increase in domestic spending triggered by the greater availability of financing has gone to imports has also contributed to this outcome. Moreover, the abundance of foreign exchange has held down the exchange rate and prices for tradeables, causing currency to appreciate in real terms, since inertial inflation is more evident in prices for non-tradeable goods and services for which demand is strictly local. All in all, exchange-rate appreciation has helped slow down inflation and has also influenced expectations. Furthermore, since the situation of the international economy is uncertain and its growth is slow, the value of the exports of most countries of the region has increased at moderate rates in the last triennium, absorbing the impact of the steady decline in the terms of trade. On the other hand, the region has again become a net importer of external financial resources, after having transferred abroad the equivalent of almost four percentage points of its output annually for the greater part of the last decade.

Perhaps the main driving force behind these flows has been the drop in international returns in dollars, coinciding with consistently high returns on capital in Latin America. However, reform processes, external debt write-offs, price stabilization and stable economic policy were the factors which made these returns attractive, by reducing the perceived risk of investing in many countries of the region, particularly the exchange-rate risk. This new climate of confidence also encouraged residents of the region to repatriate their capital through the various financial instruments available, a process which in some cases led the flow of new resources.

Massive external financing in economies that are more open to imports, greater fiscal soundness, price stability and economic recovery have combined to boster the confidence of internal and external agents in the permanence of economic policy and in the continuing reproduction of these results.

The maintenance of this new functioning of the region's economies creates some concerns and some dilemmas related to the management of economic policy however. The size of the external gap of most Latin American and Caribbean countries has tended to settle at import levels far in excess of exports, with the growth of imports exceeding immediate possibilities for the growth of exports. Capital flows have helped to finance this gap, and even to increase it by stimulating further imports.

This situation is threatening the normal functioning of many of the region's economies, given the possibility of new external shocks. A large proportion of external capital has been short-term or has entered the region for speculative purposes by means of long-term instruments. Some of these investments may be particularly sensitive to an increase in international interest rates or to the normalization of their initial returns, even without a sudden change in economic policy. Moreover, external investors pay close attention to the size of each country's external gap as an indicator of the sustainability of the basic process linking investment, growth and imports with capital inflows.

All of this gives external capital a degree of volatility that probably influences the volume of net capital inflows at a given moment more than their continuation over time. Besides, no matter how unlikely it may seem now that new external shocks will occur in the short-term, we cannot discount the possibility that they may occur at some point in the more distant future.

There is little room for manoeuvre for dealing with this eventuality. In most cases, macro-economic and fiscal regulation can operate only within relatively limited margins of intervention, at the risk of eroding confidence in its permanence and exerting a negative impact whose consequences are virtually incalculable.

Even within these margins, the size and composition of the capital flows entering the region pose difficult dilemmas for monetary and foreign-exchange policy. To the extent that these flows respond to international economic conditions or their volatility makes them essentially temporary, there is a case for sterilizing their impact on the money supply in order to gain control of monetary policy; however, this can give rise to a perverse mechanism whereby higher interest rates attract even more temporary capital.

Given this situation, it is desirable that the composition of capital flows should gradually shift away from volatile flows towards more stable capital flows and risk investments. This would justify a limited, selective regulation of external financing, following the lead of some countries of the region. Cutting back on short-term flows and eventually reducing capital flows to their more permanent components would also help to alleviate pressures forwards exchange-rate appreciation without substantially affecting investment financing.

Overcoming the above situation in the medium-term depends essentially on the rapid, sustained expansion of exports and on the international competitiveness of production structures. This will require an ongoing effort to change production patterns, increased investment in sectors that produce tradeables, and access to external markets.

Accordingly, despite the magnitude of the difficulties still faced by Latin American and Caribbean goods and services in gaining access to the markets of the industrialized countries, 1993 ended with some encouraging signs, the most significant being the intensification of intra-Latin American trade, the recent ratification of the Free Trade Agreement between Canada, the United States and Mexico and the adoption of the Final Act of the Uruguay Round of multilateral trade negotiations.

TABLE 6.1 Latin American and the Caribbean: Main Economic Indicators

Indicators	1986	1987	1988	1989	1990	1991	1992	1993[a]
Gross domestic product at market prices prices (index, base year 1980=100)	106.7	110.1	111.0	112.4	112.4	116.6	120.0	123.9
Population (millions of inhabitants)	392.8	400.9	408.9	417.0	425.1	433.2	441.3	449.0
Per capita gross domestic product (index, base year 1980-100)	93.6	94.7	93.6	92.6	91.1	92.8	93.8	95.00
			Growth rates					
Gross domestic product	4.2	3.2	0.8	0.9	0.3	3.8	3.0	3.2
Per capita gross domestic product	2.0	1.2	-1.2	-1.0	-1.6	1.8	1.1	1.3
Consumer prices	64.1	208.9	773.7	1205.7	1185.2	198.6	416.8	796.6
Terms of trade (goods)	-11.0	-0.9	-0.3	1.2	-0.9	-8.7	-5.6	-4.9
Purchasing power of exports of goods	-11.9	7.9	8.2	4.5	5.4	-2.8	2.9	3.3
Current value of exports of goods	-15.7	14.5	13.9	9.8	9.8	-0.8	5.1	4.5
Current value of imports of goods	2.5	12.6	14.0	6.6	15.8	18.2	22.7	7.7
			Bilions of dollars					
Exports of goods	77.6	88.7	101.1	111.0	121.9	120.9	127.2	132.9
Imports of goods	59.7	67.2	76.7	81.7	94.6	111.8	137.2	147.7
Trade balance (goods)	17.9	21.5	24.4	29.3	27.3	9.1	-10.0	-14.8
Net payments of profits and interest	32.4	31.3	34.0	37.6	34.8	31.0	29.2	28.9
Balance on current account[c]	-17.4	-10.9	-11.0	-6.7	-6.5	-20.2	-36.9	-42.6
Net movement of capital[d]	9.9	15.2	5.3	9.7	20.7	39.3	62.0	54.6
Global balance[e]	-7.5	4.3	-5.7	3.0	14.2	19.1	25.1	12.0
Total gross external debt	401.0	427.4	419.6	422.7	439.1	456.6	468.1	487.0
Net transfer of resources[f]	-22.5	-16.1	-28.7	-27-9	-14.1	8.3	32.8	25.7

Source: ECLAC, on the basis of official figures.

a Preliminary estimates, subject to revision. bVariation from December to December. cIncludes net unrequired private transfer payments. dIncludes long-and short-term capital, unrequited official transfer payments, and errors and omissions. eCorresponds to the variation in international reserves (of opposite sign) plus counterpart items. fCorresponds to net inflow of capital, less net payments of profits and interest.

7

DIVERSE ISSUES

7.1 HUMAN DEVELOPMENT: HUMAN DEVELOPMENT REPORT, 1993

The report, prepared by an independent team of economists for the United Nations Development Programme (UNDP), shows that ethnic minorities, the poor, rural dwellers, women, and the disabled often have little power to change their lives. This disempowerment can even extend to entire countries.

According to Mahbub ul Haq, Special Adviser to the Administrator and chief architect of the report. The basic message of human development has not changed: economic growth is imperative for a nation's development, but this growth must be translated into the lives of people. Income is essential, "but it is only a means, not the sum total of human life." People make many choices besides making money which affect their lives, in areas ranging from health and education to employment and the way they are governed.' The report ranks countries according to a Human Development Index (HDI), which combines life expectancy, educational attainment and basic purchasing power into one indicator of human development. The countries with the highest incomes are not always those with highest HDI ranking. In 1993, Japan ranks first on the HDI although sixth in real gross domestic product (GDP), Canada is second in HDI, followed in order by Norway, Switzerland, Sweden, USA (first in income), Australia, France, the Netherlands, and the United Kingdom. Among developing countries, Barbados is first with a ranking of 20, followed by Hong Kong (24), Cyprus (27), Uruguay (30), Trinidad and Tobago (31), Bahamas (32), Republic of Korea (33), Chile (36), Costa Rica (36) and Singapore (43).

The need for improved levels of human development is not limited to developing countries. To highlight the exclusion of ethnic minorities from participating fully in economic and social benefits, the 1993 report ranked the white. African-American and Hispanic populations of the United States on the HDI as if they were separate entities. The white population would rank first on the HDI, ahead of Japan, while the African-Americans, with lower life expectancy, income and education levels, would rank 31st, the same as Trinidad and Tobago. Hispanics in the U.S. would rank 35th among countries, below the Bahamas, Republic of Korea and Estonia, Studies of other countries show many other groups such as the poor, women and rural dwellers are excluded from participation as well.

Five new pillars of a people-centred world order :

(1) New concepts of human security that stress security of people, not just of nations and territory. This means accelerated disarmament, using defence cuts to boost human development. It means a new role for the United Nations, increasingly intervening to provide human security in areas such as the former Yugoslavia and in Somalia, where people are fighting within countries rather than between countries.

(2) New strategies of sustainable human development that weave development around people, not people around development.

(3) New partnerships between state and markets, to combine market efficiency with social compassion.

(4) New patterns of national and global governance. Inflexible nation-states cannot cope with the globalisation of markets on the one hand and the rising aspirations of their people on the other. Needed: more decentralisation of power, more involvement by non-governmental organizations, more empowerment of the poor.

(5) New forms of international cooperation, to focus foreign aid directly on the needs of the people rather than on the perferences of governments.

Participation as a key to human development.

Economic Participation

The starting point for economic participation is jobs. All over the world, economies are growing but the number of jobs is not keeping pace, resulting in "jobless growth". From 1960 to 1987, for example, France, Germany and the United Kingdom saw their economies more than double and their employment rates fall. The phenomenon is particularly devastating in developing countries. Less than one-third of the increase in output in developing countries in the 1960-87 period came from increased labour; more than to-third resulted from capital investment. At the same time, the labour force in the developing world grew by more than 400 million, creating legions of unemployed. In some countries, particularly in East Asia, land reform and investment in human resources have led to substantial job growth.

One way of making economies work better and increasing opportunities for participation is to reduce state regulations, unleash private creativity and sell off inefficient public enterprises. However, they must be made carefully, so as to avoid abuses. There is need for full disclosure to prevent corruption and for anti-monopoly steps so that economic power does not pass from one ruling elite to another, among other possible failings.

Political Participation

If people cannot travel miles to the seat of government to share power, government can and should move to people by decentralising, says the report. One of the few ways of measuring decentralisation is by studying where government money is spent, and by that measure, there is a long way to go. On average, central governments in developing countries allocate less than 10 per cent of total national spending to local governments and less than 6 per cent of total social expenditure. This compares with an average allocation of 40$ of all spending and 25 per cent of social spending in 15 industrialised countries studied.

it is not an easy task to change the patterns of centralised government. Even Chile, Indonesia, Morocco and Zimbabwe, which have taken large strides toward decentralisation by creating nearly autonomous levels of local government, have dispersed relatively little power. The resources controlled locally are small, local decision-making powers are narrow and many local appointments are imposed from above. Yet these countries show that decentralisation can bring government closer to the people and improve their lives. Chile assigned responsibility for basic education and primary health care to local governments in the 1980s. As a result, 30 per cent of all social spending takes pace at the local level, compared with six per cent in the capital, a reversal of the usual pattern.

Group Participation

When people organise, by definition they increase their level of participation and often increase influence over their own lives. The dramatic shift toward democracy across the developing world has led to an explosion of participatory movements and non-governmental organizations. NGOs today benefit more than 250 million people, compared to 100 million in the early 1980s, says the report. The expansion of NGO activity has been supported by aid donors who, dissatisfied with the performance of much official aid, are channelling more of the money though them. Over the past 20 years, grants by NGOs in the North (most of it from government sources) to developing countries jumped from just over $ 1 billion to $ 5 billion a year.

NGOs play a variety of roles. One is to promote democracy. Labour unions, such as Solidarity in Poland and the Congress of Trade Unions in Zambia, both played central roles in opposing one-party states and fostering multi-party elections; in both cases, union presidents were elected country presidents. NGOs are often able to reach the poorest in society, where governments are not. In Zimbabwe, agricultural groups supported by the NGOs Silveira House increased crop yields by as much as tenfold, enabling farmers to break out of subsistence agriculture and move into a cash economy. By extending loans to nearly 1 million people in 23,000 villages, the Grameen Bank in Bangladesh has proven that credit for the landless poor not only creates businesses and jobs, but can yield a loan repayment rate of 95 per cent. NGOs can also help to empower marginalised groups. In Ecuador, Indian Federations are helping indigenous people to gain secure title to their land, resulting in both material benefits and improved standing in civil society.

The growth of NGOs and their impact can obscure the fact that they still operate on a relatively small scale, notes the report. The grants channeled through Northern NGOs to Southern NGOs accounts for 13 per cent of official aid and 2.5 per cent of total resource flow to developing countries.

The Report makes a Difference

Since its first appearance in 1990, the *Human Development Report* has kept one message intact; development must centre on people, and one sure indicator of progress in development is the widening range of people's choices. The reports have argued for sharply reduced military spending and higher levels of social spending; better targeting of foreign aid; more favourable terms of trade for poorer nations; and higher levels of democracy and paticipation.

Because of the ranking of countries in the Human Development Index, reaction has been strong: in 1992, the Group of Seven Summit Meeting in Paris hailed cutting of military spending, while Heads of State of the Non-Aligned Movement meeting in Jakarta after some debate, called on governments to urgently promote international cooperation for human development. Human development has been the subject of debate in the parliaments of Italy, France, Sweden, Canada and Europe.

For many countries, the starting point is data collection. Bolivia is conducting a census to discover the human development status of its people. India, responding to the reports, started a nationwide data collection exercise at state and district levels last year to improve efforts toward poverty alleviation. An entire region moved toward people-centred development when six Central American presidents met in late 1991 to sign a commitment to "assemble all resources" for human development in their countries. Heads of three of those countries pledged to reallocate a total of $500 million a year within their national budgets to fund social sector initiatives. Bangladesh, Colombo, Ghana and Pakistan were among the first countries to request UNDP assistance to review and set costs for meeting human development targets. Ghana, for example, has drafted an elaborate human development strategy that recognises the need for change in areas ranging from macro-economic planning to protection of the poorest during periods of austerity.

More than 20 countries in one way or another have sought UNDP assistance to implement a human development approach. As a result of the more than $3 billion in UNDP programme funding for the 1992-96 period, nearly $1.2 billion or nearly 40 per cent will go to poverty alleviation and people's participation programmes.

Source : *Go Between,* Juy 1993, NGLS, Geneva.

7.2 HUMAN RIGHTS: WORLD CONFERENCE ON HUMAN RIGHTS, 1993

The second major World Conference on Human Rights to take place since the 1948 Universal Declaration of Human Rights was held in Vienna from 14-25 June 1993. The first conference was in Tehran in 1968, the 20th anniversary year of the human rights declaration. The recent conference was convened to assess progress in and obstacles to the full realization of human rights, and to reinforce UN efforts to promote respect and advancement of these rights.

Among the issues raised during the conference were the creation of a forum to identify human rights abuses, active promotion of democracy, the condition of women in the world, the right of people in Bosnia and Herzegovina to self-defence, the observation of strict impartiality in human rights matters, resources allocated to the protection of human rights, the rights of children, protection of minorities and vulnerable groups, and increased economic assistance to assist developing countries in consolidating their democracies, among other issues. The conference called on all governments to take steps to counter intolerance and related violence and stressed that those who perpetrated or authorized criminal acts associated with "eithnic cleansing" were individually responsible and accountable and should be brought to justice. Two declarations calling on the international community, particulary the Security Council, to take forceful and decisive steps to bring peace to Bosnia and Herzegovina and Angola were also adopted.

Leading up to the conference, three Preparatory Committees (PrepCom) were held in Geneva in 1991-92, with a mandate to make proposals to the General Assembly on procedures and preparatory activities. The fourth and final PreCom, in Geneva from 19 April–8 May 1993, adopted a draft final declaration with consensus on only seven of its 26 paragraphs. At Vienna, the final document was formally adopted, and now reflects the orgoing negotiations since PreCom IV. For example, the right to development (Paragraphs 6, 6 bis and 6 ter of the declaration) is now recognized. On the other hand, the proposal made in PreCom IV's final document specifying individual and collective rights was not agreed. Decision was also postponed on certain questions of concern to NGOs, such as the immediate creation of a High Commissioner for Human Rights and of an international criminal court of justice (the conference recommendation only that the General Assembly begin considering these matters).

A total of 170 countries including 11 heads of states and 70 foreign affairs ministers attended the conference, as well as some 1,000 NGOs. A number of international personalities were invited by the conference's Secretary-General including Jimmy Carter, Corazon Aquino, Rigoberta Menchu and Elena Bonner. The International Year of Indigenous People was celebrated during the conference, leading to a recommendation that the General Assembly proclaim an International Decade of Indigenous People beginning in January 1994.

The Vienna Declaration

The Final Declaration of the World Conference of Human Rights is made up of three parts: a preamble, a declaration, and a programme of action.

The *Preamble* contains 12 paragraphs and highlights the duty of all states, in accordance with the Universal Declaration of Human Rights, to develop and encourage respect for human rights and fundamental freedoms for all. The preamble is a list of principles. Paragraph 2, for example, affirms that the human being is the central subject of human rights and fundamental freedoms and consequently should be the principal beneficiary of those rights. Paragraph 7 bis was added to the final text of PreCom IV and says the conference is deeply concerned about the various forms of discrimination and violence faced by women around the world.

The *Vienna Declaration* reaffirms the universal character of human rights and freedoms. All people have the right to self-determination and by virtue of that right they freely determine their political status and freely pursue their economic, social and cultural development. While some speakers said that human rights standards must be consistent with cultural, religious and regional particularities, the conference's final document states categorically that the universal nature of human rights and fundamental freedoms is "beyond question" and while such particularities are to be borne in mind, "it is the duty of states, regardless of their political, economic and cultural systmes, to promote and protect" all such right and freedoms".

The declaration underlines that democracy, development, and human rights and fundamental freedoms are interdependent and mutually reinforcing. It reafirms that the right to development is a universal and inalienable right which is an integral and part of fundamental human rights.

The international community is called upon to continue giving high priority to alleviating and eventually eradicating extreme poverty. Also, the declaration states that the fundamental rights of women and girl children are inalienable, integral, and inseparable from universal human rights. The declaration recognize the inherent dignity of indigenous people and reaffirms the commitment made by the international community to ensure their economic, social and cultural well-being. It also reiterates the commitment to assist indigenous people in sharing in the benefits of sustainable development. The Vienna Declaration also underlines the importance of teaching human rights and invites states to include the subject in school curricula.

In paragraph 25, the declaration expresses its appreciation of the contribution made by NGOs to raising public awareness about human rights and humanitarian issues, implementing education, training and research programmes, and promoting and protecting human rights and fundamental freedoms. While the principal responsibility in setting standards lies with states, the Vienna Declaration recoginzes NGOs' significant contributions to the process. The declaration also highlights the importance of ongoing dialogue and of cooperation between governments and NGOs.

The *Programme of Action* recommends greater coordination in human rights efforts within the UN system and calls for a strengthening of the Geneva-based Centre for Human Rights. It also stresses the need to avoid a proliferation of human rights instruments and urges states to consider limiting the extent of any reservations they lodge when ratifying such instruments.

On issues relating to equality, dignity and tolerance, the action programme considers the elimination of racism and racial discrimination, particularly in its institutionalized form such as apartheid, a key objective of the international community and of a world programme to promote human rights.

The action programme also calls on states and on the international community to promote and protect the rights of ethnic, religious and linguistic minorities. It emphasizes that women should have full and equal fundamental rights and that this should be a priority for governments and for the UN. It invities the General Assembly and ECOSOC at their 1993 session to adopt rules for equal opportunity for handicapped people. The action programme also encourages the International Law Commission to continue its work to create an International Criminal Court.

With reference to follow-up, the General Assembly, the Human Rights Commission and other UN agencies should examine how to apply recommedations contained in the final declaration, including the possibility of declaring a Decade for Human Rights. The commission should also assess results obtained in the field of human rights each year.

After formal adoption of the Vienna Declaration and the Programme of Action, several delegations expressed reservations about the document, Chile, for example, would have preferred a more focused document with concrete recommendations. Turkey would have preferred more concrete measure concerning terrorism. The United States had reservations about the declaration's qualified endorsement of freedom of the press "within the framework of national laws". Denmark, on behalf of the EC, regretted that the final document did not consider minority rights collectives rights. The US, Israel and Iraq raised objections to the references to foreign occupation and denial of self-determination as a human rights violation. Both the US and Israel objected to the omission of any reference to anti-Semitism in the declaration.

NGOs and the Vienna Conference

Non-governmental organizations played an unprecedented role at the conference, and parallel NGO activities were held on the conference site itself. In another milestone, the results of the NGO Forum, held from 10-12 June, were presented in a formal meeting of the Drafting Committee by Rapporteur-General Manfred Nowak of the Boltzmann Institute. In addition to recommending the immediate creation of a senior UN human rights post and of permanent international criminal court for serious human rights violations, the forum also recommended the appointment of a special rapporteur of the Human Rights Commission on violence against women, sexual discrimination, and the establishment of mechanisms for the protection of indigenous peoples' rights.

NGOs also recommended the adoption of new human rights education strategies and called for action against violations of the rights of migrant workers, displaced persons and stateless persons.

While NGOs presence at Vienna was extensive, they were not able–as at the PrepComs–to gain access to the informal sessions of the Drafting Committee. National and international NGOs, however, did not always have the same priorities and strategies on human rights issues. They have learned to work together, however, and to recognize their mutual importance to one another. The International Service for Human Rights (Geneva) is evaluating the Vienna conference from the NGOs' viewpoints. National NGOs have also set up a liaison committee which will meet for the first time in March 1994 during the Human Rights Commission.

During the conference, 120 NGOs also organized a series of parallel activities at the Austria Centre, including seminars, working groups, concerts and exhibitions. The NGOs also contributed to the plenary debates.

Source: Go Between, July 1993, NGLS. Geneva.

7.3 INTERNATIONAL YEAR OF THE FAMILY, 1994

The United Nations General Assembly, in its Resolution 44/82 of December 1989, proclaimed 1994 as the International Year of the Family. The theme of the Year was decided as "Family: Resources and Responsibilities in a Changing World".

In United Nations instruments, the family is referred to as the basic unit of society; it is appreciated for the important socio-economic functions that it perfomrs. In spite of the many changes in society that have altered its role and functions, the family continues to provide the natural framework for the emotional, financial and material support essential to the growth and development of all its members, particulary infants and children, and for the care of other dependants, including the elderly, disabled and the infirm. The family remains as vital means of preserving and transmitting cultural values. In the broader sense, it can, and often does, educate, train, motivate and support its individual members, thereby investing in their future growth and acting as vital resources for development.

The manner in which families form, establish patterns of behaviour, function and evolve, as well as their relationships with the local community, reflect societal values and expections and, to some degree, individual choice. Societal values regarding the functions and roles of families differ both among, and within, countries. Similarly, views on the extent to which the community, or Government, should intervene and influence the decisions made in individual families also vary according to differing interpretations of what is good for society. Nevertheless, several international legal norms governing the rights of individual family members have been adopted, and most countries have subscribed to these standards. These norms include the Convention on the Elimination of All Forms of Discrimination against Women and the Convention on the Rights of the Child.

Of course, there is no simple view of the family and no easy definition of family policy; to some degree, all policies affect families. Yet, despite the major changes most societies have undergone in recent decades, policies and programmes still tend to be based on concepts and family models that may no longer reflect reality. Accordingly, while general trends may by known, there seems to be a great need to use whatever knowledge is available to create more relevant and appropriate policies directed at the family, while recognizing that many policies that are seemingly of no great relevance may indeed have unseen or long-range implications. Institutional capabilities should, therefore, be strengthened. The first goal might be to encourage organizations and agencies, whether governmental or non-governmental, national or international, to recognize that their decisions and actions will usually have an impact on how families will be formed, whether they will survive or not, and how well they function as nurturers and providers. The second goal might then be to improve the formulation and implementation of "family-sensitive" policies, assuming that they can be generally agreed in a society, and to devise appropriate means to deal with a range of specific problems related to the family as a unit.

Furthermore, the effects of economic change on family structure and on families' abilities to discharge their functions need to be better understood. Interestingly, both positive and negative economic change would seem to have a strong impact on the family. In many countries, in recent years, economic retrenchment, structural adjustment programmes and the costs associated with government provision of social welfare services have resulted in cutbacks in services. Increasing burdens are placed on families, and particularly on female members. The result has often been to weaken the fabric of family unity. Varying effects on the family have been attributed to such diverse phenomena as migration, agrarian change, urbanization and population growth. Social changes will continue and families will continue to evolve, perhaps in unpredictable ways. The family is not static and policy must continually evolve as well, if it is to remain relevant and effective.

The UN has identified some of the basis for countries to evolve their policies towards the family.

Issue One

Strengthening the Family's Ability to Meet its Own Needs

The UN believes that the family remains a primary source of nurturing, as well as a conduit for the transmission of values, culture and information , particularly to children and young people. The family should, therefore, be aided and encouraged to fulfil these important functions for the benefit of all society. For example, even limited government expenditure to educate and encourage adults to practise appropriate parenting techniques,whereby responsibility for child-rearing is shared by both parents, can result in vastly improved health, education and socialization of children, thus lowering the overall costs of social services.

Issue Two

Clarifying and Understanding the Balance between how the Family can Satisfy its Needs and what it can Expect through Public Provision of Services

Changes in economic conditions have altered and indeed, at times, undermined the ability of families to meet their needs as a unit and as individuals. This may create stress or alienation for the individual, may further weaken family relationships, or may increase the demand for public services.

At the same time, a trend towards limiting public provision of social services has placed additional burdens on families, and on female members in particular, to meet basic family needs. This may cause families to assume direct responsibility for providing needed services or it may require them to assume additional financial commitments to pay for services previously provided free.

Issue Three

Recognizing the Effect of Societal Ills on Family Relationships and Acknowledging that Government Policy Intervention may be Needed to Counter Resulting Negative Behaviour or Exploitation in the Family

Because of the intimate nature of family relationship. Negative behaviour or exploitation may be tolerated within families. In line with the concepts of equality between women and men and the rights of all individual family members, social policy may seek to educate and inform family behaviour to discourage antisocial or detrimental practices. Such policy might involve:

(a) education and activities to foster equality between women and men, including equality in their roles as spouses and parents, thereby improving the status of women in the context of the Nairobi Forward looking Strategies for the Advancement of Women and the Convention on the Elimination of All Forms of Discrimination against Women; furthermore, information and education might encourage a more equitable distribution of family resources and a more flexible sharing of household and parental responsibilities in order to improve opportunities for women within and outside the family;

(b) information, legal support and counselling to assist in the prevention of all forms of exploitation (including child labour), violence and abuse of family members, both physical and psychological;

(c) assistance and encouragement to families to nurture and protect children and facilitate the transition from adolescence to responsible adulthood and the world or work, in the context of the World Declaration on the Survival Protection and Development of Children and the Plan of Action for implementing the Declaration in the 1990s, adopted by the World Summit for Children, and the Convention on the Rights of the Child; and

(d) education to encourage and develop values and behaviour patterns that contribute to responsible citizenship, ensure equal rights for all, discourage discrimination and protect the environment.

But beyond all these, especially in the developing world, it is necessary to devote energies to human development in its various manifestations. When the stomach is hungry, then faimly ties take a back seat. The fight for food can tear families as under. We have to first address resources to poverty alleviation projects and provide education for all, in order to make families all over the world more secure and stable.

Activities for the UN International Year of the Family were structured in three phases:

(a) the preliminary phase:

in 1991, this phase was geared to setting up and mobilizing organizatioinal structures and identifying priority issues;

(b) the preparatory phase:

in 1992-93, the phase would focus on measures to tackle the priority issues and on activities to prepare for the observance of the Year;

(c) the observance phase:

in 1994, targeted activities will take place and programmes implemented to observe the Year.

Source: UN Newsletter, January 1, 1994, New Delhi.

8

SIGNIFICANT REPORTS, MEETINGS AND EVENTS*

8.1 World Education Report, 1993

In the new vision of world development that is beginning to emerge in the 1990s, knowledge, human ingenuity, imagination and goodwill are the only resources that finally matter. No lasting progress, it is realized, can be made towards peace and respect for human rights and fundamental freedoms without them. The role of education in developing them is recognized as crucial.

While this vision is deeply clouded in many parts of the world by poverty, economic dislocation, political conflict and communal violence, there is a growing realization that these conditions themselves have their origins at least partly in past policies and, strategies that neglected to give a significant priority to the human dimension of development and failed in particular to provide an approprite education and vision of human solidarity for the young.

The entire conception of development at the global level is changing. Recognition of looming threats to the ecological balance of the planet itself has given rise to a new global consciousness, and the end of the Cold War has challenged countries to redefine both their external relations and internal purposes. Where previously there was an emphasis on ensuring military security, alone or in alliance with others, the imperatives now are to ensure economic and social security and the conditions of a civil society. In every regions countries are seeking new forms of economic and political co-operation with their neighbours and trading partners. With the external military threat reduced, the last remaining arguments that were utilized to postpone democracy and some form of decentralization, subsidiary and more power for citizens to make decision for themselves.

National policy-makers are looking more closely at their education systems and at the ability of these systems to respond to the new imperatives. They are also looking outwards. There is a growing demand for better international information about education. How is it organized in different countries? What are the best practices? International legal instruments relating to education are being carefully scrutinized again (Section 8.1.1); in some of the countries now undergoing radical political reform new comprehensive educational legislation has been drafted. Philosophical outlooks on education are changing. Unidimensional views are being questioned: those which considered education to

*Other than those mentioned in previous Chapters.

be mainly an instrument of state for the moulding of a certain type of social personality have been largely abandoned, but others which stress only a certain type of productive capital are now being challenged. Increasingly there is agreement on the primordial nature of the relationship between education and culture, and on its multidimensional character: even more so in global perspective, where the challenge to provide 'education for all' implies a willingness among the difference peoples of the world to share their diverse knowledge and cultural experience as much as their material resources.

Accompanying these changes in outlook on education is a growing awareness of national and international disparities in its provision, and of the potential consequence of these disparities for the economic and social security of the poorer countries. In certain regions around half the adult population is illiterate still. The South Commission referred to 'knowledge gap' between the North and the South (Section 8.1.2). While some countries in the South are converging relatively quickly towards the levels of literacy and school participation prevailing in the advanced industrial countries, and a few, notably on the Pacific rim, are beginning to emerge as significant forces in science and technology, others are in danger of falling behind and overall progress towards the reduction of intercountry inequalities is slow. In some sub-Saharan African countries today the average 6-year-old can expect to receive little more than two years of formal education, and girls not much more than a year, compared with nearly sixteen years for boys and girls in North America.

Progress towards 'education for all' will require more than just a levelling up of years of schooling. It will also require increased scope for educational 'choice': contents, methods, delivery systems. How else, and by whom, a democratic context, are 'the basic learning needs' of all children, youth and adults to be defined? It will mean too agreed standards: those of the community and of civil society, of people learning to live together peacefully while respecting their differences.

8.1.1 The State's Responsibility to Ensure the Right to Education

1. The States Parties to the present Covenant recognize the right of everyone to education. They agree that education shall be directed to the full development of the human personality and the sense of its dignity, and shall strengthen the respect for human rights and fundamental freedoms. They further agree that education shall enable all persons to participate effectively in a free society, promote understanding, tolerance and friendship among all nations and all racial, ethnic or religious groups, and further the activities of the United Nations for the maintenance of peace.
2. The States Parties to the present Convenant recognize that, with a view to achieving the full realization of this right:

   (a) Primary education shall be compulsory and available free to all;
   (b) Secondary education in its different forms, including technical and vocational secondary education, shall be made generally available and accessible to all by every appropriate means, and in particular by the progressive introduction of free education;

(c) Higher education shall be made equally accessible to all, on the basis of capacity, by every appropriate means, and in particular by the progressive introduction of free education;
(d) Fundamental education shall be encouraged or intensified as far as possible for those persons who have not received or completed the whole period of their primary education; and
(e) The development of a system of schools at all levels shall be actively pursued, an adequate fellowship system shall be established, and the material conditions of teaching staff and shall be continuously improved.

3. The States Parties to the present Convenant undertake to have respect for the liberty of parents and, when applicable, legal guardians to choose for their children schools, other than those established by the public authorities, which conform to such minimum educational standards as may be laid down or approved by the State and to ensure the religious and moral education of their children in conformity with their own convictions.
4. No part of this article shall be construed so as to interfere with the liberty of individuals and bodies to establish and direct education institutions, subject always to the observance of the priciples set forth in paragraph 1 of this article and to the requirement that the education given in such institutions shall conform to such minimum standards as may be laid down by the State.

Source: The International Covenants on Human Rights and Optional Protocol, pp. 8-9, New York, United Nations, Office of Public Information, 1976. (Article 13 of the International Covenant on Economic, Social and Cultural Rights).

TABLE 8.1.1: Estimated Total Literate and Illiterate Populations Aged 15 and over in Developing Countries, by Region, 1990 (millions)

	Region	Literate	Illiterate
1.	Eastern Asia/Oceana	942	233
2.	Souther Asia	341	398
3.	Latin America/Caribbean	244	43
4.	Sub-Saharan Africa	125	139
5.	Arab States	64	61

8.1.2 The Challenge to the South: 'Overcoming the Knowledge Gap

We live in an age in which the role of science based technologies as a major determinant of the pace of social and economic change, as well as of global power structures, has become even more pronounced. In the past, there were great civilizations in the South that were fertile in scientific ideas, but the bulk of new knowledge now originates in the developed countries of the North.

Unless the South learns to harness the forces of modern science and technology, it has no chance of fulfilling its developmental aspirations or its yearning for an effective voice in the management of global interdependence. All its societies must therefore mount a determined effort to absorb, adapt, and assimilate new technological advances as part of their development strategies. Simultaneously, their technological economic, and social structure must acquire a built-in inducement and capacity to generate new technologies in accordance with their development needs.

The foundation for the build-up of scientific and technological capabilities in the South is an education and skilled labour force, with ample opportunities for continuing education and updating of knowledge and skills throughout the productive career. To achieve this, all countries of the South should give priority to providing a high standard of education to all children between the ages of 6 and 15 years, with basic sciences and mathematics being given the importance that is in keeping with the requirements of the modern technological age. The tree of knowledge can flourish only if it is securely planted in the educational system.

Source: *The Challenge to the South: The Report of the South Commission*, pp. 277-78, Oxford, Oxford University Press, 1990.

TABLE 8.1.2: Estimated School Life Expectancies* in Selected Countries** 1990

Country	Male	Female
Niger	2.8	1.4
Guinea	3.9	1.6
Bangladesh	5.8	4.2
Morocco	7.4	5.1
Rwanda	5.8	5.5
New Zealand	14.4	14.6
France	14.1	14.7
Norway	14.3	14.9
United States	15.1	15.8
Canada	15.5	16.5

* Expected number of years of formal education.

** The five countries with the lowest and the five countries with the highest expected number of years of formal education for girls and women, among those countries for which UNESCO has relevant data.

8.2 WORLD POPULATION PROSPECTS (2025): 1992 REVISION

The world population at mid-1992 is estimated to be 5.5 billion persons. It is now growing at a rate of 1.7 per cent per annum, which means that an additional 93 million persons were added to the world total population during 1992.

These population figures are given in the released 1992 *Revision* of the official United Nations population estimates and projections, prepared by the Population Division of the Department of Economic and Social Development. The biennial revisions provide global estimates and projections of national populations by size and its demographic components. Demographic estimates are provided for all countries and regions of the world from 1950 to 1990; the projections are provided with various assumptions of future ferility, mortality and migration from 1990 to 2025. These estimates and projections provide the standard set of population figures used throughout the United Nations system.

The world continues to be diverse in terms of population distribution, growth and size among the major areas and regions of the world.

The world population more than doubled between 1950 and 1992, from 2.5 billion to 5.5 billion persons. The annual addition to the population in 1950-1955 was 47 million persons per year (only half the current increase in size) and has been growing since then. Between 1985 and 1990, the population of the world increased by 441 million persons, or 88 million additional persons per year.

By the end of this century, according to the medium-variant projections, the total population will reach 6.2 billion, and by the year 2025, the world population may reach 8.5 billion. These momentous increase will occur even though the annual population growth rate is projected to decline from the current 1.7 per cent to only 1.0 per cent by 2025.

The world population is also projected forward to the year 2025 under three other assumptions of the course of fertility. Starting from a population of 5.3 billion in 1990 as the base, world population may reach 9.1 billion in 2025 under the high fertility assumption, compared with 8.5 billion with the medium variant. In the low-fertility variant projection, the 2025 population may reach 7.9 billion persons.

Currently, 4.3 billion persons live in the less developed regions of the world, comprising 78 per cent of the world population. In the more developed regions, the current total population size is 1.2 billion persons, or 22 per cent of the world population. The average annual population growth rate is currently about 0.5 per cent of the more developed regions and 2.0 per cent for the less developed regions.

Of the 88 million persons added to the world population each year during 1985-1990, only 8 million persons were in the more developed regions, while 80 million were in the less developed regions. In the less developed regions, 17 million additional people were added to the population of China and 16 million to the population of India.

The medium-variant projections show that the population of the more developed regions may increase by 179 million between 1992 and 2025, whereas the population of the less developed regions will increase by 2.8 billion. In other words, over the next 35 year, 94 per cent of world population increase will occur in the less developed regions of the world and only 6 per cent in the more developed regions.

In 1992, more than half the world population (59 per cent) was living in Asia. The two largest countries in the world, China and India, alone made up 64 per cent of Asia's population and 38 per cent of the world population. The population of Africa made up 12 per cent of the world population; Latin America, 8 per cent; Europe, 9 per cent; Northern America and the former USSR, 5 per cent each; and Oceania, 0.5 per cent. In terms of size, there were 3.2 billion people in Asia (1.2 billion in China and 0.9 billion in India), 682 million in Africa, 512 million in Europe, 458 million in Latin America, 283 million in Northern America, 285 million in the former USSR and 28 million in Oceania.

As a result of differences in projected growth, the distribution of the population among different major areas of the world is expected to continue changing. The share of Europe, 9 per cent of the global population in 1992, is projected to decline to 6 per cent by 2025. Northern America and the former USSR are each expected to decline from 5 per cent of the world population in 1992 to 4 per cent by 2025.

In 1985-90, all three of these major areas had annual population growth rates of 1.0 per cent or lower. By 2020-25, the growth rates of Europe, Northern America and the former USSR are expected to decline to 0.5 per cent per annum or lower. By 2025, the population of Europe is expected, under the medium-variant projection, to reach 542 million (an increase of 30 million from 1992), that of Northern America to reach 361 million (an increase of 78 million) and the former USSR to reach 344 million (an increase of 59 million).

Among the less developed regions, the population of Africa, which comprised 12 per cent of the world population in 1992, may reach 19 per cent by 2025. The countries of Latin America are expected to remain at about 8 per cent of the world population during the period 1992-2025. The share of the world population living in Asia is expected to change slightly: 59 per cent in 1992 and 58 per cent by 2025. However, within Asia, the share of China will continue to decline-from 22 per cent in 1992 to 18 per cent in 2025. The population of India, which comprised 16 per cent of the world poplation in 1992, is expected to retain its share in 2025.

During 1985-90, Africa had the highest growth rate (3.0 per cent) among all the major areas of the world. As a result, by 2025, Africa's population is expected to reach 1.6 billion, which is more than double its preset size (682 million) even though its growth rate is projected to decline to 2.2 per cent per annum by 2025. In Asia, even though the population growth rate is projected to decline from 1.9 per cent per annum in 1985-1990 to 0.9 in 2020-2025, its population may grow by a staggering 1.7 billion, from 3.2 billion in 1992 to 4.9 billion in 2025. In this scenario, China's population may increase by 352 million to 1.5 billion in 2025, and India's population may increase by 514 million (about the present size of Europe) to 1.4 billion-this, even though the growth rate of China is projected to more than halve, to 0.5 per cent per annum by 2020-2025 from its present 1.5 per cent, and India's is projected to decline to 1.0 per cent per annum by 2020-25, from 2.0 per cent.

The total population of Latin America may increase from its present 458 million to 702 million by 2025 and that of Oceania may increase from 28 million to 41 million. By 2020-25, the growth rate in both these major areas is expected to decline to 0.9 per cent per annum, from 2.0 in Latin America and 1.6 Oceania, in 1985-90.

Clearly, high growth rates (both current and in the past) have tremendous implications for future population size. Countries currently growing at a rate of about 3 per cent per annum can expect a doubing of their population in about 23 years. The *1992 Revision* shows that growth rates are still high in a number of countries in the world. Fifty-three countries had growth rates of 3 per cent per annum or more in 1985-90. These countries or areas together had a total of 585 million people, or 11 per cent of the world population in 1990. Twenty-four of these countries were in Africa, 16 in Asia, 7 in Oceania and 5 in Latin America.

Nearly half the world population (44 per cent) was living in countries or areas that had growth rates of more than 2 per cent per annum. In 1985-90 there were 114 such countries or areas. They included nearly all countries in Africa, two thirds of those in Asia, half of those in Oceania and slightly more than one third of the countries in Latin America. On the other hand, 66 countries or areas had growth rates of less than 1 per cent per annum during 1985-90, with 1.1 billion, or 23 per cent of the world population. A majority of these countries were in Europe.

In 1992, there were 10 countries with poplations of over 100 million (60 per cent of the world population) and 13 countries with population size of 50 million to 100 million (15 per cent of the world population). This means that nealry three quarters of the world population live in just 22 countries of the world. China and India, the two largest countries in the world, alone make up 38 per cent of the world population.

The dissolution of the Union of Soviet Socialist Republics has altered the ranking of the 10 largest countries in the world. The United States of America, which was the fourth largest country after China, India and the USSR in 1990, is currently the third largest country after China and India. The largest republic in the former USSR,the Russian Federation, is now the sixth largest country.

Current high growth rates in a large number of countries will result in a burgeoning population for these countries in 2025, with the result that the ranking of countries according to population size may change somewhat. Medium-variant projections show that in 2025, Japan will move from being the eighth largest country in 1992 to thirteenth in 2025, whereas the Islamic Republic of Iran may move from fifteenth place in 1992 (with a population of 62 million) to tenth in 2025 (with a population of 145 million).

The results of the *1992 Revision* reflects the demographic situation of the world in 1990 and the expectation for the future based on what is known of the world today. But what of the expectation for 1990 in the *1974* and *1984 Revisions* of world population prospects? The estimate of total world population for 1990 in the 1992 *Revision* is 47 million (0.9 per cent) higher than that of the 1982 assessment and 15 million (0.3 per cent) higher than that of the 1973 assessment. The population estimate for the more developed regions is 2 million (0.2 per cent) higher than in the 1982 assessment, but 19 million (-1.5 per cent) lower than in the 1973 assessment. For the less developed regions, the 1992 total population surpasses that of the 1973 assessment by 34 million (0.8 per cent) and that of the 1982 assessment by 45 million (1.1 per cent).

Both the 1973 and the 1982 assessments underprojected the population of Asia. At that time it was expected that the unprecedented declines in fertility that took place in China and India in the late 1960s would continue at the same pace into the 1990s. However, the late 1980s saw slowing down in the rate of fertility decline in these two large countries. Both the previous assessments also overprojected the population of Latin America: the 1973 assessment, by 9.3 per cent, and the 1982 assessment, by 2.6 per cent. The results of the 1990 censuses from the two largest countries in this major area—Brazil and Mexico—gave a population size for 1990 that was lower than anticipated.

8.2.1 Urban Agglomeration

In 1992, 13 urban agglomerations have populations exceeding 10 million people. In addition to the five mentioned above, the biggest cities are Bombay, Los Angeles, Buenos Aires, Seoul, Beijing, Rio de Janeiro, Calcutta and Osaka.

Two trends are continuing among the largest urban agglomerations. The first is a steady increase in the number of cities with populations exceeding 10 million persons. In 1950, only New York had more than 10 million inhabitants; Tokyo joined the size category by 1960, as did Shanghai by 1970. During the next decade, three more cities—Mexico City, Sao Paulo and Osaka—grew to populations of at least 10 million, making a total of six such cities in 1980. The number jumped to 13 by 1992, and Jakarta (Indonesia), Tianjin (China),and Metro Manila (Philippines) are all projected to have at least 10 million by the time the next urban agglomeration chart is released in 1994.

The second trend is an increased tendency for large cities to be located in less developed regions of the world, especially Asia. In 1980 three of the six largest cities were in more developed countries, but in 1992, nine of the 13 largest are in less developed regions, and five of the 13 are in Asia. By 2010, 26 urban agglomerations are projected to have at least 10 million residents; 21 of them will be in less developed regions. Asia will be home to 14 of these cities; five will be in Latin America, Africa will have two.

No African city is yet among the world's largest, but as the chart shows, growth rates are high for many cities in Africa. Lagos, Nigeria, for example, grew at an annual rate of 5.7 per cent between 1985 and 1990, and it is expected to grow at 4.1 per cent during 2005-10. This would result in a 1992 population of 8.7 million, more than doubling to 21.1 million in 2010.

Growth rates of cities are generally higher in less developed regions than in more developed ones. An annual growth rate of 3.5 per cent implies a doubling time of about 20 years. The chart shows many cities that far exceeded this rate in the period 1985-90, such as Brasilia (Brazil) at 7.8 per cent, Kuala Lumpur (Malaysia) at 5.5 per cent and Peshawar (Pakistan) at 7.8 per cent. Cities experiencing very rapid population growth also experience large-scale inmigration. Migrants may come from rural areas or other urban areas within the country, or they may be international refugees fleeing conflict or natural disaster in their own countries.

By contrast, cities in developed countries generally show growth rates of 1 per cent per annum or less. A number of cities—for example, London, Chicago, Osaka, Rotterdam and Rome—have virtually stopped growing; their estimated growth rates for 1985-90 are all less than 0.4 per cent per annum.

In some countries, a single "mega-city" dominates the urban structure and may contain more than half the country's urban population. A measure of population concentration is presented in the final two columns of the chart. They show the population of each agglomeration as a percentage of the country's total population and of its urban population.

Population concentration in one very large city is more common in developing countries. Of the 26 urban agglomerations projected to have more than 10 million inhabitants by 2010, seven currently have more than 30 per cent of their country's urban population, and all of them are located in less developed regions. Bangkok had the highest concentration, with 58.0 per cent of Thailand's urban population in 1992. Two cities in Latin America, Buenos Aires and Lima, each had more than 40 per cent of the country's urban population, and four other cities—Seoul, Metro Manila, Dacca and Cairo—had more than 30 per cent.

More developed regions are less likely to have primate cities. New York, for example, was home to 8.4 per cent of the United States urban population in 1992, and Los Angeles had 6.1 per cent. Japan's urban population is more concentrated, with its two largest cities, Tokyo and Osaka, having 26.7 per cent and 10.9 percent, respectively, of Japan's urban population.

The chart gives information about each of the 288 urban agglomerations in the world with a population of 1 million or more. Cities are listed alphabetically, from Aachen (Germany) to Zhengzhou (China). In addition to population size in 1992 and rank among the world's cities by size, the chart shows the projected population of each city in 2010, along with growth rates for two five-year periods and the percentage of a country's population (both urban and total) that resides in each city. Graphics present the 13 cities of 10 million or more, with bar charts showing their relative size in 1970 and 2010.

TABLE 8.2.1 : World's Largest Urban Agglomerations in 1992

Rank	Agglomeration	Country	Population (thousands)
1	Tokyo	Japan	25,772
2	Sao Paulo	Brazil	19,235
3	New York	United States of America	16,158
4	Mexico City	Mexico	15,276
5	Shanghai	China	14,053
6	Bombay	India	13,322
7	Los Angeles	United States of America	11,853
8	Buenos Aires	Argentina	11,753
9	Seoul	Republic of Korea	11,589
10	Beijing	China	11,433
11	Rio de Janeiro	Brazil	11,257
12	Calcutta	India	11,106
13	Osaka	Japan	10,535

8.2.2 PROJECTED WORLD POPULATION

TABLE 8.2.2 : Estimated and Projected Population by Region in the World, 1950-2025)

(in million)

Region	1950	1970	1990	2000	2025
World Total	2,516 (100.0)	3,698 (100.0)	5,292 (100.0)	6,261 (100.0)	8,504 (100.0)
Industrialized countries	832 (33.1)	1,049 (28.4)	1,207 (22.8)	1,264 (20.2)	1,354 (15.9)
Developing countries	1,684 (66.9)	2,649 (71.6)	4,086 (77.2)	4,997 (79.8)	7,150 (84.1)
Africa	222 (8.8)	362 (9.8)	642 (12.1)	867 (13.8)	1,597 (18.8)
North America	166 (6.6)	226 (6.1)	276 (5.2)	295 (4.7)	332 (3.9)
Latin America	166 (6.6)	286 (7.7)	448 (8.5)	538 (8.6)	757 (8.9)
Asia	1,377 (54.7)	2,102 (56.8)	3,113 (58.8)	3,718 (59.3)	4,912 (57.8)
Europe	393 (15.6)	460 (12.4)	498 (9.4)	510 (8.1)	515 (6.1)
Oceania	13 (0.5)	19 (0.5)	26 (0.5)	30 (0.5)	38 (0.4)
USSR	180 (7.2)	243 (6.6)	289 (5.5)	308 (4.9)	352 (4.1)

Source : *Population Newsletter,* November 4, 1992, The Population Division, Department of Economic and Social Development, United Nations, New York.

8.3 WHO REPORT, 1993

Important Findings

1. Instead of dying of infectious and communicable diseases, people in what is now referred to as the Thrid World will also die of the diseases wrought by lifestyles – unhealthy diets, stress, tobacco, obesity and lack of exercised.
   Though diseases of lifestyles are still thought of as exclusively an affiction of westernised nations, even now, in absolute numbers, these diseases take a higher toll in the developing than in the developed world.
   Today, in the industrialised world, about 8.2 million die yearly from lifestyle diseases, such as heart attacks, stroke, cancers and respiratory illness. More do so in the Third World – 11.7 million.
   Lifestyle diseases now account for about 45 per cent of total deaths in developing countries. By the year 2015, however, the percentage is expected to rise to 60 per cent–virtually equalling the developed world's figure of 75 per cent projected for then, says the report.
2. When life expectancy increases, infant mortality and deaths from infectious diseases decline and overall death rates drop to below 15 per 1,000 population, then, experts say, lifestyle diseases emerge.
3. "The diseases that we bring upon ourselves by unhealthy behaviour are fast becoming the world's No.1 health problem", according to Dr. Nikolai Khaltaev, manager of WHO's inter-health programme. "That's already happened in Western societies. Now it's happening elsewhere as well".
4. The WHO programme, launched publicly in 1990 in Helsinki, is based on the concept that diseases with common causes–namely unhealthy lifestyles–should be tackled together rather than separately.
5. Unlike communicable diseases where a parasite, bacterium or virus transmits a single disease, one bad habit carries multiple risks to health. The health of an able person who smokers, or a hypertensive with high cholesterol levels, is doubly at risk, the experts point out.

Here are some other examples of multiple risks to health carried by unhealthy lifestyles:

(a) *Diet:* A diet high in animal fat, salt and refined sugar, and low in fresh vegetables and fruit, carries the risk of heart attacks, stroke and hypertension; plus colorectal, stomach and breast cancers.

(b) A lack of vitamins A and C, which are found in vegetables and fruit, carries the risk of chronic pulmonary diseases, notably emphysema and chronic bronchitis. A lack of calcium, particularly in the diets of adolescent girls and post menopausal women, carries the risk of osteoporrosis, a condition of brittle bones.

Improper diets also lead to gastric ulcers, as well as to malnutriition and obesity, which in turn carries the risk of cardiovascular diseases, cancer, diabetes, and arthritis.

Immoderate drinking carries the risk of liver cirphosis, but again also of cardiovascular diseases, oral cancer, osteoporosis,cancer, diabetes and gastric ulcers.

(c) *Tobacco:* A smoker runs the risk of heart attacks, stroke, hypertension, lung and oral cancers, osteoporosis. Chronic pulmonary diseases and gastric ulcers.
(d) *Lack of physical activity:* A sedentray individual runs the risk of cardiovascular diseases, diabetes and osteoporosis.
(e) *Air pollution:* Those exposed to air pullutants run the risk of chronic pulmonary diseases and lung cancer.

6. WHO estimates of the toll in death and suffering of the major lifestyle diseases.

Cardiovascular diseases: The diseases claim some 12 million lives yearly, accounting for between a quarter and a third of all deaths globally. Far too often, victims are undr age 65, dying in the prime of life.

According to WHO estimates, mortality can be cut at least by hald with healthy lifestyle or six million lives can be saved yearly.

Contrary to popular belief, cardiovascular diseases are a bigger killer than any other major infective and parasitic disease.

Mortality is on the rise in developing nations and in eastern Europe. Despite declines in industrialised nations, notably in Australia, Canada, New Zealand and Western Europe, they are still the No. 1 killer in those nations.

Cancer: Some seven million new cases yearly and five million deaths worldwide. Lung cancer is now the most common form of the disease, overtaking stomach cancer in the mid-1980s. The third most common form is breast cancer.

Source: *WHO Report, 1993,* as reported in P.T.I Release.

8.4 SIGNIFICANT INTERNATIONAL EVENTS

April 1993

3. US announces $ 1.6 billion aid to Russia.
7. A major nuclear tank explosion in the city of Tomak–7 in Russia.
9. Macedonia becomes 181st member of UN.
18. President Gulam Ishaq Khan of Pakistan dismisses Nawaz Sharif government and the National Assembly.
26. Long times rivals Taiwan and China sign pacts for closer relations.

May

1. Sri Lanka President Ranasinghe Premadasa assassinated.
6. The Supreme Court of Pakistan reinstates in dismissed Prime Minister Nawaz Sharief.
13. President Ali Akbar Rafsanjani of Iran wins his second term getting 63 per cent votes.

June

19. Japanese Prime Minister Kiichi Miyazawa loses a no-confidence motion in the lower house of The Diet-Japanese Parliament.

July

18. Pakistan President Ghulam Ishaq Khan and Prime Minister Nawaz Sharief quit and fresh polls announced to solve the political dead lock arising out of their mutual conflict.

August

6. Japanese Ruling Liberal Democratic Party (LDP) Custed after 38 year in power. Norihirio Hosokawa new Prime Minister.
29. Teng Cheong first directly elected President with executive powers Israel–PLO sing pact on limited autonomy to Palestine.

September

15. Pop megastar Michael Jackson faces allegations of sexual abuse of minor boy.
29. Sihanouk takes oath as Cambodian King.

October

19. US embargo against Haifi begins Benazir Bhutto returns as Pakistan Prime Minister.
26. Liberals wipe out conservatives in Canadian elections.

November

1. European Union formally takes shape.
6. New Zealand has hung Parliment.

December

12. 300 killed in Philippines typhoon.
15. Historic GATT approved at Geneva.

1994
January

10. NATO offers partnership to Eastern Europe.
12. Fiji's Great Council appoints Ratu Sir Kamisese Mara as Fiji's President.
13. US and Russia agree to stop aiming long range missiles at each other.
14. Burundi National Assembly elects Mr. Cyprien Nitarya Mura as the country's and New President.

February

6. China opens biggest Daya Bay N. Plant.
24. Pakistan closes omission in Kabul.
25. An American immigrant Jewish settler armed with an automatic rifle guns down more than 50 Palestinians and wounds about 300 Muslim Worshippers kneeling in prayer in the West Bank town of Hebron.

March

1. Former coup leader Sitiveni Rabuka sworn in as Fiji's Prime Minister for a second five-year term.
4. Nepal Prime Minister Girija Prasad Koirala faints in the Pratinidhi Sabha (Parliament) when about to finish reply on the no-confidence motion.
10. Pakistan withdraws its resolution on violation of human rights in Kashmir at The United Nations Human Rights Commission's Conference at Geneva.
11. Saudi Arabia bans the use of dioh antena for receiving satellite television programmes in the country to protect its religious and social values.
25. The fourth, Three-day G-15 summit begin in India. The summit stresses that G-15 should work towards forming trans-regional mechanism in trade, investment and technology.

    G-15 are Algeria Algeria Argentina, Algeria Brazil, Algeria Bharat, Egypt, Indonesia, Jamaica, Malaysia, Mexico, Nigeria, Peru, Senegal, Yugo-Serbia, Venezuela, Zimbabwe.

PART TWO

INDIA 1993-94

9

LAND AND ITS PEOPLE

India that is Bharat covering a land area 32,87,263 sq.km is the seventh largest and the second most populous country of the world. It stretches 3,214 km from North to South between the extreme latitudes and 2,933 km from East to West between the extreme longitudes. On this 2.4 per cent of earth's surface live 15 per cent (88 crore people) of world's population.

9.1 Population

Over 160 million people are added annually to our population (President's Republic day Speech, 25th January 1989). Since 1881, the Census in India has been taken reqularly aften ten years. According to 1991 Census, the total population of India (including the projected population of Jammu and Kashmir is 846,302,688. As compared 1981 census, it showed an increase of 23.85 per cent. According to 1991 Census, the growth of urban population in the country during the decade 1981-91, slowed down by about ten per cent as compared to the earlier decade of 1971-81. However, the number of cities and towns has been consistently increasing. The urban population at present in 25.72 per cent.

9.2 Density

The average population of density of per km^2 in 1991 was 267. It varies considerably from State to State.

9.3 Sex Ratio

According to 1991 Census (Provisional) there are 43.7 crore males and 40.6 crore females; thus for every 1,000 males India has 929 females. Only Kerala has more women than men, i.e., 1,040 per 1,000 men. The lowest female ratio among the State is in Haryana i.e. 874 for 1,000 men and the lowest female ratio among the Union Territories is in Chandigarh where it is 733 per thousand.

9.4 Literacy

According to 1991 Census, the literacy percentage is 52.21. Out of this 64.13 per cent of males and 39.29 per cent of females are literate.

9.5 Major Religions and Persuasions

TABLE 9.1 : Major religions and persuasions, 1991 and 1981 (excluding Assam)

Religion Community	Population		Percentage of Total Population	
	1991	1981	1991	1981
Hindus	67,20,00,000	54,97,24,517	82.41	82.63
Muslims	54,74,00,000	7,55,71,514	11.67	11.36
Christians	1,88,00,000	1,61,74,498	2.32	2.43
Sikhs	1,62,00,000	1,30,78,146	1.99	1.96
Buddhists	63,00,000	47,19,900	0.77	0.71
Jains	33,00,000	31,92,572	0.41	0.48
Other Persuasions	31,00,000	27,56,285	0.38	0.42
Religion not stated	4,00,000	60,217	0.05	0.01

9.6 Languages

The detailed data from the 1981 Census which were made available only in 1988, enumerate the main languages spoken in the household and not the mother tongue and groups related languages under a dominant language. By this count, 106 languages are separately recognised. Of these 94 are spoken by 10,000 or more people.

There were 1562 mother tongues, 10 writing system, and 76 languages as used in the school system out of 2000 codified languages.

Eighteen languages have been specified in the Eighth Schedule of the Constitution. These are: Assamese, Bengali, Gujarati, Hindi, Kannada, Kashmiri, Konkani, Malayalam, Manipuri, Marathi, Nepali, Oriya, Punjabi, Sanskrit, Sindhi, Tamil, Telugu and Urdu.

9.7 National Flag

The National Flag is horizontally tricolour with deep saffron *(Kesari)* at the top, white in the middle and dark green at the bottom in equal proportion. The ratio of the width of the flag to its length is two to three. In the centre of the white band is a wheel, in navy blue, which represents the *Charkha.* Its design is that of the wheel *(Chakra)* which appears on the abacus of the Sarnath Lion Capital of Ashoka. Its diameter approximates to the width of the white band and it has 24 spokes.

The design of the National flag was adopted by the Constituent Assembly of India on July 22, 1947. Its use and display are regulated by a code.

9.8 State Emblem

The State Emblem of India is an adaptation from the Sarnath Lion Capital of Ashoka as preserved in the Sarnath Museum. In the original, there are four lions, standing back to back, mounted on an abacus with a frieze carrying sculptures in high relief of an elephant, a galloping horse, a bull and a lion separated by intervening wheels (Chakras) over a bell-shaped lotus. Carved out of a single block of polished sandstone, the capital is crowned by the Wheel of the Law (Dharma Chakra).

In the State emblem adopted by the Government of India on January 26, 1950, only three lions are visible, the fourth being hidden from view. The wheel appears in relief in the centre of the abacus with a bull on the right and a horse on the left and the outlines of the other wheels in the extreme right and left. The bell-shaped lotus has been omitted. The words *Satyameva Jayate* from the *Mundaka Upanishad,* meaning *'Truth Alone Triumphs'* are inscribed below the abacus in Devanagri script.

9.9 National Anthem

The song *Jana-gana-mana,* composed by Rabindranath Tagore (1861-41) was adopted by the Constituent Assembly as the National Anthem of India on January 24, 1950. It was first sung on December 27, 1911 at the Calcutta session of the Indian National Congress. The complete song consists of five stanzas. The first stanza constitutes the full version of the National Anthem. It reads:

Jana-gana-mana-adhinayaka, jaya he
Bharata-bhagya-vidhata
Punjab-Sindhu-Gujarata-Maratha-
Dravida-Utkala-Banga
Vindhya-Himachala-Yamuna-Ganga
Uchchala-jaladhi-taranga.
Tava shubha name jage,
tava shubha asisa mage,
gahe tava jaya-gatha,
Jana-gana-mangala-dayaka jaya he
Bharata-bhagya-vidhata.
Jaya he, jaya he, jaya he,
Jaya Jaya Jaya, Jaya he!

Playing time of the full version of the National Anthem is approximately 25 seconds. A short version consisting of the first and last lines of the stanza (playing time approximately 20 seconds) is also played on certain occasions. The following is Tagore's English rendering of this stanza:

Thou art the ruler of the minds of all people,
dispenser of India's destiny.
Thy name rouses the hearts of Punjab, Sind, Gujarat and Maratha
Of the Dravida and Orissa and Bengal;
It echoes in the hills of the Vindhyas and Himalayas,
mingles in the music of Jamuna and Ganges

and is chanted by the waves of the Indian Sea.
They pray for thy blessings and sing thy praise.
The saving of all people waits in thy hand,
thou dispenser of India's destiny.
Victory, victory, victory of thee.

9.10 National Song

The song *Vande Mataram,* composed by Bankimchandra Chatterji (1838-94), was a source of inspiration to the people in their struggle for freedom. It has an equal status with *Jana-gana-mana.* The first political occasion on which it was sung was the 1896 session of the Indian National Congress. The following is the text of its stanza :

Vande Mataram !
Sujalam, suphalam, malayaja shitalam,
Shasyashyamalam, Mataram !
Shubhrajyotsna pulakitayaminim,
Phullakusumita drumadala shobhinim,
Suhasinim sumadhura bhashinim,
Sukhadam, Varadam, Mataram!

The English translation of the stanza rendered by Sri Aurobindo (1872-1950) in prose[1] is:

I bow to thee, Mother,
richly-watered, richly-fruited,
cool with the winds of the south,
dark with the crops of the harvests,
the Mother!
Her nights rejoicing in the glory of the moonlight,
her lands clothed beautifully with her trees in flowering bloom,
sweet of laughter, sweet of speech,
the Mother, giver of boons, giver of bliss.

9.11 National Calendar

A uniform National Calendar based on the *Saka Era* with *Chaitra* as its first month and a normal year of 365 days was adopted from March 22, 1957 (along with the Gregorian calendar) for the following official purposes in particular :

(i) Gazette of India
(ii) News broadcast by All India Radio and T.V.
(iii) Calendars issued by the government of India, and
(iv) Government communications addressed to members of the public.

The dates of the National Calendar have a permanent correspondence with the dates of the Gregorian calendar; *Chaitra 1* falling on March 22 normally and on March 21 in a leap year.

---

1. Sri Aurobindo Butt Centinary Library, Popular Edition, Volume 8, 1972.

Chaitra 1 of *Saka Era* is the New Year Day. *Saka Era* was established in A.D. 78 by Emperor Kanishka of the Saka dynasty, who ruled in the North and North-Western India in the first century of the Christian era. The day, which has been chosen to become the first day of the New Year, is vemal equinox when the day and the night are of equal duration throughout the world. *Saka* calendar is based on *Solar Chaitra* and not on *Lunar Chaitra. Chaitra Shukla Partipada*

1. As published in *Sri Aurobindo Birth Centenary Library,* Popular edition, 1912, vol. 8. which is celebrated as New Year Day in many parts of the country, is called differently. It is *Gudi Padwa* in Maharashtra and *Yugadi* in Karnataka based on lunar calendar, etc. April 13, *Baisakhi* in Punjab, Pongal on April 14 in Tamil Nadu and *Palia Baisakhi* in West Bengal are based on solar calendar. In solar calendar this discrepancy of 22 or 23 days (between March 22 and April 13/14) has been caused by an astronomical phenomenon called the precession of the equinoxes.

9.12 National Animal

The majestic tiger *[Panthera tigris* (Linnaeus)], the national animal of India for its rich colour, illusive design and formidable power, has always been held in high esteem in India. Among the carnivores, the tiger is very georgeous and attractive with roaring voice as symbol of power. Out of eight races of the species known the world over, the Indian race is the Royal Bengal Tiger. The Royal Bengal Tiger is found throughout the country expect the North-Western region and also in Nepal, Bhutan and Bangladesh. As shrinkage of habitat in India dwindled its population to only 1,827 in 1972, the Project Tiger was launched on April 1'st 1973. Since then there is a gradual increase in its population. The tiger population 4,430 of the country according to 1989 censes was 4,339. So far 19 tiger reserve have been established covering over 29,716 sq km forest area.

9.13 National Bird

The Indian peacock *[Pavo cristatus* (Linnaeus)], the national bird of India, is one of the most beautiful birds, particularly the males having the glistering blue neck and breast, fanshape crest and long magnificent tail. The courtship dance of the male by fanning out the tail before the female is most spectacular. From time immemorial, this bird has found a profound place in Indian literature, folklore and legends.

The Indian peafowl, as the peacock is called, is widely found in the country in south and east of Indus river, Jammu and Kashmir, east Assam, south of Mizoram and the whole of Indian peninsula. It is fully protected under the Indian Wild Life (Protection) Act, 1972.

Source : India 1993.

9.14 Presidents of India

January 26, 1950 – May 13, 1962	Rajendra Prasad
May 13, 1962 – May 13, 1967	S.Radhakrishan
May 13,1967 – May 3, 1969	Zakir Husain

May 3,1969 – July 20, 1969	V.V.Giri (Acting)
July 20, 1969 – August 21. 1969	M. Hidayatullah (Acting)
August 24, 1969 – August 24, 1974	V.V.Giri
August 24, 1974 – Febuary 11, 1977	Fakhruddin Ali Ahmed
February 11, 1977 – July 25 1977	B.D.Jatti (Acting)
July 25, 1977 – July 25, 1982	N.Sanjeeva Reddy
July 25, 1982 – July 25, 1987	Zail Singh
July 25, 1987 – July 25, 1992	R.Venkataraman
July 25, 1992 –	S.D.Sharma

9.15 Vice Presidents of India

1952-1962	S.Radhakrishnan
1962-1967	Zakir Husain
1967-1969	V.V.Giri
1969-1974	G.S.Pathak
1974-1079	B.D.Jatti
1979-1984	M.Hidayatullah
1984-1987	R.Venkataraman
1987-1992	S.D.Sharma
1993-	K.R.Narayanan

9.16 Prime Minsiters of India

August 15, 1947 – May 27, 1964	Jawaharlal Nehru
May 27, 1964 – June 9, 1964	Guljari Lal Nanda (Acting)
June 9, 1964 – January 11, 1966	Lal Bahadur Shastri
January 11, 1966 – January 24, 1966	Guljari Lal Nanda (Acting)
January 24, 1966 – March 24, 1977	Indira Gandhi
March 24, 1977 – July 28. 1979	Morarji Desai
July 28, 1979 – January 14, 1980	Charan Singh
January 14, 1980 – October 31, 1984	Indira Gandhi
October 31, 1984 – December 1, 1989	Rajiv Gandhi
December 2, 1989 – November 10, 1990	V.P.Singh
November 10, 1990 – June 21, 1991	Chandra Shekhar
June 21, 1991 – February 1996	P.V.Narasimha Rao
June 1, 1996 – April 1997	H.D. Devegauda
April 21, 1997 –	I.K. Gujral

9.17 Speakers of the Lok Sabha

1952-1956	G.V.Mavlankar
1956-1962	Ananthasayanam Ayyangar
1962-1967	S.Hukam Singh
1967-1969	N.Sanjieeva Reddy
1969-1975	G.S.Dhillon
1975-1977	B.R.Bhagat
March 1977 - July 1977	N.Sanjieeva Reddy

1977-1979	K.S.Hegde
1980-1989	Balram Jakhar
November 19, 1989 – June 1991	Rabi Ray
July 10, 1991 –	Shivraj Patil

9.18 Important Days

National Youth Day	January 12
Army Day	January 15
Republic Day	January 26
International Customs Day	January 26
Martyrs' Day	January 30
National Science Day	February 28
International Women's Day*	March 8
World Consumers Rights Day	March15
World Disabled Day	March (Third Sunday of March)
International Day for the Elimination of Racial Discrimination	March 21
World Forestry Day	March 21
World Meteorological Day	March 23
National Maritime Day	April 5
World Health Day*	April 7
May Day (Worker's Day International Labour Day)	May 1
World Red Cross Day	May 8
World Telecommunication Day*	May 17
World Day for Cultural Development*	May 21
Commonwealth Day	May 24
World No-Tobacco Day*	May 31
World Envirnoment Day*	June 5
International Day of Solidarity with the Struggling People of South Africa*	June 16
World Population Day*	July 11
Hiroshima Day	August 6
Quit India Day	August 9
Nagasaki Day	August 9
International Day of Solidarity with the Struggle of Women in South Africa*	August 9
Independence Day	August 15
Teacher's Day	September 5
International Literacy Day*	September 8
International Day of Peace	September (Third Tuesday of September)
World Tourism Day	September 27
International Day for the Elderly*	October 1
University Children's Day*	October (First Monday of October)
Mahatma Gandhi Birthday	October 2
World Habitat Day	October 5

Air Force Day	October 8
Universal Postal Union Day*	October 9
Day of Solidarity with South African Political Prisoners	Octocer 11
Post Office Day	October 19
World Standard Day	October 14
World Food Day*	October 16
United Nations Day	October 24
World Development Information Day*	October 24
National Re-Dedication Day	October 31
Children's Day	November 14
National Integration Day	November 19
International Day of Solidarity with the Palestinian People*	November 29
World AIDS Day*	December 1
International Day of Disabled Persons*	December 3
Navy Day	December 4
International Volunteer Day for Economic and Social Development	December 5
Flag Day	December 7
Human Rights Day*	December 10
Kisan Day	December 23

* Proclaimed by UN System/UNESCO Associated Schools

10

INDIA SINCE INDEPENDENCE

10.1 Achievements

Going back, India that is Bharat was the richest and the most prosperous country in the world. It was then known as the *'Golden Sparrow'*. The standard of living of the common man was reasonably high. Articles of everyday needs were available in plenty. A common man could get easily things like milk, butter, ghee an foodgrains. Literally speaking 'Rivers of milk flowed'. Indain handicrafts and industrial products were known for their excellence of design and quality all over the world. From the richness of this land and from the labour and wisdom of its people had sprung great wealth, great ideas, great skills and arts. Naturally, therefore, foreigners were tempted to come to India for learning, as well as loot and plunder.

The well-knit economic organisation of the country received a serious set-back with the advent of invaders and especially with the British rulers who were primarily concerned with the governance of the country, not its growth. They wrer greatly interested in draining out wealth from India. Industrial crafts, industries and agriculture, all suffered heavily. As a result, India became a poor country. People remained underfed, ill-housed and scantily dressed.

The statement 'A rich country inhabited by the poor people' seems paradoxical and strange. But it is still true to a considerable extent though since independence we have made a spectacular progress in different fields. The giant *irrigation dams* at *Bhakra, Hirakud* and *Nagarjunasagar*, the huge steel millis at *Bhilai, Bokaro, Rourkela* and *Durgapur;* the fertilister factories at *Sindri* and *Nangal;* the 1000-tonne per day ammonia plant (said to be the largest in the world) at Tuticorin; the *aircraft factories at Bangalore, Hyderabad* and *Nasik;* the locomotive factory at Chittarajan; the atomic reactor at Trombay; the rocket launching station at Sriharikota; the ISRO's establishment like *Vikram Sarabhai Space Centre,* Trivandrum and Space Application Centre, Ahmedabad; launching of Indain Satellite *Bhaskara* and *Rohini;* three axis-stabilised Geostationary Communication Satellite; *APPLE (Ariane Passenger Payload Experiment),* establishment of *Indian National Satellite System (INSAT);* participation of an Indian Cosmonaut in a joint Indo-Soviet Flight; nuclear explosion of Pokaran, etc., are the prized possessions of the Indian Nation.

November 21, 1988 marked the 25th anniversary of Indian Space Programme. The Silver Jubilee Year saw the launching of three major programmes; IRS-1A, ASLV-02 and INSAT-1A (see relevant Chapter for details). Militarily we are among the first five countries in the world.

India is the sixth country to successfully detonate a nuclear device as part of its successful experiment for peace purposes.

We have the third largest reservoir of highly skilled scientific and technical manpower in the world.

India is the fifth nation to have its remote sensing satellite.

We have achieved self-sufficiency in foodgrains.

India is the third largest producer of books in English, next to the U.S.A and U.K.

The eradication of poverty problem of the masses became the first consideration of the government soon after we achieved independence. We decided to adopt the system of planned development for tackling our problem of poverty which was linked with rising prices, low production, unemployment and inequalities of income.

The frame a development plan for independent India, the *Planning Commission* was set up in March 1950, by a resolution of the Government of India. The aims of planning as defined by the resolution were, 'to promote a rapid rise in the standard of living of the people by efficient exploitation of the resources of the country, increasing production and offering opportunities to all for employment in the service of the community'.

The *First Five Year Plan* was initiated in April 1951. This covered the period 1951-56. So far we have had seven Five Year Plans and Three Yearly Plan. The *Eighth Five-Year Plan,* covers the period 1992 to 1997.

The most important achievement of planning in the post-independence period is our self-sufficiency in foodgrains. Now we need not import foodgrains for domestic requirements as we did till a few years ago. The production was about 172 million tonnes in 1991-92 as against 51 million tonnes 1950-51.

As a result of many multipurpose projects, area under irrigation increased from 226 lakh hectares in 1950 to 860 lakh hectares in 1990-91.

Our industry has many strengths: a wide range of products, a demonstrable ability to absorb and operate high technology, a large entrepreneurial capability and ample managerial and technical skills.

During the Plans, industrial production has made rapid strides, both in terms of quality and quantity. As per the index of *industrial production,* the growth rates achieved in the industrial sector as a whole were 8.6 per cent in 1984-85, 8.7 per cent in 1985-86, 9.1 per cent in 1986-87, 7.3 per cent in 1987-88, 8.7 in 1988-89, 8.6 in 1989 and 8.1 in 1990-91. However, there was setback in 1991-92. There was a (–) 0.9 per cent decline (April-November).

In the year 1950-51, there were only two major units producing iron and steel. Now we have eleven relevant major steel plants. Steel production rose from about one million tonnes in 1950-51, to about 13.40 million tonnes in 1990-91.

Cotton textile industry holds the second place in the production of cloth in the world. At present there are about 700 textile mills in the country.

In 1951, we had 138 sugar mills in the country. This number increased to 351 in 1987. About half the mills are in the public sector.

The production of cement increased from 2.69 million tonnes in 1951 to 10.7 million tonnes in 1990-91 (provisional).

The generation of electric power registered a twenty-fold increase.

Public sector in the field of industries has witnessed a very significant rise. In 1951, we had only 5 public undertakings whereas there were 255 public undertakings in 1991, in the Central Sector.

The road network in the country has become very elaborate system of national highways, state and district roads, and rural roads totalling about 23 lakh kms. This is five and a half times the figure of 4 lakh km of roads in 1950-51.

Between 1950-51 and 1991-92, the number of trucks rose from 82,000 to 16,85,000 and busses from 34,000 to 3,70,000.

Per captia income increased from Rs. 246 in 1950-51 to about Rs. 4,254 in 1989-90 at current prices.

Prior to Independence, average life span of an Indian was 32 years. Today it has lengthened to 58 years.

Our Constitution can be described as a charter of freedom. It enshrines the supremacy of the will of the people and their resolve to secure for all citizens: justice, social, economic and political; Equity of status and opportunity, and to promote among them all Fraternity assuring the dignity of the individual and the unity of the nation. The will of the people is exercised through universal adult franchise and a parliamentary democracy. Election to Parliament and State legislature are open contests for all political parties, and independent candidated also enjoy full scope to express themsleves.

Notwithstanding various problems and the magnitude of the task of conducting elections, we have all *general elections* with significant success. Barring the period, March 1977 to July 15, 1979 and December 1989 to May 1991 when the Janata Party and National Front were in power at the Centre, the Congress had held the reigns of the Government since the first General Election in 1951-52.

Many political changes accompanied by government changes, especially in States have taken place in the country since Independence, through peaceful and constitutional means. Transfer of power from one party to another has taken place as a natural course and in an orderly manner.

Another historic step in the development of democracy in the country was the inauguration of *Panchayati Raj* in October 1950. The Panchayati Raj aims at giving full authority and responsibility to the village people and helping them play an active role in local development through the Panchayats. There are over 228,500 Village Panchayats in the country covering partially the entire population of India.

With the Panchayati Raj, we now have parliamentary democracy in operation from the Gram Sabha to the Lok Sabha.

We have got an established judicial system.

10.2 Progress Made and Tasks Ahead

Excerpts from the text of President Shanker Dayal Sharma's address to the joint session of Parliament.

As I address you in the New Year, I sense that the country is today in a frame of mind different from the one it was in, this time last year. We faced many difficulties at the beginning of the year 1993 but our people displayed tremendous resilience as the year progressed and 1993 ended certainly on a note of optimism. There was steady progress on all fronts as evidenced from the improved law and order situation, a record foodgrain production, unprecedented levels of procurement, very high levels of foodgrains stocks, containment of the rate of inflation at a single digit level, comfortable foreign exchange reserves, considerable reduction in trade gap, buoyancy in exports, improved performance in certain essential areas of the infrastructure sector, and increased inflow of foreign investment both direct and portfolio. All these have symbolised and justified this emerging optimism. Clearly, we have regained our elan internally and our confidence globally. We have reason and justification to feel encouraged at the all round performance. But we still have a long way to go before we achieve the objectives we have set for ourselves in social and economic development. It is on this note of cautious optimism that government approaches its tasks in 1994.

There has been overall improvement in the law and order situation. The stituation in regard to insurgency in the north-east has shown improvement. The gains of last year in Punjab were consolidated. The elections to the assemblies in five States and the National Capital Territory of Delhi were peaceful. Government is determined to consolidate the gains of this improvement and address the areas of concern that still remain.

Around this time last year the Ayodhya issue had cast its long shadow on the national scene. There was a great deal of concern over the possible fall-out of the demolition and the riots that followed. Thanks to the inherent wisdom and sagacity of the Indian people, the grim predictions that were being made have been proved wrong. The atmosphere has improved considerably and we can hope for a lasting solution to the dispute. Proceedings are continuing in the Supreme Court on the reference made to it under the Constitution. Government will take appropriate measures in the light of the opinion of the Supreme Court.

The Ayodhya issue is the most convincing demonstration in recent times of the danger inherent in mixing communalism and politics. It is of utmost importance to correct this aberration and keep both religion and politics in their legitimate domains. Our secular State demands nothing less. The issue needs to be debated fully and effective measures evolved. The Government will welcome suggestions in this regard.

In Jammu and Kashmir, we pursue our policy of firm action against terrorism. The police and the security forces have gained considerable success during the year in their counter-terrorist operations. Steps have been taken to further improve their operational efficiency. Every effort is made to see that the maximum restraint is exercised in the use of force. The grave crisis that arose in the Hazratbal shrine was handled by the administration and the security forces in a commendable manner, with the cooperation of the people. The resolution of this crisis demonstrated the efficacy of Government's approach of restraint. Whenever there has been any incident suggesting excessive use of force, an inquiry has been promptly instituted and action taken. Action against the terrorists is continuing in order to restore law and order. At the same time appropriate measures are being taken to tone up the administration. Development and economic activity have been intensified to generate employment opportunities. We are deeply concerned about the difficulties of the common people and the grievance redressal mechanism has been strengthened. We are also pursuing steps to bring about effective involvement of the people in dealing with matters which concern them. Jammu and Kashmir is an inalienable part of India and we shall foil any attempt to destabilise it either from across the border or from any other quarter.

Human Rights

The National Commission on Human Rights has been set up with a former Chief Justice of India as its Chairman. Members of the Commission include a former justice of the Superme Court and one former Chief Justice of a High Court. The setting up of the Commission is indicative of our continuing determination to deal with questions of human rights with promptitude and transparency. The Commission has started its work in right earnest.

In order to strenghten the accountability of the executive of Parliament, 17 department-related standing committees of Parliament were constituted in April 1993 to make detailed examination of Bills, demands for grants, annual reports of the ministries and national basic long-term policy documents presented to the House. This will greatly facilitate the working of Parliament.

The country had its share of national calamities. However, the unprecedented scale of damage in the Maharashtra earthquake stands out among these. In all these instances, Government responded with commendable alertness and provided prompt relief. Governments of several other countries, the World Bank and other institutions promptly offered assistance and we are grateful to all of them. A massive reconstruction programme in the earthquake affected areas of Maharashtra is being taken up at an outlay of Rs. 1,000 crore. Non-governmental organisations are being appropriately associated with the reconstruction programme.

The economic reforms introduced in 1991 gained momentum last year and have been pursued consistently. Still much more needs to be done. Government is aware that the reform is an irreversible and continuous process and needs to be implemented with determination and foresight, keeping the responses and circumstances in the country constantly in view. As a result of this approach, the progress of implementation has been steady and firm and based on a general consensus. We shall hasten with care.

In drawing up the refrom package, stress has been laid by the Government on reforms in the financial sector. The financial institutions have necessarily to be restructured and strengthened to enable them to take on the new responsibility imposed by the expanded activity in the private sector. An important policy change was the unification of the exchange rate and the floating of the rupee in March 1993. The fact that the rupee has remained steady since it was floated is testimony to the good judgement of the Government in the matter.

The basic economic indicators show that although the year started in a difficult environment, the performance of the economy during 1993-94 has been satisfactory. In 1992-93, the gross domestic product (GDP) is estimated to have grown by four per cent. In 1993-94, the Government expects the rate of growth to be maintained at about the same level. The inflation rate touched a low of below six per cent for a short period during this year, the highest level being 8.4 per cent.

Global investors have shown growing confidence in the Indian market. Direct foreign investment approved since the inception of the new industrial policy till the end of 1993 is now approximately Rs. 13,000 crore in terms of equity. The total investment in these project is estimated to be of the order of Rs. 65,000 crore. The significant point of this investment is that the bulk of this, is proposed in sectors like power, oil refining, food processing, metallurgical industry, electrical equipment, chemicals, electronics and other priority areas. Only about seven per cent of the proposed investment will be for products which could be categorised as consumer goods. The investment inflow will be spread over a peroid of three to four years which is the gestation period of the mega projects.

Government continues to lay a great deal of emphasis on export promotion. The results of changes in the trade policy coupled with the floating of the exchange rate and the general liberalisation of the economy have yielded results and exports have shown good growth recording an increase of around 20 per cent in dollar terms during April-December, 1993 compared to a little over three per cent in the corresponding period in 1992.

Government attaches the highest priority to development of agriculture. The timely provision of adequate and reasonably priced inputs and the creation of a structure that provides for the timely announcement of prices which in turn promotes higher production so as to meet fully the domestic needs of the country as well as exports, are the major objectives of the Government. In keeping with the overall strategy, the Plan outlay for the Department of Agriculture and Cooperation has been raised by 26.6 per cent from Rs. 1,050 crore in 1992-93 to Rs. 1330 crore in 1993-94. The production of foodgrains during 1992-93 was 180 million tonnes which was more than the production in 1991-92 by 7.1 per cent. The kharif foodgrains production in 1993-94 is expected to be 99 million tonnes. The prospects for rabi are excellent.

As part of the agriculture policy, States have been advised to remove all intra and inter-State restrictions on the movement of foodgrains.

It is Government determination that no vulnerable section of the population–be it women, children, minorities, Scheduled Caste, Scheduled Tribes or backward classes–should remain outside the main-stream of development. In all areas of development of the poor, resource allocations were enhanced during 1993-94 compared to the previous year. The revised outlay for the Ministry of Rural Development went up by 56 per cent while the Plan outlay of the Welfare Ministry was raised from Rs. 820 crore to Rs. 980 crore. The Jawahar Rozgar Yojana has been strengthened in 120 most backward districts. The subsidies under the Integrated Rural Development Programme were enhanced by Rs. 1,000 per household. The improved tool kits to rural artisans programme started in 1992-93 was extended in 1993-94 to 100 more districts, thus covering in all 162 districts in the country benefiting 2,30,000 rural artisans. Comprehensive programmes for the welfare and development of the weavers were evolved. They include housing, work sheds, handloom development centres, quality dyeing units, training in improved practices and provision of working capital. These programmes with a total outlay of Rs. 1,372 crore were started during the year. The scheme for handloom development centres and quality dyeing units launched towards the end of 1993 seeks to merge and expand existing units and establish new ones. Against the 1993 target of 120 centres and 20 units, 213 centres and 94 units have been approved. Twentyfive centres and 25 units have already started operating.

New Schemes

Government has formulated three new and innovative schemes to benefit the poor, particularly rural women and urban youth.

The employment assurance scheme introduced in 1,752 of the most backward and remote blocks of the country, where seven crores of the country's poor people live, will provide assured wage employment for 100 days during the lean agaricultural season to the rural labour. This scheme thus expands rural employment of fuller levels.

The Mahila Samriddhi Yojana will empower rural women by enabling them to gain and exercise control over their own earnings and household resources. Already, more than 4 lakh women have opened accounts under this scheme in rural post offices. This scheme, along with the Rashtriya Mahila Kosh, would greatly enhance opportunities for self-employment among rural women.

To provide sustained employment to the educated urban youth in micro enterprises, a rozgar yojana has been launched. About 1,95,000 applications have been received so far from youth in different States. So far 41,275 applications have been processed and recommended to banks and about 2,000 of them have also been sanctioned. During the current year, the scheme will cover 40,000 beneficiaries and from 1994-95 onwards it is intended to cover 2.20 lakh beneficiaries every year, thus, covering in all 7 lakh beneficiaries during the rest of the 8th Plan period. The Reserve Bank of India has been instructed to support the programme fully. The scheme provides for 22.5 per cent reservation for the Scheduled Castes and Scheduled Tribes and 27 per cent for the other backward classes with preference for women.

Our relations with our neighbours continued to be cordial, and our interaction in various fields with Bangladesh, Bhutan, Maldives, Nepal and Sri Lanka recorded good progress during the year. In the case of Pakistan, however, its continuing support for terrorism and subversion in Jummu and Kashmir and anti-Indian activities world-wide seriously hampered our efforts at normalising relations. The Prime Minister offered Pakistan a dialogue aimed at establishing good-neighbourly relations as enshrined in the Shimla Agreement. Bilateral talks have since taken place, but the stridency of Pakistan's anti-Indian statements has grown, adversely affecting efforts at improving bilateral ties. There are no quarrels between us and the people of Pakistan. We feel that for good relations between our countries the Government of Pakistan should give up its negative approach and reciprocate our desire to normalise India-Pakistan relations in accordance with the Shimla Agreement.

Our relations with China have improved markedly. The Prime Minister's visit to China in September 1993, and the signing of the agreement on the maintenance of peace and tranquility along the line of actual control have brought them to a new stage of development. The expert group set up under this agreement held its first meeting recently, reflecting the desire of both sides to maintain and continue the interaction on this complex issue.

India values SAARC as an innstrument of regional cooperation consistent with the objectives of its charter. The Prime Minister attended the SAARC summit in Dhaka last year. SAARC has recorded progress in dealing with certain important issues of common interest such as poverty, terrorism, population growth, problems relating to the status of women, children, youth and drugs and psychotropic sustenances. We continue to pay an active role in SAARC with a view to promoting its socio-economic and other objectives in accordance with the SAARC charter.

Our interaction with the United States has traditionally ranged over a number of areas from education and science and technology to culture and sports. We have also cooperated in the UN on issued relating to disarmament such as the comprehensive test ban treaty. The response from the United States to our economic liberalisation policies has been very positive and the US investments in India in the last two years were very substantial. We look forward to working with the United States towards mutual understanding, including on those issues on which such understanding needs enhancement. This will reflect the vibrant democratic and secular ideals of our two countries.

Relations with the Russian Federation,drawing upon rich traditions of our friendship of the past, continued with mutual understanding and cooperation. Despite certain difficulties the two countries face, cooperation in the political, economic, commercial and other areas was sought to be promoted by both sides. The goodwill and understanding that underpins our relations reinforce our joint efforts at identifying possibilities of further cooperation in various areas in today's changed context.

We welcome the signing of the declaration of principles on interim self-government arrangements between Israel and the PLO in September 1993 as a notable step towards peace and stability in West Asia and the restoration of the legitimate rights of the Palestinian people.

India continues to play an active role in shaping the global agenda on issued pertaining to political and security matters, economic and social development, human rights, environment and population.

I am confident your debates and deliberations in the course of this session and beyond will take the nation forward in fulfilling the aspirations of the people. I commend you to your talks and wish you all success.

Source : Hindustan Times, February 22, 1993.

10.3 Concluding Observations

A large part of our population still remains backward. There is a wide gulf between the rich and the poor. *Unemployment* is on the increase. National integration is our urgent need. Erosion in the standard of values, in fact is the topmost blockade, which requires to be checked and a crusade for 'Clean Life, Clean Poltics and Clean Administration' is to be given first priority.

India is on the move. The tasks before us are very challenging and tremendous. But there is no causes for despair. By harnessing all our resources and working unitedly and sincerely, we can usher in an era of peace, progress and prosperity.

The 21st century beckons up holding fourth new hopes. We, the people of India, must march ahead as an integrated resurgent.

As *Gurudev Rabindranath Tagore* would advise, we must "hold the faith firm", surely "the day will dawn".

11

FIVE YEAR PLANS

11.1 Planning Commission and Planning Process

Constitued in March 1950 by a Resolution of the Government of India, the Planning Commission works under the over-all guidance of the National Development Council which is headed by the Prime Minister and includes Ministers of the Central Cabinet, Chief Ministers of all States and Union Territories and Members of the Planning Commission. Delhi Administration is represented by the Lt. Governor and the Chief Executive Councillor, and the remaining Union Territories by their respective Administrators. The Planning Commissioning consults the Central Ministers and the State Government while formulating Five Year Plans and Annual Plans and also oversees their implementation. The Commission also functions as an advisory body at the apex level.

The following functions have been assigned to the *Planning Commission*

1. Make an assessment of the material, capital and human resources of the country, including technical personnel, and investigate the possibilities of augmenting such of these resources as are found to be deficient in relation to the nation's requirements;
2. formulate a Plan for the most effective and balanced utilisation of country's resources;
3. on a determination of priorities, define the stages in which the Plan should be carried out and propose the allocation of resources for the due completion of each stagse;
4. indicate the factors which are tending to retard economic development and determine the conditions, which in view of the current social and political situation, should be established for the successful execution of the Plan;
5. determine the nature of the machinery which will be necessary for securing the successful implementation of each stage of the Plan in all its aspects;
6. appraise from time to time the progress achieved in the execution of each stage of the Plan and recommend the adjustments of policy and measures that such appraisal may show to be necessary; and
7. make such interim or ancillary recommendations as appear to it to be appropriate either for facilitating the discharge of the duties assigned to it on a consideration of prevailing economic conditions, current policies, measures and development programmes or on an examination of such specific problems as may referred to it for advice by Central or State Governments.

Besides, the Planning Commission has been entrusted with the responsibility in respect of the following matters as per the *Government of India Allocation Business Rules:*

(a) Public Cooperation in National Development;
(b) Hill area Development Programme;
(c) Perspective Planning;
(d) Institute of Applied Manpower Research; and
(e) National Informatics Centre.

Composition of the Commission

The composition of the Planning Commission as on April 1, 1993 was as follows:

Chairman:	:	Shri P.V.Narasimha Rao, Prime Minister
Deputy Chairman:	:	Shri Pranab Mukherjee
Members:	:	1. Dr.Manmohan Singh, Minister of Finance
		2. Shri Sharad Pawar, Minister of Defence
		3. Shir Balaram Jakhar, Minister of Agriculture
		4. Dr.Chitra Naik
		5. Dr.D.Swaminadhan
		6. Shri V.Krishnamurthy
		7. Dr.C.Rangarajan
		8. Dr.S.Z.Qasim
		9. Prof.J.S.Bajaj
		10. Dr.Jayant Patil.

The Prime Minster, in his capacity as Chariman of the Planning Commission, paritcipates and gives direction to the Commission on all major issues of policy.

11.2 Five Year Plans: A Recapitulation

The First Five Year Plan (1951-52 to 1955-56) was 'ground preparing' exercise which gave its primary attention to the achievement of economic stability and elimination of shortages of food and basic resources. Accordingly it accorded top priority to agriculture of which irrigation and power were deemed essential ingredients. About 44.6 per cent of the total outlay was earmarked for the agricultural sector. The annual growth targeted in this Plan was 2.1 per cent of the national income.

The Plan also aimed at increasing the rate of investment from five per cent to about seven per cent of the national income.

The Second Five Year Plan (1956-57 to 1960-61) aimed, among other things, at 25 per cent increase in the national income, rapid industrialisation with particular emphasis on development of basic and heavy industries, large expansion of employment opportunities, and reduction inequalities in income and wealth and more even distribution of economic power. The Plan laid special stress on fastening industrialisation with the aim of strengthening the capital base and productive capacity.

The Plan also aimed at increasing the rate of investment from about seven per cent of the national income to eleven per cent by 1960-61.

The Third Plan (1961-62 to 1965-66) aimed at securing a marked advance towards self-sustaining growth. Its immediate-objectives were to (a) secure an increase in national income of over 5 per cent per annum and a simultaneous evolution of a pattern of investment capable of sustaining this rate of growth during subsequent Plan period; (b) achieve self-sufficiency in foodgrains (the target of foodgrains productio stood at 100 million tonnes) and increased agricultural production to meet the requirement of industry and exports; (c) expand basic industries like steel, chemicals, fuel and power and establish machine building capacity; (d) utilise fully manpower resources an ensure a substantial expansion of employment opportunities; and (e) establish greater equality of opportunity and bring about reduction in disparities of income and wealth and more equitable dispersal of economic power. The Plan sought to increase the national income by about 30 per cent from Rs. 14,500 crore in 1960-61 to about Rs. 19,000 crore by 1965-66 (at 1960-61 prices) and per capita income by about 17 per cent from Rs. 300 to Rs. 385 during the same peroid.

The finalisation of the Fourth Plan was delayed on account of the situation created by the Indo-Pakistan War in 1965, two successful years of severe drought, devaluation of currency, general rise in prices and erosion of resources available for Plan purposes. There, three Annual Plans were formulated between 1966 and 1969.

The Fourth Five Year Plan (1969-70 to 1973-74) aimed at accelerating the tempo of development in conditions of stability and reducing the fluctuations in agricultural production as well as the impact uncertainties in foreign aid.

It sought to raise the standard of living and promote equality and social justice. The Plan laid particular empahsis on improving the conditions of the less-privilege and weaker sections of the society through gainful employment and education and on diluting the concentration through wider diffusion of wealth, income an economic power. The average annual rate of growth envisaged was 5.7 per cent.

The Fifth Plan (1974-75 to 1977-78) aimed at achieving self-reliance and adoption of measures to boom consumption standards of the people living below the poverty line. The Plan also gave high priority to bringing inflation under control and achieving stability of the economic front. The Plan targeted an annual growth rate of 5.5 per cent in national income and better capacity utilisation of industries, developing renewable sources of energy, and integration of science and technology into the main stream of development.

The Sixth Plan (1980-81 to 1984-85) assigned the highest priority to the removal of poverty. The strategy was essentially to strengthen the infrastructure for both agriculture and industry so as to create conditions for a sustained and accelerated growth in investment output and exports. It aimed at meeting the minimum basic needs of the people through special programmes and creating increased opportunities for employment, especially in the rural areas and the unorganised sector. Stress was laid on greater management efficiency and intensive monitoring in all sectors and involvement of people in formulation and speedy implementation of schemes at the local level.

The Seventh Plan (1985-86 to 1989-90) gave highest priority to food, employment and productivity. Faster movement towards the objectives of self-reliance with social justice was the core idea of the Plan. The salient features of the Plan were: decentralised Planning, maximum employment generation, self-sufficiency in food at higher levels of consumption, export-import balance, modernisation and upgrdation of technology. The Seventh Plan laid down an average annual growth rate target of 5 per cent. It also aimed at a 8.7 per cent annual growth rate for industries.

11.3 Eighth Five Year Plan (1992-97)

The formulation and implementation of the Eighth Five Year Plan was delayed by two years on account of rapid changes in the Central Government. It came into operation in 1992.

Salient Features of the Eighth Plan

The Plan has some features which distinguishes it from other Plans.

This Plan is indicative in nature. It concentrates on building a long-term strategic vision of the future and sets forth the priorities of the nations. While for the public sector the Plan goes into the details examining the alternatives and identifying the specific projects in various sectors, for the rest of the economy it works out sectoral targets and tends to provide promotional stimulus to the economy to grow in the desired direction.

The Plan recognises "human development" as the core of all developmental effort. It is only healthy and educated people who can contribute to economic growth and this growth in turn will contribute to human well being. The priority sectors of the Plan that contribute towards realisation of this goal are health, education, literacy and basic needs including drinking water, housing and welfare programmes for the weaker sections. In the Eighth Plan, Governments at the Centre and in the States will expand their role in this sphere.

For rapid economic development, the priority sectors identified for the growth of infrastructure are power, transport and communications. The basic assumption is that if we can provide these three essential ingredients in the urban and rural areas, it will lead to accelerated economic growth.

The Plan attempts to correct the fiscal imbalances from which the Sixth and Seventh Plans suffered.

This is an integrative Plan. If the results of our developmental activities so far have not been commensurate with the investments made, one of the main reasons for that has been our fragmented approach. Too many agencies trying to do too many things with a thin spread of resources has led to poor results. If we can integrate our developmental efforts, the results can be much more impressive even with these levels of investment.

The Eighth Plan recognises the essential need to involve people in the process of development.

The new role of the Government in the process of plan implementation devolution of power to peoples organisations at the district, block and village levels.

This Plan is performance oriented. It concentrates not so much on its allocative role, but on how to utilise the allocations optimally. The stress is on performance improvement, quality consciousness, competitiveness, efficiency of operations and on-time completion of the projects. In order to provide incentive for good performance and bring in result orientation the formula for giving Central assistance to States has been suitably amended.

Eighth Plan pays special attention to employment in the rural areas.

This is a flexible Plan with scope for change, innovation and adjustment. In the outlays proposed for the States and some of the central Ministries, there is a fairly large component of resources that the States and Central Ministries have to raise themselve.

The Plan proposes a growth rate of 5.6 per cent per annum on average during the Plan period. The level of national investment is proposed at Rs. 789,000 crore and public sector outlay is proposed to be at Rs. 434,100 crore.

Source : Yojana, August 15, 1992.

The Sectoral pattern of investment and its financing in the Eighth Plan is presented in Table 11.1. An outlay of Rs. 434,100 crore is planned for public sector. This will have an investment component of Rs. 361,000 crore and a current component of Rs. 73,100 crore. The public sector investment then, will amount to 45.2 per cent of the total domestic investment, allowing for a much large space for the private sector than has hither to been given. The share of Centre and States in Public Sector Plan Outlay is given in Table 11.2. The share of the Public Sector in total investment during the Fifth, Seventh and Eighth Plan is shown in Table 11.3.

TABLE 11.1 : Sectoral Pattern of Investment and its Financing in the Eighth Plan (1992-97)

(Rs. crores at 1991-92 prices)

Sector	Own Saving	Sources of Financing the Investment Transfer from Household Sector's Savings	Rest of the World	Investment	Current Outlay	Aggregate Outlay
Public Sector	68900	258400	33700	361000	73100	434100
Private Corporate Sector	68930	587770	21300	149000		
Household Sector	605170	317170	—	288000		
	743000	—	55000	798000		

Consistent with the expected resource position, the size of the States' Plans is projected at Rs. 179,985 crore and the Central Plan at Rs. 254,115 crore (including Rs. 6,250 crore for the UTs). These are shown in Table 11.4. The share of the States in the Public Sector plan which has been declining through the Fifth, Sixth and the Seventh Plans, is sought to be raised from realised level of 39 per cent in the Seventh Plan to 41.5 per cent in the Eighth Plan. The States will be required to improve their resources, curb expenditure and improve and realise a positive contribution to the resources from their enterprise particularly in the electricity and transport sectors.

TABLE 11.2 : Share of Centre and States in Public Sector Plan Outlay

Item	Annual Plan 1991-92 (at current prices)	Annual Plan 1992-93 (at current prices)	Eighth Plan at 1991-92
Central Deptts. Outlay	42,969	48,407	247,865
Budgetary Support	19,015	18,501	103,725
IEBR	23,954	29,906	141,140
States & UTs Outlay	28,107*	32,365	186,235
Union Territories Outlay	1,277*	1,291	6,250
Budgetary Support	1,277	1,291	6,250
State Outlay+	26,830*	31,074	179,985
Central Assistance	13,428	14,820	78,500
States own Resources	13,402	16,254	101,485
Total Plan Outlay	71,076*	80,772	434,100

\+ Includes outlay for Area Programme.

* Excludes Rs. 1,072 crore Plan Loans to States which were not finally agreed to by Ministry of Finance and the "Model villages" Scheme and "Equity Base for Cooperatives" which were subsequently dropped.

TABLE 11.3 : Share of Public Sector in Total Investment

	Public Sector Investment (as % of total investment)	
	Projected	Realised
Fifth Plan (1974-79)	57.6	43.4
Sixth Plan (1980-85)	52.9	47.8
Seventh Plan (1985-90)	47.8	45.7
Eighth Plan (1992-97)	45.2	—

TABLE 11.4 : *Public Sector Outlay* and its Financing by Centre and States

(Rs. Crore at 1991-92 prices)

Items	Centre	States	Total
Balance from Current Revenue	22020	12985	35005
Public Enterprises	144140	4000	148140
Ext. Com. Borrowing & Sup.			
Credit (Net of repayment)	(5000)	—	(5000)
Public Bonds by Enterprises	37300	—	37300
Government Borrowings*	117755	58300	176055
Negotiated Loans	—	26200	26200

(Contd.)

TABLE 11.4 *(Contd.)*

Items	Centre	States	Total
Net Capital Inflow from Abroad	28700	—	28700
Govt. Loans	24500	—	24500
Govt. Grants	4200	—	4200
Deficit Financing	20000	—	20000
Total Resources	336215	101435	434100
Central Assistance	-78500	78500	0
Resources for Plan	254115	179985	434100

* Includes market borrowings, small savings, other loans taken by Central & State Governments, State Provident Funds and net miscellaneous capital receipts.

Savings and Flow of Funds

The rate of saving is projected at an average of 21.6 per cent of GDP during the Plan period. The realised average rate of savings was 19.7 per cent of GDP during the Sixth Plan and 20.4 per cent during the Seventh Plan. The slow pace in increase in domestic savings during the eighties as compared to the rate of improvement in savings In the earlier decades is accounted for by two factors. While the savings of the household sector has shown a smallar rise than in the previous decades partly influenced by the larger availability of consumer goods, both durable and non-durable, the savings of the Government sector has shown a sharp deterioration. The rates of savings during the Sixth and the Seventh Plan and the projected rates of savings for the Eighth Plan are shown in Table 11.5.

TABLE 11.5 : Rates of Savings

(As percentage of GDP Pmp)

	At Current Prices			Projected (At 1991-92 Prices)		
	Sixth Plan	Seventh Plan	Average of 7 years (1985-86 to 1991-92)*	1991-92	1996-97	Eighth plan (1992-97)
1. Public Sector	3.69	2.33	2.00	1.44	2.07	2.00
2. Govt. Sector	1.10	-1.36	-1.74	-2.37	-1.08	-1.11
3. Public Enterprises	2.59	3.69	3.74	3.81	3.15	3.11
4. Private Corporate Sector	1.63	2.04	2.15	2.39	2.17	2.00
5. Household Sector	14.33	16.00	16.60	17.77	17.36	17.60
6. Gross Domestic Savings	19.65	20.37	21.75	21.60	21.60	21.60

* Based on data from Quick Estimates for 1990-91 and projections for 1991-92.
Abbreviation : GDP Pmp = Gross Domestic Product at market prices.

The savings of the household sector increased from 16 per cent of household disposable income in the Sixth Plan to 18.6 per cent in the Seventh Plan. In view of the increasing opportunities for consumption and urbanisation of the society, the increases in household savings in relation to their disposable income are not expected to be as sharp as in the previous Five Year Plan. With the increase in the proportion of financial savings in the total savings, however, the major contribution of household savings in the Eighth Plan will be towards making larger resources available for financing the investment of the private corporate sector and the *Public Sector.*

TABLE 11.6 : Domestic Investment and Eighth Five Year Plan Intersectoral Flow of Funds during 1992-97

(Rs. crore at 1991-92 prices)

Item	Public sector	Private Corporate sector	Household Sector	All Sector
Gross Investment	361000	149000	288000	798000
Financed by:				
Own Savings	68900	68930	605170	743000
	2.00%	2.00%	17.60%	21.60%
Borrowing				
From Household	258400	58770	-317170	0
	7.51%	1.71%	-9.22%	0.00%
From Rest of the World	33700	21300	0	55000
	0.98%	0.62%	0.00%	1.60%

Notes 1.: Percentage are with reference to GDP at market prices during the 5 years of the Eighth Plan.

2.: For the Eighth Plan financial savings of household sector as a percentage of total household savings is projected at about 52%.

Table 11.7 indicates the sectoral investment during the Eighth Plan.

Public sector outlay by major heads of development during the Eighth Plan–Center, States and Union territories is shown in Table 11.8

Public sector outlays by heads of development, i.e., agriculture, etc., is given in Table 11.9.

TABLE 11.7 : Eighth Plan Sectoral Investment during 1992-93 to 1996-97

(Rs. crore at 1991-92 prices)

Sector	Public	Private	Total	Share of Sector in total investment by sectors %	6th Plan	7th Plan	8th Plan
Agriculture	52000	96800	148800	34.95	15.24	11.23	18.65
Mining & Quarrying	28500	11100	39600	71.97	6.06	6.70	4.96
Manufacturing	47100	141300	188400	25.00	23.60	26.00	23.61
Electricity, Gas & Water	92000	10120	102120	90.09	12.07	13.65	12.80
Construction	3300	17240	20540	16.07	2.73	1.86	2.57
Transport	49200	38710	87910	55.97	9.42	9.93	11.02
Communication	25000	1000	26000	96.15	1.50	2.03	3.26
Services	63900	120730	184630	34.61	29.38	28.60	23.13
Total	361000	437000	798000	45:24	100.00	100.00	100.00

Note : Sixth & Seventh Plan figures are calculated at 1980-81 prices.

TABLE 11.8 : Eighth Plan Public Sector Outlay by Major Heads of Development (1992-97) : Center, States and Union Territories

(Rs. crore at 1991-92 prices)

Head of Development	Centre			States	U.T.S	Total	Eighth	Seventh
	Budget Support	IEBR	Total				plan % to total	plan % to total
Agriculture and Allied Activities	12394.00	224.00	12618.00	42135.35	239.15	54992.50	12.67	14.27
Rural Development	24170.00	0.00	24170.00	10213.26	42.10	34425.36	7.93	5.01
Special Area Programmes	0.00	0.00	0.00	6750.16	0.00	6750.16	1.55	1.75
Energy**	13136.00	5359.00	66795.00	47291.58	1474.51	115561.09	26.62	30.48
Industry and Minerals	9186.00	28353.00	37539.00	9284.89	97.86	46921.75	10.81	12.48
Transport	8636.00	32341.00	40977.00	13786.58	1161.99	55925.57	12.88	12.76
Communication	715.00	24382.00	25097.00	12.50	0.48	25109.98	5.78	3.60
Science and Technology	3739.00	200.00	3939.00	188.72	3.99	41.31.71	0.95	1.13
Ecology and Environment***	1200.00	0.00	1200.00	3654.16	55.82	49.9.98	1.13	1.27
General Economic and General Services	1040.55	44.00	1084.55	5079.04	196.41	6360.00	1.47	0.94
Social Services	29508.45	4937.00	34445.76	41588.76	2977.69	79011.90	18.20	16.31
Grand Total	103725.00	144140.00	247865.00	179985.00	6250.00	434100.00	100.00	100.00

* Includes irrigation and flood control.

** Includes allocations for integrated rural energy planning programme.

*** Includes allocations for forestry and wildlife.

TABLE 11.9 : Eighth Plan Public Sector Outlay by Heads of Development (1992-97)

(Rs. crore at 1991-92 prices)

Head of Development	Centre			States	UTs	Total
	Budget	IEBR$	Total			
1	2	3*	4	5	6	7
I. Agriculture & Allied Activities	10894.00	224.00	11118.00	11190.25	158.96	22467.21
Crop Husbandry	4681.00	0.00	4681.00	4555.88	37.93	9274.81
Soil & Water Conservation	800.00	0.00	800.00	1497.44	7.38	2304.82
Animal Husbandry	400.00	0.00	400.00	1079.55	50.86	1530.81
Dairy Development	900.00	0.00	900.00	405.71	1.80	1307.51
Fisheries	467.00	0.00	467.00	733.45	32.37	1232.82
Plantations	132.00	58.00	190.00	17.41	0.00	207.41
Food, Storage & Warehousing	320.00	166.00	486.00	58.10	0.00	544.10
Agricultural Research & Education	1300.00	0.00	1300.00	711.39	6.31	2017.70
Agricultural Financial Institutions	244.00	0.00	244.00	276.68	0.00	544.10
Cooperation	1550.00	0.00	1550.00	1485.89	21.23	3057.12
Other Agricultural Programmes	100.00	0.00	100.00	368.35	1.08	469.43
II. Rural Development	24170.00	0.00	24170.00	10213.26	42.10	34425.36
Special Programme for Rural Development	4950.00	0.00	4950.00	2866.	10.09	7817.55

(Contd.)

TABLE 11.9 : *(Contd.)*

1	2	3*	4	5	6	7
Rural Employment	18400.00	0.00	18400.00	5244.88	0.00	23644.88
Land Reforms	210.00	0.00	240.00	845.54	1.88	1087.42
Other Rural Development Programmes	580.00	0.00	580.00	1256.38	39.13	1877.51
III. Special Area Programmes	0.00	0.00	0.00	6750.16	0.00	6750.16
Hill Area	0.00	0.00	0.00	1450.00	0.00	1450.00
North Eastern Area	0.00	0.00	0.00	1160.00	0.00	1160.00
Other Special Area Programmes	0.00	0.00	0.00	4140.16	0.00	4140.16
(a) Backward Areas	0.00	0.00	0.00	2250.16	0.00	2250.16
(b) Tribal Areas	0.00	0.00	0.00	1250.00	0.00	1250.00
(c).Others	0.00	0.00	0.00	640.00	0.00	640.00
IV. Irrigation & Flood Control	1508	0.00	1500.00	30945.10	80.19	32525.29
Major & Medium Irrigation	95.00	0.00	95.00	22310.21	9.32	22414.53
Minor Irrigation	293.00	0.00	293.00	5662.47	21.79	5977.26
Command Area Development	830.00	0.00	830.00	1679.33	0.80	2510.13
Flood Control and Drainage	282.00	0.00	282.00	1293.09	48.28	1623.37
V. Energy	13136.00	53659.00	66795.00	47291.58	1474.51	115561.09
Power	8902.00	22279.00	31181.00	46961.86	1445.88	79588.74
Petroleum	527.00	23473.00	24000.00			24000.00
Coal & Lignite	2600.00	7907.00	10507.00			10507.00
Sources of Energy Non-Conventional	1107	0.00	1107.00	329.72	28.63	1465.35
VI. Industry & Minerals	9186.00	28353.00	37539.00	9284.39	97.86	46921.75
Village & Small Scale Industries	2458.00	0.00	2458.00	3803.05	73.15	6334.20

(Contd.)

TABLE 11.9 : *(Contd.)*

1	2	3*	4	5	6	7
Iron & Steel Industries	774.00	13805.00	14579.00			14579.00
Non-Ferrous Mining & Metallurgical Industries	352.00	1746.00	2098.00	813.74	0.00	2911.74
Cement & Non-metallic Mineral Industries	0.00	300.00	300.00			300.00
Fertilizer Industries	1018.00	4466.00	5484.00			5484.00
Petrochemical Industries	38.70	4543.50	4582.20			4582.20
Chemical & Pharmaceutical Industries	23.30	223.50	246.80			246.80
Engineering Industries	449.22	1771.61	2220.83			2220.83
Telecommunication & Electronic Industries	493.00	579.00	1072.00			1072.00
Consumer Industries	224.78	518.39	743.17			743.17
Atomic Energy Industries	800.00	400.00	1200.00			1200.00
Other Industries	80.00	0.00	80.00	4668.10	24.71	4772.81
Other Outlays on Industries & Minerals	2475.00	0.00	2475.00			2475.00
VII. Transport	8636.00	32341.00	40977.00	13786.58	1161.99	55925.57
Railways	5375.00	21827.00	272.00			27202.00
Port & Lighthouses	500.00	2773.00	3273.00	260.85	79.73	3613.98
Shipping	150.00	3250.00	3400.00		268.91	3668.91
Civil Aviation	107	3891.00	3998.00	45.26	40.00	4083.26
Roads & Bridges	2000.00	600.00	2600.00	9516.19	716.99	12833.18
Road Transport	264.00	0.00	264.00	3799.47	55.63	4119.10

(Contd.)

TABLE 11.9 : *(Contd.)*

1	2	3*	4	5	6	7
Inland Water Transport	240.00	0.00	240.00	91.14	0.00	331.14
Other Transport Services				73.67	0.73	74.40
VIII. Communication	715.00	24382.00	25097.00	12.50	0.48	
Postal Services	325.00	0.00	325.00		325.00	
Telecommunication Services	264.00	23582.00	23946.00			
Other CommunicationServices	26.00	8.00	826.00	12.50	0.48	
IX. Science, Technology & Environment	4939.00	200.00	5139.00	3842.88	59.81	9041.69
Atomic Energy Research	600.00	0.00	600.00			600
Space Research	1604.00	200.00	1804.00			1804.00
Oceanographic Research	115.00	0.00	115.00			115.00
Other Scientific Research	1420.00	0.00	1420.00	188.72	3.99	1621.71
Ecology & Environment	675.00	0.00	675.00	149.00	4.11	828.11
Forestry & Wildlife	525.00	0.00	525.00	3505.16	51.71	4081.87
X. General Economic Services	924.00	44.00	968.00	3540.66*	40.86	4549.52*
Secretarial Economic Services	7.00	0.00	7.00	395.03	3.37	405.40
Tourism	240.00	32.00	272.00	505.18	26.92	804.10
Foreign Trade & Export Promotion	115.00	12.00	127.00			127.00
Census, Surveys & Statistics	106.00	0.00	106.00	84.72	3.15	193.87
Meteorology	130.00	0.00	130.00			130.00
Civil Supplies	30.00	0.00	123.50	123.50	5.72	159.22
General Financial & Trading Institutions	75.00	0.00	75.00			75.00

(Contd.)

TABLE 11.9 : *(Contd.)*

1	2	3*	4	5	6	7
Technical & Economic Cooperation with other Countries	0.00	0.00	0.00			0.00
Other General Economic Services	221.00	0.00	221.00	1.70	2618.91	
XI. Social Services	29508.45	4937.00	34445.45	41588.76	2977.69	79011.90
General Education	6619.00	0.00	6619.00	9607.19	587.16	16813.35
Technical Education	824.00	0.00	824.00	1804.66	157.72	2786.38
Sports & Youth Services	350.00	0.00	350.00	509.06	30.54	889.60
Art & Culture	350.00	35.00	385.00	324.76	17.93	727.69
Medical & Public Health	1800.00	0.00	1800.00	5307.77	468.15	7575.92
Family Welfare	6500.00	0.00	6500.00			6500.00
Water Supply & Sanitation	5743.00	225.00	5968.00	9847.26	895.77	16711.03
Housing	831.35	860.00	1691.35	3409.08	172.59	5273.02
Urban Development	692.10	600.00	1292.10	3461.73	523.15	5276.98
Information and Publicity	184.05	15.00	199.05	215.68	6.78	421.51
Broadcasting	23295	3202.00	3434.95			3434.95
Welfare of SC, ST & Other Backward Clases	2549.42	0.00	2549.42	3050.97	35.09	5635.48
Labour & Employment	449.58	0.00	449.58	839.98	24.41	1313.97
Social Welfare	2373.00	0.00	2373.00	1467.72	14.49	3855.21
Nutrition	10.00	0.00	10.0	1742.40	43.91	1796.31
Secretarial Social Services				0.50	0.00	0.50

(Contd.)

TABLE 11.9 : *(Contd.)*

1	2	3*	4	5	6	7
XII. General Services	116.55	0.00	116.55	1538.38*	155.55	1810.48*
Secretariat-General Services	5.00	0.00	5.00			5.00
Stationery & Planning	0.50	0.00	0.50	85.17	6.09	91.76
Police	25.0		25.00			
Public Works	36.05	0.00	36.05	1224.99	107.21	1368.25
Other Administrative Services	50.00	0.00	50.00	198.37	42.25	290.62
Grand Total	103725.00	144140.00	247865.00	179985.00	6250.00	434100.00

*Figures may not add-up to total schematic details pertaining to one State are awaited.

$Where rules at present do not permit creation of internal resources outside the Consolidated Fund of India, IEBR has been shown in anticipation of evolution of appropriate mechanism to create such resources.

12

STATE OF INDIAN ECONOMY

12.1 Overview

The economy has emerged decisively from the crisis of 1990-91. The crisis reached its peak in the summer of 1991 when foreign currency reserves had plummeted to almost $1 billion, inflation had soared to an annual rate of 17 per cent, industrial production was falling and overall economic growth had declined to 1.1 per-cent (in 1991-92). The programme of stabilisation and the economic reform measures put in place in 1991-92 helped restore economic growth to 4 per cent in 1992-93 (Table 12.1) brought down the rate of inflation to 7 per cent, restored the level of foreign currency reserves to $ 6.4 billion and stimulated a strong recovery in exports towards the end of the financial year. The measures taken during the past two years also averted a deepening crisis in the banking sector, ensured a systematic overhaul of foreign trade and exchange rate policies, largely dismantled the cumbersome and abuse-prone system of industrial licensing, launched a more liberal policy towards foreign investment and ushered in far-reaching changes in the governance of the capital market.

The year 1993-94 saw further fruits of the initial array of reforms, the deepening of the reform efforts in some areas and the identification of new priorities for policy action. The balance of payments position has improved markedly. The current account deficit is expected to be less than 0.5 per cent of GDP in 1993-94. An inflow of over $2.5 billion on account of foreign direct and equity portfolio investments is expected. This reflects a quantum jump in such private capital inflow over previous years. Foreign exchange currency reserves, had reached $10.9 billion by February 4, 1994. The Stand-by Arrangement with the IMF negotiated in 1991, was successfully completed in June 1993. Access to foreign capital markets has been restored. Equity and bond issues by Indian companies have received a strong response in overseas markets. Inflation was running below 8.5 per cent in January 1994. Foodgrain stocks are at record levels due to good agricultural performance in two successive years and marked increases in procurement prices. The unorganised manufacturing sector and the consumer and intermediate goods segments of organised industry have shown reasonable recovery. The Advance Estimates of National Income by CSO place overall economic growth in 1993-94 at 3.8 per cent (Table 12.1).

At the same time, there were setbacks, most notably with regard to slippage in the realization of targets for fiscal deficit correction, and the associated rekindling of inflationary pressures and pre-emption of investible resources for Government borrowing. Furthermore, investment and capital goods production, which were recovering strongly in the first three-quarters of 1992-93, were detailed by the disturbances of December-March, 1992-93. For a number of reasons, the growth in this sector has remained weak and has pulled down overall industrial performance.

The most striking evidence of progress was in the external sector. Responding to the earlier changes in the exchange rate, the unification of the rate from March 1, 1993, the liberalization of trade policies and the strong fiscal deficit correction achieved in the previous two years, export growth soared to 19.9 per cent in dollar terms in the first nine months of the year after having been negative in 1991-92 and showing a weak growth of 3.8 per cent in 1992-93. Despite the earlier wise-ranging liberalization of import policy, imports declined by 1.3 per cent in dollar terms in the first nine months, partly because of the price-rationing effect of the unified, market-determined exchange rate system and also because of slow growth of production in organised manufacturing. For the full year 1993-94, the trade deficit is expected to be in the order of $ 1000 million, compared to $ 9437 million in 1990-91 and $ 4106 million in 1992-93. Similarly, the deficit in the balance of payments on current account is anticipated to be less than 0.5 per cent of GDP as compared to the unsustainable level of 3.3 per cent in 1990-91 and 2.1 per cent in 1992-93. These favourable developments in the current account, together with the growing inflows of foreign direct and portfolio investment, took the level of foreign currency reserves to $ 10.9 billion by February 4, 1994.

Latest available data indicate that real gross capital formation recovered sharply from a decline of 15.8 per cent in 1991-92 to a growth of 16.7 per cent in 1992-93 (Quick Estimates of CSO). The recovery of private investment, which provides a better measure of the incentive effects of the new policies, was also fairly significant: real private gross capital formation increased by 15.1 per cent after falling by 18.4 per cent in the previous year, while real private gross fixed investment increased by 6.7 per cent in 1992-93 after falling by 7.1 per cent the year before (Table 12.2).

The unregistered sector of manufacturing, which is very important from the employment perspective, has responded well to the policy reforms. This sector shows the fatest recovery, with growth moving from -4.3 per cent in 1991-92 to 3.7 per cent in 1992-93 (Quick Estimates of CSO).

Fiscal Deficit

The principal cause of macroeconomic concern in 1993-94 was the deterioration in the fiscal position. The key to the successful stabilisation effort of the past two years had been the reduction of the Central Government's fiscal deficit from 8.4 per cent of GDP in 1990-91 to 5.9 per cent in 1991-92 and even lower in 1992-93, despite sharp revenue shortfalls linked with the disturbances of December-March 1992-93, which entailed slippage of actual fiscal performance from the budget target of 5 per cent of GDP. In 1993-94 the Central Government fiscal deficit was budgeted to fall to 4.7 per cent of GDP. However, because of continued revenue shortfalls in indirect taxes and heavy pressures on expenditure, the deficit is expected to be substantially higher.

Reserve money increased by 16.9 per cent during 1993-94 (up to January 8, 1994), almost double the growth of 8.5 per cent over the same period in 1992-93. The growth in money supply (M3) during this period of 1993-94 at 14.1 per cent, was also higher than the 12.4 per cent growth recorded in the corresponding period of 1992-93.

12.2 Prices

The point-to-point rate of increase in the Wholesale Price Index (WPI) had fallen to 7 per cent by March, and averaged 7 per cent from March to July. It rose to a higher plateau of 8 per cent in August and stood at 8.2 per cent (provisional) on January 29, 1994.

National Income

The Advance Estimates of National Income by CSO put growth of GDP (at factor cost) at 3.8 per cent in 1993-94, with agriculture growing at 2.3 per cent, manufacturing at 2.5 per cent and the growth of utilities and other service sectors ranging from 3.8 to 8.1 per cent. While the estimate of overall economic growth is more than three times higher than the growth in 1991-92, it is below the 5.6 per cent rate projected in the Eighth Five Year Plan. At the macro-economic level, the challenge for policy is to stimulate higher growth, while acting firmly to dampen the build-up of inflationary potential in the economy.

Net State Product and Per capita state Domestic Production is given in Tables 12.3 and 12.4.

Agricultured production: Despite a good year, agricultural production will show lower growth in 1993-94 because of the peak levels attained in 1992-93.

Industrial Production : The aggregate performance of the industrial sector appears poor because of the sharp setback suffered by the reduction in peak custom tariffs to 85%, and general machinery rates to 35 per cent.

Revenue : Revenue realisation in 1993-94 have been substantially short of targeted levels, because of a number of factors

12.3 Government Borrowing

Government borrowing from commercial and cooperative banks in the form of sale of securities and Treasury bills, has increased by 25.5 per cent during 1993-94 (till January 7, 1994). This is almost twice the 14.1 per cent rate of growth in 1992-93.

12.4 Balance of Payments

The year saw a remarkable recovery in the balance of payments position. Exports have increased by 19.9 per cent in US dollars terms during April-December 1993. Imports have shown a decline of 1.3 per cent despite liberalization of import policy and lowering of imports duties. The trade deficit at $ 732 million during April-December is less than a fifth of the level in 1992. By

TABLE 12.1 : Key Indicators

	1990-91	1991-92P	1992-93 P	1993-94P	1990-91	1991-92P	1992-93P	1993-94P
	Absolute Values				per cent change over previous year			
1	2	3	4	5	6	7	8	9
Gross national product (Rs. thousand crore)								
At current prices	468.1	540.1	616.5Q		16.2	15.4	14.Q	
At 1980-81 prices	207.5	208.7	217.6Q	225.9E	4.7	0.6	4.3Q	3.8E
Gross domestic product (Rs. thousand crore)								
At current prices	475.6	551.6	627.9Q		16.4	16.0	13.8Q	
At 1980-81 prices	211.3	213.6	222.1Q	230.4E	4.9	1.1	4.0Q	3.8E
Agricultural production (1)	192.2	188.5	195.8	194.0A	3.2	-4.5	6.9	-0.5A
Foodgrain production (million tonnes)	176.4	168.4	180.0	179.1A	3.0	-1.9	3.9	-0.9A
Industrial Production (2)	212.6	212.5	216.3	209.8 (3)	8.3	0.0	1.8	1.6 (3)
Electricity generated (TWH)	264.6	287.0	301.4	237.8 (8)	7.8	8.5	5.0	7.4 (8)
Wholesale price index (4)	191.8	217.8	233.1	251.1 (5)	12.1	13.6	7.0	8.2 (5)

(Contd.)

TABLE 12.1 *(Contd.)*

1	2	3	4	5	6	7	8	9
Consumer price index for industrial workers (6)	201.0	229.0	243.0	264. (7)	13.6	13.9	6.1	8.6 (7)
Money supply (M3) (Rs. thousand crores)	265.8	317.5	362.7	413.9 (10)	15.1	19.4	14.2	14.1 (11)
Imports at current prices								
(Rs. Crore)	43198	47851	63375	51477 (8)	22.3	10.8	32.4	8.4 (8)
(US$ million)	24075	19411	21882	16414 (8)	13.5	-19.4	12.7	-1.3 (8)
Exports at current prices								
(Rs. Crores)	32553	44041	53688	49182 (8)	17.7	35.3	21.9	31.8 (8)
(US$ million)	18143	17865	18537	15682 (8)	9.2	-1.5	3.8	19.9 (8)
Foreign currency assets								
(Rs. crores)	4388	14578	20140	34225 (9)	-24.2	232.2	38.2	69.9 (9)
(US$ million)	2236	5631	6434	10904 (9)	-33.6	151.8	14.3	69.5 (9)
Exchange rate Rs/US #) #+	17.94	24.65	28.96	31.36 (8)	7.2	27.2	14.9	9.0 (8)

Note : GDP and GNP figures are at factor cost.

A—Anticipated; P—Provisional; Q—Quick estimates E—Advance estimates.
+ Per cent change indicates the rate of depreciation of the Rupees.
# Composite rate from March, 1992 to February, 1993.

(1) Index of agricultural production (Principal crops) with base triennium-ending 1969-70=100. (2) Index of industrial production 1980-81=100. (3) Average index for April-October, 1993. (4) Index with base 1982-82=100. (5) As on January 29, 1994. (6) Index with base 1982=100. (7) As in December, 1993 (8) April-December, 1993 (9) As on February 4, 1994 for 1993-94 and at the end of March for previous years. (10) As on January 7, 1994 (11) April 1, 1993-January 7, 1994.

TABLE 12.2 : Trends in Saving-Investment

	1987-88	1988-89	1989-90	1990-91	1991-92P	1992-93Q
1	2	3	4	5	6	7
			As percentage of GDP at current market prices			
Gross Domestic Savings	21.5	22.0	24.0	24.0	23.1	22.3
Public	2.2	2.0	1.6	1.0	1.7	2.1
Private	19.3	20.0	22.4	23.0	21.4	20.2
Gross Domestic Investment*	23.6	25.1	26.7	27.4	24.2	24.5
Public	10.5	10.7	10.6	10.5	10.0	10.3
Private	13.2	14.9	15.0	16.2	14.0	14.6
Gross Domestic Investment*	23.6	25.1	26.7	27.4	24.2	24.5
GFCF	21.7	21.6	22.5	22.8	22.0	21.3
Change in stocks	2.1	4.0	3.1	3.9	2.0	3.7
Saving-Investment Gap	-2.0	-3.1	-2.7	-3.4	-1.0	-2.2
Public	-8.4	-8.6	-9.0	-9.5	-8.3	-8.2
Private	6.2	5.0	7.4	6.8	7.4	5.5

(Contd.)

TABLE 12.2 *(Contd.)*

1	2	3	4	5	6	7
Growoth Rate of Capital Formation (at 1980-81 prices) (per cent)						
GDCF*	18.6	19.8	6.0	11.2	-15.8	16.7
Public	-8.3	8.4	6.0	6.1	-7.1	26.4
Private	18.6	31.0	-4.1	17.3	-18.4	15.1
GFCF	11.0	7.1	8.7	8.8	-4.1	1.7
Public	-3.0	4.7	0.6	6.5	0.2	-4.8
Private	27.0	9.2	15.5	10.5	-7.1	6.7

Notes : (i) Gross domestic investment denotes Gross Domestic Capital Fomation (GDCF).
(ii) Figures may not add up due to rounding off.
* Adjusted for errors and omissions.

GFCF: Gross Fixed Capital Formation.
P Provisional estimates.
Q Quick estimates.

Sources : (i) Central Statistical Organisation.
(ii) *Economic Survey 1993-94*. Ministry of Finance, Government of India, New Delhi, 1994, Chap 1.

TABLE 12.3 : Net State Domestic Products at Current Prices (New Series)

		1980-81	1984-85	1985-86	1986-87	1987-88	1988-89	1989-90	1990-91	1991-92
	1	2	3	4	5	6	7	8	9	10
1	Andhra Pradesh	7324	11962	13412	14242	17375	22089	24991	30168	36102
2	Arunachal Pradesh	97	196	237	267	284	335	336	426	484
3	Assam	2356	4725	5118	5476	5993	6563	7749	8680	9562
4	Bihar	6360	11363	12357	14115	15311	18622	19565	22736	25455
5	Delhi	2297	3710	4718	5252	6061	7223	8385	9855	*
6	Goa	316	542	509	608	671	781	920	987	1032
7	Gujarat	6585	11757	12037	13883	12663	18421	20890	23810	26533
8	Haryana	3032	4747	5788	6077	6744	8915	9943	12263	14437
9	Himachal Pradesh	723	1031	1237	1363	1539	1873	2184	2429	2798
10	Jammu & Kashmir	1050	1747	1929	2134	2086	2601	2702	2951	3167
11	Karnataka	5616	9767	10330	11852	13559	15834	17833	20847	25435
12	Kerala	3823	6142	6503	7354	8258	9182	10665	12062	13543
13	Madhya Pradesh	6887	10257	12047	12528	16212	19023	21416	26349	27355
14	Maharashtra	15113	22833	26464	28120	33283	40124	48639	56856	62098
15	Manipur	201	353	377	431	508	610	642	694	761
16	Meghalaya	180	302	342	386	472	513	664	729	798
17	Mizoram	62	122	157	194	259	260	281	*	*

(Contd.)

TABLE 12.3 *(Contd.)*

	1	2	3	4	5	6	7	8	9	10
18	Nagaland	110	220	242	269	340	387	469	558	674
19	Orissa	3225	4801	5936	6206	6521	8433	9105	11228	12913
20	Punjab	4449	7381	8347	9174	10816	12495	15055	16830	19621
21	Rajasthan	4126	6983	7669	8341	9437	12892	13837	17804	19502
22	Sikkim	49	95	113	135	156	167	185	203	224
23	Tamil Nadu	7218	12028	13682	15305	18166	19632	22975	25916	28868
24	Tripura	268	442	485	512	589	767	835	970	*
25	Uttar Pradesh	14012	21514	24669	27237	30481	36009	41260	48962	56381
26	West Bengal	8720	14640	15699	17499	20151	23823	27255	31386	35827

P Provisional.
Q Quick estimates.
- Not available.

Note : Owing to differences in methodology and source material used, the figures for different States are not strictly comparable.

Source : Directorate of Economics & Statistics of respective State Governments.

the end of the year, the trade deficit is expected to be about one billion dollars and a small surplus is expected on the invisible account. Based on this, the current account deficit in 1993-94 is likely to be less than 0.5 per cent of the GDP, the lowest since 1977-78.

Foreign currency reserves with the RBI stood at $10.9 billion on February 4, 1994. The year could end with reserves close to $12 billion. This represents nearly 6 months of import cover-as compared to 2 weeks of cover in May, 1991.

Conclusion

Once of the worst economic crises in decades was successfully met by a combination of macro-adjustment measures and policy reforms. Far-reaching policy reforms have been introduced with a view to transforming the structure and competitiveness of the economy and setting it on a path of fast labour intensive growth. Considerable success has been attained on the balance of payments and inflation fronts and economic growth has been rekindled. But the task ahead is long and arduous and the pressures for fiscal laxity and business-as-usual are ever present. The alternatives to fiscal responsibility and sustained reform will bring higher inflation, low growth, recurrent balance of payments problems and the accentuation of poverty. They must be firmly resisted if the goals of fast labour intensive growth, employment generation and poverty reduction are to be successfully pursued and attained.

Notes : 1. *Economic Survey 1993-94* Ministry of Finance, Government of India, New Delhi, 1994
2. Captions to paragraphs inserted.

TABLE 12.4 : Per Capita Net State Domestic Product at Current Prices (NEW SERIES)

		1980-81	1984-85	1985-86	1986-87	1987-88	1988-89	1989-90	1990-91 (P)	**1991-92** (Q)
1		2	3	4	5	6	7	8	9	10
1	Andhra Pradesh	1380	2086	2296	2394	2869	3584	3986	4731	**5570**
2	Arunachal Pradesh	1561	2793	3274	3575	3680	4212	4467	5046	**5551**
3	Assam	1200	2182	2313	2420	2589	2772	3589	3932	**4230**
4	Bihar	919	1506	1604	1793	1904	2266	2330	2650	**2904**
5	Delhi	3759	5126	6252	6677	7393	8456	9425	10638	—
6	Goa	3145	4931	4522	5277	5696	6501	7505	7890	**8096**
7	Gujarat	1948	3204	3218	3644	3264	4663	5210	5850	**6425**
8	Haryana	2370	3325	3948	4044	4387	5679	6120	7516	**8690**
9	Himachal Pradesh	1704	2249	2649	2870	3185	3813	4375	4790	**5355**
10	Jammu & Kashmir	1776	2669	2874	3099	2954	3591	3636	3872	**4051**
11	Karnataka	1529	2432	2520	2835	3181	3645	4031	4631	**5555**
12	Kerala	1510	2261	2352	2615	2888	3162	3617	4032	**4618**
13	Madhya Pradesh	1333	1805	2071	2103	2657	3045	3347	4021	**4077**
14	Maharashtra	2427	3366	3825	3992	4647	5519	6594	7598	**8180**
15	Manipur	1429	2270	2362	2636	3040	3568	3674	3893	**4180**
16	Meghalaya	1361	2047	2250	2479	2955	3118	3863	4190	**4458**

(Contd.)

TABLE 12.4

	1	2	3	4	5	6	7	8	9	10
17	Mizoram	1289	2139	2658	3165	4077	4026	4135	—	—
18	Nagaland	1448	2453	2591	2781	3385	3709	4333	4977	**5810**
19	Orissa	1231	1707	2072	2128	2194	2793	2965	3596	**4068**
20	Punjab	2674	4123	4578	4940	5719	6487	7674	8423	**9643**
21	Rajasthan	1222	1849	1978	2095	2310	3075	3217	4035	**4361**
22	Sikkim	1571	2635	3023	3472	3886	4241	4686	5063	5416
23	Tamil Nadu	1498	2341	2620	2885	3374	3594	4150	4619	5018
24	Tripura	1323	1962	2108	2177	2444	3121	3328	3569	—
25	Uttar Pradesh	1278	1784	2000	2158	2362	2730	3061	3557	**4012**
26	West Bengal	1611	2498	2627	2873	3247	3769	4236	4794	**5383**

P Provisional
Q Quick estimates
— Not available

Note : Owing to differences in source material used, the figures for different States are not strictly comparable.

Source : Directorate of Economics and Statistics of respective State Governments.

13

POVERTY ALLEVIATION AND EMPLOYMENT

13.1 Poverty

13.1.1 Incidence of Poverty

Alleviation of poverty and unemployment continue to be the long run objectives of economic and social development in our country. The Planning Commission has been preparing estimates of the proportion and number of poor in the country. Such estimates were prepared for 1972-73, 1977-78, 1983-84 and 1987-88. These were based on the concept of the poverty line and data on household expenditure obtained through National Sample Survey Rounds. Following the recommendations of the Task Force on Projection of Minimum Needs and Effective Consumption Demand (1979), the Poverty Line was defined as the per capita monthly expenditure needed to obtain the consumption basket corresponding to the calorie norms of 2400 per capita per day in rural areas and 2100 per capita per day in urban areas in the base year 1973-74. The poverty line so defined was Rs. 49.10 for rural areas and Rs.56.60 for urban areas. The same poverty line was updated for subsequent years using suitable indicators of change in cost of living.

The estimates of poverty at the national level for the years 1972-73, 1977-78, 1983-84 and 1987-88 are given in Table 13.1.

These estimates show a continuous decline in the poverty proportions.

In view of the methodological issues raised in respect of the estimates on poverty and also poverty alleviation being an objective of economic and social development, the Planning Commission constituted and Expert Group in September 1989 to consider methodology and computational aspects of estimation of proportion and number of poor in the country. The Expert Group, while retaining the concept of poverty line as recommended by the Task Force, suggested changes in the price deflator to update the poverty line for use in later years. It suggested use of State specific price indices which can reflect the changes in cost of consumption basket of the people around the poverty line. It relied exclusively on the National Sample Survey (NSS) data on consumption expenditure to assess the incidence of poverty without adjusting the NSS Consumption to that obtained from macro-aggregates of the national accounts.

The estimates of percentage of population living below the poverty line arrived at by the Expert Group are in Table 13.2.

The report of the Expert Group which was submitted in July 1993 was released by the Planning Commission, and its recommendations are under consideration. The Expert Group estimates also confirm a steady decline in the proportion of population living below the poverty line. Yet, a substantially high proportion of people continue to be living below the poverty line. This underscores the need for rapid growth of output and employment coupled with strengthening of the special programmes of poverty alleviation and employment generation.

13.1.2 Poverty Line

Nearly 40 per cent of Indians live below the poverty line, according to experts, the Rajya Sabha was told on December 1, 1993.

An expert group, on the basis of alternative methodology, had estimated the percentage of people below poverty line in 1987-88, the details of which were available now at 39.34 per cent.

An earlier estimate had put the percentage of people below the poverty line at 29.9 per cent.

However, as per both estimates, Orissa and Bihar were ranked as the poorest States in respect of both urban and rural poverty in 1987-88.

Orissa headed the list with 55.61 per cent below the poverty line, while Bihar had 53.37 per cent.

Others with high percentage were Tamil Nadu, Andaman and Nicobar Islands, Pondicherry, West Bengal, Uttar Pradesh, Madhya Pradesh, Maharashtra, with the figure ranging between 40 and 45 per cent, he added.

Source : *Rajya Sabha Proceedings,* December 21, 1993.

13.1.3 Reports on Poverty in India

Following recent reports throw considerable light on the magnitude of poverty in India:

1. Lakadwala/Dandekar Panel Report, 1993.
2. Bread for the World Institute (Washington) Annual Report, 1993.
3. UNDP Project Report, 1994.

13.1.3.1 Lakadwala/Dandekar Panel Report, 1993

The expert panel of economists was appointed with Prof. D.T. Lakadwala as its chairman following recommendations of the task force as early as 1979. After Prof. Lakadwala's sudden demise about a year ago, the chairmanship of the group was passed on to Prof. V.M. Dandekar who himself is an expert of poverty studies in the country. The report has thrown up some very revealing details. Contrary to the general impression that the bulk of the people below the poverty line live in the countryside, it has put the percentage of the rural poor at 39.06 or 230 million (as per the 1987-88 NSS data) while the number of the urban poor is 40.12 per cent or 312 million. The two figures together prove that the Government's earlier projections of the poverty level were off the mark by a good 10 percentage points or 75 million in absolute terms.

Rather than depending solely on the calorie intake for poverty criteria, the expert group has attempted to broadbase the definition to assess the overall consumption levels. More significantly, it has separately determined the consumption norms for such sections of the population as the farm labourers, industrial workers and non-manual workers. Equally significantly, State-wise disaggregation of the poverty levels has been worked out to evolve area-specific profiles. Thus, the number of people below the poverty line is as high as 55.61 per cent in Orissa and 53.34 per cent in Bihar as against only 12.71 per cent in Punjab and 16.66 per cent in Haryana.

Source : *Hindustan Times,* October 16, 1993.

13.1.3.2 Bread for the World's Institute (Washington) Annual Report, 1993

Highlights

The Poverty rate in India dropped from 48 per cent in 1977-78 to 25 per cent in 1992 but the number of poor increased to 210 million because of population growth.

In contrast with India, in China the number of people living in absolute poverty fell from 275 million to 100 million and in Indonesia from 70 to 27 million.

"Progress against hunger in the region", "stems not just from rapid economic growth in East and South-East Asia but fron anti-poverty policies".

A number of countries that had depended on food aid, including India, had achieved self-sufficiency but still nearly half the adult population in India regularly consumed an inadequate number of calories.

Half of the world's anaemic women were found in South Asia while over 50 per cent of the people suffering from iodine deficiencies lived in China and India.

More than half of the world's underweight children under the age of five years were found in South Asia despite the fact that the proportion of the sub-region's children who were underweight fell from 68 per cent in 1975 to 62 per cent in 1990. The figure for Bangladesh of 65 per cent "is the highest in the World".

Malnutrition persisted among South Asian children, the report said, despite declining poverty rates in India and Pakistan, gains in per capita food production throughout South Asia, large-scale child survival programmes in India and Sri Lanka and progress in reducing the percentage of the population with inadequate diets.

"Many South Asian families provide girls less food, health care and education than boys".

Preliminary data on malnutrition among women of child-bearing age indicated that 60 per cent women in South Asia and 45 per cent in South-East Asia (Myanmar or Burma, Thailand, Malaysia, Singapore, Indonesia, the Philippines, Brunei, Cambodia, Laos and Vietnam) were underweight due to malnutrition.

This made them more likely to have underweight babies and die in childbirth, the report said, adding that 18 per cent of Asian women had their first baby at the age of 18.

Success in boosting food grain output has contributed to high and apparently rising rates of anaemia among South Asian women, as farmers have abandoned cultivation of iron-rich vegetables such as beans and lentils in favour of rice and wheat".

Source: *Economic Times*, October 16, 1993.

13.1.3.3 UNDP Project Report, 1994

The report has been prepared under a project sponsored and funded by the United Nations Development Programme (UNDP), within technical services programme.

As regards the medium-term effects of structural adjustment on employment and poverty, the problem is one of reviving growth, that is, of boosting aggregate demand in the economy. Since expansionary fiscal policies are not on the cards, revival of growth depends on the degree of success in boosting exports and attracting foreign direct investment. Success in these areas, unfortunately, depends not only on domestic policies but also on developments in the international economy.

Employment generation and poverty alleviation will depend not only on economic growth but also on other policies designed to influence the pattern of growth and distributional changes.

"Indeed, in the absence of these other policies, even a revival of growth will not be enough to renew the processes of employment generation and poverty-alleviation in the medium term. For although a revival of growth and the associated growth of export orientation of the economy should have positive effects on employment and poverty, some of the structural adjustment measures themselves (or the absence of) are likely to have negative effects".

Restructuring of the sick enterprises and public sector reforms are most likely to lead to substantial redundancies in the organised sector: the lack of clear policies towards the rural economy may lead to an acceleration in the rural-urban migration and so on.

Moreover, inflow of foreign direct investment and the increasing openness of the economy are likely to create pressures for modernisation leading to a growth of a capital intensity in industries.

The experts noted that the reforms programme was planned to be implemented in two phases. The first phase, which is virtually over, concerned stabilisation and principally involved in restraining the growth of aggregate demand. The second phase, that of structural adjustment, is under way and pertains to reforms in the basic structure of the economy and its growth.

Stabilisation measures have induced industrial recession and have led to cuts in public expenditure on anti-poverty programmes. As such, there can be little doubt that the employment generation and poverty-alleviation processes, operative in the 1980s, have been reversed in the course of stabilisation.

The project was coordinated by Ajit K. Ghose of the International Labour Organisation (ILO), and the Asian Regional Team of Employment Promotion (ARTEP), who led the initial mission in which S.V. Sethuraman and Manueal Tomei of ILO, Geneva, also participated.

Dr. Ghose and Sudipto Mudel of the Institute of Public Finance and Policy, New Delhi, wrote the report.

The leading social scientists who prepared the background papers were: Amit Bhaduri, S. Tendulkar, K. Sundaram, L.R. Jain, Abhijit Sen, Jyoti Ghosh, Amitav Kundu, S. Gangopadhya, W. Wadhwa, Deepak Nayyar, Y.K. Alagh, Water Fernandez, Shoma Chaudhury, Manish Rao and Nita Mishrs.

Source : *Hindustan Times, February 17, 1994.*

13.1.4 Rural Poverty

A study of the Jawahar Rozgar Yojana (JRY) by the Planning Commission has revealed that a little over 90 per cent of the rural poor (population below poverty line) live in the 10 major states – Andhra Pradesh, Bihar, Karnataka, Madhya Pradesh, Maharashtra, Orissa, Rajasthan, Tamil Nadu, Uttar Pradesh and West Bengal.

The study was taken up in these States covering 20 districts, 40 gram panchayats, and 598 beneficiaries who got jobs under JRY between April 1, 1989 and Sept. 30, 1991.

The study, inter-alia, says that the record of number of persons who actually got employed under JRY was not maintained at any level. But the percentage achievement in terms of mandays of employment generation was more than the percentage utilisation of funds available during 1989-90 and 1990-91 at the State, district and gram panchayat levels.

Although the proportion of mandays of employment of the Scheduled Castes and Scheduled Tribes to total mandays of employment generated was more than 50 per cent, the women's share remained 22 to 25 per cent upto the district level. At the gram panchayat level, it was 15 to 18 per cent.

During the first nine months of 1991-92 (upto December '91), the financial achievements remained less than 50 per cent at the all-India and State levels. This shows that more than 50 per cent of the available funds would be utilised only during the last quarter and major works would have to be taken up during the terminal quarter.

Of the 40 selected gram panchayats, two in 1989-90 and six in 1990-91 did not utilise the funds at all. In the first half of 1991-92, 19 gram panchayats did not report any utilisation of funds.

The gram panchayats which utilised the funds could provide employment to a person for an average number of 11.44 and 15.68 days during 1989-90 and 1990-91 respectively.

All the selected beneficiaries (598) did not get employment in all the years under study.

It was observed in the case of 75 per cent of selected gram panchayats that the illustrative list of works as per JRY manual has become an exhaustive list at the operational level.

The quality of assets was not up to the mark in 56 per cent of the gram panchayats. Eighty-nine per cent of the selected beneficiaries had expressed the view that assets created were useful. However, the maintenance of assets had not been given due attention.

At the gram panchayat level, it was felt that the wage; material ratio was not workable. The panchayat secretary was over-worked and the action plan, instead of being prepared by the gram panchayats was formulated by the block agency in some cases, thereby ignoring the felt needs of the area.

It was gathered that technical guidance was not available, measurement of works was delayed, and the operational areas of the junior engineer was too large. Other problems reported at the gram panchayat level were lack of proper maintenance of muster rolls and factions in the gram panchayats.

Source : *Hindustan Times,* March 30, 1994.

13.2 Employment

13.2.1 Process

Unemployment is a major socio-economic problem which must be tackled on a priority basis. At the outset of the Eighth Five Year Plan (1992-97), employment was estimated to be 301.7 million. The open unemployment was estimated at 17 million, of which the educated accounted for 7 million. Severe underemployment was estimated as 6 million. The backlog of unemployment for planning purposes was thus reckoned at 23 million in April 1992. As the net additions to labour force during the Eighth Five Year Plan and during the period 1997-2002 were estimated at 35 million and 36 million respectively, the task of reducing unemployment to negligible levels by 2002 implied that employment should grow at the average annual rate of about 2.6 to 2.8 per cent over the ten year period 1992-2002.

The Eighth Five Year Plan seeks to achieve 2.6 per cent rate of growth of employment corresponding to an average annual rate of growth of GDP of 5.6 per cent envisaged in the plan. This is sought to be achieved by laying emphasis on a crop-wise and geographic diversification of agricultural growth wasteland development promotion of agro-based activities rural non-farm activities including rural industries the decentralised and small scale sector of industry, the urban informal sector and the services sector, expansion of rural infrastructure, housing and health and educational services especially in rural areas revamping of the training system and streamlining of the special employment porogrammes to integrate them with area development plans. Additional employment opportunities of the order of 8 to 9 million per year, on an average, during the Eighth Plan period and of the order of 9 to 10 million per year, on an average, during the period 1997-2002 are expected to be generated.

It is estimated that 6 million additional employment opportunities were generated during 1992-93 showing an improvement over 1991-92 when only 3 million additional employment opportunities are estimated to have been created. However, this fell short of the average annual number of additional employment opportunities envisaged in the Plan and also of the estimated average annual net addition to labour force. Open unemployment may thus have increased by about a million during 1992-93.

The number of applicants on the live register of employment exchanges at the end of November 1993 was 362.52 lakh (provisional) as against 367.75 lakh at the end of November, 1992, i.e. a decrease of 1.4 per cent. The vacancies notified during April-November, 1993 were 2,66 lakh against 2.76 lakh during the same period in 1992. The placements effected during April-November, 1993 was 1.57 lakh as against 1.49 lakh during April-November, 1992. The educated job-seekers (Matriculation and above) constitute over 60 per cent of the registered. However, it may be conceded that employment exchange statistics do not provide a full coverage on the one hand, and include a substantial proportion of persons who might be actually employed or having multiple and advance registrations, on the other.

In view of the importance of tackling the unemployment problem, a Committee of the NDC was appointed in early 1991 to suggest ways and means of achieving the goal of near-full employment in a ten year period. The Committee submitted its report in September, 1992. The NDC endorsed the recommendations of the Committee at its meeting held on the 18th September 1993 and directed that the recommendations be implemented by the Central Ministries and State Governments and that this may be monitored by the Planning Commission.

NDC Committee on Employment

Major Recommendation

* Besides creation of additional productive employment opportunities, the strategy should focus on augmentation of existing employment in terms of productivity and incomes.
* The augmentation strategy is particularly useful in States where stimulation to agricultural growth, diversification of the economics and movement out of agriculture is needed. In States with higher agricultural productivity and more open unemployment strategies favouring faster expansion of secondary and tertiary activities would be desirable. More specific strategies are called for in areas with special problems.
* In the realm of sectoral strategies, thrust areas should be diversification of agriculture, irrigation, stimulation to rural non-agricultural employment, small scale industries and cottage industries, large scale programmes of construction faster growth of the services and the informal sector.
* Vast regional variations in work requirements and structure, needs of women, marginal farmers and labourers, etc. re-emphasise micro-planning.
* A three-pronged strategy for educated employment is needed comprising development of employment – intensive sectors; promotion of self-employment; and raising responsiveness of education and training to labour-market.
* A national wage policy may be evolved for removing irrational and inequitous disparities in wages and salary levels and to induce efficiency, and for bringing unorganised sector within its purview.
* Increased access of educated women to employment and training, creation of special cells/branches in banks to meet their credit needs and fixing for them a minimum coverage in self-employment.
* A major restructuring of on-going special programmes is needed. Significant part of rural development outlay may be utilised for building rural infrastructure. Redesigned and expanded programme of Integrated Development of Small & Medium Towns for generating wage employment in smaller towns may be taken up.

In order to achieve the employment goals of the Eighth Plan, over 9 million additional employment opportunities would have to be generated per year on an average during the period 1993-97. This is a stupendous task and underscores the significance of achieving a higher average annual growth rate of the economy than envisaged in the plan and vigorous pursuit of the employment strategies envisaged in different sectors in the Plan.

13.2.2 Studies in Unemployment

A study entitled Unemployment and the Financing of Relief Employment in a period of stabilisation in India 1992-94, conducted by Dr. Sudipto Mundle, Professor at the National Institute of Public Finance and Policy (NIPFP), has estimated that the number of persons 'openly unemployed' was around 18 to 22 million in 1992-93. The figure was expected to rise to 19 to 25 million in 1993-94.

It is based on two sets of assumptions–a high growth variant and low growth variant. This, however, is linked to what happens on the foreign trade front, total unemployment comprises open unemployment and "disguised" unemployment.

If the policies being pursued for switching expenditure from imports to domestic production are successful, alongwith the structural adjustment policies in steadily decreasing the current account deficit, the economy would proximate the high growth rate scenario, the study says.

Even under these favourable conditions, the unemployment rate will rise from less than three per cent in 1990-91 to around five per cent in 1993-94. This implies total open unemployment of about 18 million persons in 1992-93 and 19 miollion the year after.

After allowing the cost of administration, a total cost of Rs. 57.6 billion is required in order to extend some relief to 20 million unemployed persons in 1992-93. By 1993-94 this could go up to around Rs. 60 billion. Allowing for an additional two million unemployed and some upward revision of statutory minimum wages or administrative cost.

The Central Government is already spending about Rs. 28 billion or rural employment schemes. Therefore, the problem of financing relates only to an additional expenditure of around Rs. 30 billion in 1992-93, going up to about Rs. 33 billion in 1993-94. The corresponding levels of Central Government expenditure, consistent with the announced fiscal deficit targets, would be of the order of Rs. 1100 billion to Rs. 1200 billion in 1992-93 and Rs. 1200 billion to Rs. 1500 billion in 1993-94.

Though in absolute sums the money looks large, the financing of an enlarged relief programme is "really a problem of adjustment at the margin," accounting for only 2.5 per cent of total Central Government expenditure.

The items in this regard relate to reduction in interest payments, reduction in nonstatutory transfers to States, reduction in subsidies and reduced budgetary support to public undertakings.

The study has worked out the amounts that can be affected on each of these counts.

Source : *Hindustan Times,* June 8, 1993.

13.2.3 Educated Unemployed Persons

As educational avenues muitiply and organised sector witnesses a sharp downslide, two to nine million educated people would be looking for employment by the end of the Eighth Plan, according to different projections.

While the Planning Commission estimates are on the lower side – at about two million, the Institute of Applied Manpower Reseaıch (IAMR) estimates 8.72 million educated could still be waiting in the queue in 1997.

According to Dr. T.S. Papola, Advisor to the Planning Commission on labour, employment and manpower, there was a backlog of seven million educated unemployed in April 1992.

The Planning Commission's current estimates say that three million educated are added to the labour market every year, which means about 15 million will enter the labour market in 1992-97, taking the net demand to 22 million.

The Eighth Plan seeks to ensure 8.5 million jobs annually and "our past experience shows that 45 per cent of the jobs created go to the educated, which means four million jobs for the educated (out of 8.5 million) will be created every year to total about 20 million by 1997 as against the expected demand of 22 million".

Or, a backlog of just about two million in 1997.

It might not be possible to specify any dater for elimination of unemployment among the educated as the ideal scenario in terms of 5.6 per cent GDP growth and sectoral growth along the lines envisaged may not work.

Besides, supply of educated unemployed to the labour market may increase substantially from the current annual figure of three million with the expansion of educational facilities.

For example, in 1991-92, due to vartious factors, the GDP grew at 1.2 per cent only and the total employment grew at a mere three million, which was the lowest in past 8-10 years.

"While the overall employment growth has been around two percent per annum over the years, employment among the educated grew at 6.5 per cent to seven per cent."

However, the growth is offset by the fact that the educated labour force grew even faster–at eight per cent per annum.

IAMR projections, on the higher side, say that 8.72 million people will be in search of jobs by 1997.

According to a recent IAMR study–the status paper on educated umemployment in India–a backlog of six million educated unemployed was there in the beginning of 1992. And the addition to the labour force was expected to increase to 22.10 million by 1997 with the joining of 16.10 million in the next five years.

Painting a gloomy picture, the study authored by the joint chief of the HRD study unit of IAMR, Mr. N.K. Soni, and four other researchers, says that the labour market might fulfil the requirement of only 13.38 million of these, leaving 8.72 million groping in the dark.

While these varying projections may not make matters easy, one unmistakable trend is that the growth of employment among the educated labour force has been faster than the overall employment growth.

This is not surprising as the IAMR study says that enrolment for higher education increased from 1.7 lakh in 1950-51 to 39.5 lakh in 1988-89, registering 8.6 per cent annual growth rate.

And at the secondary stage in the corresponding period, it increased from 18 lakh to 185 lakh, growing at 6.32 per cent per annum, the study adds.

A steady decline of vocational education has also led to many educated not getting jobs.

The proportion of vocational education decreased almost by half in 30 years–from 13.78 per cent in 1950-51 to 7.48 per cent in 1988-89, says the study.

In higher education, 85 per cent enrolment in general subjects declined just fractionally to 81.5 per cent in 1988-89, and urban bias in terms of location of colleges was visible as more than 70 per cent colleges were in urban areas.

According to a working paper of the Planning Commission on past trends in employment and prospects for 1990s, the downslide in the rate of employment growth has been sharp, particularly in the organised sector.

Source : *Hindustan Times,* July 24, 1993.

13.2.4 Employment Elasticity

Against the analysis of negative employment elasticity, the Eighth Plan Paper's calculations to achieve full employment by 2000 seem to be ambitious, as it assumes that manufacturing in the small industry (10 per cent) will be much higher than the organised sector (5 per cent).

This is not going to be easy since in the first place, the difference in growth rates as between any two industries has never been so large. Secend, all indications suggest that following structural reforms, the organised industry is likely to grow at a relatively faster rate than in the past, consume a higher amount of capital and generate more employment.

The emphasis on non-household, tiny and micro enterprise for promotional policies will have to be the answer, but it will take a while before the series of physical handicaps, they are faced with, are got over.

However, if the eighth plan targets fail to materialise the scenario will be much more depressing.

Two disconcerting features are deceleration in the growth rate to around two per cent in 1983-88 in manufacturing employment and that the relatively favourable employment in the sector has mainly been the result of high growth in the unorganised sector. Within the organised sector, the employment elasticity with respect to output has been higher in respect of the small sector.

The future employment strategy must place emphasis on small and decentralised sectors of manufacturing as a major sources of industrial and employment growth.

Source : *Occasional Papers,* Reserve Bank of India, Bombay, quoted in *Economic Times,* October 26, 1993.

13.3 Employment and Poverty Alleviation

13.3.1 ILO Report

The ILO Report, prepared under a project sponsored by the United Nations Development Programme (UNDP) has cautioned the Government of India that if its economic restructuring programme has to acquire "a human face", a great deal of attention will have to be paid to employment generation and poverty alleviation during the adjustment period.

Pointing out that employment in the organised industrial sector will tend to stagnate in the medium term, the ILO has made out a strong case for incorporation of specific policies in the reform package to minimise the social costs of adjustment, even if growth remains sluggish for a while. These policies need not frustrate revival efforts.

The ILO has come out with the opinion that there is no need for India to modify its employment security regulations. Simultaneously, it has highlighted the need for an "intelligent and sensitive handling" of the problem of-restructuring sick industries in private and public sectors alike."

The existing employment security regulations are not responsible for the phenomenon of industrial sickness in India. Nor are they real obstacles to restructuring the sick units.

The real reasons for sickness, the report emphasises, lie in unsound financial structure of enterprises. In the case of public enterprises, the complicating factor has been "inappropriate labour recruitment practices" that have led to considerable overmanning. However, with the government already having the power to retrench labour or close down units, there is no need to change the law.

While dealing with the contentious issue of restructuring sick industries, the ILO feels this move has the portents to create "a new group of unemployed and poor." At the same time, it concedes that the problem of sick units cannot be wished away as these units, after all, constitute a drain on investible resources.

It has taken not of the establishment of the National Renewal Fund (NRF), which is intended to provide a social safety net for workers affected by industrial restructuring. However, since issues relating to the appropriate course of restructuring and deployment of NRF are still being debated, the ILO has said the problem will require "intelligent and sensitive handling."

The stabilisation measures, constituting the first phase of the economic reforms programme, have "induced industrial recession and have involved cuts in public expenditure on anti poverty programmes."

"There can be little doubt that the employment generation and poverty alleviation process, operative in the eighties, have been reversed in the course of stabilisation." Both the level of underemployment and the incidence of poverty have very probably increased since 1991 although this cannot be empirically confirmed."

While the first phase of stabilisation is over, the second phase of structural adjustment currently under way involves wide ranging reforms, affecting the basic structure and the growth path of the economy. The stabilisation phase, initiated in mid-1991 in the wake of the grave foreign exchange crisis, has principally involved restraining the growth of aggregate demand.

As regards the medium term effects of structural adjustment on employment and poverty, even if growth is revived in the immediate future, employment in the organised segment of the economy is likely to stagnate. Revival of growth itself will largely hinge on the degree of success in boosting exports and in attracting foreign direct investment.

"With no changes in policies towards the rural sector, the employment elasticity in agriculture is unlikely to be high and the dynamism in the rural non-agricultural sector observed in the eighties, will very probably be missing in the nineties, the report says and visualises a situation of increasing migration to cities and worsening urban informal employment conditions. "The incidence of poverty may well rise under these conditions."

By way of a possible strategy for the future, essentially from the standpoint of employment and poverty alleviation policies "whose effect do not depend on developments in the international economy" are necessary. Implementation of these policies "will involve restructuring of public expenditure, but this will be well within the Government's realm of control."

As for policies towards agriculture, the report has suggested a "shift of emphasis from subsidisation of inputs to public investment in irrigation." This will mean promoting agricultural growth outside the green revolution belt in North India. Concentration of public investment in Central and Eastern India, it opines, will have "the strongest effects on employment and poverty."

Source : *Hindustan Times,* April 4, 1993.

13.3.2 Special Employment and Anti-Poverty Programmes

A number of special employment programmes for encouraging self and wage employment are being implemented both in rural and urban areas. These include Integrated Rural Development Programme (IRDP). Training of Rural Youth for Self Employment (TRYSEM), Jawahar Rozgar Yojana (JRY), Nehru Rozgar Yojana (NRY), and the Scheme for Self-Employment for Educated Unemployed Youth (SEEUY). Special employment programmes are also being implemented by some of the State Government like the Employment Guarantee Scheme (EGS) in Maharashtra and the Self Employment Scheme for Registered Unemployed (SESRU) in West Bengal.

In the current year, to give a fillip to employment generation, the following two new programmes have been launched : (i) Employment Assurance Scheme (EAS), and (ii) Prime Minister's Rozgar Yojana (PMRY) for the Educated Unemployed Youth.

The EAS is being implemented in the 1752 backward blocks in which the Revamped Public Distribution System is in operation. The scheme aims at providing 100 days of unskilled manual work to the rural poor who are seeking employment. Its funding pattern is 80.20 by the Centre and the States respectively. It is targeted at the poor especially during the lean agricultural season in rural areas. The works undertaken are run departmentally and no contractors are hired. Part of the wages may be paid in terms of foodgrains.

The PMRY scheme for Educated Unemployed Youth has been designed to provide employment to more than one million persons by setting up seven lakh micro-enterprises during the Eighth Five Year Plan in industry, service and business. The scheme covers urban areas only during 1993-94, and would subsequently cover both the urban and rural areas. From 1994-95 onwards, the present Scheme for Self-Employment for Educated Unemployed Youth (SEEUY) will also be integrated into PMRY. The target for 1993-94 is to assist 40,000 beneficiaries, from 1994-95 to 1996-97, the annual target will be 2.2 lakh beneficiaries. Project up to Rs. 1 lakh are covered under the scheme in the case of individuals. If two or more eligible persons enter into a partnership, projects with higher cost can be assisted provided the share of each person in the project-cost does not exceed Rs. 1 lakh. An entrepreneur is required to contribute 5 per cent of the project-cost as margin-money in cash. Unemployed educated persons in the age group 18-35 are eligible for assistance subject to certain educational, income and other criteria. Preference is being given to those belonging to weaker sections and women. The scheme envisages 22.5 per cent reservation for Scheduled Castes/Scheduled Tribes and 27 per cent for other Backward Classes (OBCs). The loan does not require any collateral guarantee. The Government of India provides subsidy at the rate of 15 per cent of the project-cost subject to a ceiling of Rs. 7,500/- per entrepreneur. The scheme also envisages training for entrepreneurs after the loan is sanctioned.

Broad achievements of the special programmes are given in Table 13.3.

Bringing about qualitative improvements in the special programmes involving better targeting, judicious selection of assets cost-effectiveness, infrastructural support and integration with sectoral and area development plans has acquired added significance in the present-day context. It must be emphasised that the special employment programmes play only supplementary and short-term role, and the lasting solution to the problems of unemployment and poverty lies in faster generation of productive employment in the growth process. Slow employment growth in the past is partly due to the growth of capital intensive methods of production which was, to some extent, induced by the protective labour laws. Other factors responsible for slow growth of employment are mismatch between skill requirements and employment opportunity low productivity occupational shifts from artisans to unskilled labour and declining trend of labour absorption in.

TABLE 13.1: Percentage of Population living below the Poverty Line

Areas	1972-73	1977-78	1983-84	1987-88
1	2	3	4	5
Rural	54.1	51.2	40.4	33.4
Urban	41.2	38.2	28.1	20.1
Combined	51.5	48.3	37.4	29.9

Source : Planning Commission.

TABLE 13.2 : Percentage of Population Living Below the Poverty Line – Expert Group Estimates

Areas	1973-74	1977-78	1983-84	1987-88
1	2	3	4	5
Rural	56.4	53.1	45.6	39.1
Urban	49.2	47.4	42.2	40.1
Combined	54.9	51.8	44.8	39.3

Source : Planning Commission – Report of the Expert Group on Estimation of Proportion and Number of Poor, July 1993.

TABLE 13.3 : Achievement of Special Employment and Anti-Poverty Programmes

(in Lakh)

Programmes	1992-93 Target	1992-93 Achievement Oct. 1993	1993-94 Target	1993-94 Achievement
1	2	3	4	5
A. Programmes in Rural Areas				
1. IRDP–Families assisted	18.8	20.7	25.7	9.48
2. TRYSEM–Youths trained	3.0	2.8	3.5	0.74
3. DWCRA–				
(a) Group formed	0.075	0.090	0.10	0.04
(b) Membership	–	1.3	–	1.01
4. JRY–Mandays of employment generated	7538	7821	10805	3093*
B. Programmes in Urban Areas				
1. Nehru Rozgar Yojana (NRY)				
(a) Scheme of Urban Micro Enterprises. (SUME)–Families Assisted	0.92	1.20	1.23	0.65
(b) Scheme of Urban Wage Employment (SUWE)/ Scheme of Housing and Shelter Upgradation (SHASU) Employment generated	158.20	133.89	143.00	52.99
(c) Persons trained under SUME and SHASU	0.48	0.32	0.58	0.18
C. Urban and Rural Areas				
1. Scheme for Self Employment for Educated Unemployed youth (SEEUY)	1.0	0.72	1.26	N.A.

* Up to September, 1993. N.A. Not available.

Sources: (i) Ministeries of industry Rural and Urban Development.

(ii) *Economic Survey, 1993-94* Ministry of Finance, Government of India, New Delhi, 1994.

14

INFLATION AND PRICES

The annual inflation rate (as measured by the Wholesale Price Index (WPI) which entered double digits in November, 1990 (10.5 per cent) kept rising sharply to reach a peak of 16.3 per cent in September 1991. It declined to single digit level by August 1992 (Table 1). Thereafter, the WPI fell continuously (barring temporary interruption in October 1992) to reach 7.1 per cent in March 1993. This level was maintained till the end of June. The trend was reversed in August with an inflation rate of 8 per cent led mainly by the spurt in primary product prices. Based on the final index this had reached 8.8 per cent by September 1993. Since then there has again been some slight moderation and the provisional inflation rate by January 15, 1994 was 8.4 per cent and by January 29, 1994 it came down to 8.2 per cent.

Inflation in terms of the Consumer Price Index for Industrial Workers CPI (IW) moved almost in tandem with the wholesale price index (WPI) during the past 3 years (Table 14.1). The rate of inflation based on CPI (IW) decelerated from a peak of 16.1 per cent in January 1991 to 8.4 per cent in November 1992, and thereafter fell sleeply to 6.1 per cent by March 1993. Its continued decline to a low of 4.5 per cent in July 1993 reflected mainly the fall in prices of primary commodities which have a relatively higher weight in CPI than in WPI. With the sharp increase in primary product prices from August 1993 and the rise in the WPI, the CPI(IW) growth has also risen to 8.6 per cent in December 1993. Movements in the Consumer Price Index for urban non-manual employees, CPI(UNME), have been similar to the CPI(IW).

Agricultural labourers had faced the highest inflation till October 1992, as per the consumer price index for them. They have also gained the most from the control of inflation. From December 1992, the rise in CPI(AL) has been much less than in the other two CPI series (Table 4.1). Between April to August 1993 the growth rate of CPI (AL) became negative, reflecting a fall in prices of coarse grains and edible oils.

The differences in inflation as measured by the different price indices are due to differences in the commodity basket composition and weighting diagrams. The WPI has the most comprehensive coverage of commodities ranging from consumer goods, consumer durables, basic raw materials, intermediate and capital goods. The coverage of food articles and products is much more comprehensive and their weights are higher in the CPI(IW) and CPI(AL).

The wholesale price index (WPI) for all commodities reached 250.7 (provisional) on January 15, 1994, as against 233.1 at the end of March 1993. This represents an increase of 7.6 per cent in the general price level so far in this fiscal year. The magnitude of change by groups and sub-groups, the detailed data for which is available till January 15, 1994 is shown in Table 14.2

Primary Articles and Inflation

Primary commodities accounted for a higher annual inflation rate this year as their prices rose 8.1 per cent compared to a rise of 2.5 per cent last year. Within the primary group of commodities, foodgrains recorded a higher rise of 11.6 per cent on annual point-to-point basis compared to a decline of 2.1 per cent last year. This is rather surprising given the good harvest. Much of this increase was on account of 8.1 per cent rise in wheat price and 6.9 per cent rise in price of rice. An upward revision of issue prices under PDS for wheat (from Rs. 280 to Rs. 330 per quintal) and for rice (from Rs. 377 to Rs. 437 per quintal) in January 1993 and the higher minimum support price (MSP) payable to farmers for wheat and rice were apparently the main factors for this uptrend. Thus, administered prices operating under Public Distribution System (PDS) and the MSP (or procurement price) provided a floor below which foodgrain prices could not have fallen even though improved production and supply situation warranted a price fall. Vegetable prices rose by 39.1 per cent over last year, with onion prices rising by 134.7 per cent by January 15 over same date last year. Price of tea was up by about 7.5 per cent and coffee by about 28.3 per cent over last year. Eggs, fish and meat was up by 9.8 per cent but condiments and spices were down by about 24 per cent. Fruit prices also showed a decline of 12 per cent over last year.

The annual inflation in non-food articles component of the primary groups was 14 per cent this year, compared to a fall of 4.6 per cent last year. Very high rise was seen in raw jute (120.8 per cent), raw cotton (41 per cent), rape and mustard seed (16.7 per cent) and sugarcane (11.7 per cent). Even though the revision in the petroleum product prices was reflected in the index in September 1992, changes in crude oil prices were not fully reflected in the index of petroleum prices last year.

Primary Articles and Inflation : This group accounted for 40.4 per cent of the increase in the general price level since April 1993 compared to only 23.4 per cent for the same period last year. Share of foodgrains in total price rise since April 1993 was 14 per cent this year as against a drop of 1 per cent last year. Non-food articles (which include sugarcane, oilseeds and fibres) contributed 22.1 per cent to inflation in financial year 1993-94. One can therefore, conclude, that relatively higher rise in foodgrains as also in non-food articles (oilseeds and fibres) this year was the main reason for the sharp rise in primary articles.

The contribution of primary articles to the annual point-to-point inflation rate (8.4 per cent as on January 15, 1994) was, 31.6 per cent compared to 11.7 per cent compared to last year. Contribution of foodgrains was about 11.4 per cent to total inflation as against a decline of 2.6 per cent last year. Non-food articles contributed 16.8 per cent to this year's annual inflation rate thus providing the main thrust for the primary articles to rise this year, though the magnitude of rise was more pronounced during the financial year.

Coal prices are still administered and this year (1993) the price revision raised the WPI of coal by about 18 per cent. There was a major hike in electricity rates by most of the SEBs' pushing up the index of electricity prices by about 38 per cent. Hence the fuel group registered an annual inflation rate of 13.9 per cent.

Manufactured products : Manufactured products was the only major sub group which registered a lower inflation rate of 7.5 per cent as on January 15, 1994 as against 9.5 per cent last year. The increase may have been even lower except for the unprecedented 29.7 per cent price rise in sugar, khandsari and gur. Even though price of groundnut oil rose by over 11 per cent, other oils were steady or declined and hence average price of edible oils group was only slightly higher (0.4 per cent) compared to 8.4 per cent decline last year. Textiles registered over 11 per cent increase and leather products were up by 9.4 per cent. There was decline in price of non-ferrous metals but iron and steel prices were up by 9 per cent. Prices of machinery and machine tools showed an increase of 1 per cent. Transport equipment and parts rose by a modest 2.3 per cent. Overall, the rise in manufactured goods prices was rather modest at 7.5 per cent. Thus the uptrend seen in the annual inflation rate since August this year was driven mainly by the rise in primary product prices.

Manufactured products : This group contributed 46.7 per cent to inflation since April as against 60 per cent last year. On annual basis, manufactured products accounted for half the rise (50.3 per cent) in this year's general price level compared to 71.8 per cent in 1992-93.

Fuel, Power, Light and Lubricants : This group contributed 13.1 per cent to inflation since April compared to 16.9 per cent in the corresponding period last year. Much of this year's increase was due to increase in electricity prices effected by most of the SEBs'. The price index for electricity is up by a step 37.5 per cent over January last year, and 26.3 per cent since April 1993.

Essential Commodities : The group of 30 essential commodities which have a weight of 21.77 per cent in WPI accounted for 31.8 per cent of total inflation since April 1993 as against only 16.6 per cent for the same period last year. Last year, primary articles including most of the foodgrains had shown an absolute decline in prices but this year, the prices of almost all essential commodities rose except jowar, chillies, coconut oil and laundry soap. Comparable CPI (IW) and WPI based price indices for 30 essential commodities show that annual rate of inflation in essential commodities (November 1993 over November) 1992) was higher this year (13.2 per cent) based on WPI compared to 5.7 per cent last year. Retail prices (CPI), however, registered 9.7 per cent inflation this year, compared to 5.3 per cent in 1992. Since April, 1993, however, both retail (CPI) and wholesale prices (WPI) for the 30 essential commodities were higher this fiscal year compared to last year.

TABLE 14.1 : Annual Rates of Inflation in WPI and CPI

(per cent)

Year/Month		Base	WPI 1981-82	CPI (IW) 1982	CPI (UNME) 1984-85	CPI (AL) 1960-61
1			2	3	4	5
1990-91	April		9.1	7.8	8.6	3.2
	May		8.7	7.7	9.3	3.3
	June		9.5	8.8	9.2	3.1
	July		9.6	9.9	9.7	4.6
	August		8.1	9.2	8.9	4.6
	September		7.5	8.5	8.2	2.6
	October		8.9	10.8	9.5	3.5
	November		10.5	12.5	11.6	8.4
	December		12.0	13.7	13.0	10.0
	January		12.9	16.1	15.0	13.9
	February		13.5	15.4	15.0	17.3
	March		12.7	13.6	13.4	16.6
1991-92	April		11.6	12.2	12.6	14.7
	May		11.8	12.1	11.8	13.7
	June		12.2	13.0	12.3	15.4
	July		13.1	13.2	13.3	15.9
	August		16.1	14.2	15.1	18.3
	September		16.3	15.7	15.7	23.1
	October		14.7	14.4	14.2	23.1
	November		14.7	13.6	14.0	21.2
	December		14.3	13.1	13.3	21.7
	January		13.6	12.9	12.4	20.4
	February		12.9	13.4	13.0	20.6
	March		13.6	13.9	13.6	21.9
1992-93	April		13.8	14.4	13.5	22.6
	May		13.8	14.7	14.0	23.9
	June		13.0	12.9	13.2	21.9
	July		11.7	13.1	12.8	20.6
	August		9.4	11.5	10.9	19.0
	September		9.6	10.0	10.9	14.1
	October		10.6	9.4	10.8	11.0
	November		9.1	8.4	9.6	8.6
	December		8.5	8.0	9.6	5.9
	January		7.6	5.7	7.3	1.9
	February		7.6	5.7	7.9	5.0
	March		7.1	6.1	6.8	0.7

(Contd.)

TABLE 14.1 (*Contd.*)

1993-94	April	6.9	6.1	6.7	-0.7
	May	6.9	5.1	6.2	-1.9
	June	7.0	5.9	6.6	-1.0
	July	7.3	4.5	5.4	-2.0
	August	8.0	5.8	5.9	-2.3
	September	8.8	6.6	6.4	0.1
	October	8.5	7.4	6.3	3.2
	November	8.6	8.6	7.3	6.5
	December	8.3*	8.6		
	January	8.2*			

*Provisional

TABLE 14.2 : Price Movements in Major Groups as on Jan. 15, 1994

(per cent)

	Weight	Financial Year		Annual (pt-to-pt)	
Group/subgroup	(%)	1993-94	1992-93	1993-94	1992-93]
1	2	3	4	5	6
All Commodities	**100.00**	**7.6**	**6.2**	**8.4**	**7.3**
(i) Primary articles	**32.30**	**9.5**	**4.3**	**8.1**	**2.5**
Food articles	17.39	5.0	6.3	4.1	6.5
Foodgrains	7.92	13.1	-0.6	11.6	-2.1
Rice	3.69	8.4	1.2	6.9	3.5
Wheat	2.25	9.3	3.8	8.1	-6.7
Fruit & Vegetables	4.09	-4.2	3.8	1.2	9.5
Non-food articles	10.08	17.2	1.4	14.0	-4.6
(ii) Fuel, Power, etc.	**10.66**	**8.8**	**10.0**	**13.9**	**12.1**
(iii) Manufactured products	**57.04**	**6.2**	**6.6**	**7.5**	**9.5**
Food products	10.14	10.2	5.8	11.2	5.3
Sugar	2.01	11.5	3.5	22.6	12.0
Edible oils	2.45	6.7	-1.2	0.4	-8.4

Source : *Economic Survey 1993-94,* Ministry of Finance, Government of India, New Delhi, 1994, Chapter 4.

15

FISCAL POLICY, BUDGET AND UNION FINANCES

15.1 FISCAL POLICY AND BUDGET, 1994-95

The results of the fiscal adjustment undertaken in 1991-92 and 1993-93 which were just beginning to emerge at the time of the reporting in the last year's Economic Survey, are now clearly visible. It is therefore, an appropriate time to review the experience of the past in the light of our recent success, and to lay out a clear direction for the future. Under this programme the Central fiscal deficit came down by about 3.2 per cent of GDP over a period of 21 months (RE). The primary deficit which excludes interest payments declined by about 3.8 per cent of GDP (Table 15.1). This is a better measure of the adjustment effort made by the Government, as it excludes the inescapable liability due to the past debt. This reduction represents a significant achievement, and compares well with efforts made in this respect world-wide.

Gross and Net Primary Deficit

- Macro-economic stability is measured in terms of the behaviour of key macro variables such as fiscal deficit, balance of payments and inflation. These are closely linked, with the fiscal deficit now commonly recognised to be the key driving force. A stable fiscal deficit is defined in terms of the ratio of Public Debt to GDP. Stability means that other things remaining the same, Debt-GDP ratio declines over time.
- Fiscal stability depends, *inter alia,* on the primary deficit, appropriately defined.
- Fiscal deficit is equal to revenue receipts minus expenditure. Excess of expenditure is met by borrowing (gross), thus adding to debt. Governments, besides borrowing to finance this shortfall, also lend to others which earns interest and would be rapid in future. The issue here is whether 'net lending' that is the flow of such lending minus related loan repayments should be treated as outflows and be added to normal expenditures. The other possibility is to treat them as a financing item, and substract them from (gross) borrowing.
- The net fiscal deficit is defined as a change in net liabilities and is calculated by subtracting net lendings, from (gross) public borrowings. The corresponding Primary deficit can be obtained by substracting net interest payments from net fiscal deficit. The gross fiscal deficit is defined as a change

in gross liabilities, i.e. taking only the borrowing side into account. It is calculated by subtracting revenues from "Expenditure plus net lending". The corresponding primary deficit is obtained by subtracting gross interest payments from gross fiscal deficit.

* The definition on 'Net' basis is the one directly related to the concept of stability. These concepts have, however been developed for the total public sector consisting of Centre, States and PSUs. Table 15.1 shows the deficit of the Centre which is a sub-set of the total public sector. Most of the lending is made to the States and PSUs. In this situation, deficits on 'gross' basis may be a more accurate reflection of the total public sector deficit.
* A third method, which may be called 'Hybrid', calculates the primary deficit by subtracting 'net' interest payments from 'gross' fiscal deficit. This method appears to be neither logically consistent nor related to the concept of fiscal stability.

A rapid adjustment of this magnitude was essential for achieving quick control over the balance of payments deficit and over inflation. The success of this policy has been amply demonstrated by: (a) the fall in the current account deficit from 3.3 per cent of GDP in 1990-91 to 2.1 per cent in 1992-93 and; (b) the fall in inflation from a peak annual (point to point) rate of over 16 per cent in August-September, 1991 to less than 7 per cent in April-May, 1993. Such a rapid pace of decline in the fiscal deficit cannot be maintained indefinitely, and was bound to slow down. One of the factors in the reduction of fiscal deficit was the increase in revenues Tax revenues have increased only gradually (Table 15.2). The second factor in the decline of the fiscal deficit was non-interest expenditure. This declined by 2.2 per cent of GDP over the adjustment period as per revised estimates (Table 15.3).

Savings and Capital Formation. Gross savings of the Central Government have increased by 1.2 per cent of GDP over the two years of macro economic adjustment.

Government Debt and Interest Payments. Increasing resort to borrowing over the years has led to a continuous growth in the total outstanding debt of the centre. Internal liabilities registered a sharp increase in the 1980's from 35.6 per cent of GDP in 1980-81 to 53.2 per cent of GDP in 1990-91 (Table 15.4 reflects the present position in relation to previous years).

The increasing fiscal deficit and consequent borrowing from the domestic private sector was associated with higher average interest rates. The average rate of interest on internal liabilities rose from 7.1 per cent in 1986-87 to 8.2 per cent in 1990-91 (Table 15.5) and further to 9.1 per cent in 1992-93 (RE) because of the continued replacement of old lower-interest debt by new higher-interest debt. Another noteworthy feature is the reduction of the difference between the interest rate on market borrowings and other internal liabilities (small savings, provident funds, etc.).

Budget Deficit

The budget deficit was to be reduced from Rs. 7202 crore in 1992-93 (RE) to Rs. 4314 crore in 1993-94 (BE). Except for the first two weeks of April 1993, the deficit has been higher than the deficit prevailing during the corresponding weeks of the last two years. There has, however, been a steep decline in the budget deficit from the week ending October 15, 1993: Budget deficit for the week ending December 31, 1993 was lower than the deficit prevailing on this date during the last year. However, the budget deficit increased during the next two weeks and was marginally higher for the week ending January 14, 1994 than the deficit prevailing on this date during the last year. The fiscal deficit has also been higher. It was Rs. 19694 crore at the end of June 1993, which is 62 per cent higher than the corresponding level last year. The fiscal deficit rose still further to Rs. 28978 crore at the end of August 1993.

Revenue and Expenditure : The aggregate resources of the Centre (including PSUs) in 1993-94 (BE) are 13.1 per cent higher than those in 1992-93. While tax revenue is estimated to grow by 7.8 per cent non-tax revenue is estimated to increase by 25.2 per cent. Internal resources of PSUs which increased by 35.2 per cent in 1992-93 (RE) are estimated to increase further by 42.8 per cent in 1993-94. Aggregate disbursements are estimated (BE) to grow at a slower rate (10. 8 per cent) than the resources (13.1 per cent). The pattern of disbursement was also budgeted to change; the rate of growth of developmental expenditure was to increase from 14.2 per cent in 1992-93 (RE) to 19.3 per cent in 1993-94 (BE). Non-developmental expenditure was estimated to increase by only 1.1 per cent against 27.0 per cent in 1992-93 (RE). The overall gap in the resources of the Centre and its PSUs is estimated at Rs.67657 crore.

Fiscal Resources : The next effect of various fiscal measures in 1993-94 Budget was an estimated loss of Rs. 4522 crore; Rs. 3273 crore on account of customs and Rs. 1249 crore on account of reduction in excise duties. The net loss to the Centre after reducing the share of States by Rs. 541 crore came to Rs. 3981 crore. The Railway Budget for 1993-94 proposed increase in charges adding up to Rs. 1848 crore. Thus, the net loss of revenue to the Centre was Rs. 2133 crore.

As per the Economic and Functional Classification of the Central Budget, gross dissavings are to be reduced further from Rs. 5515 crore during 1992-93 (RE) to Rs. 2848 crore in 1993-94 (BE). The gross dissaving were, therefore, budgeted to improve by 0.4 per cent of GDP (Table 16.4). The rate of growth of gross capital formation was estimated to increase from 10.4 per cent in 1992-93 (RE) to 13.4 per cent in 1993-94 (BE). This would raise the share of gross capital formation in total expenditure to 31.9 per cent from 30.4 per cent in 1992-93(RE). The share of expenditure on physical assets in total expenditure is expected to increase from 9.3 per cent in 1992-93 (RE) to 10.7 per cent in 1993-94 (BE). The share of expenditure on financial assets (21.2 per cent) is also marginally higher (21.1 per cent) than in 1992-93 (Table 15.3).

Centre, States and Union Territories : 1993-94

The budget deficit of the Centre, States and Union Territories in 1993-94 (BE) is placed at Rs. 6271 crore, 23.1 per cent lower than in 1992-93 (RE). Aggregate receipts including borrowing are budgeted to increase by 11.4 per cent to Rs. 252206 crore while aggregate expenditure is estimated to increase by 10.2 per cent to Rs. 258477 crore development expenditure is projected to rise by

14.6 per cent and non-development expenditure by 4.2 per cent. The current revenue is estimated to increase by13.2 per cent to Rs. 178958 crore. The gap between current revenue and disbursement which denotes the total gap in the resources of the States and the Centre, is estimated at Rs. 79519 crore, or 10.0 per cent of GDP.

Annual Plan

The Annual Plan for 1993-94 provides for a total out-lay of Rs. 100120 crore for the Centre, States and Union Territories. This is 29.8 per cent higher than in 1992-93 (RE) (Table 15.6). Of this, the allocation for the Central Plan at Rs. 63936 crore in 28.6 per cent above 1992-93 (RE). The allocation for States and Union Territories is 36.1 per cent of the total outlay (Rs. 36184 crore). With a view to minimise the burden of adjustment on the poor, greater emphasis has been placed on social services. Central Plan outlay (BE) for the Department of Rural Development has been increased by 39.2 per cent over 1992-93 (RE). The outlay for education has been increased by 29.5 per cent and that for family welfare by 22 per cent over the previous year.

The Plan outlay of the Central Public Sector Enterprises (CPSEs) for 1993-94 Annual Plan amounts to Rs.47235 crore or 73.9 per cent of the Central Plan outlay of Rs.63936 crore (excluding UTs.) The proportion of budget support in the Plan outlay of the CPSEs during 1993-94 works out to 13.8 per cent as against 36.4 per cent in respect of the overall Central Plan. The contribution of internal resources to the financing of the Plan of the CPSEs during 1993-94 is estimated to be 40.4 per cent, while the extra-budgetary resources, comprising bonds/debentures, external commercial borrowing/suppliers credits and others (inter-corporate transfers, deposits rised by companies, etc.) account for 45.8 per cent of their Plan outlay. Though in 1992-93, the CPSEs could mobilise only around 20 per cent of the estimated amount through bonds due to adverse capital market conditions, they are expected to perform better during 1993-94.

In the pattern of financing of the Annual Plan 1993-94 it is envisaged that domestic resources would finance 81.9 per cent of the outlay and that net inflow from abroad would contribute another 12.1 per cent. The remaining 6.0 per cent is estimated to be met by the budget deficit. The contribution of the balance from current revenue is estimated to be Rs. 3823 crore.

TABLE 15.1 : Central Government Deficit
(per cent of GDP at current market prices)

	Budget Deficit	Revenue Deficit	Monetised Deficit	Gross Fiscal Deficit	Gross Primary Deficit
1	2	3	4	5	6
1975-76	0.5	1.1	0.0	4.1	2.5
1980-81	1.8	1.5	2.6	6.2	4.3
1981-82	0.9	0.2	2.0	5.4	3.4
1982-83	0.9	0.7	1.9	6.0	3.8

(Contd.)

1	2	3	4	5	6
1983-84	0.7	1.2	1.9	6.3	4.0
1984-85	1.6	1.8	2.6	7.5	5.0
Average Sixth Plan	1.2	1.1	2.2	6.3	4.1
1985-86	2.0	2.2	2.4	8.3	5.5
1986-87	2.8	2.7	2.4	9.0	5.8
1987-88	1.7	2.7	2.0	8.1	4.7
1988-89	1.4	2.7	1.6	7.8	4.2
1989-90	2.3	2.6	3.0	7.8	3.9
Average Seventh Plan	2.1	2.6	2.3	8.2	4.8
1990-91	2.1	3.5	2.8	8.4	4.4
1991-92	1.1	2.6	0.9	5.9	1.6
1992-93 (RE)	1.0	2.4	0.8	5.2	0.6

Note : The 'budget deficit' is the difference between all receipts and expenditure, both revenue and capital. The 'revenue' deficit denotes the difference between revenue receipts and revenue expenditure. The 'monetised' deficit is the increase in net RBI credit to the Central Government comprising of the net increase in the holdings of Treasury Bills of the RBI and its contribution to the market borrowings of the Government. The 'fiscal deficit' is the excess of total expenditure over revenue receipts and grants. The 'primary deficit' is the fiscal deficit less interest payments.

TABLE 15.2 : Centre's Revenue Receipts and Revenue Expenditure (As per cent of GDP)

	1980-81	1988-89	1989-90	1990-91	1991-92	1992-93 (RE)	1993-94 (RE)
1	2	3	4	5	6	7	8
1. Tax revenue (Net of States' share)	6.9	8.5	8.4	8.1	8.1	8.3	8.4
2. Non-tax revenue	2.5	2.8	3.4	2.6	2.9	3.3	3.1
3. Total current revenue(1+2)	9.4	11.4	11.8	10.7	11.1	11.5	11.5
4. Total current expenditure	10.9	14.0	14.4	14.2	13.7	13.9	13.7
(a) Interest payments	1.9	3.6	3.9	4.0	4.3	4.6	4.8
(b) Subsidies	1.2	2.0	2.4	2.0	1.7	1.4	1.0
(c) Defence expenditure	2.4	2.4	2.1	2.0	1.9	1.8	1.7
(d) Grants to States & UTs	2.1	2.5	1.9	2.5	2.6	2.6	2.5
(e) Others	3.4	3.5	4.1	3.6	3.3	3.5	3.8
5. Revenue Account Surplus (+)/deficit (-)[3-4]	-1.5	-2.7	-2.6	-3.5	-2.6	-2.4	-2.2

Note : The figures may not add up to the total because of rounding off.

TABLE 15.3 : Economic Classification of Total Expenditure of Central Government

(Rs. in Crore)

	1980-81	1988-89	1989-90	1990-91	1991-92	1992-93 (RE)	1993-94 (BE)
1	2	3	4	5	6	7	8
1. Consumption expenditure	5174	18763	20784	22359	24466	27218	29936
(a) Defence	3571	13237	14298	15319	16251	17384	19057
(b) Other Government administration	1603	5526	6486	7040	8215	9834	10879
2. Transfer payments (current)	6912	31399	37877	45134	51378	59072	62358
(a) Interest payments	2253	13347	16525	19949	24955	30278	35903
(b) Subsidies	1912	7859	10862	10728	10326	10188	7731
(c) Grants to States & UTs (including local bodies)	1810	5831	5725	7664	8797	10058	10121
(d) Others	937	4362	4765	6793	7300	8548	8603
3. Gross capital formation out of budgetary resources	9012	28977	33012	35058	35165	38820	44016
(a) Physical assets	1907	7056	8136	8602	9259	11916	14773
(b) Financial assets	7105	21921	24876	26456	25906	26904	29243
4. Others	1397	2263	3376	2422	1722	2643	1718
5. Total expenditure	22495	81402	95049	104973	112731	127753	138028
As per cent of GDP		**(per cent)**					
1. Consumption expenditure	3.8	4.7	4.5	4.2	4.0	3.9	3.8
(a) Defence	2.6	3.3	3.1	2.9	2.6	2.5	2.4
(b) Other Government administration	1.2	1.4	1.4	1.3	1.3	1.4	1.4
2. Transfer payments (Current)	5.1	7.9	8.3	8.5	8.3	8.4	7.8
(a) Interest payments	1.7	3.4	3.6	3.7	4.1	4.3	4.5
(b) Subsidies	1.4	2.0	2.4	2.0	1.7	1.4	1.0
(c) Grants to States & UTs (including local bodies)	1.3	1.5	1.3	1.4	1.4	1.4	1.3
(d) Others	0.7	1.1	1.0	1.3	1.2	1.2	1.1
3. Gross capital formation out of budgetary resources	6.6	7.3	7.2	6.6	5.7	5.5	5.5
(a) Physical assets	1.4	1.8	1.8	1.6	1.5	1.7	1.9
(b) Financial assets	5.2	5.5	5.4	5.0	4.2	3.8	3.7
4. Others	1.0	0.6	0.7	0.5	0.3	0.4	0.2
5. Total expenditure	16.5	20.6	20.8	19.7	18.3	18.1	17.3
As per cent of total expenditure				**(per cent)**			
1. Consumption expenditure	23.0	23.0	21.9	21.3	21.7	21.3	21.7
(a) Defence	15.9	16.3	15.0	14.6	14.4	13.6	13.8
(b) Other Government administration	7.1	6.8	6.8	6.7	7.3	7.7	7.9

(Contd.)

TABLE 15.3 *(Contd.)*

1	2	3	4	5	6	7	8
2. Transfer payments (Current)	30.7	38.6	39.8	43.0	45.6	46.2	45.2
(a) Interest payments	10.0	16.4	17.4	19.0	22.1	23.7	26.0
(b) Subsidies	8.5	9.7	11.4	10.2	9.2	8.0	5.6
(c) Grants to States & UTs (including local bodies)	8.0	7.2	6.0	7.3	7.8	7.9	7.3
(d) Others	4.2	5.4	5.0	6.5	6.5	6.7	6.2
3. Gross capital formation out of budgetary resources	40.1	35.6	34.7	33.4	31.2	30.4	31.9
(a) Physical assets	8.5	8.7	8.6	8.2	8.2	9.3	10.7
(b) Financial assets	31.6	26.9	26.2	25.2	23.0	21.1	21.2
4. Others	6.2	2.8	3.6	2.3	1.5	2.1	1.2

TABLE 15.4 : Outstanding Liabilities of the Central Government

(Rs. Crore)

	1980-81	1988-89	1989-90	1990-91	1991-92	1992-93 (RE)	1993-94 (RE)
1	2	3	4	5	6	7	8
1. Internal liabilities	48451	204025	239849	283033	317714	355264	393988
(a) Internal Debt	30864	114498	133193	154004	172750	193035	208671
(b) Market borrowings	15676	55161	62565	70565	78075	81745	85445
(b) Others	15188	59337	70628	83439	94675	111290	123226
(b) Other Internal liabilities	17587	89527	106656	129029	144964	162229	185317
2. External debt (outstanding)*	11298	25746	28343	31525	36948	41218	46452
3. Total outstanding liabilities (1+2)	59749	229771	268192	314558	354662	396482	440440
4. Amount due from Pakistan on account of share of pre-partition debt	300	300	300	300	300	300	300
5. Net liabilities (3-4)	59449	229471	267892	314258	354362	396182	440140
6. Total assets	58999	184303	209623	236740	261478	288465	314795
7. Excess of liabilities over assets (5-6)	450	45168	58269	77518	92884	107717	125345
As per cent of GDP at current prices				**(per cent)**			
1. Internal liabilities	35.6	51.6	52.5	53.2	51.6	50.4	49.5
(a) Internal Debt	22.7	28.9	29.2	28.9	28 1	27.4	26.2
(b) Other Internal liabilities	12.9	22.6	23.3	24.3	23.5	23.0	23.3
2. External debt (outstanding)*	8.3	6.5	6.2	5.9	6.0	5.8	5.8

(Contd.)

TABLE 15.4 *(Contd.)*

1	2	3	4	5	6	7	8
3. Total outstanding liabilties	43.9	58.1	58.7	59.1	57.6	56.2	55.3
6. Total assets	43.4	46.6	45.9	44.5	42.5	40.0	39.6
7. Excess of liabilities over assets (5-6)	0.3	11.4	12.8	14.6	15.1	15.3	15.7
Memorandum items							
External Debt (Rs. crore) @	13479	46839	54158	65208	109746	121149	123860
(as per cent of GDP)	9.9	11.8	11.9	12.3	17.8	17.2	15.6
Total outstanding liabilities	61930	250864	294007	348241	427460	476413	517848
(as per cent of GDP)	45.5	63.4	64.4	65.5	69.4	67.5	65.1

* External debt figures represented borrowings by Central Government from external resources and are based upon historical rates of exchange.

@ Converted at current year end exchange rates. For 1980-81 the rates prevailing at the end of March, 1981. For 1986-87, the rates prevailing at the end of March, 1987 and so on. However, for 1993-94 the rates pertain to end-september, 1993.

TABLE 15.5 : Interest on the Outstanding liabilities of Central Government

(Rs. Crore)

	1980-81	1988-89	1989-90	1990-91	1991-92	1992-93 (RE)	1993-94 (RE)
1	2	3	4	5	6	7	8
1. Interest on internal liabilities	2373	13036	16241	19637	23892	28878	34054
(a) Internal Debt	1369	6913	8273	9814	11317	13602	15423
(i) Market borrowings	808	4506	5368	6366	7355	7950	8680
(ii) Others	561	2407	2905	3448	3962	5652	6743
(b) Other internal liabilities	1004	6123	7968	9823	12575	15276	18631
2. Interest on external debt	231	1242	1494	1834	2704	3622	3946
3. Gross interest payments	2604	14278	17735	21471	26596	32500	38000
4. Net interest payments	809	7297	9269	12687	15674	20064	23468
Average rate of interest		**(per cent)**					
1. Internal liabilities	N.A.	7.6	8.0	8.2	8.4	9.1	9.6
(a) Internal debt	N.A.	7.0	7.2	7.4	7.3	7.9	8.0
(i) Market borrowings	N.A.	9.6	9.7	10.2	10.4	10.2	10.6
(ii) Others	N.A.	4.6	4.9	4.9	4.7	6.0	6.1

(Contd.)

1	2	3	4	5	6	7	8
(b) Other Internal liabilities	N.A.	8.3	8.9	9.2	9.7	10.5	11.5
2. External debt	N.A.	5.3	5.8	6.5	8.6	9.8	9.6
3. Total liabilities	N.A.	7.3	7.7	8.0	8.5	9.2	9.6

N.A. Not Available

Note : The interest liabilities indicated above are on cash basis and not on accrual basis.

TABLE 15.6 : Annual Plan Outlay : Centre, States and Union Territories

Heads of Development	1992-93 (RE)	1993-94 (BE)	1992-93 (RE)	1993-94 (BE)
1	2	3	4	5
	(Rs. crore)		**(Per cent)**	
1. Agriculture and Allied Activities	4373	5409	5.7	5.4
2. Rural Development	5010	6187	6.5	6.2
3. Special Area Programme	1154	1406	1.5	1.4
4. Irrigation and Flood Control	4419	5854	5.7	5.8
5. Energy	23412	30920	30.4	30.9
6. Industry and Minerals	9271	11363	12.0	11.3
7. Transport	10515	13947	13.6	13.9
8. Communications	4968	6248	6.4	6.2
9. Science, Technology and Environment	956	1317	1.2	1.3
10. General Economic Services	827	1501	1.1	1.5
11. Social services	11938	15430	15.5	15.4
12. General Services	284	538	0.4	0.5
Total	77127	100120	100.0	100.0

Source : *Economic Survey, 1993-94*, Ministry of Finance, Government of India, New Delhi, 1994, Chapter 2.

15.2 REKHI COMMITTEE ON INDIRECT TAXES, 1993

The Committee headed by Shri K.L. Rekhi submitted its report to the Finance Minister Manmohan Singh on May 24, 1993. The Committee recommended that the government should move to the system of valuation on the basis of invoice price of transactions value provided it is fair and genuine.

The Committee observed that tariff value may be fixed for as many products as convenient and these could be revised at yearly or six monthly intervals.

According to the Committee, there need be only one common tariff for

Customs and Central Excise duties which should be fully aligned. Rates of Customs duty and Central Excise duty can be indicated in separate columns against each heading/sub-heading. The exemption notifications relating to (i) Customs and (ii) Central Excise can be printed in two separate sections at the end of the statutory text of the common tariff.

Further number of exemption notifications should be reduced to the minimum possible level, more so, after the passing of annual Budget. Description of products in the exemption notifications may be the same as one used in the tariff itself.

The Rekhi Committee said that notifications with fixed time validity may not be withdrawn before the stipulated date except in circumstances of an exceptional nature. Also end-use based notifications may be kept to the barest minimum.

According to the Committee, small scale units eligible to the general SSI exemption who desire to add a new product to their line of manufacture may be granted the benefit of exemption of provisional basis on their furnishing an affidavit of the latest value of plant and machinery installed in their unit, pending addition of the new product in the SSI Unit's Registration Certificate.

With regard to the exemption in respect of bulk drugs, actual end-use of each individual consignment need not be verified where the Drugs Controller (India) has certified that the bulk drugs in question are solely or pre-dominantly used for manufacture of medicines.

The Committee said that the scale of depreciation allowed on second hand machinery which is now contained in departmental instructions may be notified so that it is known to the trade also.

Further, production of foreign manufacturer's invoice may be insisted upon under rule 10 of the Valuation Rules only in those cases where goods are shipped by the foreign manufacture direct to the Indian importer but sale invoice to the Indian importer is raised by a third party in another country and where the price variation noted is substantial.

The Committee said that specific rate of duty or tariff values may be considered for imported products which are prone to heavy underinvoicing.

In the case of imports from foreign collaborators, there should be no loading of import price by 5% as a routine while making initial provisional assessment. The loading should be restricted to the figure actually noticed in past cases (1 per cent, 1.5 per cent or so).

Source : *Hindustan Times,* May 26, 1993.

15.3 BUDGET SPEECH, FEBRUARY 28, 1994 : SUMMARY OF PART B

The peak rate of customs duty has been reduced from 85 per cent to 65 per cent for making available capital goods at a reasonable cost and enhance the competitiveness and promote investment, the Finance Minister has proposed a package of measures which include, reduction in basic customs duty on project imports and general capital goods from 35 per cent to 25 per cent. The facility of project import is being extended to port development. All this will help to reduce cost of investment and modernisation in Indian industry.

Import duty on parts, whether imported as parts of original equipment, or as spares is also being reduced to 25 per cent from the present rates varying from 25 per cent to 85 per cent. Import duty on fertilise, projects and power projects will continue at nil rate and 20 per cent, respectively without any countervailing duty.

The Finance Minister has accepted the demands of the domestic suppliers of capital goods an has proposed countervailing duty on imports of capital goods equivalent to the excise duty on domestic capital goods, to enable the domestic capital goods to compete with imports.

The customs duty on steel, a key input, has been reduced from a range of 75 per cent to 85 per cent at present to 50 per cent. Import duties to primary forms of major non-ferrous metals copper, zinc, and lead are also being unified at 50 per cent for giving a strong boost to investment in the economy and help the domestic capital goods industry, in particular.

Duty on Ores Cut

To help domestic metal producers, the import duties on all ores and concentrates have been reduced and lunified at 10 per cent. Import duty on machine tools has been reduced.

The import duty structure for coal and petroleum has been simplified. Crude petroleum and coal will attract import duty of 35 per cent as against Rs. 1500 per metric tonne and 85 per cent, respectively. Duty on coke has been reduced from 85 per cent to 25 per cent. LPG and other petroleum gases will attract import duty at 15 per cent. Naphtha and kerosene will continue to be exempted from basic customs duty.

The import duties on DM, PTA and MEG have been reduced from 70 per cent to 60 per cent and on intermediates like xylenes and toluence, the duty has been reduced from 40 per cent to 30 per cent.

Duty Cut on Leather

Import duty on a large number of items of machinery and raw material used in the leather industry has been reduced. The tariff structure for electronics and telecommunication sectors has been rationalised. The import duty on certain items for watch industry has been reduced from 50 per cent at present to 25 per cent.

In order to remove certain anomalies in the import structure of medical equipment, the system of certification for charitable hospitals has been abolished and free import of specialised medical equipment at 15 per cent without any countervailing duty has been permitted. In the pharmaceutical sector, import duty on a large number of raw materials has been reduced.

Major reforms in the present excise tax structure include extension of MODVAT to capital goods and petroleum products and spun yarns, shift in the bulk of excise taxation from specific to ad valorem rates, reduction in total number of ad valorem tax rates to about half the existing number and continuing the process of lowering rates when they are unduly high. These concessions aim at promoting growth of manufacturing output and employment, make tax administration easier, less discretionary and also reduce the scope for misclassification, disputes and evasion.

Handlooms Exempted

Duty rates have been adjusted in some cases to compensate for loss of revenue because of the extension of MODVAT. However, the Union Finance Minister has ensured that items of mass consumption are not burdened by higher taxes. For example, full exemption continues for many goods such as handloom products, unbranded drugs, domestic electric bulbs, bicycles, baby food, cooking oil, spices, jams, jellies, sauces, tea and coffee. Care has also been taken not to raise the rate on essential items of consumption of the comman man.

There is a switch over to ad valoram rates of 5 per cent, 10 per cent and 20 per cent on cotton and manmade fabrics from the numerous specific and ad valorem rates currently prevailing. In order to simplify and rationalise the present complicated excise duty structure on fibre and yarn, the Union Finance Minister has proposed a uniform excise duty of 20 per cent on all fibres of blended ore or spun yarns. On cotton yarn, excise duty is, however proposed at 5 per cent only instead of the present complex and varying specific rates depending on the count of the yarn.

A uniform duty of 15 per cent has been proposed on all metals except on aluminium whereas the duty has been reduced from the present 25 per cent to 20 per cent.

Exemption for Drugs

Schedule-I drugs which are for the national health programme and are under price control will continue to be fully exempted from excise duty.

In order to simplify the duty structure for various chemicals and chemical based products like dyes, paints, tanning preparations, etc., a uniform duty of 20 per cent has been proposed.

Duty on Cigarettes

The duty rate of 70 per cent applicable to cosmetics and similar personal care products has been reduced to 50 per cent as these form part of the consumption basket of ordinary people.

For the first time the distinction between registered and non-registered units under the exemption scheme in the general small scale industries has been done away with.

For the ship breaking industry, all goods obtained from such breaking up are also proposed to be exempted from excise duty so that ship breaking activity is completely outside the excise control.

Duties on cigarette which have remained unchanged for two years despite an increase in price have been increased by about 12 per cent. However, in a bid to help to tobacco growers, the excise duty for upto 60 mm category in the non-filter segment is being reduced from Rs. 120 per thousand of Rs. 60 per thousand.

Telephone Tax

A modest effort in imposing a tax on the services sector as recommended by the tax reforms committee has been made by imposing a 5 per cent tax on services of telephones, non-life insurance and stock brokers.

Income Tax

The income tax exemption limit has been raised to Rs. 35,000, adjusted the tax slabs which have not been changed for two years. The Union Finance Minister has proposed a rate of 20 per cent tax on the first slab of Rs. 35,000 to Rs. 60,000. The second slab will be from Rs. 60,000 to Rs. 1,20,000 with a rate of 30 per cent tax and a maximum tax rate of 40 per cent has been proposed for income above Rs. 1,20,000.

Rebate for Senior Citizens

The surcharge of 12 per cent on non-corporate income has been withdrawn. The tax rebate admissible to senior citizens has been raised from 20 per cent of the tax due to 40 per cent and the benefit is also extended to senior citizens having income upto Rs. 1,00,000.

Interest on Borrowed Capital

In order to give relief to those living in their own houses and as an incentive for house construction, the deduction on account of interest on borrowed capital for house construction has been raised from Rs. 5,000 to Rs. 10,000 for purposes of income tax.

Uniform Tax Rate

The distinction between tax rates for widely held and closely held domestic companies has been done away with and a single rate of 40 per cent has been proposed for both. At present, widely held companies are taxed at 45 per cent, while other domestic companies attract 50 per cent tax.

The Finance Minister has continued the levy of surcharge at the rate of 15 per cent on the incomes of domestic companies exceeding Rs. 75,000 due to revenue constraints. The tax on companies incorporated abroad, but earning income in India has been reduced to 55 per cent.

The Finance Minister has lowered the rate of capital gains tax on domestic companies to 30 per cent from 40 per cent.

Tax Holiday

As a stimulus to new investment in backward districts, the Finance Minister has extended the concession of five-year tax holiday in respect of certain States announced last year, to backward districts. The guidelines for the determination of such backward districts will be prescribed soon.

While declaring the continuance of presumptive scheme of taxation for the assesses in the unorganised sector, the Finance Minister announced a new estimated income scheme for contractors with a turnover of upto Rs. 40 lakh and for truck-owners who own upto ten trucks.

With a view to boosting tourism the rate of expenditure tax of hotels is proposed to be reduced from the present 20 per cent to 10 per cent. The exemption limit of gift tax on the occasion of marriage of a dependent relative has been raised from Rs. 30,000 to Rs. 1 lakh.

Source : *Hindustan Times,* March 2, 1994.

TABLE 15.7 : Union Budget at a Glance

(Rs. crore)

	1992-93 Actual	1993-94 Budget Estimates	1993-94 Revised Estimates	1994-95 Budget Estimates
Revenue Receipts	74128	84209	76166	86084
Capital Receipts	36178	42800	58646	59615
Total Receipts	110306	127009	134812	145699
Non-Plan Expenditure	85958	90072	97846	105117
Plan Expenditure	36660	41251	46026	46582
Total Expenditure	122618	131323	143872	151699
Revenue Deficit	18574	17630	34058	32727
Budgetary Deficit	12312	4314	9060	6000
Fiscal Deficit	40173	36959	58551	54915
Primary Deficit	9138	(-) 1041	21051	8915

TABLE 15.8 : Where the Rupees comes from and Where it Goes

Rupees comes from

1.	Internal borrowings	25 p
2.	Excise	21 p
3.	Customs	15 p
4.	Non-tax revenue	13 p
5,	Corporation Tax	07 p
6.	Non-debt capital receipts	06 p
7.	Income tax	06 p
8.	External borrowing	03 p
9.	Borrowing from Reserve Bank of India (91 days treasury bills)	03 p
10.	Other tax	01 p
	Total	1.00 (Re one)

Rupees goes to

1.	Interest	26 p
2.	Central Plan	16 p
3.	States' share of taxes and duties	14 p
4.	Defence	13 p
5.	State & Union Territory Plan Assistance	11 p
6.	Other non-Iplan expenditure	11 p

7.	Subsidies	05 p
8.	Non-plan assistance to States and Union Territory Governments	04 p
	Total	100 p (Re one)

15.4 HIGHLIGHTS OF THE BUDGET

* Excise duty reduced on cosmetics, detergent powder, cooking ranges, washing machines, lamps and light fitting, VCR and VCP computer parts, typewriters, plastic, dyes.
* Excise duty also reduced on plastic based paints flush doors, safes and strong boxes, glazed ceramic tiles, carpets and floor coverings, white cement, aluminium.
* Excise duty lowered on cars for physically handicapped, taxis and parts of motor vehicles.
* Filter cigarettes to cost more.
* Introduction of 5 per cent tax on services of telephone, non-life insurances and stock brokers.
* Exemption limits on gifts on marriage of dependent relatives raised from Rs. 30,000 to Rs one lakh.
* Hotel expenditure tax halved to promote tourism.
* Special measures to boost electronics, telecommumications, leather and watch industry.
* Tax relief for senior citizens and the handicapped.
* Exemption continues for items of mass consumption like tea, coffee, unbranded drugs, domestic electric bulbs and refined cooking oil.
* Modvat scheme extended to captial goods, petroleum products and spun yarns.
* Duty converted to ad valorem on petroleum products, aerated waters, TV sets, refrigerators, air conditioners, fibre and yarns.
* General small scale industry exemption scheme extended to tyres, tubes, certain textile goods, specified metals and their articles.

15.5 EXCISE DUTY HIGHLIGHTS

* Scheme of filling and approval of price list abolished
* Massive reduction in number of exemption notifications
* Drastic reductioin in numbers of ad valorem rates
* Removal of end use exemptions in most cases

Extension of Modvat to

* Capital goods
* Spun yarns
* Petroleum products

Customs

* Maximum customs duty level slashed to 65% with certain exceptions
* Countervailing duty on most items of import
* Substantial reduction in the number of exemption notifications
* Reduction/Removal of anomalies in import duties on raw materials and components being higher than on finished products
* Removal of certification procedure in most cases

15.6 INCOME TAX HIGHLIGHT

TABLE 15.9 : Income tax Rates

Income slab	*Existing rates*	*Income slab*	*Proposed rates*
Upto Rs. 30,000	Nil	Upto Rs. 35,000	NIL
Rs. 30,001 - Rs. 50,000	20%	Rs. 35,001 - Rs. 60,000	20%
Rs. 50,001 - Rs. 1,00,000	30%	Rs. 60,001 - Rs. 1,20,000	30%
Above Rs. 1,00,000	40%	Above Rs. 1,20,000	40%

Total income	*Existing Tax Liabilities*	*New tax Liabilities*	*Proposed Relief Amount*
35,000	1,000	Nil	1,000
40,000	2,000	1,000	1,000
50,000	4,000	3,000	1,000
60,000	7,000	5,000	2,000
75,000	11,5000	9,500	2,000
1,00,000	19,000	17,000	2,000
1,20,000	30,240	23,000	7,240
1,50,000	43,680	35,000	8,680
2,00,000	66,080	55,000	11,080
5,00,000	2,00,480	1,75,000	25,480

TABLE 15.10 : **Union Finances**
Table 1 : Provision

	1994-95 Budget	1993-94 Received	1993-94 Budget	1992-93 Actuals
(1) Revenue receipts	86084 (13.0) [9.5]	76166 (2.7) [9.6]	84209 (13.6) [10.6]	74128 (12.3) [10.5]
(a) Tax revenue (net to centre)	62742 (15.2) [6.9]	54473 (0.8) [6.8]	62739 (16.1) [7.9]	54044 (7.9) [7.7]
(b) Non-tax-revenue	23342 (7.0) [2.6]	21693 (8.0) [2.7]	21470 (6.9) [2.7]	20084 (25.8) [2.8]
(2) Capital receipts	59615 (1.7) [6.6]	58646 (62.1) [7.4]	42800 (18.3) [5.4]	36178 (-6.1) [5.1]
(a) Recovery of loans	6700 (0.7) [0.7]	6655 (4.7) [0.8]	6655 (4.7) [0.8]	6356 (5.6) [0.9]
(b) Other receipts	4000 (60.0) [0.4]	2500 (27.5) [0.3]	3500 (78.5) [0.4]	1961 (-35.5) [0.3]
(c) Borrowing and other liabilities	48915 (-1.2) [5.4]	49491 (77.6) [6.2]	32645 (17.2) [4.1]	27861 (-5.5) [3.9]
(3) **Total receipts (1+2)**	**145699 (8.1)** [16.1]	**134812 (22.2)** [16.9]	**127009 (15.1)** [16.0]	**110306 (5.5)** [15.6]
(4) Non-Plan expenditure	105117 (7.4) [11.6]	97846 (13.8) [12.3]	90072 (4.8) [11.3]	85958 (6.8) [12.2]
(a) On revenue account	90749 (8.2) [10.0]	83870 (15.0) [10.5]	77654 (6.5) [9.8]	72925 (8.5) [10.3]

(Contd.)

TABLE 15.10 *(Contd.)*

	1994-95 Budget	1993-94 Received	1993-94 Budget	1992-93 Actuals
of which				
(a.1) Interest payment	46000 (22.7) [5.1]	37500 (20.8) [4.7]	38000 (22.4) [4.8]	31035 (16.7) [4.4]
(b) On capital account	14368 (2.8) [1.6]	13976 (7.2) [1.8]	12418 (-4.7) [1.6]	13033 (-1.5) [1.8]
(5) Plan expenditure	46582 (1.2) [5.1]	46026 (25.5) [5.8]	41251 (12.5) [5.2]	36660 (18.40 [5.2]
(a) On revenue account	28062 (6.5) [3.1]	26354 (33.3) [3.3]	24185 (22.3) [3.0]	19777 (31.2) [2.8]
(b) On capital account	18520 (-5.9) [2.0]	19672 (16.5) [2.5]	17066 (1.1) [2.1]	16883 (6.3) [2.4]
(6) **Total expenditure (4+5)**	**151699 (5.4)** [16.7]	**143872 (17.3)** [18.1]	**131323 (7.1)** [16.5]	**122618 (10.1)** [17.4]
(a) Revenue expenditure (4.a + 5.a)	118811 (7.8) [13.1]	110224 (18.9) [13.8]	101839 (9.9) [12.8]	92702 (12.7) [13.1]
(b) Capital expenditure [4.b+5.b]	32889 (-2.3) [3.6]	33648 (12.5) [4.2]	29484 (-1.4) [3.7]	29916 (2.7) [4.2]
(7) Revenue deficit (1 - 6a)	32727 [3.6]	34058 [4.3]	17630 [2.2]	18574 [2.6]
(8) Budgetary deficit (3 - 6)	6000 [0.7]	9060 [1.1]	4314 [0.5]	12312 [1.7]

(Contd.)

TABLE 15.10 *(Contd.)*

	1994-95 Budget	1993-94 Received	1993-94 Budget	1992-93 Actuals
(9) Fiscal deficit (2c + 8) or (1 + 2a + 2b - 6)	54915 [6.1]	58551 [7.4]	36959 [4.6]	40173 [5.7]
(10) Primary deficit (9 - 4.a1)	8915 [1.0]	21051 [2.6]	-1041 [-0.1]	9138 [1.3]
Memo Items				
Budget support for central Plan outlay	27278 (9.1) [3.0]	25012 (23.9) [3.1]	23241 (15.2) [2.9]	20180 (18.0) [2.9]
Internal and external budgetary resources of public enterprises, etc.	42863 (17.6) [4.7]	36442 (21.9) [4.6]	40695 (36.1) [5.1]	29906 (32.9) [4.2]
Total Centtral Plan only	70141 [14.1]	61454 [22.7]	63936 [27.7]	50085 [26.5]
GDP at current market prices	[7.7] 907301*	[7.7] 795878*	[8.0] 795878*	[7.1] 705566

* *Projected*

Notes : (1) Figures in round brackets next to absolute numbers are per cent variations over the previous year.
(2) Figures in square brackets are percentages to GDP at current market prices.
(3) Data for internal and external budgetary resources of public enterprises are as per revised estimates up to 1993-94.

Source: *Economic and Political Weekly.*

16

BALANCE OF PAYMENTS, FOREIGN TRADE AND EXTERNAL DEBT

16.1 OVERVIEW

The year 1993-94 has seen a significant improvement in the country's balance of payments. Exports are expected to increase by 20 per cent in dollar terms. Import growth will be limited to four per cent despite large scale liberalisation of import policy over the last two years. The trade deficit (DGCI & S) in the first nine months of 1993-94 was only $ 732 million which was less than one fourth of the level in the corresponding period of 1992-93. The current account deficit in 1993-94 is expected to be less than 0.5 per cent of the DGP. The year has also seen a sharp increase in inflow of foreign investment. The total quantum of foreign investment flows during 1993-94 could be about $ 3 billion as compared to $ 585 million in 1992-93 and $ 148 million in 1991-92. As a result of these improvements in trade, current account and capital flows, foreign currency assets of the Reserve Bank of India had built up to $ 10.9 billion on February 4, 1994. It is expected that these reserves could climb as high as $ 12 billion by the end of March 1994. This will imply a build up of about 5.5 billion during 1993-94.

16.2 RECENT DEVELOPMENTS IN BALANCE OF PAYMENTS

Key indicators of India's balance of payments from 1990-91 onwards are given in Table 16.1 , using the new balance of payments format adopted by the Reserve Bank in line with the recommendation of the High Level Committee of Balance of Payments.

Balance of Trade : The trade balance has shown a significant improvement in the first half of 1993-94 as compared to the previous year. The trade deficit of $ 846 million (Rs. 2653 crore) during April-September 1993 was less than one third of the trade deficit during these months in 1992 when it was $ 3132 million (Rs. 8941 crore). This improvement on the trade account was primarily due to a growth of 21 per cent in dollar value of exports and a decline in imports of 3.5 per cent. Exports were estimated to be $ 10590 million (Rs. 33210 crore) during the first half of 1993-94. Imports at $ 11436 million (Rs. 35863 crore) were substantially below expected levels. Taking seasonality factors into account, exports appear to be on track for a 20 per cent growth in dollar terms during 1993-94. Imports appear to be heading for less than 4 per cent growth in 1993-94. As a result, the trade deficit is expected to be about $ 1000 million in 1993-94.

Current Account: The current account during 1993-94 reflects the improvement in the country's balance of trade and invisibles account. The current account deficit, it may be recalled, had risen to 3.3 per cent of the GDP during 1990-91 compared with 2.3 per cent on average over the Seventh Plan. These were unsustainable levels and were the principal underlaying cause for the external sector crisis which over-took the economy in 1990-91. With the help of strong fiscal stabilisation measures of the last two years, the current account deficit was brought down to 2.1 per cent in 1992-93. It was estimated at $ 938 million (Rs. 2942 crore) in the first half of 1993-94 as compared to $ 3468 million (Rs. 9901 crore) during the same period of 1992-93. Given the likely trends in trade and invisibles flow, the current account deficit is expected to be less than 0.5 per cent of GDP in 1993-94.

External Assistance: Over the years the contribution of external assistance to capital inflows has come down significantly as gross inflows have tended to rise only marginally and principal repayments of past disbursements, falling due have increased. Net inflows of external assistance (excluding grants) have consequently declined from $ 2.2 billion in 1990-91 to $ 1.8 billion in 1992-93.

In the first half of the current year only $ 59 million of external assistance (excluding grants) accrued on a net basis in comparison to $ 259 million during the same period last year. Utilisation levels have come down during the past three years. Fiscal stringency of the past three years, and extensive procedural difficulties faced by implementing agencies have contributed to the decline in utilisation levels.

External Commercial Borrowing: The growth of external commercial borrowings (ECB) during the 1990s has come down. During 1990-91 and 1991-92 this was on account of lack of access to international credit markets. Since 1992-93 ECB has been brought down as part of the policy to reduce the country's external debt. Gross disbursements have been about $ 1.8 billion per annum during the 1990s, as compared to $ 2.3 billion per annum during 1986-87 to 1989-90. In 1992-93, gross disbursements of $ 1.2 billion were short of repayments resulting in a negative net inflow of $ 451 million. In 1993-94 gross disbursements have increased and are expected to be about $ 3 billion by the end of the year. These include Euro-convertibles. In the first half of the current year, a net inflow of only $ 254 million has occurred on account of ECB and for the full year 1993-94 the net inflow is expected to be about $ 1 billion.

Borrowing from IMF: The stand by arrangement negotiated with the IMF continued to be operational during 1991-92. Under this arrangement a net inflow of $ 1288 million (Rs. 3363 crore) was available during 1992-93. This facility due to a clsoe with the release of its last tranche in June 1993 which amounted to $ 325 million as compared to $ 781 million (Rs. 20.77 crore) in 1991-92.

Non-Resident Deposits: During 1991-92, non-resident deposits showed a decline of $ 454 million. In 1992-93, those deposits grew by $ 1.9 billon.

16.3 FOREIGN INVESTMENT

* The approvals of direct foreign investment proposals rose from $ 73 million (Rs. 128 crore) in 1990 to $ 235 million (Rs. 535 crore) in 1991, to $ 1318 million (Rs. 3888 crore) in 1992 and to $ 2091 million (Rs. 6577 crore) during January-October, 1993.
* Actual inflows under total foreign investment rose from $ 165 million during the financial year 1990-91 to $ 585 million during 1992-93 and is expected

to rise sharply to $ 3.0 billion during 1993-94.

* In 1993-94, direct foreign investment is expected to be about $ 600 million, portfolio investment by foreign institutional investors (FIIs) of $ 1.2 billion and inflows through Euroequity issues of about $ 1.2 billion.
* In the current financial year up to December 1993 the country received foreign investment flows of $ 1.8 billion consisting of a direct investment of $ 425 million, portfolio investment by FIIs of $ 1.0 billion (up to mid-January 1993) and Euroequity issues of $ 358 million (Table 16.2).

Foreign Exchange Reserves: A summary ane overall evaluation of the country's balance of payments and external sector condition is perhaps provided by the state of foreign exchange and foreign currency assets. Foreign exchange reserves including gold held by the RBI and SDR balances held by the Government, increased from $ 9.2 billion (Rs. 23850 crore) at the end of March 1992, to $ 9.8 billion (Rs. 30744 crore) by the end of March 1993. They were $ 13.9 billion (Rs. 43434 crore) at the end of December 1993. Foreign currency assets of the RBI recorded an increase of $ 3.4 billion in 1991-92. By the end of March 1993, foreign currency assets had reached $ 6.4 billion as compared to $ 2.2 billion at the end of March 1991 (and $ 1.1 billion in June 1991). Thus, the loans from the IMF under the standby and earlier arrangements had been used effectively to build up the country's foreign exchange reserves and place the external sector on a more stable footing.

During the current year, between April to November 1993, foreign currency assets have increased by $ 1.8 billion to reach a level of $ 8.2 billion. They crossed $ 10 billion and stood at $ 10.9 billion on February 4, 1994. This build up was achieved at a time when there was a net outflow of $ 1.7 billion (excluding accrued interest) from the FCNRA scheme by the end of January 1994, a repayment of $ 1.1 billion (between April and October 1993) on account of State Bank of India liabilities taken on behalf of IOC during 1991-92, and a settlement of all outstanding swaps with a net sale of $ 1.2 billion between April and October 1993. Thus, the build up in reserves has occurred alongwith a marked improvement in the quality of these reserves.

16.4 MERCHANDISE TRADE

Exports

The slow growth in total exports during 1992-93 was commented upon in last year's Survey. Various economic and other factors combined to keep export growth down to 3.8 per cent. This was achieved despite a 62 per cent decline in exports to the Rupee Payment Area (mainly markets of erstwhile Soviet Union) which followed upon a decline of 42 per cent in 1991-92. The collapse of India's exports of Russia and East Europen countries is best revealed by noting that monthly exports to these markets were on an average about $ 56 million (Rs. 162 crore) during 1992-93 as compared to $ 255 million (Rs. 458 crore) per month during 1990-91. It can be safely expected that this performance will improve during the current and succeding years.

Exports to the General Currency Area (GCA) increased by 10.8 per cent in dollar terms during 1992-93 which was a distinct improvement over a 6.3 per cent growth in 1991-92. Excluding the two month of December 1992, and January 1993, during which exports were adversely affected by post-Ayodhya developments, exports to GCA recorded an average growth of 13.1 per cent during 1992-93. This provided a sound basis to build up export performance during 1993.94.

The current year started with export growth of 27.8 per cent, in dollar terms, during the first quarter. To some extent this was due to a spill-over from the previous quarter when disturbances in Bombay had disrupted supplies and shipments. But it also represented the positive effects of policy changes of the previous two years. The export growth was adversely affected in August and September 1993 by the transporters' strike reinforcing the seasonal downturn. The exports growth of 19.9 per cent in dollar terms in the first nine months of 1993-94 is markedly higher than that of 3.4 per cent during the same period in 1992-93 and of 9.2 per cent in 1990-91. Exports appear on track for a 20 per cent growth in 1993-94.

Manufactures accounted for 74.6 per cent of total exports in 1991-92. Their share increased to 76.3 per cent in 1992-93. Share of agricultural and agro-processed products declined from 17.9 per cent in 1991-92 to 16.4 per cent in 1992-93 (Table 16.3). These trends are apparently being reversed in 1993-94. Agricultural exports increased by 38 per cent while manufactured exports grew by 19 per cent during first half of 1993-94 (Table 16.4).

Imports

Imports reached a level of $ 21.9 billion during 1992-93 showing a growth of 12.7 per cent during that year. The current year is expected to end up with an import growth of less than four per cent. Imports during April-December 1993 were $ 16.4 billion as compared to $ 16.6 billion in the corresponding period of 1992. This represents a decline of 1.3 per cent. The overall trade deficit which stood at $ 3536 million in April-December 1992 has dropped to $ 732 million during April-December 1993, showing an improvement of $ 2.88 billion.

POL imports reached a level of $ 6100 million during 1992-93 showing a growth of 20.9 per cent. During the first nine months of 1993-94, POL imports were $ 4291 million representing a decline of 10.1 per cent over the corresponding period of previous year. Imports of POL have constituted an increasing share in total imports in the past few years. In 1989-90 they accounted for 17.8 per cent of total imports and this increased to 27.9 per cent in 1992-93 (Table 28.5). During the first half of 1993-94, POL imports at $ 3045 million accounted for 28.2 per cent of total imports The increase in imports share of POL has coincided with the decline in domestic production specially from off-shore fields. It is important for balance of payments reasons to reverse the decline in domestic production. Table 16.6 provides details of import of commodities group wise. India's exports and Imports is shown in Table 16.7 , Table 16.8 and Table 16.9.

Direction of India's foreign trade has undergone a significant change with the collapse of Russian and some of the East European trading arrangements. This directional change both in exports and imports was reported in the previous year's Survey and has continued during 1992-93. Exports to Russia (former Soviet Union) accounted for as much as 16.1 per cent of India's total exports in 1990-91. This came down to 9.2 per cent in 1991-92 and further to 3.2 per cent in 1992-93. This decline continued during the first half of 1993-94 with exports to Russia now constituting only 2.4 per cent of total exports. The collapse of the

Russian market has been a major shock to our export effort.

The data for the first half of 1993-94 indicate an increase in the share of developing countries, including OPEC, in India's exports. Their share increased to 35 per cent from 29 per cent in the first half of 1992-93. The table reveals a substantial growth in dollar terms in India's exports to OPEC (34 per cent) and non-OPEC developing countries (54 per cent) during the first half of 1993-94. It may also be noted that exports to selected East Asian countries (Indonesia, Malaysia, Hongkong, South Korea, Singapore, Thailand, and Chinese Tapei) have boomed, increasing on the average by 61 per cent in dollar terms during the first six months of 1993-94. The percentage export growth to these countries is about three times the overall export growth.

The share of foreign trade in the country's GNP has been rising over the years. It was 11.7 per cent in 1985-86, 14.5 per cent in 1990-91 and 16.9 per cent in 1992-93. In 1993-94 with plausible growth scenarios its share would be close to 19 per cent. It still remains one of the lowest in comparison with other developing countries.

External Debt: The total outstanding stock of the country's external debt (including defence) increased sharply by $ 8.1 billion in 1990-91 to $ 83.96 billion Table 16.10. This increase coincided with a decline in the foreign exchange reserves of $ 1.3 billion. This signifies the gravity of the external payments crisis faced by the country in that year. In 1991-92 the growth of external debt was limited to $ 1.4 billion. This small increase in total ??? was despite a net borrowing from the IMF of about $ 800 million. The increase was limited on account of a decline in short-term debt of $ 1.5 billion in 1991-92. At the same time, foreign exchange reserves were built up by $ 3.6 billion. This reflects the success of Government policy in not only restraining the growth of external debt but using it for building up the country's foreign exchange reserves. In 1992-93 total debt increased by $ 4.8 billion yielding an average growth of total external debt of $ 3.1 billion for the two years 1991-92 and 1992-93. In the first half of 1993-94 the increase in external debt has been marginal of $ 296 million. This is a result of conscious Government policy which has limited the growth of external commercial borrowing, reduced defence debt and encouraged non-debt creating equity flows.

TABLE 16.1 : Balance of Payments: Key Indicators

(US $ Million)

	1990-91*	1991-92**	1992-93***	April-Sep*** 1992	April-Sep*** 1993
1	2	3	4	5	6
1. Exports	18477	18223	18789	8720	10590
2. Imports	27914	20347	22895	11852	11436
-Oil	6028	15364	6100	3133	3045
-Non-oil (DGCI & S)	18045	14047	15626	8038	7747
-Non-DGCI & S	3841	936	1169	681	644
3. Trade balance (1-2)	-9437	-2124	-4106	-3132	-846

(Contd.)

1	2	3	4	5	6
4. Invisibles balance	-242	-11	-815	-336	-92
5. Current account (3+4)	-9679	-2135	-4921	-3468	-938
6. External assistance (net)	2210	2916	1842	259	59
7. Commercial borrowings (net)	2249	1647@	-451	-82	254
8. NRI deposits (net)+	1536	-454	1949	1705	657
9. Rupee debt service	-1193	-1332	-977	-458	-690
10. Foreign investment	165	148	585	392	608
11. Other capital (net)++	2221	2004	1413	926	1007
12. Capital account (6 to 11)	7188	4929	4361	2742	1895
13. Overall balance (5+12)	-2491	2794	-560	-726	957
14. IMF borrowing (net)	1214	781	1288	468	235
15. Official reserves (-increase + decrease)	1277	-3575	-728	258	-1192
Memo items:					
		(As per cent of GDP)			
Exports	6.2	7.3	7.7		
Imports	9.4	8.1	9.3		
Trade balance	-3.2	-0.9	-1.6		
Invisible balance	-0.1	-0.0	-0.4		
Current account balance	-3.3	-0.9	-2.1		

* Preliminary estimates ** Provisional estimates *** Quick estimates

@ Includes India Development Bonds of US $ 1627 million + Including FC (B & O) deposits.

++ Other capital movements in banking capital, bilateral balance, short-term credit, etc.

Note: Balance of payments for 1992-93 and 1993-94 exclude gold and silver brought in by returning Indians under the liberalised baggage rules.

TABLE 16.2 : Foreign Investment Flows by Different Categories

(US $ million)

	1991-92	1992-93	1993-94*			
			Apr-Jun	Jul-Sep	Oct-Dec	Apr-Dec
A. Direct investment	148.0	343.5	161.4	137.5	126.4	425.3
a. RBI automatic route	0.2	42.6	4.9	18.6	26.8	50.3
b. SIA/FIPB route	85.4	239.9	89.6	75.9	50.2	215.7
c. NRIs (40% & 100% schemes)	62.4	61.0	66.9	43.0	49.4	159.3

(Contd.)

	1991-92	1992-93	1993-94* Apr-Jun	Jul-Sep	Oct-Dec	Apr-Dec
B. Portfolio investment	-	241.5	45.5	263.8	1050.7	1360.0
a. FIIs	-	1.0	45.5	194.8	761.7#	1002.0#
b. Euroequities		240.5	0.0	69.0	289.0	358.0
Total (A+B)	148.0	585.0	206.9	401.3	1177.1	1785.3

* Provisional # Up to January 13, 1994.

TABLE 16.3 : Composition of Exports

(Percentage share)

Commodity Group	1991-92	1992-93	1992	1993
1	2	3	4	5
I. Agriculture & allied, of which	17.9	16.4	15.7	17.8
1. Tea	2.8	1.8	1.9	1.6
2. Tobacco manufactured	0.1	0.2	0.2	0.2
3. Oil meals	2.1	2.9	2.2	2.9
4. Sugar & molasses	0.4	0.2	0.3	0.4
5. Processed fruits & juices	0.2	0.2	0.3	0.2
6. Cotton raw incld. waste	0.7	0.4	0.1	1.6
II. Ores and minerals, of which	5.2	4.0	3.6	3.9
7. Coal	0.0	0.1	0.0	0.0
III. Manufactured goods, of which	74.6	76.3	77.0	75.5
8. Leather & manufactures	4.5	4.7	5.0	4.0
9. Footwear of leather	2.6	2.1	2.2	2.1
10. Gems & jewellery	15.3	16.5	16.1	18.1
11. Plastic & linoleum products	0.6	0.8	0.7	1.3
12. Manufactures of metals	2.7	3.2	2.9	3.1
13. Transport equipment	2.8	2.8	3.0	2.5
14. Iron & steel bar/rod, etc.	0.3	0.8	0.5	0.4
15. Primary & semifinished iron & steel	0.5	0.8	0.8	2.2
16. Ready-made garments	12.3	12.9	13.3	11.7
17. Handicrafts	4.7	4.6	4.8	4.2
IV. Crude & petroleum products	2.3	2.6	2.8	2.3
V. Other & unclassified items	0.0	0.7	1.0	0.5
Grand Total	100.0	100.0	100.0	100.0

Source: DGCI & S, Calcutta.

TABLE 16.4 : Growth of India's Exports by Commodity Groups

(US $ million)

Commodity Group	1991-92	1992-93	Apr.-Sep. 1992-94	Apr-Sep 1993-94	Apr. - Sep. 1992-93 (per cent change)	1993-94
1	2	3	4	5	6	7
I. Agriculture & allied, of which	3193.5	3035.3	1338.3	1846.1	-5.0	37.9
1. Tea	491.5	335.8	158.1	164.5	-31.7	4.0
2. Tobacco manufactured	25.5	40.6	14.3	16.3	58.9	13.8
3. Oil meals	373.8	531.2	190.1	301.9	42.1	58.8
4. Sugar & molasses	63.8	37.1	21.5	46.5	-41.8	116.3
5. Processed fruits & juices	33.8	42.9	21.7	23.7	26.9	9.1
6. Cotton raw incld. waste	124.1	67.5	8.1	164.7	-45.6	1920.9
II. Ores and minerals, of which	929.7	740.9	309.2	408.4	-20.3	32.1
7. Coal	6.1	17.6	2.8	3.9	188.6	40.4
III. Manufactured goods, of which	13325.5	14151.1	6567.8	7812.6	6.2	19.0
8. Leather & manufactures	804.9	867.2	427.3	410.4	7.7	-4.0
9. Footwear of leather	463.8	390.5	191.3	212.4	-15.8	11.0
10. Gems & jewellery	2738.2	3051.9	1371.2	1875.0	11.5	36.7
11. Plastic & linoleum products	112.1	148.1	61.3	134.1	32.1	18.9
12. Manufactures of metals	484.2	585.5	251.3	325.7	20.9	29.6
13. Transport equipment	496.4	524.3	255.8	256.3	5.6	0.2
14. Iron & steel bar/rod etc.	62.0	140.2	39.4	39.1	126.3	-0.7
15. Primary & semi-finished iron & steel	1299.3	1356.4	640.2	718.6	4.4	12.2
16. Ready-made garments	2199.2	2388.7	1137.5	1215.7	8.6	6.9
17. Handicrafts	835.9	848.9	413.2	437.1	1.6	5.8
IV. Crude & petroleum products	414.7	476.2	237.2	236.7	14.8	-0.2
V. Others & unclassified items	2.0	17.1	82.0	47.3	743.8	-42.3
Grand Total	**17865.4**	**18537.1**	**8534.6**	**10351.1**	**3.8**	**21.3**

Source: DGCI & S, Calcutta.

TABLE 16.5 : Composition of India's Imports

(percentage share)

Commodity Group	1991-92	1992-93	Apr.-Sep. 1992	1993
1	2	3	4	5
I. Food and allied products, of which	2.2	3.2	2.5	2.0
1. Cereals	0.4	1.5	0.7	0.6
2. Pulses	0.5	0.5	0.5	0.6
3. Edible oils	0.6	0.6	0.6	0.4
II. Fuel, of which	29.8	30.1	30.6	30.2
4. Coal	2.2	2.2	2.5	2.0
5. POL	27.6	27.9	28.1	28.2
III. Fertilizers	4.9	4.5	5.5	3.6
IV. Paper board, manufactures & news print	1.0	0.8	0.5	0.8
V. Capital goods, of which	21.8	20.4	19.7	23.1
6. Transport equipment	1.9	2.1	1.5	4.7
7. Project goods	7.6	5.5	5.7	5.4
VI. Others, of which	23.6	24.1	24.4	24.1
8. Chemicals	7.8	7.4	8.3	5.8
9. Pearls, precious and semi-precious stones	10..1	11.1	10.4	13.2
10. Iron & steel	3.6	3.3	3.5	2.9
11. Professional instruments, optical goods, etc.	2.1	2.3	2.2	2.1
VII. Unclassified items	16.6	17.0	16.8	16.2
Grand Total	100.0	100.0	100.00	100.0

Source: DGCI & S Calcutta

TABLE 16.6 : Growth of India's Imports by Commodity Groups

(US $ million)

Commodity	1991-92	1992-93	1992	1993	1992	1993
1	2	3	4	5	6	7
I. Food and allied products, of which	430.7	702.9	274.9	211.9	63.2	-22.9
1. Cereals	70.3	320.1	83.0	64.1	355.1	-22.8

(Contd.)

1	2	3	4	5	6	7
2. Pulses	103.6	109.1	59.2	62.5	5.3	5.6
3. Edible oils	100.5	59.5	35.6	14.3	-40.8	-60.0
II. Fuel, of which	5784.4	6576.2	3415.0	3259.4	13.7	-4.6
4. Coal	420.4	476.2	282.0	214.4	13.3	-24.0
5. POL	5364.0	6100.0	3133.0	3045.0	13.7	-2.8
III. Fertilizers	954.2	976.1	612.9	386.8	2.3	-36.9
IV. Paper board, manufactures & news print	197.9	166.6	58.4	85.3	-15.8	46.1
V. Capital goods, of which	4231.8	4463.1	2191.2	2496.1	5.5	13.9
6. Transport equipment	371.1	461.2	172.1	502.6	24.3	192.0
7. Project goods	1470.5	1194.7	633.9	579.8	-18.8	-8.5
VI. Others, of which	4585.6	5274.9	2724.6	2601.1	15.0	-4.5
8. Chemicals	1515.1	1619.8	924.1	628.0	6.9	-32.0
9. Pearls, pcs and semiprcs stones	1957.1	2420.6	1164.3	1428.3	23.7	22.7
10. Iron & steel	706.4	722.3	391.0	314.7	2.3	-19.5
11. Profit instrmts, optical goods etc.	407.1	512.3	245.2	230.1	25.8	-6.1
VII. Unclassified items	3225.9	3722.2	1872.0	1751.0	15.4	-6.5
Grand Total	**19410.5**	**21882.0**	**11149.1**	**10791.6**	**12.7**	**-3.2**

Source: DGCI & S, Calcutta

TABLE 16.7 : Destination of Exports Country

(% of export)

Country	1991-92	1992-93 (Apr-Sep)	1993-94 (Apr-Sep)
U.K.	6.5	7.4	6.3
Germany	7.7	7.5	6.9
U.S.A.	18.8	19.5	18.6
Japan	7.7	7.7	7.7
Russia	3.2	3.6	2.4
Other East Europe	1.3	1.3	0.9
OPEC	9.5	9.4	10.4
Other EC	14.0	13.4	12.1
Others	11.0	10.9	10.4
Other LDC's	20.3	19.4	24.3

TABLE 17.8 : Commoditywise Exports

in $ million

Items	Target	1992-93 Actual	% change	1993-94 Target
Textiles	6193	5311	-14.2	7400
Gems and Jewellery	3236	3052	-5.7	3455
Engineering goods	2057	2246	+9.2	2500
Agriculture Products	2000	1904	-4.8	2255
Chemical Products	2222	1871	-15.6	2168
Leather Products	1480	1275	-13.0	1490
Ores & Minerals	940	741	-21.2	809
Marine Products	615	602	-2.11	450
Plantation Crops	557	462	-17.1	500
Petroleum Products	452	476	+5.31	269
Total	**20132**	**18420**	**-8.5**	**22139**

TABLE 17.9 : Commodity Exports

Country	% of exports 1992-93	1992-93 (Apr-Sep)	1993-94 (Apr-Sep)
U.K.	6.3	6.6	6.9
Germany	7.5	8.3	7.3
Other E C	16.3	15.9	17.7
U.S.A.	9.7	10.1	10.6
Japan	6.4	4.3	5.8
Russia	1.2	0.9	1.0
Other East Europe	1.4	1.4	0.6
OPEC	21.7	21.7	24.9
Other LDCPs	15.1	15.5	13.7
Others	14.5	15.3	11.7

TABLE 17.10 : External Debt and Debt Servicing

	1989-90	1990-91	1991-92	1992-93	Apr-Sep 1993 (P)
1	2	3	4	5	6
Peroid-end outstanding debt stock US $ billion	75.90	83.96	85.33	90.09	90.39
Rs. thousand crore	130.28	163.31	253.03	280.98	282.90
Change is debt stock US $ billion		8.06	1.37	4.76	0.30
Debt service payments US $ billion	7.60	8.13	8.22	8.17	
Debt as per cent of GDP*	28.5	30.7	41.1	39.8	
Debt service as per cent of current receipts**	31.7	31.9	31.2	30.8	

P Provisional.

* This is computed by dividing the year-end debt numbers in repees by GDP numbers of corresponding years.

** Current receipts include gross receipts under merchandise exports and invisibles except official transfers.

Note: The data on external debt and debt servicing differ from what had been published earlier as the latter was based on estimated accrued interest credited to FCNRA deposits whereas the former is based on actual accrued interest obtained from an initial census count which are being subjected to a further special audit by the RBI.

17

MONETARY TRENDS

17.1 OVERVIEW

Objective Instruments and Targets : Inflation control remained the primary objective of monetary policy in 1993-94.

Monetary policy and monetary expansion in the past have been largely determined by the government's borrowing requirement and as such the distinction between objectives and instruments has been blurred. Historically, SLR and CRR have been the main instruments of monetary policy. Rising fiscal deficits over the eighties made the monetised deficit a major factor driving money supply growth. The aim should be to gradually delink budget and fiscal deficit from net RBI credit to government so that the latter becomes an independent instruments for non-monetary policy.

In the light of these objectives and constraints, monetary expansion in 1993-94 was originally targeted by RBI at about 12 per cent. Bit it was subsequently revised to 14 per cent in October 1993.

Interest Rate Policy : The floor commercial bank lending rate was also reduced in line with falling inflation. The interest rate on advances of scheduled commercial banks to borrowers with credit limits over Rs. 2 lakh, was lowered from 18 per cent to 17 per cent from March 1,1993. It was further reduced to 16 per cent from June 24 and then to 15 per cent from September 2, 1993. The real lending rate which had exceeded 10 per cent in January-May 1993, declined gradually since July 1993 and was of the order of 7 per cent in January 1994. There has also been an accompanying adjustment of the rates charged by financial institutions.

Cash Reserve Ratio (CRR) : CRR was reduced in two phases-from 15 per cent to 14.5 per cent effective April 17, 1993 and further to 14 per cent effective May 15, 1993.

Statuatory Liquidity Ratio (SLR) : The phased reduction of the SLR is designed to bring down the level of pre-emption of resources by the Government at below market rates. This is accompanied by an effort to make Government securities an attractive instrument for banks and financial institutions to hold voluntarily. As part of this policy, SLR was reduced from 37.55 per cent at the beginning of 1993-94 to 37.5 pr cent on August 21, and to 37.25 per cent on September 18, 1993. The net demand and time liabilities (DTL) base to which this ratio was to be applied was shifted to September 17, 1993 from April 3, 1992 with effect from October 16, 1993 and SLR was further reduced to 34.75 per cent. The incremental SLR on any increase in net DTL above the

September 17, 1993 level was fixed at 25 per cent. Over time, this is expected to bring down the average SLR on net DTL of the banks to 25 per cent.

Monetary Trends in 1993-94

Reserve money growth and net RBI credit to Government have seen a sharp increase in 1993-94 (Table 17.1 and 17.2). During financial year 1993-94, till January 7, 1994 reserve money has grown by 16.9 per cent, compared to 8.5 per cent during the corresponding period of 1992-93.

Non-Food Credit : Total credit of the scheduled commercial banks grew by 5.7 per cent during 1993-94. Non-food credit growth was negligible (2.9 per cent). The major component of growth in bank credit was food credit, which grew by 64 per cent in 1993-94 (Table 17.3 and 17.4). Expansion in food credit in consistent with the rising ratio of currency with public (CWP) to demand deposits from 1.3 to 1.4 and of CWP to aggregate deposits from 22.3 per cent to 23.9 per cent.

The new income recognition and provisioning norms, and accounting procedures and format, which were among the measures announced in April, 1992, took effect from the year 1992-93. They have revealed the true extent of the deterioration in the profitability of the banks (Table 17.5). Apart from State Bank of India and its subsidiaries, only seven other public sector banks declared profits. During the current financial year, provisioning requirements of the banks will be much higher than in 1992-93 and, therefore, a larger number to banks are expected to report net losss at the end of this year.

Profits as a percentage of working funds also declined for private sector banks, foreign banks and all public sector banks excepting the SBI Group. For the SBI Group, it remained constant at a low level of 0.2 per cent. Except for SBI group, expenses as a percentage of working funds have increased for all categories of banks (Table 17.6).

17.2 BANKING AND FINANCIAL REFORMS, 1991-92 AND 1993-94

* Statutory Liquidity Ratio (SLR) on incremental net demand and time liabilities (DTL) reduced from 38.5 per cent to 25 per cent SLR and on net total DTL reduced from 38.5 per cent to 34.75 per cent. Expected to fall to 33 per cent by March.
* Incremental Cash Reserve Ratio (ICRR) of 10 per cent removed. One third of the impounded cash balances under incremental CRR was released, implying a reduction in CRR by 0.6 per cent. CRR on net total DTL reduced from 15 per cent to 14 per cent.
* Number of interest rate slabs on bank advances reduced from about 20 in 1989-90 to 3 in the current financial year. Controlled floor interest rate on bank advances and ceiling interest rate on term deposits reduced by 4 percentage points 3 percentage points, respectively.
* Prudential norms for income recognition classification of assets and provisioning for bad debts introduced. Banks to complete provisioning for doubtful and substandard assets by end March, 1994.
* Introduction of capital adequacy norms requiring 4 per cent to be attained by all bank by March 31, 1993 and 8 per cent by March 31, 1996. Foreign

banks operating in India and Indian banks with branches abroad must attain 8 per cent by March 31, 1993 and March 31, 1994, respectively.

* Budgetary support of Rs. 5700 crore for capitalisation of banks released after the nationalised banks entered into performance agreements with RBI for strengthening bank management and ensuring efficiency improvement.
* State Bank of India (SBI) Act amended to enable the bank to access the capital market and allow 10 per cent voting rights to share holders. SBI raised over Rs. 1400 crores as equity (including premium) and Rs. 1000 crores as bonds through a public issue. The RBI shareholding is now 67 per cent as against 99 per cent earlier.
* Bill to enable nationalised banks to access the capital market for debt and equity, introduced in Parilament.
* Banks given freedom to open new branches and upgrade extension counters on attaining capital adequacy norms and prudential accounting standards. They are permitted to close non viable branches other than in rural areas.
* New Bank of India merged with Punjab National Bank.
* 'In principle' approval given to seven proposals for setting up of new private sector banks. Banks allowed to raise capital contribution from foreign institutional investors upto 20 per cent and from Non-Resident Indians upto 40 per cent.
* A new Board of Financial Supervision being set up within RBI to strengthen the supervisory system of banks and financial institutions. A new department viz. Department of Supervision, established in RBI as an independent unit effective December 22, 1993 for supervision of commercial banks.
* 'Recovery of debts due to banks and financial institutions Act, 1993' passed to set up Special Recovery Tribunals to facilitate quicker recoveries of loan arrears.
* Bank lending norms liberalised and banks gives freedom to decide levels of holding of individual items of inventories and receivables.
* Ordiance promulgated amending Banking Regulation Act, 1949 to enable a banking company to have a non-executive Chariman and upto three directors from among the directors of promoting insitituion and to raise the ceiling for the exercise of voting rights for a shareholder upto 10 per cent and to raise the penalties for contravention of the act.
* Union agreement in October 1993 paves way for faster computerisation in banks.
* Scope of mandatory consortium arrangements narrowed to 76 large borrowal accounts in place of 934 accounts hitherto, borrowers allowed to induct new banks into a consortium and banks permitted to leave consortium after two years.
* 'Financial institutions' access to SLR funds reduced and they are encouraged to approach captial market for funds.
* IFCI convered into a company and its maiden public issue raised over Rs. 6000 crore as equity (including premium).
* Convertibility clause no longer obligatory for assistance sanctioned by term lending institutions.
* Ceiling on interest rate on debentures and bonds removed except for that

on tax-free PSU bonds.

* Auction of 91 days treasury bills and Government securities commenced from January 8, 1993 and June 3, 1992, respectively. Auction of 364 day treasury bills started from April 28, 1992 and replaced auction of 182 day treasury bill. Repo auctions in Government securities introduced in December 1992. Term can now be up to 14 days.

17.3 CREDIT POLICY MEASURES, 1993-94

* Floor interest rate on bank advances of over Rs. 2 lakh brought down in stages from 17 to 15 per cent and the number of interest rates on bank advances reduced from four to three.
* Interest rates on Rupee export credit reduced across the board by one percentage point.
* The ceiling interest rate on domestic term deposits of commercial banks reduced in stages from 12 per cent to 10 per cent and the interest rate on domestic saving deposits reduced from 6 per cent to 5 per cent.
* Ceiling interest rate on term deposits under NRER account reduced from 13 per cent to 11 per cent. Interest rate on saving deposits under these accounts reduced to 5 per cent.
* Minimum maturity period of FCNR deposits raised to two years and above but less than three years.
* A new FCNR (Banks) Scheme exempt from CRR and SLR with exchange rate guarantee by banks introduced.
* Authorised dealers allowed to rediscount export bills at rates linked to international interest rates and scope of preshipment export finance in dollar extended. Refinance limits for Export Credit (Rupee) refinance and postshipment export credit denominated in U.S. dollar reduced.
* 32 per cent of net bank credit stipulated as priority sector credit target for foreign banks with sub-targets of 10 per cent each for credit to SSI sector and to export sector, to be reached by end March 1994.
* Direct and indirect advances for agriculture clubbed within 18 per cent target for agricultural advance for domestic banks.
* Definition of small scale industries for priority sector advance revised to include units with investment in plants and machinery upto Rs. 60 lakh.
* 40 per cent of the total credit to SSI by each bank to flow to cottage, khadi and village and tiny industries.
* Package of measures to boost flow of bank credit to SSI units introduced including annual credit budget at branch level in consultation with SSI Units; minimum of 20 per cent of annual turnover as working capital finance for units requiring fund-based credit upto Rs. 50 lakh institutional framework for redressal of grievances and working captial finance for their marketing companies.
* Selective credit controls removed from bank advances against wheat, cotton/kapas and relaxed on bank advances against paddy and rice.
* Concession given to Certificates of Deposit (CD) in the form of exemption from CRR withdrawn.
* Companies allowed to issue commercial papers for maturities between 3 month and less than one year (in place of 6 months earlier) from the date of issue, and both the minimum net worth and minimum working captial (fund based) limit for eligibility of a company for issuing CP reduced from

Rs. 5 crore to Rs. 4 crore.

* Stipulation regarding minimum rate of interest of 14 per cent per annum on inter-bank participations (IBP) on risk-sharing basis withdrawn.
* Select All India financial institutions permitted to borrow from the term money market for three to six months.
* General Line of Credit from RBI to NABARD raised to Rs. 3700 crore from Rs. 3100 crore.
* Banks allowed to finance hire purchase and equipment leasing companies upto four times the net owned funds.
* Minimum margin on bank advances against shares and debenture/bonds reduced from 75 per cent to 50 per cent.
* Ceiling for investment by banks in public sector bonds/deposits raised from 1.5 per cent to 5 per cent of the incremental aggregate deposits of the previous year.

17.4 CAPITAL MARKET REFORMS, 1992-93 AND 1993-94

* Capital Issues (Control) Act, 1947 repealed and the office of the Controller of Capital Issues (CCI) abolished control over price and premium of shares removed. Companies are now free to approach capital market after clearance by SEBI.
* Securities and Exchange Board of India (SEBI) armed with necessary authority and powers for regulation and reform of capital market.
* Indian companies permitted to access international capital markets through Euro-equity shares.
* Companies required to disclose all material facts and specific risk factors associated with their projects while making public issues.
* Merchant banking statutorily brought under the regulatory framework of SEBI and merchant bankers required to abide by a code of conduct.
* Private mutual funds permitted and a few already set up. All mutual funds allowed to apply for firm allotment in public issues.
* Investment norms for NRIs liberalised allowing companies to accept capital contribution and issue shares or debentures to NRIs or overseas corportate bodies without prior permission of RBI.
* Foreign Institutional Investors (FII) permitted to invest in Indian capital market on registration with SEBI. Common application forms simplified for them and foreign brokers permitted to assist them.
* Over the Counter Exchange of India (OTCEI) commenced operations and a number of shares already lists with it.
* SEBI notified several regulations for intermediaries in the secondry market bringing these intermediaries within regulatory framework for the first time.
* SEBI introduced new reforms in the primary market for improving the disclosure standards, introducing prudential norms and simplifying issue procedurs.
* The procedures for lodgement of securities for transfer was considerably eased for domestic and foreign institutional investors through the introduction of a 'jumbo' transfer deeds and consolidated payment of stampe duty.
* SEBI introduced a code of advertisement for public issues for ensuring fair and truthful disclosures.
* SEBI introduced a number of meaures for streamlining the functioning of

the secondary market, such as reconstitution of the governing boards of the stock exchanges, capital adequacy norms for brokers, and for providing transparency in client/broker relationships.

* National Stock Exchange of India with nationwide stock trading facilities, electronic display, clearing and settlement facilities being set up by financial institutions and banks.

Source: *Economic Survey 1993-94,* Ministry of Finance, Government of India, New Delhi, 1994, Chapter 3

TABLE 17.1 : Source of Change in Money Stock

	Variation during					
	1992-93 Mar.31 to Mar.31	1992-93 Mar.31 to Jan. 8	1993-94 Mar.31 to Jan. 7	1992-93 Mar.31 to Mar.31	1992-93 Mar.31 to Mar.31	1993-94 Mar.31 to Jan. 7
1	2	3	4	5	6	7
		(Rs. crore)			*(Per cent)*	
I. M 1 Money supply with the public	8440	3619	17923	7.3	3.2	14.5
II. M 3 (Aggregate monetary resources)	45184	39370	51279	14.2	12.4	14.1
(i) Currency with the public	7414	5031	10999	12.1	8.2	16.1
(ii) Demand deposits with banks	408	-2829	6749	0.8	-5.5	12.7
(iii) Time deposits with banks	36744	35751	33356	18.1	17.6	13.9
(iv) Other deposits with RBI	618	1477	175			
III. Source of change in M 3 (1+2+3+4-5)						
1. Net bank credit to Government (a+b)	17826	16532	28448	11.3	10.4	16.2
(a) RBI's net credit to Government (i+ii) @	4433	7491	8686			
(i) Central Government	4257	8724+	10167			
(ii) State Governments	176	-1233	-1481			
(b) Other banks' credit to Government	13393	9041	19762			

(Contd.)

1	2	3	4	5	6	7
2. Bank credit to commercial sector (a+b)	28380	24439	13089	15.1	13.0	6.0
(a) RBI's credit to commercial sector *	-1040	-1239	75			
(b) Other banks'credit to commercial sector	29420	25678	13014			
3. Net foreign exchange assets of the banking sector #	3809	-3261	11270	17.4	-15.4	45.1
3a. Excluding revaluation of gold	2369	-3110	9450	11	-14.7	37.8
4. Government's currency liabilities to the public	94	89	81	5.5	5.2	4.5
5. Banking sector's net non-monetary liabilities other than time deposits (a+b)	4925	-1571	1609	9.4	-3.0	2.8
(a) Net non-monetary liabililties of RBI	641	-2836	-1763			
(b) Net non-monetary liabilities of other banks (residual)	4284	1265	3372			

$ Variations in respect of scheduled commercial banks are based on data for last reporting Friday of March. Data for RBI and other are for March 31. All figures are provisional.

* Excludes, since the establishment of NABARD, its refinance to banks.

@ Includes special securities

\# Inclusive of appreciation in the value of gold following its revaluation close to international market price since October 17, 1990. Such appreciation has a corresponding effect on RBI's net non-monetary liabilities.

\+ Includes Rs. 751.64 crore (equivalent of SDRs 211.95 million) incurred on account of Reserve Asset subscription to the IMF towards the quota increase.

TABLE 17.2 : Sources of Change in Reserve Money

	Outstanding as on March 31, 1992	Vartiations+ 1992-93 Mar. 31 to Mar. 31	1992-93 Mar. 31 to Jan.8	1993-94 Mar. 31 to Jan. 7	1992-93 Mar. 31 to Mar.31	1992-93 Mar. 31 to Jan. 8	1993-94 Mar. 31 to Jan. 7
1	2	3	4	5	6	7	8
		(Rs. crore)				Percent	
1. Net RBI credit to Government $	94016	4433	7491	8686	4.7	8.0	8.8
2. RBI credit to banks @	5103	4783	2565	-3144	93.7	50.8	-31.8
3. RBI credit to commercial sector*	7260	-1040	-1239	75	14.3	-17.1	1.2
4. Net foreign exchange assets of RBI #	18838	3809	-3261	11270	20.2	-17.3	49.8
4a. Excluding revaluation of gold		2369	-3110	9450	12.6	-16.5	41.7
5. Government's currency liabilities to the public	1787	94	89	81	5.5	5.2	4.5
6. Net non-monetary liabilities of RBI	127415	641	-2836	-1763	2.3	-10.3	-6.3
7. Reserve Money (1+2+3+4+5+6)	99505	11438	8481	18731	11.5	8.5	16.9

\+ Variations are worked out on the basis of March 31 data after closure of Government accounts. All figures are provisional.

@ Includes claims on NABARD.

* Excludes, since the establishment of NABARD, its refinance to banks.

$ Includes special securities.

\# Variations are inclusive of apperciation in the value of gold following its revaluation close to the international market price since October 17, 1990. Such appreciation has a corresponding effect on RBI's net non-monetary liabilities.

TABLE 17.3 : Scheduled Commercial Banks - Selected Indicators

Item	1991-92 Mar. 22 1991 to Mar 20 1992	1992-93 Mar. 20 1992 to Mar. 19 1993	Variation during 1992-93 Mar. 20 to Jan. 8*	1993-94 Mar. 19 to Jan. 7*
1	2	3	4	5
		(Rs. crore)		
1. Aggregate deposits (a+b)	38216	37814	31549	35410
(a) Demand deposits	11895	1373	-1827	6079
(b) Time deposits	26321	36441	33376	29331
2. Borrowings with RBI	-2891	1042	2536	948
3. Cash in hand	204	285	85	-14
4. Balances with R.B.I.	10318	-5644	1856	15820
5. Net balances with R.B.I. (4-2)	13209	4602	-680	14872
6. Money at call and short notice	904	1293	2367	-1040
7. Bank Credit (a+b)	9291	26390	21085	8592
(a) Public food procurement credit	164	2073	824	4336
(b) Non-food bank credit	9127	24317	20261	4256
of which to Priority Sector #	2510	4333	1304+	-210++
8. Investments in approved securities	15131	15460	10999	19640
(a) Governments securities	12729	13218	8764	18796
(b) Other approved securities	2402	2242	2235	844
9. Balances with other banks in current account	621	-192	385	-290
		(per cent)		
10. Credit-Deposit Ratio	54.4	56.6	55.9	52.8
11. Investment-Deposit Ratio	39.1	39.3	38.6	41.2

* Provisional

\+ Up to August 28, 1992

++ Up to August 27, 1993

\# Data relate to 48 banks accounting for more than 90 per cent of bank credit.

TABLE 17.4 : Sectoral Deployment of Gross Bank Credit

	Variations during*							
					April-August		April-August	
	1991-92	1992-93	1992-93	1993-94	1991-92	1992-93	1992-93	1993-94
1	2	3	4	5	6	7	8	9
I. Gross bank credit	7986	21066	7159	-1249	6.8	16.7	5.7	-0.8
1. Public food procurement	164	2073	-710	2309	3.6	44.4	-15.2	34.2
2. Gross non-food credit (a+b+c+d)	7822	18993	7869	-3558	6.9	15.7	6.5	-2.5
(a) Priority Sector (i+ii+iii)	2510	4333	1304	-210	5.8	9.5	2.9	-0.4
(i) Agriculture	1407	1727	656	132	8.4	9.5	3.6	0.7
(ii) Small scale industry	969	1877	327	-40	5.6	10.3	1.8	-0.2
(iii) Other priority sectors	134	729	321	-302	1.5	8.0	3.5	-3.1
(b) Medium and large industries	2582	11537	5202	-1921	5.8	24.5	11.0	-3.3
(c) Wholesale Trade (excluding food procurement)	244	755	413	-551	4.1	12.3	6.7	-8.0
(d) Other sectors	2486	2368	950	-876	12.3	10.4	4.2	-3.5
II. Export credit +	1108	5054	1369	539	12.1	49.1	13.3	3.5
Priority Sector advances as proportion of net bank credit. @					38.7	35.0	37.1	34.4

* All figures after 1991-92 are provisional.

@ In the last month of each period. Advances include inter bank participation.

\+ Also included in non-food credit.

Note: Data relate to 50 scheduled commercial banks which account for about 95 per cent of the credit of all scheduled commercial banks. Gross bank credit date exclude bills rediscounted with RBI, IDBI, Exim Bank and other approved financial institutions.

TABLE 17.5 : Provisions and Profits in 1992-93

(Rs. crore)

Banks	Gross Profit	Provision	Net Profit
1	2	3	4
(a) SBI Group	2164	1984	280
(b) Other Public sector banks	805	4453	(-) 3648
(c) All Public sector banks	2969	6437	(-) 3368

TABLE 17.6 : Working Results of Scheduled Commercial Banks for 1991-92 and 1992-93

Item	SBI Group		Other public sector banks		Private sector banks		Foreign banks		All banks	
	1991-92	1992-93	1991-92	1992-93	1991-92	1992-93	1991-92	1992-93	1991-92	1992-93
1	2	3	4	5	6	7	8	9	10	11
A. Rupees crore										
A. Income 13428	13963	21018	22126	1298	1595	3674	4009	39418	41693	
(i) Interest	11775	12166	18975	19945	1160	1410	2829	3700	34739	37221
(ii) Other incomes	1653	1797	2043	2181	138	185	845	309	4679	4472
B. Expenditure	13184	13683	20459	25774	1221	1520	3354	4851	38218	45828
(i) Interest	7392	8416	13630	15696	708	987	1845	2570	23575	27669
(ii) Other operating expenses	2864	3283	5020	5625	375	417	570	858	8829	10183
(iii) Provisions and contingencies	2928	1984	1809	4453	138	116	939	1423	5814	7976
C. Profit 244	280	559	-3648	77	75	320	-842	1200	-4135	
D. Working Funds	115081	124567	186636	211614	11917	15111	25103	31678	338737	382970
B. Per Cent of Working Funds										
A. Income 11.7	11.2	11.3	10.5	10.9	10.6	14.6	12.7	11.6	10.9	
(i) Interest	10.2	9.8	10.2	9.4	9.7	9.3	11.3	11.7	10.3	9.7
(ii) Other incomes	1.4	1.4	1.1	1.0	1.2	1.2	3.4	1.0	1.4	1.2

(Contd.)

TABLE 17.6 *(Contd.)*

1	2	3	4	5	6	7	8	9	10	11
B. Expenditure	11.5	11.0	11.0	12.2	10.2	10.1	13.4	15.3	11.3	12.0
(i) Interest	6.4	6.8	7.3	7.4	5.9	6.5	7.3	8.1	7.0	7.2
(ii) Other operating expenses	2.5	2.6	2.7	2.7	3.1	2.8	2.3	2.7	2.6	2.7
(iii) Provisional and contingencies	2.5	1.6	1.0	2.1	1.2	0.8	3.7	4.5	1.7	2.1
C. Profit 0.2	0.2	0.3	-1.7	0.6	0.5	1.3	-2.7	0.4	-1.1	

18

AGRICULTURE, ANIMAL HUSBANDRY AND DAIRY DEVELOPMENT

18.1 AGRICULTURE

Overall Production

The performance of agricultural production during the last years and the prospects during 1993-94 are given in Table 18.1.

TABLE 18.1: Agricultural Production-Principal Crops
(Million Tonnes)

	1989-90	1990-91	1991-92	1992-93		1993-94	
			(Revised)	Target	Final	Target	Final
1	2	3	4	5	6	7	8
Rice	73.6	74.3	74.7	77.3	72.6	78.0	74.0
Wheat	49.8	55.1	55.7	57.0	56.8	58.5	56.9
Coarse Cereals	34.8	32.7	26.0	34.3	37.0	36.0	33.7
Pulses	12.8	14.3	12.0	14.4	13.6	15.5	14.5
Total Foodgrains	**171.0**	**176.4**	**168.4**	**183.0**	**180.0**	**168.0**	**179.1**
Kharif	101.0	99.4	91.6	103.3	100.5	105.5	98.9
Rabi	70.0	77.0	76.8	79.8	79.5	82.5	80.2
Oilseeds	16.9	1.6	18.6	19.0	20.3	21.0	20.5
Sugarcane	225.6	241.0	254.0	243.0	230.8	250.0	231.0
Cotton @	11.4	9.8	9.7	12.0	11.6	12.5	10.6
Jute & mesta	8.3	9.2	10.3	9.3	9.0	9.3	8.3

(Contd.)

TABLE 18.1 *(Contd.)*

1	2	3	4	5	6	7	8
Rice	4.4	1.0	0.5		-2.8		1.9
Wheat	-7.9	10.6	1.1		2.0		0.2
Coarse Cereals	10.5	-6.0	-20.5		42.3		-8.9
Pulses	-7.2	11.7	-16.1		13.3		6.6
Total Foodgrains	**0.6**	**3.2**	**-4.5**		**6.9**		**-0.5**
Kharif	5.6	-1.6	-7.8		9.7		-1.6
Rabi	-5.8	10.0	-0.3		3.5		0.9
Oilseeds	-6.1	10.1	—		9.1		1.0
Sugarcane	11.1	6.8	5.4		-9.1		0.1
Cotton @	31.0	-14.0	-1.0		19.6		-6.6
Jute & mesta $	5.1	10.8	12.0		-12.6		-7.8

@ Bales of 170 kg each
$ Bales of 180 kg each

Foodgrains

The production of foodgrains during 1992-93 reached a record level of 180 million tonnes which was higher by about 7 per cent over the previous year. This was mainly due to a quantum jump in the production of coarse cereals which was higher by 11 million tonnes over 1991-92. The production of wheat also attained a new height at 56.76 million tonnes during 1992-93. The increase in production of foodgrains has been rather modest during the last three years.

Rice

Area under rice during 1992-93 was 41.64 million hectare, 2.4 per cent less than the previous year. With only 45.1 per cent of the total rice area under irrigation, the country still depends heavily on south-west monsoon rain. Total production of rice in 1992-93 at 72.61 million tonnes declined by 2.8 per cent from the previous year's record output of 74.68 per million tonnes due to a decline in both area and yield.

Kharif 1993 rice area is expected to be at last year's level but production may be higher at 65.50 million tonnes. With summer (rabi) rice production expected at 8.50 million tonnes, the total output of rice (kharif and rabi) during 1993-94 is expected to be 74 million tonnes (about 2 per cent gain over 1992-93).

Wheat

In 1992-93, production of wheat reached a record level at 56.76 million tonnes which was 2 per cent higher than that of previous year. The area under wheat increased by 5 per cent from 23.26 million hectares in 1991-92 to 24.43 million hectares in 1992-93. The production target of wheat for 1993-94 has been fixed at 58.50 million tonnes. The cumulative rainfall has been satisfactory during the post monsoon season in all the major wheat growing areas of Punjab, Haryana, Rajasthan, Madhya Pradesh, Uttar Pradesh, besides Bihar plains. A good spell of widespread rain in January is likely to result in a higher wheat output even though current estimate of likely production is 56.9 million tonnes.

Coarse Cereals

Jowar, bajra, maize, ragi, small millets and barley constitute coarse cereals. Area under total coarse cereals at 34.8 million hectare in 1992-93 was 4 per cent higher than the preceding year. Production of coarse cereals in 1992-93 rose to a spectacular level at 37.04 million tonnes from the previous year's 26.99 million tonnes, registering an increase of 42.5 per cent, much of it due to extremely favourable weather effect. Production in the current year is likely to fall back to its normal growth trend and hence kharif 1993 output of coarse cereals may be 27.40 million tonnes. With the likelihood of normal production of rabi coarse cereals (i.e., jowar, maize, and barley) at 6.30 million tonnes for 1993-94, the total production of coarse cereals may be around 33.7 million tonnes against the target of 36.0 million tonnes.

Pulses

Production of pulses during 1992-93 increased significantly to 13.60 million tonnes from 12.02 million tonnes in 1991-92 recording an increase of 13.1 per cent. The increase in production of pulses during 1992-93 was the result of an increase in both area and yield. Output of pulses during kharif season in 1993-94 may be 6 million tonnes compared to 5.85 million tonnes in 1992-93. If rabi season turns out to be reasonably satisfactory, the total production of pulses during 1993-94 may reach 14.5 million tonnes, which should reduce the pressure for imports of pulses.

Oilseeds

Production of nine oilseeds (groundnut, rapeseed and mustard, soyabean, sunflower, seasamum, castorseed, nigerseed, linseed and safflower) is estimated at 20.27 million tonnes during 1992-93 against the preceding year's production of 18.60 million tonnes, registering an increase of 9 per cent. The increase in production of oilseeds was mainly due to an increase in yield from 719 kg. per hectare in 1991-92 to 793 kg. per hectare in 1992-93. Production of safflower, groundnut, soyabean, sesamum and castroseed increased by 70.0 per cent, 24.8 per cent, 24.9 per cent, 19.7 per cent and 7 per cent, respectively, in 1992-93 over 1991-92. On the contrary, production of rapeseed and mustard, lineseed and sunflower declined by 17.0 per cent, 6.8 per cent and 0.8 per cent respectively, during the same period. It is interesting to note that the production of groundnut and seasamum increased significantly during 1992-93 despite decline in area by 3.7 per cent and 10 per cent respectively Table 18.2.

TABLE 18.2: Production of Oilseeds

(Million Tonnes)

Oilseeds	1986-87	1987-88	1988-89	1989-90	1990-91	1991-92*	1992-93**	1993-94 Target	1993-94 Likely
1	2	3	4	5	6	7	8	9	10
Groundnut	5.88	5.85	9.66	8.10	7.51	7.09	8.85	8.20	7.15
Kharif	4.43	4.18	7.49	6.10	5.12	4.99	6.58	6.00	4.90
Rabi	1.45	1.67	2.17	2.00	2.39	2.10	2.27	2.20	2.25
Castorseed	0.23	0.20	0.41	0.52	0.72	0.58	0.62	0.70	0.50
Seasmum	0.45	0.58	0.68	0.74	0.84	0.71	0.85	0.90	0.80
Rapeseed & Mustard	2.60	3.46	4.38	4.12	5.23	5.87	4.87	5.70	6.25
Linseed	0.32	0.39	0.36	0.33	0.33	0.29	0.27	0.40	0.30
Nigerseed	0.13	0.18	0.18	0.19	0.19	0.18	0.18	0.20	0.20
Safflower	0.35	0.46	0.44	0.49	0.32	0.20	0.34	0.40	0.40
Sunflower	0.42	0.63	0.37	0.63	0.87	1.19	1.18	1.40	1.40
Kharif	0.25	0.38	0.22	0.27	0.33	0.36	0.42	0.60	0.60
Rabi	0.17	0.25	0.15	0.36	0.54	0.83	0.76	0.80	0.80
Soyabean	0.89	0.90	1.55	1.80	2.60	2.49	3.11	3.10	4.50
Total	**11.27**	**12.65**	**18.03**	**16.92**	**18.61**	**18.60**	**20.27**	**21.00**	**20.50**
Kharif	6.38	6.42	10.53	9.62	9.80	9.31	11.76	11.50	11.50
Rabi	4.89	6.23	7.50	7.30	8.81	9.29	8.52	9.50	9.00

* Revised estimates
** Final estimates.

Sugarcane

Since 1985-86 production of sugarcane had maintained uptrend until it touched 254.0 million tonnes in 1991-92. In 1992-93, it declined to 230.8 million tonnes mainly due to a decline in area from 3.84 million hectares in 1991-92 to 3.62 million hectares in 1992-93. During 1993-94, the acreagae under sugarcane is expected to decline further by 3 per cent, though the production is expected to be around last year's level.

Cotton

In spite of a decline in area under cotton by 1.5 per cent during 1992-93 over 1991-92, the production of cotton increased significantly by 19.2 per cent from 9.71 million bales (of 170 kg each) to 11.58 million bales in 1992-93. The increase in production of cotton during 1992-93 was, therefore, exclusively due to an increase in yield. Because of floods in Punjab and Haryana in July and deficient rains in Gujarat during August/September, production of cotton during 1993-94 may be just 10.6 million bales.

Jute & Mesta

Production of jute and mesta at 9 million bales (of 180 kg each) in 1992-93 registered a decline of 12.6 per cent over the previous year's production of 10.29 million bales mainly due to a decline in area, both under jute and mesta, by about 12.6 per cent and 11.5 per cent respectively. The area under jute in 1993-94 is expected to have declined further as dry weather prevailed at the time of the sowing of the crop in the jute growing eastern region. The crop coverage under mesta was, however, reported to be satisfactory. The total production of jute and mesta may be around 8.3 million bales in 1993-94.

Plantation Crops

Tea

Tea is an important traditional item of export. The domestic demand for tea in the last decade has risen at a faster pace compared to production thus resulting in a decline in exportable surplus. Due to unfavourable climatic factors, production of tea declined marginally from 727 million kgs. in 1991-92 to 721 million kgs in 1992-93. In consequence, export of tea was of the order of 177.80 million kgs valued at Rs. 993.4 crore during 1993-94 as compared to 216.45 million kgs valued Rs. 1212.27 crore during 1991-92. The production target for 1993-94 has been set at 730 million kgs and export target at 210 million kgs.

Coffee

The production of coffee varies considerably with the fluctuations in wheather conditions. However, from a small quantity of 18893 tonnes in 1950-51, it had gone up to an all time high of 215000 tonnes in 1988-89. The production during 1992-93 was 161500 tonnes. Unlike tea, the bulk of coffee is exported. The domestic demand had been stagnating at around 55000 tonnes per annum. Exports of coffee amounted to 1.13 lakh tonnes valued at Rs. 381 crore during 1992-93 compared with 1.11 lakh tonnes valued at Rs. 349 crore in 1991-92.

Rubber

Production of natural rubber increased from 2.6 lakh tonnes in 1988-89 to 3.95 lakh tonnes in 1992-93. The total area under rubber is estimated to be 4.66 lakh hectares, out which Kerala alone accounts for 85 per cent. The increase in production was due to an increase in both area and yield. Rubber is now being grown in non-traditional areas of Karnataka, Maharashtra, Tripura, Meghalaya, Mizoram, Manipur, Assam, Nagaland, Andaman & Nicobar Islands, Goa and Orissa. Most of the rubber plantations are small, the average size being 0.5 hectare. Consumption of rubber is expected to increase from 4.14 lakh tonnes in 1992-93 to 4.5 lakh tonnes in 1993-94. To meet the gap between demand and supply, some quantity of natural rubber continues to be imported.

Irrigation

The country's irrigation potential has increased from 22.6 million hectares in the pre-Plan period to 83.4 million hectares at the end of 1992-93 comprising of 31.3 million hectares under major and medium irrigation projects and 52.1 million hectares in minor irrigation projects. The target for 1993-94 is 86.1 million hectares comprising 32.0 million hectares under major and medium projects and 54.1 hectares under minor irrigation projects. Irrigation sector continues to be a priority sector for development in the Eighth Five Year Plan.

The problem of under utilisation of created irrigation potential, particularly in major and medium irrigation projects continues to persist. At the end of 1992-93 utilisation was 75.1 million hectares against a created potential of 83.4 million hectares. This leaves a gap of 8.3 million hectares (4.5 million hectares in major and medium and 3.8 million hectares in minor irrigation). The main reasons for the gap are delays involved in the development of on-farm works like construction of field channels, land levelling and adoption of the 'warabandi system' (network of distributories and minors over the command area) and finally the time taken by the farmers in switching over to the new cropping pattern, i.e., from dry farming to irrigated farming.

Minor irrigation schemes include ground water and surface water projects. While ground water schemes include dugwells, shallow tubewells and pumpsets, the surface water schemes include tanks and reservoirs diversion schemes have been accorded special attention under the Special Foodgrains Productions Programme. For 1993-94, the targets for irrigation potential created and utilisation are 2.0 m.ha. and 1.7 m. ha respectively. Because of shorter gestation lags and lower investment costs, emphasis is being laid on creation of minor irrigation schemes to cover both surface and ground water. Because of advantageous water table levels, the eastern sector is being given special attention for exploration of minor irrigation during the Eighth Plan.

The details of development of irrigation potential and their utilisation are listed in Table 18.3.

TABLE 18.3: Development of Irrigation Potential and its Utilisation

(Million hectares)

	At the end of Seventh Plan	During 1990-92	At the end of 1991-92	1992-93 (Likely)	1993-94 (Target)
1	2	3	4	5	6
1. Major & medium irrigation					
Potential	29.9	0.8	30.7	0.6	0.7
Utilisation	25.5	0.9	26.4	0.5	0.6
2. Minor Irrigation					
Potential	46.6	3.7	50.3	1.8	2.0

(Contd.)

TABLE 18.3 *(Contd.)*

1	2	3	4	5	6
Utilisation	43.1	3.4	46.5	1.7	1.7
3. Total					
Potential	76.5	4.5	81.0	2.4	2.7
Utilisation	68.6	4.3	72.9	2.2	2.3

Note: Irrigation projects with a Cumulative Comman Area (CCA) of more than 10000 hectares are classified as major projects and projects with CCA of more than 2000 hectares and up to 10000 hectares as medium projects.

Seeds

Availability of quality seeds is essential for achieving higher production. Accordingly, high yielding variety programme (HYV) started in 1966-67 has remained a major instrument of agricultural strategy to increase foodgrains production in the country. The HYV programme is supported by 'mini kit demonstration' programme for rice, wheat and coarse-cereals for popularising newly identified varieties suitable for different agro-climatic zones.

During 1992-93, 5.85 million quintals of certified quality seeds were distributed to farmers as against 5.75 million quintals during 1991-92. The distribution of certified seeds is expected to reach the level of 7 million quintals by the end of Eighth Plan. The progress of area covered under HYV seeds under different crops and their share in the total area are listed in Table 18.4.

TABLE 18.4: Area Under High-Yielding Varieties of Seeds

(Million hectares)

Crop	1966-67	1988-89	1989-90	1990-91	1991-92*	1992-93 (Estimated)	1993-94 (Target)
1	2	3	4	5	6	7	8
Paddy	0.9	25.4	26.2	28.1	28.0	28.3	31.0
Wheat	0.5	20.2	20.3	20.4	20.5	22.2	22.8
Jowar	0.1	6.1	6.9	6.7	6.8	6.9	9.0
Bajra	0.1	5.9	5.6	5.1	5.4	5.6	6.9
Maize	0.2	2.5	2.3	2.6	2.8	3.0	3.5
Ragi	—	—	—	1.0	1.2	1.1	1.1
Total	1.8	60.1	61.2	63.9	64.7	67.1	74.3
(Percentage of HYV area to Total Area under the crop)							

(Contd.)

TABLE 18.4 *(Contd.)*

1	2	3	4	5	6	7	8
Paddy	2.6	60.9	62.1	65.8	65.7	68.0	
Wheat	3.9	83.8	86.4	84.3	88.1	90.8	
Jowar	0.6	41.8	46.6	46.5	55.0	52.6	
Bajra	0.8	49.2	51.4	48.6	53.8	52.9	
Maize	3.9	42.4	39.0	44.1	47.8	49.8	
Ragi	—	—	—	45.5	56.3	53.4	

*Revised

The National Seeds Project Phase-II launched in March 1990 with the assistance of the World Bank for strengthening the public and private seed sector is continuing. The project is scheduled to receive an assistance of US$ 150 million up to June 1995.

Fertilisers

Use of fertilisers remains of the principal determinants of crop yield. The consumption of fertiliser, which was only 0.13 million tonnes in 1955-56, increased to 12.2 million tonnes in 1992-93. At this level the consumption was lower by 4.52 per cent as compared to 1991-92. This was mainly due to a fall in the consumption of phosphatic and potassic fertilisers in the wake of price decontrol and consequent rise in prices in August 1992. Fertiliser consumption since 1985-86 is shown in Table 18.5.

TABLE 18.5: Consumption of Chemical Fertilisers

(Million Tonnes of nutrients)

Year	Nitrogenous	Phosphatic	Potasic	Total
1	2	3	4	5
1985-86	5.7	2.0	0.8	8.5
1986-87	5.7	2.1	0.9	8.7
1987-88	5.7	2.2	0.9	8.8
1988-89	7.3	2.7	1.1	11.1
1989-90	7.4	3.0	1.2	11.6
1990-91	8.0	3.2	1.3	12.5
1991-92	8.0	3.3	1.4	12.7
1992-93	8.4	2.9	0.9	12.2
1993-94*	9.6	3.2	1.0	13.8

*Target

Consumption in appropriate mix of the three plant nutrients-Nitrogen (N), Phosphate (P) and Potash (K) is essential for increasing crop yields. The ideal average NPK ratio aggregated for the country as a whole is 4:2:1, which is substantially at variance with the observe all-India NPK consumption ratio as shown in Table 18.6.

TABLE 18.6: All India NPK Consumption Ratio

Year	N	P	K
1	2	3	4
1955-56	10.8	1.3	1
1960-61	7.2	1.8	1
1965-66	7.5	1.7	1
1970-71	6.5	2.0	1
1975-76	7.7	1.7	1
1980-81	5.9	1.9	1
1985-86	7.0	2.5	1
1990-91	6.0	2.4	1
1991-92	5.9	2.4	1
1991-92*	6.4	2.6	1
1992-93	9.5	3.2	1
1992-93*	15.1	4.6	1

*.Rabi

There was some narrowing down of NP ratio of consumption from 5.9:1.9 in 1980-81 to 5.9:2.4 in 1991-92. However, this trend seems to have been reversed during 1992-93 as the Nitrogen to Phosphate ratio has increased to 9.5:3.2 in 1992-93. This is attributed to the distortion in fertiliser pricing policy. The impact of distortion is more visible in the rabi seasons as N to P ratio has significantly increased from 6.4:2.6 in 1991-92 (Rabi) to 15.1:4.6 in 1992-93 (Rabi). This is not a healthy trend as this imbalance in NPK consumption may aggravate soil fertility problems and affect productivity adversly in future crop seasons.

The production of nitrogenous and phosphatic fertilisers during 1992-93 stood at about 9.74 million tonnes exhibiting a marginal decline of about one per cent over the previous year. During the year 1993-94, however, the production of nitrogenous and phosphatic fertilisers is expected to increase. Details of production, imports and subsidies are given in Table 18.7.

Domestic fertiliser industry has begun to face greater competition following the decontrol and decanalisation of non-nitrogenous fertilisers and trade policy changes introduced in 1992-93. The custom duty on imports of phosphoric acid, the main intermediate used in manufacture of DAP, has been abolished. To offset the sharp increase in the price of Diammonium Phosphate (DAP), the Government has provided a subsidy of Rs. 1000 per tonne on the sale of indigenous DAP and proportionate concession on indigenous complex

TABLE 18.7: Fertiliser Production, Imports and Subsidy

	Production (N+P) (000 tonnes)	Imports (N+P) (000 tonnes)	Subsidy (Rs. crore) On imported fertiliser	On domestic fertiliser	total
1	2	3	4	5	6
1985-86	5756	3399	324	1600	1924
1986-87	7070	2310	197	1700	1897
1987-88	7131	984	114	2050	2164
1988-89	8964	1608	201	3000	3201
1989-90	8543	3114	771	3771	4542
1990-91	9045	2758	659	3730	4389
1991-92	9863	2769	1300	3500	4800
1992-93	9740	2986	996	4800	5796
1993-94 (Budgeted)	10000	2938	570	3430	4000

fertilisers in 1992-93 and 1993-94. This subsidy of Rs. 1000 per tonne is also available on sale of imported Muriate of Potash (MOP). A concession of Rs. 340 per tonne has also been allowed on single super phosphate during 1993-94. Thus apart from the budgeted provision Rs. 3500 crore as fertiliser subsidy, demand was approved for supplementary appropriation for Rs. 430 crore arising on account of Rs. 1000/tonne subsidy on indegenous DAP. Additional import of urea involving Rs. 70 crore subsidy has also been provided for. The total subsidy, therefore, would amount to Rs. 4000 crore in 1993-94.

Seeds

During 1992-93, 5.85 million quintals of certified quality seeds were distributed to farmers as against 5.75 million quintals during 1991-92. The distribution of certified seeds is expected to reach the level of 7 million quintals by the end of Eighth Plan.

Plant Protection

Need-based and judicious application of pesticides has been promoted through integrated Pest Management (IPM). The strategy is to adopt environmentally safe and cost-effective plant protection measures. This technology harmonises with other segments of crop husbandry for achieving higher productivity. The IPM includes pest monitoring promotion of biological control of pests, organising demonstrations and training of extension workers and farmers especially on crops such as, rice, cotton, oilseeds and pulses by 26 Central

Integrated Pest Management Centres in collaboration with the State Departments of Agriculture, State Agricultural Universities, Krishi Vikas Kendras and Indian Council of Agricultural Research Institutes.

Agricultural Credit

Availability of adequate credit/finance to the agricultural sector is one of the most important factors for achieving the objectives of increased foodgrains production/productivity. The institutional framework for present rural credit system consists of cooperative banks, regional rural banks (RRBs), rural branches of commercial banks and National Bank for Agricultural and Rural Development (NABARD). The institutional agencies advance loans for a variety of purposes such as agriculture, agro-industry and rural artisans and target groups under integrated Rural Development Programme (IRDP). The loans are of short, medium and long-term duration depending upon the end-use of the funds.

The total quantum of agricultural loans provided by cooperatives, commercial banks and RRBs has increased from Rs. 7005 crore in 1985-86 to Rs. 11308 crore in 1991-92 and to Rs. 13000 crore in 1992-93. The target for 1993 94 is Rs. 15100 crore.

Crop Insurance

From kharif 1985 to the end of rabi 1992-93 season, 365.55 lakh farmers have been covered over an area of 637.08 lakh hectares insuring a sum of Rs. 8458.85 crore. Claims amounting to Rs. 948.56 crore were paid to the farmers (of which Gujarat alone accounted for more than half the amount) against a premium income of Rs. 141.91 crore.

Agricultural Research and Extension

Department of Agriculture has reorganised extension services in major States including North-Eastern States and other Union Territories. Training infrastructure in the Central and State sector has been developed substantially. National institution of Agricultural Extension Management, 4 Extension Education Institute and 15 Advanced Training Institutes have been established for training of extension personnel at various levels. To improve farmer-scientist interaction two new schemes, namely, 'Agricultural Extention through Voluntary Organisations' and 'Women in Agriculture', are in the pipeline.

Agricultural Marketing

The marketing of agricultural produce through cooperatives has registered substantial growth from Rs. 1950 crore in 1980-81 to Rs. 6503 crore in 1991-92. The National Agricultural Cooperative Marketing Federation of India (NAFED) is an apex cooperative organisation. The number of regulated agricultural produce markets in the country was 6742 on March 30, 1994.

TABLE 18.8: Agricultural Export in Crores of Rupees

	1990-91	1991-92	1992-93
Marine products	89.3	1375	1840
Rice	461.57	754.98	971.43
Cashew	441.9	668.45	745.13
Spices	233.94	370.40	332.00
Sugar & Molasses	35.57	144.23	325.09
Wheat	31.13	121.47	—
Floriculture	7.07	13.16	13.2
Total	2819.38	4373.53	5585.39

Source: Third concept, December 1993.

18.2 ANIMAL HUSBANDRY AND DAIRY DEVELOPMENT

India is endowed with livestock resources of considerable genetic diversity to withstand environmental stress and inadequate levels of nutrition and management. The gross value of output from this sector is estimated at Rs. 51600 crores in 1991-92 compared to Rs. 43659 crore in 1990-91 accounting for 25.5 per cent of the value of total agricultural output (excluding the contribution of animal draught output).

India ranks second in the world in milk production, with an estimated production of 58.6 million tonnes in 1992-93, about 3.5 per cent higher over 1991-92. Success in raising the level of milk production is ascribed to the Operation Flood Project, world's largest integrated dairy development programme started in 1970 by the National Dairy Development Board (NDDB). This programme is basically designed to link rural milk producers with urban consumers and is currently in its third phase of implementation with financial assistance from the World Bank and commondity assistance in the form of skimmed milk powder and butter oil from European Economic Community (EEC). Over 65300 Dairy Cooperative Societies have been organised in 170 milk sheds involving about 8.4 million former members.

Poultry

Production of eggs in 1992-93 is estimated at 23.1 million.

Fisheries

Production of fish reached 4.36 million tonnes in 1992-93, registering 5 per cent growth over 1991-92. This comprised 2.58 million tonnes of marine fish and 1.78 million tonnes of inland fish. Production of fish is expected to be 4.75 million tonnes in 1993-94.

TABLE 18.9: Foreign collaboration in hybrid seed industry in India since 1988: Some Examples

Year	Indian company	Foreign collaborator	Activity	Type of collaboration
1988	ITC Agrotech Ltd., Secundrabad	Continental Grains, Australia	Hybrid seeds	Technical
1988	Bihar Seeds Corporation, Champaran	Pacific Seeds, Australia	Hybrid sunflower seeds	Technical
1988	Nath Seeds Pvt. Ltd., Aurangabad	Dobi Gon & Co., USA	Hybrid sunflower seeds	Technical
1990	Bisco Seed Tech., Delhi	Agripro Bio Sciences, USA	Hybrid seeds	Technical
1990	Nath Seeds Ltd., Aurangabad	Royal Sluis BV, The Netherlands	Hybrid vegetable seeds	Financial
1990	Maharashtra Hybrid Seed Co. Ltd., Bombay	Asgrow Seeds Co., USA	Hybrid vegetable seeds	Technical
1990	ECL Agrotech, Calcutta	Controcco-op, Yugoslavia	Hybrid seeds	Technical
1992	Raunaq International, New Delhi	University of Agriculture, NOVISAT, Yugoslavia	Hybrid seeds	Technical/Financial
1992	Intercrop Inds. Ltd., New Delhi	Rustica Semences, France	Hybrid seeds	Technical
1993	Southern Petro Chemical Industries Corporation, Madras	Pioneer Overseas Corporation, USA	Hybrid seeds	Financial
1993	Proagro-PGS India (P) Ltd., New Delhi	Plant Genetic Systems International NV, Belgium	Hybrid oilseed rape and vegetables seeds	Technical/Financial
1993	Micro Planate Ltd., Bombay	Kemira OY, Finland	Hybrid and synthetic seeds	Technical

Source: *Papers presented at the National Conference on Seeds*, February 1993, by the Ministry of Agriculture, Government of India, and the Department of Agriculture, Government of U.P. India Investment Centre (1993), Monthly Newsletter, various issues as reports. Biotechnology and Department Moniter, June 1994.

18.3 AGRICULTURE AND GATT

During the run up to the GATT agreement, which was finalised in December 1993, fears were expressed that India's interest in agriculture will be adversely affected as a result of the proposed agreement on agricultural issues in the Uruguay Round. There were apprehensions that we may be foreced to reduce the subsidies available to our farmers; phase out the public distribution system and compulsorily open up to agricultural imports. It was also feared that the traditional rights of the farmers to retain and exchange seds may also be constrained. A thorough analysis of the agreement, as finalised in December, leads to the conclusion that on the whole the country's interests will not only be protected but India may expect to benefit as a result of agriculture being brought into the fold to the GATT. The agreement has stipulated that countries with an aggregate subsidy of more than 10 per cent of the value of agricultural produce will have to lower them. The current level of subsidy for Indian agriculture is well below this level and this stipulation will, therefore, not affect us. It has also been clarified from the GATT that consumption subsidies for targetted groups of population, as under our public distribution system which is targetted primarily for the rural and urban poor, are permitted and can, therefore, continue. Farmers' interests will be completely protected once the proposed *sui generis* legislation to protect plantt varieties comes into effect. Under the proposed legislation, farmer's right to retain and exchange seeds will not be affected. The central feature of the agreement on agriculture is the reduction in production subsidies paid by developed countries to their farmer and the rolling back of some of the non-tariff barriers which have restricted agricultural trade. These measures will benefit India as our agricultural exports enjoy a comparative and competitive advantage. India's agricultural exports will, therefore, receive a welcome stimulus, at a time when the incentive structures in the domestic economy are beginning to work to their advantage.

Source: *Economic Survey 1993-94*, Ministry of Finance, Government of India, New Delhi, 1994, Chapter 5.

18.4 HYBRID SEEDS

Among developing countries, India occupies a prominent placo with respect to the development of hybrid seeds. While the initial impetus for introducing hybrids came exclusively from the government, the last years are characterized by an increasing involvement of the private sector. However, some farmers are refusing the new seeds, and are developing their own alternatives.

Promotion of hybrids

In order to meet the growing food demand, the Indian Council for Agricultural Research (ICAR), in collaboration with the Rockefeller Foundation (USA), started in 1957 the All India Coordinated Crop Improvement Project, which market the beginning of an intensive in India.

Farmers' movements against hybrids

Although the Indian government has promoted the use of hybrids and other High Yield Varieties (HYV) to achieve higher agricultural output and the acreage under hybrids is increasing every year, not all farmers have accepted the new seeds. The opposition is not to the hybrid seeds as such but to the adverse impact they could have in terms of loss of biodiversity and loss of ability of seeds saving, which forces farmers to buy new seed every year.

One of the opponents to the adoption of hybrids is the non-government organization Navadanya. Initiated in 1991 by the Research Foundation for Science, Technology and Natural Resource Policy, northern India, aiming at preventing erosion of biodiversity and monitoring the social and ecological impact of monocultures in agriculture and forestry.

The *Navdanya* network has collected and distributed local varieties of cereals, pulses, oilseeds and vegetables. The organization is also developing a network to support other centres working on conservation of indigenous genetic resources, such as *Navdshanam*, Bangalore, south India, *Annapurnain Aurovilla*, south eastern India, and the *centre for Tropical Ecosystems*, Sirsi, northern India.

19

CULTURE

19.1 NATIONAL POLICY ON CULTURE

Text of the Approach Paper on the National Policy on Culture, issued recently by the Department in Education and Culture, Ministry of HRD, Government of India.

Introduction

Culture permeates every sphere of human activity, determines and governs life and pattern of Indian society in diverse regions and equally diverse fields. It is a crucial part of development deserving careful attention and substantial investment. Although the Government of India have spent in the last 35 years six hundred thousand crores on development, the amounts spent on culture have usually been round 0.11 per cent of its annual expenditure. It is evident that investment in improving that aspect of the quality of life namely the cultural dimension has not been commensurate with the broad social needs and its intrinsic value.

The country has reached stage in its economic and technical development when the cultural dimension needs to be brought into sharper focus and strengthening.

The cultural underpinning the developmental effort has now been internationally recognised. As a report accepted by UNESCO's Inter-Government of the World Decade for Cultural Development has stated.

> "It is most important to understand the term development in its philosophical and conceptual meaning. Development has all too often been perceived as modernisation patterned after a particular dominant design, while in fact, there is a need for a multi-cultural and pluralistic conception in which different ways of living, different belief systems, (and) values are accommodated to reach the ultimate goals of various communities. Modernisation does not mean the mechanical imitation of a particular way of life. The concept of development has to be redefined in these terms. In particular, it would be necessary also to emphasise the linkage of the development elements to cultural elements, including local relevance, relevance to geographical and environmental factors, historical traditions, traditional knowledge and skills, etc. The importance of the aesthetic and artistic dimension of life should also be fully

> recognised... The motivation of the people who are the beneficiaries and participants in the development process is of utmost importance in successful design and implementation of programmes. Cultural factors play an important role in energising the motivation calling forth requisite participation and are thus crucial to sustainable development in which new concepts and ideas are absorbed in a permanent manner.

Final Report of the Inter-Governmental Committee of the World Decade for Cultural Development.

A stage in development has arrived when the importance of culture has to be clearly and candidly defined, the area of public intervention in culture identified, the role of State in culture assessed and readjusted, importance of societal and voluntary efforts in this area recognised and further incouraged.

With this aim in view the Government of India have decided to formulate a National Policy on Culture, basically to outline conditions conducive to more satisfactory self-expression and participation in cultural life by the Indian people at large. The policy recognises the need to develop strategies to sensitise people, particularly the young to creative expression in a framework of values which are generally accepted as those which enrich the quality of life.

It is also to devise strategies to promote the development of the various forms of creative expression; to preserve what of abiding value in the manifestations of creative expression through the centuries; to document forms of expression which may be changing or giving way to others; and to recognise the diversity in these forms which taken together constitute what can be called the culture of India.

More actively the policy proposes that as far as possible the State should play only a catalytic role in the development and progress of culture, its role being what may be called "arm's length intervention". It also should resist the wide-spread coarsening of vast sensibility, loss of sense of values, erosion of pluralistic vision and reduction of vast masses into passive recipients rather than active participants in processes of culture.

Culture is a central instrument of discovering, integrating and asserting the national identity of India which is truly and inevitably pluralistic. Our culture, while being Indocentric, has always been open to global influences and interaction. While resisting any colonization of mind, the policy believes, our culture should remain in constant dialogue with the world at large in the realm of ideas, perceptions, media and expressions.

Cultural enrichment can only take place if values of complexity, subtlety, elegance, beauty are cared for. Essentially there is no antipathy between aesthetic sensibility and scientific temper. The policy would lay stress on this more wholesome view.

In the current context of dissension and growing intolerance, it is imperative that the composite character of our culture, the crucial contribution made by various communities to it and its inclusive, humane and humanising ethos are highlighted and widely brought home to all. The policy would insist that Indian culture cannot be identified with any single tradition and consists of an ever enriching multiplicity of many traditions.

Growth has frequently been conceived in quantitative terms, without taking into account its necessary qualitative dimension, namely the satisfaction of man's spiritual and cultural aspiration. Any cultural policy should restore to development its profound, human significance and should democratically provide for enjoying of artistic excellence by all communities and the whole population.

Objectives

While attention to and investment in culture may have been far below expectation, it has to be recognised that there is a cultural pattern in India where interaction has taken and continues to take place amongst regions, between different are disciplines and levels of society, from the most affluent to the most weaker sections of the society at the urban, rural and tribal levels. Dialectics of continuity and change, of stability and innovation, and of individuality and inter-dependence have been the defining feature of cultural processes in our time. The policy is an attempt to delineate a blue print for areas which need urgent attention and public support. Large areas broadly covered in culture are engaging both attention and action by individuals, the creative community and numerous voluntary agencies. The policy recognises, therefore, that it shall be dealing not with the total spread and complexity and culture but only with some of its aspects and segments.

India's cultural diversity is too well known to need discovery of recognition. However, this enriching diversity should be recognised in all plans for development and the strategies for the protection and promotion of culture. There should be not attempt to give any single direction or ideological orientation or prescribe any standards in culture which is indeed the true area of societal action and consensus. While diversities and multiplicities must be allowed free play, this should happen in an overall context of harmony and consonance.

In keeping with the various changes and mutations which have come about, there is need to revive and reintegrate the holistic vision of culture in India in such a way that no segment, area or community feels excluded and each one is encouraged to freely contribute towards identifying, promoting, fostering and projecting cultural growth and enrichment. Care would have to be taken for promoting and projecting cultural contribution of the weaker section and minorities in all parts of India.

The old notion that patronage should be replaced by that of public support and there should that be effective coordination between the activities of various agencies in the States and Centre with a clear recognition that more than anywhere else decentralisation is a key factor in cultural promotion and than an important role is and should continue to be played by individuals and voluntary agencies.

Both education and media of mass communication are playing important role and participating in the society at large and are crucial culturising agencies. One of the objectives of the policy is to constantly emphasise the cultural consequences of education and media, and to deepen and strengthen their cultural components. It would also aim to see that consumerist tendencies are not allowed to create cultural distortions and tensions.

As stated in the National Policy of Education, 1986, "deculturalisation, dehumanism and alienation must be avoided at all costs and education must bring about a fine synthesis between change oriented technologies in the country's comminity of cultural traditions. Efforts should be made particularly to enable children and youth to develop sensitivity to duty harmony and refinement". Stress would have to be laid on the growth of cultural literacy along with verbal literacy. It would also aim "at interweaving into the formal and non-formal systems of education at all levels, of the content of culture and escalation and sharpening of cultural inputs in educational curricula with a view to arouse deeper interest in cultural heritage, to provide free creativity and to foster elements of composite culture". Respect and striving for creativity and excellence must be inculcated from early level of education.

It would be necessary to ensure community participation at all levels including formal, non-formal and informal agencies sich as panchayats, local bodies, etc. Literacy is an essential condition for people's cultural development.

NPE would promote evaluation of a dynamic relationship between tradition, including the pan Indian and Asian traditions, and modernity.

It would wish to preserve cultural heritage in its different ways recognising the need of preserving and documenting those aspect of classical, rural, tribal and community and culture traditions which are in danger of extinction on account of social change, market forces, technological onslaught etc., particularly of those elements which have so far been sustained through oral communications.

It would promote concrete steps to be taken to provide wider opportunities to citizens both rural and urban of meaningful and continuing exposure to various forms of cultural manifestations.

It would aim at use of existing infrastructural facilities in a more coordinated manner to provide multi points for promotion, exploration and conservation of various forms of creative expression. For better and maximal use of funds and infrastructure duplication of work should be scrupulously avoided.

It would recognise the need to preserve the tradition as also the need for new ideas, new combinations, original interpretation etc. It would encourage openness to new forms and manifestations. Photography, cinema and contemporary architecture need to be seen as a new cultural expressions.

20

DEFENCE

20.1 DEFENCE PRODUCTION

A network of ordnance factories (presently 39 number) catered to the requirements of the Armed Forces. However, alongside the basic responsibility for catering to the needs of the Armed Forces, it was realised that the defence technological base could also be utilised to cater to a wider and diversified range of applications. Such a role required, inter-alia, a flexible form of organisation and decentralised management, with adequate operational autonomy. This led to the increasing use of the public sector concept of management in defence production. The eight Defence Public Sector Undertakings (Defence PSUs) currently functioning under the administrative control of the department are:

Hindustan Aeronautics Ltd. (HAL)
Bharat Electronics Ltd. (BEL)
Bharat Earth Movers Ltd. (BEML)
Mazagon Dock Ltd. (MDL)
Garden Reach Shipbuilders & Engineers Ltd. (GRSE)
Goa Shipyard Ltd. (GSL)
Bharat Dynamics Ltd. (BDL) and
Mishra Dhatu Nigam Ltd. (MIDHANI)

In addition, the capacities available in the Civil Sector, wherever they can be made use of for defence production, are also utilised.

In recent years, on account of reduced off-take by the Armed Forces due to budgetary constraints, the defence production units have been trying to diversify their activities into civil trade. While the Ordanance Factories have diversified their production mainly for the paramilitary organisations, the Defence PSUs have raised their production for export and the non-defence sector. This explains a substantially higher level of production by the ordnance factories and the Defence PSUs in 1992-93 compared to that of 1991-92, inspite of the funds constraint. The following figures give an idea of the increasing trend of sales to the non-defence sector by the ordnance factories and the Defence PSUs:

TABLE 20.1: Civil Trade by Ordnance Factories and the Defence PSUs

(Rs. in crore)

Year	Ordnance factories	Defence PSUs
1991-92	170.00	1260.44
1992-93	262.00	1566.00
1993-94 (Target)	375.00	1762.21

Such increased production for the non-defence sector, besides improving the capacity utilisation in the defence production units, has had the effect of bringing down the unit cost production for the armed forces.

Concerted efforts have also been made by the department during the last few years to increase the export of defence items. The steps taken in this direction include policy and procedural liberalisation, marketing efforts through our missions abroad/other export agencies, sales/publicity measures such as participation in exhibitions abroad, and the exchange of delegation etc. As on December 31, 1993, the export performance of the ordnance factories and the Defence PSUs is of the order of Rs. 250.44 crore (Rs. 67.78 crore as direct and Rs. 182.66 crore as deemed). The export target of Rs. 300 crore (Rs. 132 crore as direct and Rs. 168 crore as deemed) fixed for the current year is expected to be achieved. The organisation-wise performance during the last two years is shown in the table below:

TABLE 20.2: Organisation-wise of Production Performance

(Rs. in crore)

Name of the Organisation	1991-92		1992-93	
	Direct	Deemed	Direct	Deemed
HAL	15.00	0.17	19.23	—
BEL	5.48	32.47	12.73	0.15
BEML	23.00	21.00	26.23	44.41
MDL	—	—	—	123.50
GRSE	0.57	—	0.25	0.57
BDL	—	—	0.61	—
OFB	1.98	1.57	5.13	—
Total	46.03	55.21	64.18	168.63

Besides the ordnance factories and the defence PSUs, the department also controls the following five allied organisations:

(i) Directorate General of Quality Assurance
(ii) Directorate of Technical Development and Production (Air)
(iii) Directorate of Standardisation
(iv) Directorate of Planning and Co-ordination
(v) Defence Exhibition Organisation

20.2 DEFENCE RESEARCH AND DEVELOPMENT

Achievement Highlights

The Main Battle Tank ARJUN has been accepted for induction into the Army. Bulk orders for 5.56 mm INSAS rifles have been placed by the Army. A world class phased array radar has been developed to provide multiple target handling capability to the medium range surface-to-air missile system, AKASH. Flight trials of the third generation anti-tank missile, NAG, have show good results and a millimeter wave radar seeker has been developed. A major discovery was made by a DRDO laboratory concerning emission of bright red light from junction diodes made of porous sillicon. The material is likely to find new opto-electronic applications.

Defence Public Sector Undertaking

The defence PSUs were set up to augment the production infrastructure of defence stores capable of supplying critical weapons and equipments of modern technology at economic prices. The technological base available in the Defence PSUs is also being utilised to cater to the need of the non-defence sector. The aggregate value of production in defence PSUs is likely to increase by 7 per cent in 1993-94, as compared to the previous year. The defence PSUs are likely to earn about Rs. 232 crore as profit before tax during 1993-94.

The value of production, sales and investment of 8 defence PSUs in the last 2 years, as also the estimated value in the year 1993-94, is given in the tables 20.3 and 20.4.

TABLE 20.3: Value of Production and Sales

(Rs. in crore)

	1991-92		1992-93		1993-94 (Estimate)	
Name of the PSU	Value of Production	Value of Sales	Value of Production	Value of Sales	Value of Production	Value of Sales
HAL	970.67	1024.41	1051.05	1085.99	956.17	1032.00
BEL	706.93	716.78	817.74	773.77	874.35	850.60
BEML	829.50	799.00	948.95	900.66	1041.41	1050.00
MDL	285.54	429.56	498.06	295.66	551.66	457.29

(Contd.)

TABLE 20.3 *(Contd.)*

Name of the PSU	1991-92 Value of Production	1991-92 Value of Sales	1992-93 Value of Production	1992-93 Value of Sales	1993-94 (Estimate) Value of Production	1993-94 (Estimate) Value of Sales
GRSE	196.20	226.44	228.39	141.13	254.45	123.28
GSL	85.89	66.70	106.38	35.16	120.00	106.17
BDL	137.03	125.76	111.33	112.68	221.02	171.47
MIDHANI	60.46	54.26	61.92	63.38	72.02	73.33
Total	3272.22	3442.91	3823.82	3408.43	4091.08	3864.14

Note: The sale proceeds of the shipyards (MDL, GRSE, GSL) are dependent of ships/vessels (which take 4-7 years to build). No high value ship was delivered to customers in 1992-93, hence a drop in sales and compared to 1991-92.

Investments

Of the 8 Defence PSUs, HAL, MDL, GRSE, BDL and MIDHANI are wholly owned by the Government of India. The total capital investment in the Defence PSUs has marginally gone up from Rs. 1330.68 Crore in 1991-92 to Rs. 1338.22 Crore in 1992-93. The PSU-wise details of investments as they stoods in the last three years and as estimated for 1993-94 are shown in the table below:

TABLE 20.4: PSU-wise Details of Investments

Name of the PSU	1990-91 Equity	1990-91 Govt. Loans	1991-92 Equity	1991-92 Govt. Loans	1992-93 Equity	1992-93 Govt. Loans	1993-94 (Estimated) Equity	1993-94 (Estimated) Govt. Loans
HAL	120.50	122.47	120.50	137.45	120.50	139.06	120.50	133.83
BEL	80.00	95.67	80.00	86.66	80.00	76.82	80.00	86.45
BEML	30.00	99.20	30.00	86.65	30.00	87.10	37.00	78.30
MDL	168.70	126.63	178.20	125.74	188.20	124.86	193.20	130.04
GRSE	111.19	45.56	117.84	40.70	121.84	38.88	121.84	38.75
GSL	8.42	6.72	11.32	5.74	12.93	4.86	12.93	4.03
BDL	115.00	45.62	115.00	57.54	115.00	60.83	115.00	58.43
MIDHANI	137.34	—	134.34	—	137.34	—	137.34	—
Total	771.15	541.87	790.20	540.48	805.81	532.41	817.81	529.83

21

EDUCATION

21.1 EXPANSION OF EDUCATIONAL FACILITIES

The country has made considerable progress in the sphere of education over the past four decades. The Gross Enrolment Ratio (GER) in the Primary Stage (Class I-V) increased from 42.6 per cent in 1950-51 to 105.7 per cent in 1992-93 and in the Upper Primary Stage (class VI-VIII) from 12.7 per cent to 67.5 per cent. The proportion of children moving up from the Primary to Upper Primary Stage has also increased steadily—from 16.3 per cent in 1950-51 to about 34 per cent in 1991-92. Substantial progress in literacy levels and in the spread of education institutions has been attained (Tables 21.1 and 21.2). In technical education, about 230 recognised institutions at the first degree level and more than 600 polytechnics at the diploma level have annual admission capacity of 45,000 and 88,000 students, respectively. Besides, about 150 institutions offer post-graduate and specialised research facilities with an annual capacity of 10,000 students.

TABLE 21.1: Progress in Literacy Rate (per cent)

Year	Total	Male	Female
1951	18.33	27.16	8.86
1961	28.31	40.40	15.34
1971	34.45	45.95	21.97
1981	43.56	56.37	29.75
1991	52.21	64.13	39.29

Notes: 1. Literacy rates for 1951 to 1971 relate of population aged 5 years and above and subsequently to 7 years and above.

2. The 1981 rates exclude Assam and 1991 rates exclude J&K.

TABLE 21.2: Growth of Recognised Educational Institutions

(Number as on 31st March)

Type	1951	1961	1971	1981	1991@	1993@
1. Primary schools	209671	330399	408378	494503	558392	572541
2. Upper primary schools	13596	49663	90621	118335	146636	153921
3. Secondary schools/ Pre-degree colleges	7416	17329	37051	51624	78619	84086
4. Colleges for general education	370	967	2285	3421	4862	5334
5. Colleges for prof. education	208	852	992	1156	886*	989*
6. Universities	27	45	82	110	146	149

@ Provisional

* Includes only Engineering, Medical and Teachers Training institutions whereas data for previous decades also includes Physical Education, Mid-wifery, Agriculture, Veterinary and Music etc.

Source: Ministry of Human Resource Development.

According to the 1991 census, the literacy rate in the country (in the age-group 7 years and above) was 52.2 per cent. There are, however, vast inter-state variations in educational attainments. The literacy rate among females is only 39.3 per cent (as against 64.1 per cent for males), it is only 44.2 per cent in rural area (compared to 73.1 per cent in the urban areas) and it is significantly lower for the Scheduled Castes (37.4 per cent) and the Scheduled Tribes (29.6 per cent) population.

Univerlisation of elementary education and eradication of illiteracy in the age group 15.35 years are basic objectives of education in the Eigth Plan. About 19 to 24 million children in the age-group 6-14 and over 121 million adult illiterates in the age-group 15-35 (with over 60 per cent females in both cases) are estimated to constitute the target group in this context. The strategies adopted include a phased reduction in the ratio between primary and middle schools from the existing 4:1 to 2:1 adoption of a decentralised approach to curriculum development, quality improvement in the process of teaching learning emphasis on child-centred and activity-based approach and reduction of curricular load.

Spread of education faces complex socio-economic, administrative and financial problems. It is realised that along with investment and provision of infrastructure, a holistic planning and management approach, covering aspects of access, specially for girls and disadvantaged groups; non-formal education; increasing learning competence of children; raising teachers' abilities; and convergence of education, health, welfare and related services at micro-level, are required. The NDC Committee on Literacy, which gave its report in 1993, has also, among other things, emphasised these aspects. The report of the Committee was generally endorsed by the NDC in its meeting in September 1993 and it was resolved that a meeting of the Chief Ministers will be convenced for discussion and working out an action plan for effective implementation of the report.

21.2 HIGHER EDUCATION AND RESEARCH

Growth of the Higher Education System

At the beginning of the year 1993-94, the total student enrolment in universities and colleges was 48.05 lakh. This was 1.94 lakh more than the enrolment in the previous year. The enrolment in the university departments was 7.95 lakh and that in the affiliated colleges was 40.09 lakh.

Enrolment in the faculty of arts constituted 40.0 per cent of the total enrolment. In the faculties of science and commerce the percentage was 19.6 and 21.9 respectively. Enrolment at the first degree level was 42.33 lakh (88.1%); at the post-graduate level 4.56 lakh (9.5%); at the research level 0.53 lakh (1.1%) and at the diploma and certificate level 0.62 lakh (1.3%). The number of teachers increased to 2.78 lakh during the year. Of these, 0.63 lakh were in the university departments/university colleges and the rest in the affiliated colleges. Of the 62716 teachers in the universities, 8029 were Professors, 16431 were Readers, 35748 were Lecturers and 2508 were Tutors/Demonstrators. In the affiliated colleges, the number of senior teachers was 29917, the number of Lecturers was 175846 and that of Tutors/ Demostrators was 9471.

TABLE 21.3: Stagewise Enrolment in Higher Education, 1991-92

Stage	University Deptt./ University Colleges	Affiliated Colleges	Total	% in Affiliated Colleges
Graduate	495611	3566774	4062385	87.5
Post Graduate	190554	247501	438055	56.5
Research	43115	7608	50723	15.0
Diploma Certificate	33929	26015	59944	43.0
Total	763209	3847898	4611107	83.4

TABLE 21.4: Faculty-wise Enrolment, 1991-92

	Faculty	Enrolment	% of Total
1.	Arts (including Oriental Learning)	1865605	40.4
2.	Science	903776	19.6
3.	Commerce	1009832	21.9
4.	Education	106055	2.3
5.	Engineering/Technology	225944	4.9
6.	Medicine	156777	3.4
7.	Agriculture	48908	1.1
8.	Venterinary Science	11550	0.3
9.	Law	244388	5.3
10.	Others	38272	0.8
	Total	4611107	100.0

Upto November 1993 the total number of universities in the country was 155 and the total number of institutions deemed to be universities was 34.

Higher Education among Women

The enrolment of women students at the beginning of the year 1993-94 was 15.90 lakh as against 15.12 lakh in the previous year. At the post-graduate level, the enrolment of women was 34.9 per cent of the total enrolment. The enrolment of women students was the highest in Kerala (53.3%) followed by Punjab (48.5%), Delhi (46.6%), Haryana (42.5%), Meghalaya/Nagaland/ Mizoram (39.3%), Tamil Nadu (38.8%) and West Bengal/Tripura/Sikkim (38.7%). The enrolment of women was the lowest in Bihar (16.1%).

21.3 TECHNICAL EDUCATION

Technical Education is one of the most crucial components of Human Resource Development with great potential for adding value to products and services and for improving the quality of life of the people. As a result of the efforts made during the successive Five Year Plans in the past on the development of technical education, the expansion of technical education in the country has been phenomenal during the past four decades.

There are, at the present, over 200 recognised technical education istitutions at the first degree level and more than 500 at the diploma level with the annual admission capacities of 40,000 and 80,000 students respectively. Facilities for Masters and Doctoral Programme in engineering and technology have also been created in 140 institutions with an intake of about 10,000 per year. The vast network of institutions includes IITs, RECs, technical universities, deemed universities, university departments of engineering and technology, State and private engineering colleges recognised by the AICTE specialised institutions in the field of mining, architecture, industrial engineering, foundry and forge technology, etc. The Indian Institutes of Management, University departments and professional bodies cater to the needs of managerial manpower.

Some professional bodies in the fields of engineering, technology and management conduct formal and non-formal education/training programmes for fresh students as well as the working professionals and also contribute to professional development in their respective areas of activities.

The NPE, 1986 underlined the need for re-organising the technical and management education system to effectively deal with the changes in the economy, social environment, production and management processes and rapid expansion of knowledge and advances in science and technology. The NPE, 1986 laid specific guidelines for the qualitative and quantitative development of the technical and management education sectors; establishment of linkages amongst the concerned agencies; manpower assessment and technical education forecasting; increasing effectiveness of technical education management system; proper delivery systems, measures to achieve greater cost effectiveness and generation of resources through suitable means.

Source: Census of India, 1991-Paper No. 2 of 1992.

22

ENERGY

An Overview

The growth and development of a modern economy is significantly dependent on the availability of commercial energy. India is quite deficient in the very natural resources which result in the production of commercial energy. We have 6 per cent of the world's proven reserves in coal, 0.59 per cent of the proven reserves in oil and 0.59 per cent of the proven reserves in natural gas. We have an abundant supply of solar energy. Yet, the technology for the commercial use of solar energy is nowhere close to being cost effective. Wind energy could supplement India's energy needs. But again the technology in this area is not highly efficient and costs are not very competitive. Hopes in the long run could be pinned to the abundance of thorium in the sands of Kerala (84% of the world's proven reserves).

Source: Seminar, February, 1991.

Coal

Coal resources of India (upto a depth of 1200 metres) have been estimated by the Geological Survey of India at 196891.87 million on January1, 94. The figure stood at 19377713 million tonnes as a January 1, 1993.

Currently lignite deposits in the country have been estimated at 26000 million tonnes, most of which occurs in Tamil Nadu. Other States where lignite deposits have been located are Rajasthan, Gujarat, Kerala, Jammu & Kashmir and the U.T. of Pondicherry.

Coal Planning

The planning exercise for Coal India projects is done in Central Mine Planning & Design Institute Ltd. (CMPDIL). One new project is SCCL. Five Revised cost estimates of Projects in CIL and three Advance Action Plans were sanctioned in the coal sector by the Govt. till December 31, 93.

Coal Production

Coal production (upto December 31, 1993) was 165.60 million tonnes. Companywise details are given in Table 22.1.

TABLE 22.1: Coal Production

Million Tonnes

Company	Target utp Dec. '93	Achievement upto Dec. '93
CIL	142.87	145.19
SCCL	17.83	17.10
Others: TISCO, IISCO, DVC	3.41	3.31
Total	164.11	165.60

Companywise break up of production in respect of CIL subsidiaries is given in Table 22.2 (upto 31.12.93).

TABLE 22.2: Companywise Breakup Production

Million Tonnes

Company	1993-94	
	Target (Full year)	Achievement (upto 31.12.93)
ECL	25.50	15.51
BCCL	28.10	19.20
CCL	33.50	21.10
NCL	31.40	20.81
WCL	26.00	17.67
SECL	46.60	33.31
MCL	23.80	16.86
NEC	1.10	0.73
Total	216.00	145.19

About 89 per cent of the total coal production in the country comes from the collieries of Coal India Limited. The CIL therefore is also the biggest supplier of coal in the country. During the period April-December, 1993 the

Coal India Limited supplied the following quantities of coal to various consumers.

Power

Power Generation Highlights

The total energy generation in the country during 1992-93 was 301.06 Billion Units (BUs) showing an increase of 5.0 per cent over the generation in 1991-92. The increase in thermal generation during 1992-93 over the previous year was 7.6 per cent. The hydro generation was, however, less by 3.8 per cent during 1992-93 over the last year due to less favourable monsoon.

For the year 1993-94, the generation target of 316.700 BUs has been fixed, comprising 243.200 BUs thermal, 6.00 BUs nuclear and 67.500 BUs hydro power. This envisaged an increase of about 5.2% over the generation achieved during 1992-93. The actual generation during the year 9up to December 1993) has been 237.76 BUs which is 7.4 per cent more than the generation during the corresponding period of the previous year and 0.7 per cent more than target. The actual generation during the period, as compared with the target is given below:

April to December, 1993

Figures in Million Units

	Target April-Dec. '93	Actual April-Dec. '93	% of Prog	% age of the corresponding period/last year
Thermal	178106	178461	100.2	109.9
Nuclear	4575	4239	92.7	88.55
Hydro	53550	55067	102.8	101.5
Total	236231	237767	100.7	107.4

Plant Load Factor (PLF) of Thermal Stations

Thermal capacity, at present constitutes about 70 per cent of the total installed capacity in the country, and contributes about 74 per cent of the total power generation. At the beginning of the Sixth Five Year Plan, the performance of the thermal power stations was unsatisfactory with the All India average PLF of 44.3 per cent only. To improve their performance, a number of measures were taken to achieve the optimum utilisation of the existing thermal units. At the beginning of Seventh Five Year Plan i.e. 1985-86, the All India average PLF improved to 52.4 per cent and furthr increased to 56.5 per cent in 1987-88 (which was the highest achieved in any year). During 1992-93 the PLF was 57.1 per cent which is the highest ever achieved. During the period April, 1993 to November, 1993, the All India PFL has been 58.1 per cent. During this period, the following State Electricity Boards/Corporations achieved PLF higher than the All India average of 58.1 per cent.

Sl. No.	State Electricity Boards/Corporations	PLF (%)
1.	Rajasthan	74.5
2.	Punjab	61.6
3.	Maharashtra	61.5
4.	Andhra Pradesh	62.2
5.	Tamil Nadu	68.5
6.	Karnataka	65.4
7.	West Bengal Power Development Corporation	68.9
8.	NTPC	74.1
9.	Ahmedabad Electric Co.	70.7
10.	Calcutta Electric Supply Co.	73.6

In the State Sector, Kota Thermal Power Station of RSEB, Anpara TPS of UPSEB, Sikka of GEB, Khaperkheda II of MSEB, Vijayawada of APSEB and Mettur of TNEB achieved highest PLF of more than 70 per cent during this period. In the Private Sector, Ahmedabad Electric Company achieved the highest Plant Load Factor of 70.7 per cent during the same period. In the Central Sector, Singrauli Super Thermal Power Station on NTPIC achieved the highest PLF of 80.1 per cent during the same period.

Generating Capacity during 1992-93

An aggregate capacity of 4458.02 MW consisting of 879.1 MW hydro, 3358.92 MW Thermal and 220 MW Nuclear was targeted for commissioning during the year 1992-93. Again targeted capacity the total generating capacity commissioned/rolled during the year 1992-93 was 3537.27 MW consisting of 372.95 MW hydro, 2944.32 MW thermal and 220 MW nuclear.

Figures in MW

Type	Programme for 1992-93				Achievement during 1992-93			
	CS	SS	PS	Total	CS	SS	PS	Total
Hydro	540	321.10	18	879.10	115	239.95	18	372.95
Thermal	1920	1438.92	—	3358.92	2140	804.32	—	2944.32
Nuclear	220	—	—	220	220	—	—	220
Total	2680	1760.02	18	4458.02	2475	1044.27	18	3537.27

23

HEALTH AND ENVIRONMENT

23.1 Medical and Health Care

India is a signatory to the Alma Ata Declaration of 1978 and has set for itself the goal of Health for All (HFA) by 2000 A.D. through emphasis on primary health care. Accordingly, the National Health Policy was adopted by Parliament in 1983. Within the HFA strategy, health for the under-privileged is to be promoted consciously and consistently through community-based systems.

Over the years, there has been considerables expansion of infrastructure for health services. A three-tier system comprising Community Health Centres (CHC), Primary Health Centres (PHC) and Sub-centres, has been established. The targets of one Sub-centre for a population of 5000 and one PHC for a population of 30,000 in general and one Sub-centre for a population of 3000 and one PHC for population of 20,000 in hilly and tribal areas, have already been achieved.

Between 1951 and 1992, life expectancy at birth increased from 32.1 years to 60.3 years, birth-rate came down from 39.9 to 29 per thousand, death rate fell from 27.4 per thousand to about 10 per thousand and infant mortality declined from 139 per 1000 births in 1972 to 79 in 1992. Small-pox has been eradicated and plague is no longer a problem. Morbidity due to malaria, cholera, etc. has very considerably declined. But much progress is still to be made to bring health standards and medical facilities in the country at par with even many of the developing countries. Considerable rural-urban and inter-state disparities are also observed in the achievements in this sector. Inspite of special efforts and perceptible progress make, the incidence of diseases like tuberculosis, malaria, leprosy and kala-azar continues to be significant. The biases in favour of curative a vis-a-vis preventive, and of secondary and tertiary health-care facilities rather than primary, need to be corrected. An all-round improvement in services and delivery systems is also desirable.

23.2 Water Supply and Sanitation

The Seventh Five-Year Plan which targeted to provide all the 1,61,722 identified hardcore no-source problem village with the facility of safe drinking water, left a back-log of 8365 villages. During 1990-93, about 7615 villages from these were covered and out of the remaining 750 villages targeted for the year 1993-94, 78 were covered by October 1993.

TABLE 23.1: Expansion of Health Services

in number

	Item	1951	1961	1971	1981	1991	1992
1.	Medical Colleges @	28*	60	98	111	128	146$
2.	Hospitals**	2694	3094	3862	6804	11174	N.A.
3.	Dispensaries**	6515	9406	12180	16751	27431	N.A.
4.	Community Health Centres @	0	0	0	217	2071	2193
5.	Primary Health Centres @	725	2565	5112	5740	20450	20719
6.	Sub-Centres @	0	0	28489	51405	130958	131464
7.	Hospital beds (all types)	117178	230000	348655	569495	810548	N.A.
8.	Doctors**	61840	83756	151129	268712	394068	405253
9.	Dentists**	3290	3582	5512	8648	10751	11300
10.	Nurses**	16550	35584	80620	154280	340208	N.A.

* Pertains to 1950

** As on 31st December.

NA - Not available $ - As on August 1993. @ As on 31st March.

Source: Ministry of Health and Family Welfare.

The coverage of the population in rural and urban areas under safe drinking water supply and sanitation facilities is given in Table 23.2. The coverage under water-supply has shown considerable progress since 1985, mainly due to efforts made during the International Drinking Water Supply and Sanitation. Decade (1981-91) under sanitation in rural areas, 3.15 per cent coverage of population by March 1993 corresponds to Government assisted programmes only. However, according to the National Sample Survey (44th Round, July 1988-June 1989), 10.96 per cent of rural population has access to sanitation facilities, including coverage through private initiative.

23.3 Drinking Water Supply in Rural Areas

Provision of safe drinking water facilities in rural areas is primarily the responsibility of the States. However, the Central Government has been giving top priority to this core sector of meeting one of the fundamental needs of rural masses. Technical financial assistance has been provided under the Accelerated Rural Water Supply Programme (ARWSP) which was introduced in 1972-73. With the introduction of rural water supply under the Minimum Needs Programme (MNP) in 1974-75, ARWSP was withdrawn but this was re-introduced in 1977-78. In order to give a further boost to the programme, National Drinking Water Mission was launched in 1986. The Mission has now been renamed, as Rajiv Gandhi National Drinking Water Mission.

TABLE 23.2: Population Covered with Drinking Water and Sanitation Facilities

Percentage coverage as on 31st March

Item/Area	1985	1990	1993
Drinking Water Supply			
(a) Rural	56.3	73.9	78.4
(b) Urban	72.9	83.8	84.9
Sanitation Facilities			
(a) Rural	0.7	2.4	3.15
(b) Urban	28.4	45.9	47.9

Note: *Provisional.

With the joint effort of the States/UTs under State sector MNP and the Central assistance under ARWSP and the Mission, it has been possible to provide safe drinking water facilities to 75.41 per cent of the rural population by the end of 1991-92. This has been possible with the special central assistance of about Rs. 178 crore given specifically for coverage of No Source problem villages.

With the coverage of about 94,000 problem villages till the beginning of Sixth Plan and resurvey carried out by States and Union Territories for identification of problem villages, about 2.31 lakh problem villages remained to be covered as on 1.4.1980 out of which 1.92 lakh villages were covered in the Sixth Plan and the balance 0.39 lakh spilled over to the Seventh Plan. PVs were again identified through a fresh survey conducted in 1985 and as a result 1.62 lakh PVs remained as on 1.4.1985 to be covered in Seventh Plan.

About 1.54 lakh problem villages were covered during the Seventh Plan, in addition to 1.92 lakh villages covered during the Sixth Plan. Out of the balance of 8,365 problem villages of the total of about 5.83 lakh villages in the country, 3,032 were covered in 1990-91 and 2168 in 1991-92. The target for coverage of 'No Source' problem villages in 1992-93 is 2,968 and partially covered villages as 31,500. The actual achievement reported by the States/UTs based on the reports received upto February, 1993 is 1,469 'No Source' problem villages and 23,500 partially covered villages. About 600 problem villages are likely to spill over to 1993-94. However, the target for partially covered villages is likely to be achieved. The target for 1993-94 has been provisionally fixed at 42,000 villages including spill over 'No Source' problem villages.

Under the scheme, a total of Rs. 2,961 crores has been utilised during the Seventh Plan and in 1990-91 and 1991-92. In addition, an expenditure of Rs. 3,751 crore has been utilised under the MNP in the State Sector. For 1992-93, an outlay of Rs. 460 crore was provided under ARWSP, Rajiv Gandhi National Drinking Water Mission, etc. in addition to the outlay of

Rs. 811.31 crore under MNP in the State Sector. For 1993-94, an outlay of Rs. 740 crore has been provided and Rs. 819.85 crore is under MNP in the State Sector. Allocations for Eighth Plan for Drinking Water Supply in rural areas is Rs. 4,954.52 crore under the State Sector MNP and Rs. 5,100 crore under the Central Sector.

Special emphasis is given on provision of drinking Water facilities for SCs and STs. Apart from the provision under the State sector special component plan and tribal sub-plan and earmarking of funds under ARWSP for a minimum of 25 per cent for SCs and 10 per cent for STs, the Central Government has also been giving special assistance in order to accelerate the coverage of the weaker sections with safe drinking water facilities. Special assistance of Rs. 19.80 crore was given in March 1990. Similarly, special assistance of Rs. 58.94 crore was released in 1991-92 and early part of 1992-93 as part of Dr. Baba Saheb Ambedkar Centenary Programme.

Special emphasis is also given on the quality of drinking water supply. Under the Sub-Mission on Eradication of Guineaworm, it has been possible to bring down the number of affected villages to 1906 and affected cases to 563 as on 1.1.93. The problem is likely to be eradicated by the end of 1993.

Under the Sub-Mission on Control of Fluorosis, setting up of 481 defluoridation plants was approved. Out of this, more than 260 plants have already been commissioned. An awareness campaign for imparting health education and the importance of use of drinking water free from excess fluoride had been launched in 150 districts in 15 States.

Source: Yojana, July 15, 1993.

24

HUMAN DEVELOPMENT

Human development is the ultimate goal of our development programmes and is also crucial for the long-run success of economic reforms. Sound, long-term development of social sectors, such as education and health, is crucial for sustaining higher rates of overall economic growth in an increasingly integrated world economy. Significant progress has been made over the years in human resource development which is reflected in improved demographic indicators, literacy and educational levels, health care services and other social overhead facilities. However, considerable ground remains to be covered in view of the continuing heavy demographic pressure, regional and class disparities in access to social infrastructure, and our still low levels of attainment in social sectors compared to even several developing countries in Asia. It is, therefore, necessary to pursue a conscious policy to strengthen development in social sectors and to protect the interests of the poor and vulnerable sections of society during the period of transition to a path of sustainable, broad-based growth.

The Government recognises the need to minimise the short-term social costs which may arise in the process of reform and adjustment. Allocations for social sectors were significantly stepped up in 1993-94 following the manoeuvrability gained through overall fiscal correction (Table 24.1). The ongoing programmes of poverty alleviation and employment generation and other social sector programmes are being strengthened and re-oriented in favour of the poor and more deserving groups. The public distribution system has been revamped in 1752 blocks in remote and backward areas to support the essential consumption of the poor. The National Renewal Fund, established in 1991-92, is supplementing the existing Social Safety Net by financing schemes of compensation, retraining and re-deployment of workers affected by economic restructuring.

TABLE 24.1: Central Plan Outlay for Important Programmes of Human Resource Development

Rs. crore

Item	1992-93 (BE)	1993-94 (BE)	per cent increase (col. 3 over (col. 2)
1. Elementary Education	284	442	55.6
2. Adult Education	120	178	48.3
3. Health	302	483	59.9
4. Family Welfare	1000	1270	27.0
5. Jawahar Rozgar Yojana	2046	3306	61.6
6. Integrated Rural Development Programme	375	630	68.0
7. Water Supply and Sanitation in Rural and Urban Areas	553	832	50.5
8. Integrated Child Development Services	360	474	31.7

Source: Budget Papers, 1993-94.

The Eighth Five Year Plan also enjoins that the provision of basic elements which help development of human capital, vis. employment generation, population control, literacy, education, health, drinking water supply, and provision of food and basic infrastructure, remain the primary responsibility of the Government. The April and September 1993 meetings of the National Development Council (NDC) brought out gaps in our performance in some of the most important areas of human development and outlined additional measures for promotion of family welfare, literacy and employment.

There has, indeed, been significant progress in human development in the country as reflected in its broad indicators (Table 24.2). Since 1950-51, a very significant improvement in educational attainments, health coverage and in the provision of basic social infrastructure has come about. Considering the dimensions and complexities of the problems and overall constraints of resources, these are not insignificant achievements.

TABLE 24.2: Basic Indicators of Human Development

Year	Life expectancy at birth @ (years)	Literary rate @ @ (per cent)	Births rate * (per thousand)	Deaths rate * (per thousand)	Infant mortality rate * (per thousand) live births	Per capita NNP at 1980-81 Prices # (Rs.)
1951	32.1	18.3	39.9	27.4	146	1127
1961	41.3	28.3	41.7	22.8	146	1350
1971	45.6	34.5	36.9	14.9	129	1520
1981	54.4	43.6	33.9	12.5	110	1630
1991	55.9	52.2	29.5	9.5	80	2199
1992 (P)	60.8**	N.A.	29.0	100	79	(Q)2216

@ Relates to middle of Census decade period except for 1992.

* Data for 1951 & 1961 relate to Census estimates and for 1971 onwards correspond to Sample Registration Scheme.

** Relates to 1992-93.

@ @ As on 1st March 1951 & so on. For 1950-51 to 1970-71, literacy rate relates to population aged 5 years and above, and subsequently to 7 years and above in 1981, it excludes Assam and in 1991 Jammu & Kashmir.

# Relate to financial year 1950-51, 1960-61 and so on.
P = Provisional Q = Quick estimates.

Source: Registrar General & Census Commissioner of India and Central Statistical Organisation.

25

INDUSTRY

There has been a modest recovery of industrial growth at 1.8 per cent during 1992-93 and 1.6 per cent during the first seven months of 1993-94 from an almost stagnant output during 1991-92. Although the present rate of industrial growth is below expectation, there has been an uptrend since July 1993; with the Index of Industrial Production (IIP) recording a growth rate of 2.7 per cent during July-October 1993. Basic goods, intermediate goods and consumer goods segment of the manufacturing industries, with a total weight of 60.7 per cent in the IIP, registered a growth of more than 4.5 per cent in the first seven month of 1993-94. Since July 1993, these sectors have achieved a growth rate of 6.1 per cent. Transport Equipment, Chemical Products and Cotton Textiles have continued to record substantial growth. Consumer durables and intermediate goods, in general, are performing well. The poor performance of the capital goods industry is, however, a matter of concern. Major policy initiative taken in the year included delicensing of white goods and motor car industries. The 13 minerals hitherto reserved for the public sector were opened for private sector participation.

Table 25.1 represents the monthly growth rates since January 1993 for the three major sectors and the general index.

TABLE 25.1: Trends on Monthly Growth Rates of Industrial Production

per cent

Period (Weights)	Mining & Quarrying (11.46)	Manufac-turing (77.11)	Electricity (11.43)	General (100)
1	2	3	4	5
1993:				
January	-0.7	-6.7	6.8	-4.2
February	-3.1	-8.7	5.3	-6.3
March	2.0	-0.9	5.3	0.2

(Contd.)

TABLE 25.1 *(Contd.)*

1	2	3	4	5
April	-7.4	-1.2	6.4	-0.9
May	-11.4	0.4	9.4	0.2
June	3.6	-0.6	9.3	1.2
July	3.6	3.5	7.3	4.1
August	2.2	3.6	13.3	4.9
September	2.0	-1.6	5.5	-0.2
October	-1.2	3.0	2.3	2.4

Reforms in Industrial Sector

* With effect from March 26, 1993, the 13 minerals, earlier reserved for the Public Sector, have been opened for the private sector. Consequently, the number of industries reserved for the public sector is reduced to 6, viz. defence products, atomic energy, coal and lignite, mineral oils, railway transport, minerals specified in the schedule to the Atomic Energy Order 1953.
* 'Motor car' and 'white goods' industries were delicensed with effect from April 28, 1993. Raw hides and skins, leather and patent leather, excluding chamois leather, also stand delicensed. Hence, the number of items, in respect of which industrial licensing is compulsory, has been reduced to 15.
* The manufacture of readymade garments—an item reserved for exclusive manufacture by the ancillary/small scale industrial undertaking is now open to large scale undertaking through a notification dated July 29, 1993, subject to an export obligation of 50 per cent and investment in fixed assets in plant and machinery of the large unit not exceeding Rs. 3 crore.
* In June 1993, the Development Commissioners for Export Promotion Zones (EPZs) were delegated some specific powers for 100 per cent Export Oriented Units (EOUs) and EPZs. These powers earlier rested with the Zonal Authorities under Ministry of Commerce. This will bring down the levels at which clearances are required.
* Excise duties on capital goods were rationalised and import duties were reduced further to lower capital costs and stimulate investment.
* A concessional tax rate of 30 per cent on short-term capital gains for foreign institutional investors was introduced to enhance the level of foreign investment in Indian stocks.
* A five-year tax holiday for new industries in industrially backward States and Union Territories and for power generation any where in India was introduced.
* Export credit refinance limits were augmented; 90 per cent of refinance credit is now available in US Dollars.
* The limit for compulsory consortium lending was raised from Rs. 5 crore to Rs. 50 crore. This will give greater flexibility to corporate investors to choose their bank and take advantage of increased

competition.

* CRR and SLR were reduced to 14 per cent and 34.75 per cent respectively to make more credit available for the commercial sector.
* Minimum lending rate for the highest credit slab was reduced to 15 per cent.
* Sick Industrial Companies (Special Provision) Act, 1985 (SICA) amended in December, 1993 to facilitate early detection of sickness in companies and speedy enforcement of remedial measures.

Industrial Production 1993-94

Industrial production during the first 7 months of 1993-94 as recorded by the IIP has shown a modest growth of 1.6 per cent (provisional). This growth rate resulted from a negative growth of 1.6 per cent in the mining and quarrying sectors, and a growth of 1 per cent in the manufacturing sector. Electricity generation continued to perform well with the growth rate at 7.6 per cent during these seven months of 1993-94 (Table 25.1).

An analysis of the 17 sub-sectors within manufacturing reveals that only three groups with a combined weight of 11.9 per cent have registered negative growth rates. These sectors are food products, other textile products and electrical machinery. Amongst these, the worst performance was recorded by the food product. This is however, due to a large weight of sugar industry, within this sub-sector, which showed a decline of more than 55 per cent in April-October 1993 as compared to April-October 1992. This somewhat misleading because it does not reflect the actual decline in sugar production for the whole yea which will be limited to about 5 per cent in the sugar year 1993-94 as compared to the previous year. The other fourteen sectors, with a weight of 62.5 per cent achieved a growth rate of 5.2 per cent during April-October 1993-94. The industrial recovery, though still weak, can be seen to have spread across the majority of manufacturing industries. It may, therefore, be expected that this recovery would be strengthened in the second had of 1993-94. The expectation is further reinforced by the observation that the industrial growth in the second quarter of 1993-94 is 2.8 per cent.

TABLE 25.2: Annual Growth Rates in Major Sectors of Industry

per cent

Year (weight)	Mining (11.46)	Manufacturing (77.11)	Electricity (11.43)	General (100.00)
1	2	3	4	5
1981-82	17.7	7.9	10.2	9.3
1982-83	12.4	1.4	5.7	3.2
1983-84	11.8	5.7	7.6	6.7

(Contd.)

TABLE 25.2 *(Contd.)*

1	2	3	4	5
1984-85	8.8	8.0	12.0	8.6
1985-86	4.1	9.7	8.5	8.7
1986-87	6.2	9.4	10.3	9.2
1987-88	3.8	7.9	7.6	7.3
1988-89	7.9	8.7	9.5	8.7
1989-90	6.3	8.6	10.8	8.6
1990-91	4.5	8.9	7.8	8.3
Average (1980-81 to 1990-91)	8.4	7.6	9.0	7.9
1991-92	0.1	-1.5	8.5	0.0
1992-93	1.5	1.2	5.0	1.8
April-June	8.2	4.6	6.0	5.2
July-Sept.	1.2	2.9	2.7	2.7
Oct.-Dec.	-1.9	4.2	5.5	3.6
Jan.-March	-0.6	-5.2	5.8	-3.3
April-October				
1991-92	-0.2	-2.5	9.6	-0.6
1992-93	3.9	3.9	4.3	4.0
1993-94	-1.6	1.0	7.6	1.6

The sectors in which a negative growth rate occurred are Food Products (-15.1 per cent). Other Textile Products (-11.4 per cent), and Electrical Machinery (-13.1 per cent). Expect these groups all other groups have registered higher growth rates during April-October 1993 than in April-October 1992 and so the recovery in the industrial sectors has been broad based. The following groups registered positive growth rates of more than 5 per cent: Beverages, Tobacco & Tobacco Products (13.2 per cent), Cotton Textiles (6.2 per cent), Jute-Hemp-Mesta Textiles (19.5 per cent), Leather & Leather Products (12.1 per cent), Basic Metal & Alloy Industry (6.5 per cent) and Chemicals and Chemicals Products (6.7 per cent). The sectors which registered rates of growth between 2 to 5 per cent include Wood and Wood Products (4.1 per cent), Paper (2.8 per cent), Non-Metalic Mineral Products (2.2 per cent), Non-Electrical Machinery (2.9 per cent) and Transport Equipment (3.1 per cent). Table 25.3 on industrial growth rates by use-based industrials.

Classification indicates that intermediate and consumer durables industries have come out of the recession phase. During April to October 1993, these industrial segments recorded growth rates of 10.4 and 14.3 per cent respectively. The contribution of growth in consumer durables to overall industrial growth rate is perhaps under estimated due to the low weight assigned to it and which has not been changed since the beginning of 1980s. While the consumer non-durables suffered a decline of 1.6 per cent during the first seven months of the current year, this disguises the fact that this segment includes the seasonal downturn in the sugar industry, which will change, when the production for the full sugar year 1993-94 is available.

Small Scale and Village Industries

The number, employment and output in the small scale sector as estimate by the Office of Developing Commissioner. Small Scale Industries, are given in Table 25.3.

TABLE 25.3: Small Scale Industries—Number, Output and Employment

	1991-92 Actual	1992-93 Provisional
1	2	3
Number of SSI units (lakh)	20.82	22.35 (7.3)
Employment (lakh)	129.8	134.06 (3.3)
Output (Rs. crore)	178699	209300 (17.1)

Note: Figures in parenthesis indicate the percentage increase over the last year.

In real terms the growth rate of the SSI output during 1992-93 is estimated to be about 5.6 per cent compared with only 1.8 per cent growth of the overall industrial production. Research studies indicate that the SSI sector accounts for 35 per cent of the value added by the entire manufacturing sector, 6.9 per cent of net domestic product and 30 per cent of country's exports.

The Nayak Committee was set up to examine the problems of credit, sickness and other related issues in the SSI sector. The Committee submitted its Report in September 1992. The RBI vide their circulars dated April 17, 1993 and July 3, 1993 announced a special package of measures to ensure adequate and timely credit to SSI sector. The salient features of this package are:

(a) Banks should give preference to village industries, tiny industries and other small scale units in that order, while meeting the credit requirement of the small scale sector;
(b) The banks should step up the credit flow to meet the legitimated requirement of the SSI sector in full during the Eighth Five Year Plan;
(c) An effective grievance redressal machinery within each bank which can be approached by the SSI in case of difficulties would be set up; and
(d) Banks should adopt the single window clearance scheme of SIDBI for meeting credit requirements of small scale units.

Khadi and Village Industries

The Khadi and Village Industries Commission (KVIC) covers about 2.1 lakh villages throughout the country. Over the years, the main thrust of KVI activities has been to provide a larger share of employment to SC/STs and women. At present, SC/STs comprise nearly 30.3 per cent of workers and women constitute 46 per cent of the work force. It is provisionally estimated that during 1992-93 the KVI sector produced goods worth Rs. 2670.45 crore and provided employment to 51.05 lakh persons. During 1993-94 the production levels is expected to go up Rs. 2698.53 crore and employment to 52.46 lakh persons.

PUBLIC SECTOR ENTERPRISES (PSEs) COMMITTEE REPORT, 1993

The Committee on PSEC disinvestment headed by C. Rangarajan, Governor Reserve Bank of India submitted its report to Finance Minister Manmohan Singh.

The Committee has recommended disinvestment in PSEs upto 74 per cent of equity holdings in non-reserved category and upto 49 per cent for reserved groups.

The committee has expressed its view against rigedly prescribing year-wise target for disinvestment but has stressed the need for envolving clear cut action plans for divesting equity in PSEs.

The committee has recommended that 10 per cent of the proceeds of disinvestment may be considered to be set up apart by the Government for lending to the PSEs on concessional terms to meet their expansion/ rationalisation needs. It has also recommended for consideration use of part of the proceeds of disinvestment in social sectors like literacy, health and employment creation in rural areas.

In the light of the international experience, the committee has suggested that the Government may consider creation of a standing committee on public enterprise disinvestment with full-time and part-time members drawn from the Government, PSE's financial sector and academic world. Such a committee could recommend specific action for reform, restructuring and disinvestment as well as monitoring and evaluating the process of implementation.

The committee has recommended a number of preparatory steps for disinvestment. These include conversion into company from wherever necessary, deciding the desirable level of equity and restructuring the financials with a proper debt equity gearing, assessing the ongoing investment plans of PSEs and examining the scope of issuing convertible bonds as a measure of resource mobilisation for PSEs. The committee has suggested setting up of an independent regular commission for the concerned sector if necessary.

As regards valuing PSE equity, there are three common methods in vogue based on net asset value, profit earning capacity and discounted case flow.

The choice of method, however, needs to take into account special circumstances affecting PSE's operations such as past focus of PSEs on social responsibilities rather than pure commercial considerations, financial performance being conditioned by a regime of administered prices and so on. The debt/equity structure of most PSEs has also not followed the commercial norms.

The committee has identified two acceptable and transparent process for disinvestment: (i) Offering shares to the public at a fixed price, and (ii) sale through auction amongst a pre-determined clientele. In addition, it has also identified a third method, (iii) transfer of controlling interest in an enterprise to a specific firms or person.

The committee has noted that all these three methods have their own merits and demerits, (i) it is difficult to fix the price. A pre-requisite of this method is that the shares should have an established track record of trading.

The committee has expressed the view that in the case of PSEs for which the first sale is yet to be made, or where the track records yet to be established, method (ii) would be advantageous.

The committee has recommended that once a reasonable market price is established in a normal trading atmosphere over a reasonable period of time, the fixed price method would be appropriate. In all other cases, the auction method with wide participation may be adopted.

The committee has suggested adoption of a scheme of preferential offer of shares to workers and employees in PSEs with an individual ceiling of 200 shares making up a total reservation of 5 per cent of equity.

In the case of PSEs engaged in certain non-manufacturing and skill-based sectors like consultancy services, the ceiling could go upto 20 per cent. While NRIs and foreign investors could be offered equity, it should be on par with general principles governing their participation in the Indian equity market with no reservation of concession.

Some countries have tailored disinvestment to an informed process of managing the external debt by allowing PSEs to swap a portion of their debt for equity. While this might help to reduce the debt service burden and achieve a better debt equity gearing for the PSE, the committee feels that it is not relevant for India since there is no comparable debt problem for the country. However, where a PSE finds unique advantages in adopting this approach, it may be unable to do so, according to the committee.

Source: Hindustan Times, June 27, 1993.

OVERRUNNING COST OF CENTRAL SECTOR PROJECTS

While inaugurating a 4-day National Workshop on the Project Management Approach, at New Delhi on December 20, 1993 the then Minister of State for Programme Implementation Giridhar Gomango stated that 180 of the 354 central sector projects being monitored by the Department of Programme Implementation were running behind scheduled as on Nov. 1, 1993.

The delays in their completion contributed to cost overruns to the extent of 71 per cent.

Studies carried out by the Department of Programme Implementation indicated that the time overrun was the single most important factor contributing to cost overrun. "If we can control time overrun to a great extent". The anticipated cost of all these projects is Rs. 127,000 crore, he said. The workshop was organised by the Department of Programme Implementation in association with the Project Management Associates. Top, management officials of various Government departments and national undertakings are participating in the workshop.

Mr. Gomango said that project management encompasses technology, business, people and environment. The change in technology, business trends and the attitude of people due to transnational communication networks and changes in socio-political, economic and ecological environment are going to have a far reaching impact on the concepts project management.

The Minister observed that changes in excise, customs duties and sales tax, variation in foreign exchange rates, and higher rates in disturbed areas and some of the major reasons of cost and time overruns which is common to the private sector industries as well.

The Central Government's initiatives to boost investment in the private sector and to improve the performance of the public sector cannot fully succeed unless the right technique of project management is adopted, he observed.

The Minister was confident that the project managers attending the workshop will get the much needed professional direction from Dr. Kerzner who has pioneered the technique.

Secretary of the Department of Programme Implementation C.D. Tripathi outlined the concept of project management before the participants. Mr. Gomango called for a scientific management of projects to present cost and time overruns.

Source: Hindustan Times, December 21, 1993.

26

POLITY

Party Position in the Lok Sabha and Rajya Sabha (August 23, 1993)

LOK SABHA		RAJYA SABHA	
Congress	258*	Congress	99
BJP	119	BJP	31
Janata Dal	40	Janata Dal	27
Janata Dal(Ajit)	13	CPI (M)	16
CPI (M)	35	SJP	14
CPI	14	DMK	9
AIADMK	11	AIADMK	6
Telugu Desam	7	Telugu Desam	5
JMM (Soren)	4	CPI	5
JMM (Mardi)	2	RSP	2
RSP	4	Janata Party	2
AIFB	3	National Conference	2
BSP	3	AGP	1
Samajwadi Party	3	NAGP	1
Janata Party	2	Forward Bloc	1
Shiv Sena	2	Muslim League	1
Muslim League	2	Shiv Sena	1
Congress (S)	1	Sikkini SP	1
AIMEIM	1	Nagaland PC	1
ASDC	1	HSPDP	1
AGP	1	Independent	5
HVP	1	Nominated	4
Kerala Cong. (M)	1	Vacancies	10
MPP	1	Total	**245***
SSP	1		
Independent	1	*For two-thirds support,	
Nominated	2	Government needs 163 votes if	
Vacancies	11	all members are present	
Total	**554***		

* Including Speaker.

** For Two-thirds support, Government needs 363 votes if all members are present.

Source: Hindustan Times, August 24, 1993.

November 1993 State Assembly Election Results

Party/State	Delhi	Himachal Pradesh	Mizoram	Rajasthan	Madhya Pradesh	Uttar Pradesh
Total Seats	70	68	40	200	320	425
BJP	49	8	–	93	116	177
CPI	–	1	–	0	2	3
CPI(M)	–	–	–	1	1	1
Congress	14	53	16	77	174	28
BJP	–	–	–	–	12	68
SP	–	–	–	–	–	108
Ind. and Others	3	6	2	22	11	8
J.D	4	–	8	6	4	28
Janata Party	–	–	MJD 14 MNF	–	–	01
Total	70	68	40	199	320	422

MJD - Mizoram Janata Dal
MNE - Mizoram National Front

April 1993 Tripura Assembly Election Results

Total Seats 60		
1.	Left J.D. Front	49
(i)	CPI (M)	44
(ii)	RSP	2
(iii)	Forward Bloc	1
(iv)	THPP	1
(v)	Janata Dal	1
2.	Congress TUJS Coalition	11
(i)	Congress	10
	TUJS	1

(Contd.)

POLL RESULT

Former Chief Minister Bhairon Singh Shekawat romped home in his constituency of Bali, where he defeated Meetha Lal Jain of the Congress. He lost of Janata Dal rival Surendra Singh Rathore in Sriganganagar.

In Himachal Pradesh, two former Congrees Chief Minister Virbhadra Singh and Thakur Ram Lal were declared elected yesterday. Mr Shanta Kumar of the BJP lost. Mr Virbhadra Singh won from Rohru and Thakur Ram Lal from Jubbal Kothkai.

In the most pupulous State of Uttar Pradesh, former Chief Minister Kalyan Singh of the BJP and Samajwadi Party chief Mulayam Singh Yadav were declared elected from Kasganj and Nidhauli Kalan respectively.

Mr. Mulayam Singh Yadav also won from two other constituencies namely Jaswant Nagar and Atrauli.

In Rajasthan, Mr Harideo Joshi made a record 10th entry into the Rajasthan Vidhan Sabha with a good win in Banswara, but two other former Congress Chief Ministers received a drubbing.

Mr Jagannath Pahadia lost in his new constituency of Kekri in Ajmer district and Mr Heerala Deopura was defeated Mr Surendra Singh Rathore of the Janata Dal.

Other prominent losers were former Himachal Pradesh Assembly Speaker Vidya Stokes, who lost to BJP nominee Rakesh Verma in Theog.

Source: Hindustan Times, November 29, 1993.

ANTULAY COMMITTEE, 1993

A Joint Parliamentary Committee, headed by Shri A.R. Antulay to suggest the facilities and recommandation to MPs in India so as to ensure that they stood on a footing which was not too adverse as compared to their counter parts in other countries and state legislation in India, made the following recommendations.

1. A sum of Rs. 2 crore every year for development of the constituency of each Member of Parliament may be placed at the disposal of an MP within his sole discretion.
2. The provision for signing of attendance register for claiming daily allowance during the session might be dispensed with by amending the relevant law. It also wanted restoration of quota facility for MPs in DDA housing scheme, which was scrapped in 1977.

   Alternatively, each MP may be provided with a flat or plot in the central area. Flats may be made for former MPs and given on payment of nominal rent. The Maharashtra model in this regard could be followed, the committee suggested.
3. Each MP should be provided a separate secretary, whose office should be co-terminus with his terms. The secretary may be of the rank of research assistance well versed in handling computers. He should be paid directly by the Government.

   The person suggested for employment as research assistant by MP should not be a member of his family, dependent on him.

4. Besides this, a bilingual stenographer may also be provided to each MP working in the capacity of private secretary to MP. Such a secretary and stenographer should also be given second class AC-two tier pass to travel with the MP.

The secretary and stenographer may, if an MP so choses, be drafted from outside Lok Sabha and Rajya Sabha Secretariats or Government service. He may belong to even a State cadre and in that eventuality he may be drafted on deputation.

This would not, however, prevent an MP from enlisting the service of any one in whom the MP had the confidence provided the basic qualifications laid down for such recruitment in Government service were met even though such a person was not in Government or semi-Government service.

Tranking machines, in quite good number, should be installed in Parliament House post office from where MPs could avail of this free facility. The only restriction in this regard might be that the envelopes bearing the names of MPs from whom letters were issued should alone be franked.

5. The ceiling on water and electricity consumption should be removed and made free with retrospective effect from the time the present Lok Sabha was constituted. The same date for this facility shall hold good for MPs of Rajya Sabha.
6. The number of calls should be increased from 50,000 to three lakhs. There may be a provision for carrying forward the balance of unused calls to the next year quota of an MP from the date of constitution of the present Lok Sabha. The same date for this facility shall hold good for MPs of Rajya Sabha. Telephone with STD facility may be provided at three places – one each in constituency, State headquarters and Delhi.
7. If an MP has travelled in economy class by air he should be permitted to cover extra distance within the business class air fare entitled to him for that particular journey. Further for a particular journey, an MP should be permitted to break the same enroute for a maximum period of four days. Even with a break, such a journey be treated as one.

   Out of 28 air journeys, the balance unutilised air journeys by MP should be credited to the next year quota of the MP for his use and this should continue till the end of the term. Over and above 28 air journeys an MP may be entitled to any number of air journeys on payment of difference between first class train fare and economy or business class fare.
8. More concession should be given on furniture rent, sofa covers and curtains should be washed every three months. Bathrooms and kitchens should have tiles for maintaining cleanliness.
9. The car allowance should be raised from Rs. 50,000 upto the actual price of the diesel ambassador car prevalent at the time when MP applies for the advance. The rate of interest may be five per cent.
10. MP should be entitled to a coupe for travel by first class AC when he is undertaking the journey with either the spouse of companion.
11. There should be no restriction on period of membership for eligibility of pension. A member once elected may be entitled to pension for full one term even if the Lok Sabha is dissolved any time earlier. So also if a

member is falling short to say upto three months to be entitled to get the pension of five, 10,15 and 20 years it should be treated as no shortfall and he should be treated at par with an MP who has actually completed these periods.

At present an MP gets a salary of Rs. 1500 per month in addition to Rs. 3000 per month as constituency allowance and Rs. 1000 per month as office expense allowance during the whole term of office.

He also gets a daily allowance of Rs. 200 per day for the period of residence on duty. Member is entitled to daily allowance only when he signs the register maintained for the purpose.

Besides travelling allowance and 28 single air journeys during a year to be availed of during session and inter-session periods with companion or spouse, an MP is entitled to a free non-transferable air condition two-tier pass for travel throughout the country any time with a companion.

A member is now entitled to have two free telephones, one at his residence or office in Delhi and the other at his usual place of residence in his constituency or the State in which he resides. 25,000 local calls during a year are free to a member on each of the telephones – 50,000 local calls clubbed together.

While he is entitled to a conveyance advance of Rs. 50,000 for purchase of a conveyance, recovery will be in 60 equal instalments from his salary.

Accommodation in the form of a flat is free throughout the term of office of an MP. However, licence fee is charged on bungalow.

Source: Hindustan Times, Janauary 4, 1994.

27

POPULATION AND FAMILY WELFARE

High growth rate of population has been a major problem facing the country. The 1991 Census (Tables 27.1 and 27.2) places the population at 846.3 million as against 683.3 million in 1981, i.e., a growth of 23.9 per cent over the decade. Thee annual exponential growth rate works out to 2.14 per cent during the decade 1981-91 which is marginally lower than 2.22 per cent during 1971-81.

The containment of population growth has been accorded priority in the Eighth Plan. It aims at reducing the crude birth rate from 30.2 per cent thousand in 1990 (provisionally estimated at 29.0 per thousand in 1992) to 26 per thousand by 1997. The infant mortality rate is also to be brought down from 80 per thousand live births in 1990 (provisionally estimated at 79 in 1992) to 70 over the same period. The target of achieving a Net Reproduction Rate (NRR) of unity by the turn of the century, included in the Population Policy of 1983 and the Seventh Five Year Plan, has been shifted to period 2011-2016 A.D. as per the Eighth Plan. Policy interventions must eventually develop into a popular mass movement for containing population growth. This would also require due attention being paid to increasing female literacy, raising age at marriage of girls, creating employment opportunities for women and raising their status in society. The recommendations of the NDC Committee on Population, whose report was presented to NDC in April 1993, are relevant in this connection. In its meeting on 18th September, the NDC endorsed the report of the Committee and directed the Ministry of Health and Family Welfare to initiate further action.

Recommendations are given below:

NDC Committee on Population—Major Recommendations

* The outreach and quality of family welfare programme be improved by removing the backlog and strengthening of health care infrastructure [Sub-centres, Primary Health Centres (PHCs) and Community Health Centres (CHCs)] and improving availability of drugs and other supplies.
* Medical Termination of Pregnancy/sterilisation facilities be created at each CHC/PHC and sub-divisional hospital. All district/sub-divisional hospitals to have Post-Partum units.
* Strengthening of pre-service and in-service training of family welfare staff by involving national and regional institutions.

TABLE 27.1 : Population of India - 1991

	Total	Male	Female	Rural	Urban	Scheduled Castes	Scheduled Tribes
1	2	3	4	5	6	7	8
INDIA	846302688	439230458	407072230	628691676	217611012	138223277	67758380
States							
1. Andhra Pradesh	66508008	33724581	32783427	48620882	17887126	10592066	4199481
2. Arunachal Pradesh	864558	465004	399554	753930	110628	4052	550351
3. Assam	22414322	11657989	10756333	19926527	2487795	1659412	2874441
4. Bihar	86374465	45202091	41172374	75021453	11353012	12571700	6616914
5. Goa	1169793	594790	575003	690041	479752	24364	376
6. Gujarat	41309582	21355209	19954373	27063521	14246061	3060358	6161775
7. Haryana	16463648	8827474	7636174	12408904	4054744	3250933	–
8. Himachal Pradesh	5170877	2617467	2553410	4721681	449196	131028\96	218349
9. Jammu & Kashmir	7718700	4014100	3704600	5879300	1839400	N.A.	N.A.
10. Karnataka	44977201	22951917	22025284	31069413	13907788	7369279	1915691
11. Kerala	29098518	14288995	14809523	21418224	7680294	2886522	320967
12. Madhya Pradesh	66181170	34267293	31913877	50842333	15338837	9626679	15399034
13. Maharashtra	78937187	40825618	38111569	48395601	30541586	8757842	7318281
14. Manipur	1837149	938359	898790	1331504	505645	37105	632173
15. Meghalaya	1774778	907687	867091	1444731	330047	9072	1517927
16. Mizoram	689756	358978	330778	371810	317946	691	653565
17. Nagaland	1209546	641282	568264	1001323	208223	–	1060822

(Contd.)

TABLE 27.1 *(Contd.)*

1	2	3	4	5	6	7	8
18. Orissa	31659736	16064146	15595590	27424753	4234983	5129314	7032214
19. Punjab	20281969	10778034	9503935	14238744	5993225	5742528	–
20. Rajasthan	44005990	23042780	20963210	33938877	10067113	7607820	5474881
21. Sikkim	406457	216427	190030	369451	37006	24084	90901
22. Tamil Nadu	55858946	28298975	27559971	36781354	19077592	10712266	574194
23. Tripura	2757205	1417930	1339275	2335484	421721	451116	753345
24. Uttar Pradesh	139112287	74036957	65075330	111506372	27605915	29276455	287901
25. West Bengal	68077965	35510633	32567332	49370364	18707601	16080611	3808760
Union Territories							
1. Andaman & Nicobar Islands	280661	154369	126292	205706	74955	–	26770
2. Chandigarh	642015	358614	283401	66186	575829	105977	–
3. Dadra & Nagar Haveli	138477	70953	67524	126752	11725	2730	109380
4. Daman & Diu	101586	51595	49991	54043	47543	3891	11724
5. Delhi	9420644	5155512	4265132	949019	8471625	1794836	–
6. Lakshadweep	51707	26618	25089	22593	29114	–	48163
7. Pondicherry	807785	408081	399704	290800	516985	131278	–

NA – Not available.

– Nil population.

Note: 1. The Census was not conducted in J&K in 1991. The figures for J&K are projected population figures for the year 1991. The projected figures of SCs and STs for J&K are not available hence those have not been included in columns 7&8 of the statement for J&K as well as in all India.

Source: Census of India, Series-1, Paper 2 of 1992-Final Population Totals–Brief Analysis of Primary Census Abstracts.

TABLE 27.2 : Features of Population of India - 1991

	Annual eexponetial growth rate 1981-91 (per cent)	Population aged 0-6 years as percentage of total population	Density (population per sq. K,m.)	Literacy rate* (per cent)			Workparticipation rate total workers as percentage of total population)		
				Total	Male	Female	Total	Male	Female
1	2	3	4	5	6	7	8	9	10
INDIA	2.14	17.94	274	52.21	64.13	39.29	37.45	51.55	22.25
States									
1. Andhra Pradesh	2.17	16.49	242	44.09	55.13	32.72	45.05	55.48	34.32
2. Arunachal Pradesh	3.14	21.12	10	41.59	51.45	29.69	46.24	53.76	37.49
3. Assam	2.17	19.73	286	52.89	61.87	43.03	36.09	49.45	21.61
4. Bihar	2.11	20.57	497	38.48	52.49	22.89	32.16	47.92	14.86
5. Goa	1.49	11.74	316	75.51	83.64	67.09	35.28	49.56	20.52
6. Gujarat	1.92	16.53	211	61.29	73.13	48.64	40.23	53.57	25.96
7. Haryana	2.42	18.98	372	55.85	69,10	40.47	31.00	48.51	10.76
8. Himachal Pradesh	1.89	16.25	93	63.86	75.36	52.13	42.83	50.64	34.81
9. Jammu & Kashmir	2.54	NA	NA	NA	NA	NA	NA	NA	NA
10. Karnataka	1.92	16.63	235	56.04	67.26	44.34	41.99	54.09	29.39
11. Kerala	1.34	13.19	749	89.81	93.62	86.17	31.43	47.58	15.85
12. Madhya Pradesh	2.38	19.78	149	44.20	58.42	28.85	42.82	52.26	32.68
13. Maharashtra	2.29	17.11	257	64.87	76.56	52.32	42.97	52.17	33.11

(Contd.)

TABLE 27.2 *(Contd.)*

1	2	3	4	5	6	7	8	9	10
14. Manipur	2.57	16.69	82	59.89	71.63	47.60	42.18	45.27	38.96
15. Meghalaya	2.84	22.18	79	49.10	53.12	44.85	42.67	50.07	34.93
16. Mizoram	3.34	18.60	33	82.27	85.61	78.60	48.91	53.87	43.52
17. Nagaland	4.45	17.15	73	61.67	67.62	54.75	42.68	46.87	37.96
18. Orissa	1.83	16.89	203	49.09	63.09	34.68	37.53	53.79	20.79
19. Punjab	1.89	16.30	403	58.51	65.66	50.41	30.88	54.22	4.40
20. Rajasthan	2.50	20.13	129	38.55	54.99	20.44	38.87	49.30	27.40
21. Sikkim	2.51	18.37	57	56.94	65.74	46.69	41.51	51.26	30.41
22. Tamil Nadu	1.43	13.33	429	62.66	73.75	51.33	43.31	56.39	29.89
23. Tripura	2.95	18.03	263	60.44	70.58	49.65	31.14	47.55	13.76
24. Uttar Pradesh	2.27	20.27	473	41.60	55.73	25.31	32.20	49.68	12.32
25. West Bengal	2.21	16.98	767	57.70	67.81	46.56	32.19	51.40	11.25
Union Territories									
1. Andaman & Nicobar Islands	3.97	16.51	34	73.02	78.99	65.46	35.24	53.32	13.13
2. Chandigarh	3.52	14.92	5632	77.81	82.04	72.34	34.94	54.34	10.39
3. Dadra & Nagar Haveli	2.89	20.46	282	40.71	53.56	26.98	53.25	57.50	48.79
4. Daman & Diu	2.52	15.53	907	71.20	82.66	59.40	37.63	51.63	23.17
5. Delhi	4.15	17.06	6352	75.29	82.01	66.99	31.64	51.72	7.36
6. Lakshadweep	2.51	18.30	1616	81.78	90.18	72.89	26.43	44.17	7.60
7. Pondicherry	2.90	13.67	1642	74.74	83.68	65.63	33.08	50.55	15.24

N A – Not abailable.

* Relates of pupulation aged seven years and above.

Note: Census was not conducted in J&K in 1991 and includes projected population for J&K in 1991. However, the rates in cols, 4 to 11 exclude J&K.

Source: Census of India 1991, Series-1, Paper-2 of 1991. Final Population Totals–Brief Analysis of Primary Census Abstract.

* Integrated inter-sectoral coordination at grass-root (village) level by involving Panchayats, women and youth organisations to carry out family welfare programme as part of overall development programme. It should be made a people's movement.
* Review and strengthening of Village Health Guides (VHGs) and Traditional Birth Attendents (TBAs) to usefully involve them in family welfare programme.
* Differential approaches and area-specific strategies to family welfare may be adopted.
* Allowing requisite flexibility in programme planning and implementation in view of area-specific socio-economic and demographic differentials. Concentrating on micro-planning, in the first instance, in 90 districts with birth-rates over 39 per thousand. Development of district level Health Management Information System.
* Evolving new and innovative approaches in Information, Education and Communication (IEC) and establishment of their valildity for local suitability.
* Strengthening mechanisms for monitoring, evaluation, research support and securing commitment and support of leadership.
* Attention to social determinants, such as, age at marriage of girls; literacy; health status and employment of women, etc.
* Gradually increasing allocation for family welfare programme to about 3 per cent of total public sector plan outlay.
* Formulation of a National Population Policy to take a long-term holistic view of various aspects and for effective implementation of strategies.

28

SCHEDULED CASTES, SCHEDULED TRIBES AND OTHER BACKWARD CLASSES AND WEAKER SECTIONS

DEMOGRAPHIC DATA

The number of people belonging to the Scheduled Castes and Tribes has grown much faster during 1981-91 than other people in the country put together. While the overall growth of population during the decade was 23.79 per cent, it was much higher in the case of Scheduled Castes (30 per cent), Scheduled Tribes (25.67 per cent). In the case of all others (non-Scheduled Castes and Tribes), the population growth during the last 10 years was 22.11 per cent.

The highest growth in the population of Scheduled Castes during period was in several States including Andhra Pradesh, Madhya Pradesh, Maharashtra, West Bengal and Orissa. The growth of the tribes was highest in some other States like Gujarat and Rajasthan.

Kerala is the only State in the country where the growth rate has been the highest among the tribes. As against this, the decadal growth in the population of all other sections of people (non-Scheduled Castes and Tribes) was high in States like Bihar and Uttar Pradesh. According to the latest analysis of the population figures (Paper-2 of 1992) published by the Census Commissioner.

But the demographic chart of the country makes a rather baffling reading in another respect. The proportion of Scheduled Tribes in the total population has sharply declined in at least 12 States. It has, however, gone up in another one dozen States whereas it has remained static in one State. The tribes have been listed or scheduled in only 25 States in the country.

Of these, the sharpest decline in the population of the tribes was recorded in Arunachal Pradesh. There, it went down from 69.82 per cent in 1981 to 63.66 per cent 10 years later. But in other north-eastern States, like Mizoram, Meghalaya, Nagaland and Tripura, the proportion of the tribal, population went up, though marginally (nearly one per cent).

It poses a question: is the population growth and the share of the Scheduled Tribes correctly recorded? Or, does it show an element of bias in recording the real position? The census document states that in 1981, the St constituted 7.83 per cent of the total population in the country. And, at the end of 1991, the figure was slightly higher i.e., 7.95 per cent.

The position or pattern is different in respect of the Scheduled Castes. Their proportion in the population has improved in all States, except Uttar Pradedh and Kerala. While in Kerala, the percentage of the Scheduled Castes has suffered a drop of 10 points, in UP it went down by 9.92 per cent. But the increase has been marginal, of one per cent or more in States like Andhra Pradesh, Maharashtra and Karnataka. Overall, in 1981, the SC constituted 15.81 per cent of the total population, and a decade later they were 16.73 per cent.

Consequently the proportion of all other people put together (non-SC/ST population was 76.36 per cent, at the end of the next decade, it dropped to 75.32 per cent. The decline was quite noticeable in States like Andhra Pradesh, Maharashtra, Punjab and West Bengal. The pattern was, however, different and went up in other States including Arunachal Pradesh, Bihar and Sikkim.

The sex ratio in the overall population went adversely for women. It was more so in the case of SC and ST in the country. The national position was that for every 1,000 males, there were 935 women in 1981 and 927 at the end of 1991. A drop of eight points. But it was more pronounced in the case of SCs – where it dropped by 10 points, and by 11 points in the case of STs. Interestingly while the ratio of females against males in the population among both the SC and ST went down, the decadal growth of population in these two groups was higher than other groups put together. Does it indicate a high rate of fertility among those people.

Another noteworthy aspect was, that while the influx of non-SC/ST to cities came down during 1981-91 by 1104 per cent, it went up though marginally in the case of both the SC and ST.

Source: Qureshy Ahtesham, *Hindustan Times,* April 20, 1993.

SCHEDULED CASTES AND SCHEDULED TRIBES AND OTHER BACKWARD COMMUNITIES

Welfare

For the development and welfare of weaker sections of the society like Scheduled Castes, Scheduled Tribes, backward classes and physically handicaped and disabled persons, various schemes are in operation. The Special Component Plan for Scheduled Castes is in operation in 21 States and 3 Union Territories. There are 21 State Scheduled Caste Development Corporations to assist entrepreneurs to procure loans, for taking up bankable projects. Fifty per cent of the families to be assisted under IRDP and 30 per cent of employment generation under JRY are reserved for SC/STs. Against this, the actual coverage was over 51 per cent under IRDP and over 56 per cent under JRY. In addition, under Indira Awaass Yojana and Million Wells Scheme of JRY, houses are constructed free of cost and free boring of wells is done for persons belonging to SC/ST and freed bonded labourers. For the development and Welfare of Scheduled Tribes, Tribal Sub-plans are in operation since 1975 and 193 Integrated Tribal Development Projects are functioning in 18 States and 2 Union Territories. Tribal Cooperative Marketing Development Federation facilities marketing of tribal produce, especially minor forest produce. National

Scheduled Castes and Scheduled Tribes Finance and Development Corporation serves as a national institution to support the activities of State SC and ST Development Corporations. Since its inception in February, 1989 it has sanctioned over 480 income generating projects covering over 1.74 lakh SC and ST beneficiaries.

Some important initiatives taken recently to improve the well-being of the Scheduled Castes and Scheduled Tribes, as well as Other Backward Classes, include: (i) Reservation of 27 per cent of jobs for Other Backward Classes (OBCs) in the Central Government and Public Sector Undertakings, excluding the creamy layer. (ii) Setting up a National Commission for Backward Classes (iii) A scheme for educational complexes in low literacy pockets for improving literacay among tribal women. (iv) Setting up of a National Backward Classes Finance and Development Corportion with an authorised capital of Rs. 200 crore to promote economic and other development activities of the backward classes. (v) Raising of the share capital of the National Scheduled Castes and Scheduled Tribes Finance Development Corporation from Rs. 75 crore to Rs. 125 crore.

REPORT ON "CREAMY LAYER"

Justice Prasad Committee

The then Union Welfare Minister Sitaram Kesari on March 16 announced in both Houses of Parliament the Government's acceptance of the Justice Ram Nandan Prasad Committee report which dealt with the identification of the "creamy layer" among the socially and educationally backward classes (SEBC). Though the expert committee had submitted its report a few days ago, it was tabled today, following an assurance by Mr Kesari last week in the Lok Sabha that the members would shortly have it once the Government had studied it and formulated its response. The report identified the creamy layer among the SEBC for excluding it from the list of Mandal, beneficiaries, following the Supreme Court verdict on the controversial Mandal report last year.

The Justice Prasad committee report states that only when the creamy layer is substantial and stable, formed after crossing the rubicon of social backwardness, then and then alone can it be made the basis for disentitlement. However, it says certain constitutional posts of President, Vice-President, Judges of the Supreme Court and High Courts, chairman and members of the UPSC and state public service commissions, chief election comissioner, comptroller and auditor general of India, governers, ministers and membership of legislatures, the last three being temporary ones. The rule of exclusion, it says, covers class one officers of central and state services (direct recruits), public sector undertakings, armed forces and paramilitary forces, professional class including trade, business, and industry, and property owners. It excludes from the list of reservation beneficiaries those having gross annual income of Rs. one lakh and above.

In the service category, the rule of exclusion will apply if either husband or wife is a class one officer. Where both are class one officers and if one of them dies, the rule of exclusion is still applicable. But if both dies, then the rule of exclusion becomes invalid. Permanent incapacitation is treated as death by the committee and it follows the above logic in the application of the rule of exclusion. Thus, the committee says that if before the unfortunate event of death of either of or both such spouses occurs, either of the spouses has had the benefit of employment in any international bodies like the United Nation, IMF, World Bank for a period of not less than five years, then exclusion from the benefits of reservation would continue to apply to the offspring.

Source: The Hindustan Times, New Delhi.

MANDAL JOB QUOTA

The Government has decided to extend reservation to weaker sections of society in public sector units and banks. A notification to this effect was issued on Sept. 8 by the Government along with the controversial notification reserving 27 per cent jobs for other backward classes (OBCc), excluding the "creamy layer" from the benefits. Announcing this 'politically significant' decision, the then Welfare Minister, Mr Sita Ram Kesri, said the Government had decided to extend reservation to public sector units including banks. A similar notification would be issued in respect of public sector undertakings and financial institutions including banks. The notifications have been issued with immediate effect.

According to Mr Kesri, the Government would review the order within two years to ensure that it was being implemented effectively. It would also try to find out whether the 'creamy layer' grabbed jobs meant for the real beneficiaries, the Minister said. With this, nearly 1,200 castes and communities found common in the lists of the Mandal Commission and the state governments would get the benefits Mr Kesri said, adding that a list of such castes and communities would be issued separately by his Ministry. The notification made it clear that the candidates belonging to OBCs recruited on the basis of merit in an open competition on the same standards prescribed for the general candidates would not be adjusted against the reservation quota of 27 per cent.

About the first appontment under the Mandal Commission, Mr Kesri said "the order comes into force with immediate effect and they will get jobs". The notification said the rule of exclusion will not apply to persons working as artisans or engaged in hereditary occupations. A list of such occupations is being issued separately by the Welfare Ministry. Mr Kesri, who held discussions last week with the leaders of various political parties on the issues, and said in deference to their unanimous view, the Government decided to increase the cut-off percentage for eligibility in the case of agriculturists from 65 per cent (in terms of irrigated land ceilings prescribed under state land ceiling laws) to 85 per cent. The other parameters of the expert committee, which had been set up by the Government to identify 'creamy layer', would remain unchanged, he said, clarifying that it was the Supreme Court which in its judgment on the job Quota issue in November last directed exclusion of 'creamy layer'.

The children of the President, the Vice-President, judges of the Suprme Court and High Courts, chairmen and Union members and state public service commissions, Chief Election Commissioner and Comptroller and Auditor General would be treated as 'creamy layer' and would not be entitled to the benefits. He said the Government would review within two years the criteria for 'creamy layer' in the light of experience gained in the implementation of the job quota for OBCs, he said in reply to a question.

Source: Financial Express, New Delhi.

29

SCIENCE AND TECHNOLOGY

PRITHVI MISSILE LAUNCHED

India's medium range surface to surface missile, Prithvi, was on June 12, 1993 successfully test fired in its full operational mode with an enhanced range.

The 11th launch of the 350 km range missile which was test fired over high seas at 12.20 p.m. had accomplished all "mission requirements with an accurate impact over a predetermined range" traced by radars of naval warships.

"Today's(June 12) missile launch was the first from the production batch and had used land-based mobile launcher and mobile control", the spokesman said.

The mission requirements were observed by user services, the Army and the Navy, whose teams had been positioned closer to impact site at sea, he added.

According to reports, Prithvi has already been deployed in some selected forward locations close to border with Pakistan with specialised trained Army units who are using the just tested mobile launchers.

The early deployment of the missile, according to reports, had been necessitated following Pakistan's reported rapid progress with the Hatf range of surface to surface missiles.

According to Defence Ministry officials, the Prithvi missiles are already in production at Bharat Dynamics, Hyderabad, which is the prime production agency in partnership with Hindustan Aeronautics, Ordnance Factories, Bharat Electricals, Bharat Earth Movers Limited and a number of other public and private sector units.

The officials said the successful test firing of the missile would herald user trials of the missile with the Army.

Mr.A.P.J. Abdul Kalaam, Scientific Advisor to the Defence Ministry, who witnessed the launch, congratulated Mr.V.K. Saraswat, Prithvi project director and team of scientists of the Defence Research and Development Organisation (DRDO) in realising the "operations systems" of the Prithvi missile.

Prithvi is one of the five main missile systems being developed by the DRDO. The other four being the technology demonstrator medium rante ballistic missile, Agni, the surface to air, Trishul and Akash missile and the third generation anti-tank missile, Nag.

Source : Hindustan Time, June 13, 1993.

TABLE 29.1: Financial Summary

Table giving the Actuals 1992-93, BE 1993-94, RE 1993-94 and BE 1994-95 of various plan and non-plan schemes (headwise/broad catagorywise)

Rupees in crore

Sl. No.	Head of Development Project Programmes/ Schemes	Actual Plan	1992-93 Non-Plan	Total	Budget Plan	Estimate Non-Plan	1993-94 Total	Revised Plan	Estimates Non-Plan	1993-94 Total	Budget Plan	Estimates Non-Plan	1994-95 Total
1.	Assistance to Council of Scientific and Industrial Research	99.96	162.11	261.77	126.50	166.28	292.78	126.50	194.07	320.57	140.00	198.50	338.50
2.	Technology Promotion Development and Utilisation Programme	12.15	0.00	12.15	11.00	0.00	11.0	10.97	0.00	10.97	14.10	0.03	14.13
3.	Research and Development	1.72	0.00	1.72	2.20	0.00	2.20	2.20	0.00	2.20	2.10	0.00	2.10
4.	Investmentin Public Enterprises												
4.1	Central Electronics Limited	2.58	0.00	2.58	4.00	0.00	4.00	4.00	0.00	4.00	2.25	0.00	2.25
4.2	National Research Development Corporation	0.10	0.00	0.10	0.15	0.00	0.15	0.15	0.00	0.15	0.15	0.00	0.15
	Total	2.68	0.00	2.68	4.15	0.00	4.15	4.15	0.00	4.15	2.40	0.00	2.40
5.	Loans of Public Enterprises												
5.1	Central Electronics Limited	2.58	4.56	7.14	4.00	0.00	4.00	4.00	0.00	4.00	2.25	0.00	2.25
5.2	National Research Development Corporation	0.10	0.00	0.10	0.15	0.00	0.15	0.15	0.00	0.15	0.15	0.00	0.15
	Total	2.68	4.56	7.24	4.15	0.00	4.15	4.15	0.00	4.15	2.40	0.00	2.40
	Total Ihvestments & Loans	5.36	4.56	9.92	8.30	0.00	8.30	8.30	0.00	8.30	4.80	0.00	4.80
6.	Secretariat Economic Services	0.00	0.82	0.82	0.00	0.87	0.87	0.00	0.90	0.90	0.00	0.92	0.92
	Grand Total	118.89	167.40	286.30	148.00	167.15	315.15	147.97	194.97	342.94	161.000	199.45	360.45

AGNI MISSILE LAUNCH SUCCESSFUL

Agni, India's intermediate range ballistic missile, was successfully testfired from the interim test range (ITR) on Saturday evening (February 19, 1994).

Defence ministry officials announced that the blast off was flawless. A network of telemetry and tracking stations at ITR, SHAR, Car Nicobar and naval ships followed the flight sequence throughout till the payload impacted at the designated target.

The white hot object was tracked by the naval ships confirming the success of the mission.

The third launch of the test vehicle was aimed at achieving longer range and advanced manoeuvrability during the re-entry phase of the flight for greater accuracy in guiding the payload to a designated target at long range, an official release said.

The first two launches of the sophisticated missile were on May 22, 1989 and May 29, 1992. Though the first one was successful, the second one met with partial success because of some problems at the re-entry stage.

The estimated range of Agni is between 1,500 km and 2,500 km for payloads ranging between 500 kg and 1,000 kg. It consists of a solid propellant first stage (essentially and SLV-3) and a liquid propellant second stage which are joined together by distinct trusses. These are akin to Chinese and Soviet missiles of this class.

During the second test of the Agni two years ago, the first stage had performed as expected, but there was a hitch in the second stage that led to the vehicle straying off course.

There were no problems with the direction (Azimuth) of the missile.

Source: Indian Express, February 20, 1994.

INDIAN SCIENCE CONGRESS MEET, JANUARY 1994

The 81st Session of the Indian Science Congress was held at the University of Rajasthan, Jaipur on 3-8 January 1994. Inaugurating the Session, the Prime Minister, Mr. P.V. Narasimha Rao, expressed fears that in the liberalised post-GATT scenario, crucial technologies may be withheld from India to stunt her progress in various fields. This was in spite of the fact that the new GATT deal ensures further opening up of national economies and erosion of national borders as a consequence of internationalisation of business, innovation and technological development.

His speech was devoted mainly to stress the importance of technology in the post-GATT (General Agreement on Tariffs and Trade) world environment Mr Rao said that though the new global agreement on ensuring free trade would affect many fields, its impact would be high only in some key areas.

Identifying these areas as textiles and clothing, agriculture, trade related intellectual property rights (TRIPs) and services, including research and development services, he said such sectors required a strong base in indigenous R and D and Science and technological capabilities.

"With our vast reservoir of S and T personnel and comparatively lower manpower costs, it was possible to meet such challenges through appropriate R and D inputs. To make this happen, industry has to play a dominant part",

Mr Rao stressed, referring to the successful examples of industrialised nations.

However, private industry contributed less than 15 per cent of national R and D investments. This should change, said the Prime Minister, and industry should come forward to define the goal areas and set targets for the scientific community.

While creation of wealth was important, it was even more crucial to ensure its equitable distribution, said Mr Rao. He attributed increasing social tensions to the perpetuation inequity in economic development. Quoting a Sanskrit verse, he said prosperity for all should be the purpose of our developmental programmes.

Referring to the theme of the session, "Science in India: excellence and accountability," he said he shall not judge the performance of scientists in terms of conventional yardsticks that are used to assess productivity. It will be left to scientists' own methods of judgment.

At the same time, there can be no judgment according to which concrete results were ignored. He quoted noted scientist Prof. S. Chandrasekhar to stress this point :" One's place in science, as posterity will duly assign, depends largely on one's continuous exertion, at the edge of one's ability.

Deftly side-stepping issues of declining government investment in the R and D sector and allocations for the educational institutions voiced by the scientific community, the Prime Minister said industry should step up investments in universities too and also ensure involvement of high quality manpower in programmes of their interest.

Prof P.N. Srivastava, in his presidential speech, regretted "complete neglect of the education of science".

Quoting recommendations of senior scientists made to the government in 1990, Prof Srivastava regretted that programmes to provide excellence in science education by establishing consortia of universities to work in collaboration with higher institutions of learning and utilising their superior human and material resources were not initiated.

He suggested at least ten per cent of the science and technology budget should be embarked for training of manpower in universities and colleges. The scientific activities of the UGC should be supported by various concerned agencies and the departments of science and technology. Proper improvement will have to be made in primary and secondary schools as well. "If we do not do this, we will only be strengthening the tip of the pyramid, whose bottom is weak. In such a situation, we will never be able to compete with the world in the 21st century," Prof Srivastava cautioned.

He lauded the role of agricultural scientists, due to the efforts of whom a "green revolution" was possible at a time when a famine was anticipated by the Western world. "India is better prepared to face droughts now", he said.

On the scientific achievements in India, Prof. Srivastava listed the following:

- On atomic energy, capabilities spanning the entire nuclear cycle-exploration, mining, extraction, purification and conversion of nuclear materials, processing of spent fuel-had been acheived.
- The space research programme had made a tremendous success with the successful launching of many communication and multipurpose satellites. Despite the failure of the PSLV in September 1993, there was no

need for despondency.

- On the health front, the infant mortality rate has come down to 95 per thousand from 140 per thousand, while longevity has increased from 32 years to 60. Population growth, too, is showing a decline.
- In the electronics and communications field, notable developments had occurred.
- In the fields of oil, natural gas and petrochemicals, impressive growth had been achieved, especially with regards to pipeline facilities, manufacture of offshore rigs and platforms and underwater technologies, etc.

But Prof. Srivastava warned against complacency and said the per hectare rice production in China was much higher than that in India, at 5,712 kg as compared to India's 2,624 kg.

'While it was true that scientists have not failed the country, we just cannot yet satisfy the nation by repeated assertions on what science has done," he said adding "there has been native enthusiasm for doing what every man in doing in the West, without having goal-directed activities, especially needed for the country.

India's indigenous cryogenic rocket engine programme had made some progress but it would have been better if the Indian scientists had embarked on this endeavour a few years earlier, he said.

Commenting on the deficiencies, Prof.Srivastava said "there has been a serious lacuna that a truly critical and unbiased assessment of our track record has never been made, be it of national laboratories, including those for atomic energy, space research or those at universities, etc". Many meaningful recommendations had been scuttled on one pretext or the other, he claimed.

"It has been truly pointed out that we have very few peaks of excellence both in terms of men and institutions. This is not only due to insufficiency of funds and facilities, but also partly because of the depressing atmosphere the scientists have created for themselves. We easily compromise with mediocrity", he said.

The chief minister, Mr Bhairon Singh Shekhawat, asked the scientists to suggest ways to solve the problem of drinking water in Rajasthan. The governor, Mr Baliram Bhagat, also said Rajasthan was rain deficient state having two major rivers – Chambal and Mahi. Scientists should help the policy-makers in overcoming water shortage in the state. The Union Minister of state for science and technology, Mr Bhuwanesh Chaturvedi, and the Rajasthan minister for science and technology, Mr Lalit Kishore Chaturvedi, also spoke on the occasion.

Speaking on the focal theme of the Indian Science Congress, Excellence and Accountability, Prof M.G.K. Menon, eminent scientist and former minister of state for science and technology said "lack of motivation, scant respect for scholarship and a growing tendency to contend with mediocrity are some of the major reasons for the failure of Indian scientists, in the post-independence period, to match with the best in the world". He said the first half of the 20th century–when scientists like P.C. Ray, J.C. Bose and Megnad Saha (to name a few) strode the Indian scene–was the renaissance period for Indian science.

"This was because they were fired by the spirit of the time and the all-pervading spirit of the time was one which was associated with the freedom struggle", he said, adding that "the air then induced people to strive for greatness" with a certain degree of selflessness.

The situation had changed now, which the driving force now being money and power. Every-body was more interested in cushy jobs, promotions and a better pay packet.

Prof. Menon, however, said it would be unfair for anybody to expect that science would work and function in isolation of the major trends of the day. "Do we any more have great leaders like Gandhi, Nehru, Tilak and Gokhale?" he asked. He said even the science in the West had progressed in an atmosphere of liberalisation and when people began to question the all-pervading authority of the church.

In contrast, leaders in India were again taking us back to religious themes and were instrumental more in dividing the people of the country than acting as agents of cohesion, he said.

But the eminent scientist defended the scientific community in so far as economic accountability was concerned and said the Indian scientists had not committed any securities scam thus far and there had never been a need to appoint a joint parliamentary committee to look into their conduct. At the same time, he pointed, one must admit that science too was a part of the society.

Ruing the fact that the tradition of respect for scholarship and also the *guru-shishya parampara* had all put evaporated from the national scene, Prof Menon said it would be improper to talk of excellence and accountability sitting in an ivory tower.

While stating that failure of education in the country was the main cause for science not taking off in a big way in the country, the former Union Minister said university teachers and scienctists should also introspect whether they had served society and the country and whether they could do much more and how.

Source: University News, February 7, 1994.

30

STOCK MARKET SCAM

Joint Parliamentary Committee Report on the Bank Securities

The Joint Parliamentary Committee presented its report to Parliament on December 21, 1993. The 30-Members Committee was headed by JPC Chairman Ram Niwas Mirdha. The report is a Consenus, document and is a product of 16 months, probe. There is a note appended to the JPC Report, given by 13 members belonging to the opposition parties in the committee which demanded an inquiry to be set up under the Commission of Enquiry Act.

The Committee has recommended the setting up of two expert committees to determine the exact amount involved in the scam and to trace its end-users. The 344-page report, including six separate notes by various members of the 30-member committee, asserted the emergence of a culture of non-accountability has permeated all sections of the government and banking system over the years. These grave irregularities persisted for so long that eventually it was not the observance of regulations but their breach that came to be regarded and defended as market practice, the report commented.

Briefing newsmen, JPC chairmen Ram Niwas Mirdha justified the Committee's failure to determine the volume of the scam and identifying its end-users on the ground that the Committee neither had sufficient time nor it was the part of its terms of reference. Referring to the end-use of monies, the Committee has noted that if the movement of monies through brokers is traced to the end-user, than the entire inter-connected ramifications of the scam would be revealed. The committee has regretted that it has not been possible for it to do this. "The tracing of monies to their final destination, particularly when large sums were involved and when intricate mechanics have been employed to cloak transactions, was the task of a team comprising of specialists in the field of accountancy, taxation, and criminal investigation. The Committee had no such expertise and were not equipped for this purpose. They had hoped that the other investigating agencies of the government would be able to at least partially complete this task before the Committee finalised their report and share the information with the Committee. However, that has become possible. This committee, therefore, recommends that such a team be constituted under the overall coordinating responsibility of the ministry of finance and with due and proper representation of such other agencies as it may deem fit, the task of identifying the end-use of monies been trusted to this Committee it may be directed to report within six months of appointment and the report also be presented to Parliament".

The Committee has concluded that most of their regularities in securities transactions that took place in 1991 and 1992 was the handiwork of banks. Explaining the reasons for not specifiying the exact amount of scam funds, the report said that the Committee did not independently attempt this exercise as three separate specialists bodies had already attempted it. The Committee is of the view that it is the duty fo the Ministry of Finance to undertake this responsibility. According to the JPC's estimates, the total figure is around Rs. 3650.60 crore. Indicating Health Minister B. Shankaranand, the Committee held that he dad not discharged his responsibility in consonance with the high office held by him in connection with investment decisions when he was chairman of the Oil Industry Development Board as Petroleum Minister.

Critical references have also been made against the Minister of State for Rural Development, Rameshwar Thakur, for not dealing with the income tax file of Harshad Mehta with necessry promptitude while serving in his erstwhile capacity as then Minister of State for Finance. On the alleged Rs. 1 crore pay-off to Prime Minister P.V. Narasimha Rao by stockbroker Harshad Mehta, the committee has recounted the evidence placed before it but made no reference of the issue in its chapter on observations, conclusions and recommendations. The Committee, however, recommended to the Lok Sabha speaker to consider contempt proceedings against Harshad Mehta for breach of privilege for "prevaricating, giving false evidence or willfully suppressing truth or persistently misleading" the Committee.

Strictures against Five Important Individuals

The JPC report has failed to create a political tornado, but it has willy nilly nailed five individuals who held offices of importance at the peak of the scam. Those who failed to escape the JPC net include the Union Health Minister (then Petroleum Minister) Mr. B. Shankaranand, the Minister of State for Rural Development Mr. Rameshwar Thakur, former RBI Governor Mr. S. Venkataramanan, Deputy Governors of RBI, Mr. Amitava Ghosh and Mr. R. Janakiraman. The rest of the blame has been placed at the doors of financial institutions, investigating agencies and Public Sector Undertakings. The CBI has been subjected to severest reprimand. The Enforcement Directorate and Central Board of Direct Taxes (CBDT) have been named for non-coordination, willful in-action or wanton negligence.

On Dr. Manmohan Singh

"It is good to have a Finance Minister who does not lose his sleep but one would wish that when such cataclysmic changes take place all around some alarm would ring to disturb his slumber"

On B. Shankaranand

"The two Chairmen (Shankaranand and S.P.Malaviya) of OIDB during the relevant period did not discharge their responsibilities in consonance with the high office held by them. Further, it is the expectation of the committee that the Government will take necessary corrective action".

On Big-bull Harshad Mehta

"Tried to mislead the committee".

On Rameshwar Thakur

Indicted Mr. Thakur for delay in investigation of cases and failure to launch a single prosecution.

On S. Venkataramanan

Shri S. Venkataramanan as the Governor of the Bonk (RBI) during this crucial period must be held no less responsible. The suggestion to treat the foreign banks differently, the delay in the issue of the circular of July, 1991, failure to incorporate all the deficiencies noticed even in this circular and absence of any follow up action subsequently, the noticed delay in the issue of the bill discounting circular for 22 months, his recommendation to appoint people in top positions which proved to be a liability, subsequently, display of unusual interest in the account of Mr. Harshad Mehta, his acts of omission and commission cannot be overlooked in any of their ramifications".

On PSUs

"While most of the companies were issuing instructions and getting confirmatory letters periodically from banks/finance companies with regard to investment of funds in many cases instructions to banks were not given at the time of placement of funds. In the case of PSUs like STC, MMTC, OIL, NPCIL and KRIBHCO funds were invested without issuing specific instructions to banks/ finance companies as to how their funds should be invested by them. Thus the funds of these organisation were exposed to risk by leaving the discretion with banks about the manner of investment of their funds."

Strictures against FM

Contrary to the general expectation, the Joint Parliamentary Committee (JPC) has retained various strictures against the Finance Minister, Dr Manmohan Singh, and the Ministry of Finance (MoF) in its final report submitted to Parliament. The Commitee observed that the 'responsibility and accountability of the FM to Parliament cannot be denied'.

In response to the controversial remark of the Finance Minister, "but that does not mean that I should lose my sleep simply because stock market goes up one day and falls the next day", the Committee observed that , 'it is good to have a Finance Minister who does not lose his sleep easily but one would wish that when such cataclysmic changes take place all around some alarm bell would ring to disturb his slumber'. The report stated that the Finance Minister has addressed the presidents of Stock Exchanges on March 28, 1992 regarding better control of stock exchanges. At the meeting, the Minister has expressed the need for proper administration of exchanges to prevent price rigging and better transparency, need for maintaining capital adequacy norms, increasing corporate membership etc.

Mr Mirdha regretted that despite all the exposure done in the JPC, the stock exchanges in the country continued to be highly disorganised, and they resisted any change. The Bombay stock exchange-which prominently figured in the scam and was century-old–was as "antiquated as its birth", Mr Mirdha added. He hoped that the work done by the JPC would help the Government and other authorities to take drastic action for reforms of such institutions and the whole system so that a scam did not occur again. Mr Dasgupta deplored that the Andhra Pradesh Government has not yet granted the sanction to the CBI to launch prosecution against those found "guilty" in the Gold Star affair in Hyderabad. He also noted that similarly no Government permission had yet been granted for proceeding with a criminal' case initiated against Mr S. Krishnamurthy, former Planning Commission Chairman, though the case was registered way back in 1986. Speaking about his book, Mr Dasgupta said what was more serious and worrisome than the scam was an "operation cover-up" launched to protect the key players, and to condone the criminality.

Action against Foreign Banks Recommended

The Joint Parlimentary Committee has recommended stringent penalties including suspension of licences of the foreign banks keeping in view the extent of irregularities indulged into by each of them. In its final report the JPC has desired that special scrutiny may be carried out by the Reserve Bank of India in all the foreign banks involved in the recent irregularities and the question of disallowing repatriation of profits through irregular securities transactions and other malpractices be considered. Legal action should be persued both in India and the foreign country concerned. The Committee examined in particular the securities transactions of four foriegn banks viz. SCB, ANZ Grindlays Banks, BOA and Citibank. The examination by the Committee of securities transaction in banks has, revealed that foreign banks particularly have been deeply involved in the irregularities in securities transactions, they have acted in an unbecoming manner, indulged in large scale security deals, highly disproportionnate to their normal requirements.

Venkataramanan's Deposition

The alleged "acts of omission and commission" on the part of the fomer Governor of the Reserve Bank of India, Mr S. Venkataramanan, considered by the Joint Parlimentary Committee on the securities scam, include "reactivation", in April 1992, of the current account of Harshad Mehta in the State Bank of India (Main Branch) in Bombay. This allegation, according to the deposition of Mr. Venkataramanan and his clarifications to the committee, was misconceived because there was in the first instance no freezing or deactivation of the account by the RBI but only an order to monitor the flow of firms. (The RBI has no power to freeze a current account except under legal procedures like implementation of a "garnishee order" from a court or' on issuing a show-cause notice to the account holder).

What had happened in the case of the Harshad Mehta account, according to the defence put up by the former RBI Governor, was that on March 16, 1992, extracts from the current account of Harshad Mehta with the SBI were brought to the attention of Ms Viswanathan, Executive Director of the RBI, by

Mr.M.N. Goiporia, Chairman of the SBI. This itself was the result of a query made by the RBI Governor at a meeting held in the RBI on March 10, 1992, as to the source of funds of Harshad Mehta.

The information from the SBI Chariman on the Mehta account was shown by Ms Viswanathan to Mr Venkataramanan on the same day (March 16, 1992), whereupon the latter reiterated over the telephone his instructions to Mr Goiporia to monitor the account. Ms Viswanathan, on her part, instructed RBI officials to scrutinise voucher entries on the Mehta account on a top priority basis. Harshad Mehta did not operate the account between March 16 and April 1, 1992, but again operated it from April 2 to 8,1992. Whatever the reasons which impelled Harshad Mehta to operate or not operate his current account, the fact was that there were no orders form the RBI to the SBi for freezing or defreezing the account or to withdraw the monitoring of the same, Mr Venkataramanan is understood to have told the JPC.

Jankiraman Refutes Charges

Reserve Bank of India Deputy Governor R. Jankiraman, who had operated as the "radiologist of the securities scam" and has been indicated by the Joint Parliamentary Committee (JPC) on Dec. 24 issued a lengthy "statement of innocence". The statement explained, at lenght, the various RBI procedures, to claim that he could not have had access to information and as such the JPC was not justified in rubbing him hard for acts with which he was not even remotely concerned. Mr Jankiraman, who is known for being exceptionally sensitive to criticism pointed out that he was made Director of National Housing Bank (NHB) in April 1992 and the first meeting of the Board was held on June 11, 1992 (after the scam broke out) which was attended by him.

Referring to the JPC strictures against him as a Director of State Bank of India, he has explained that the observation of the JPC that "the RBI nominees–virtually have access to a mine of information available within the RBI in the form of reports of financial inspection, scrutinies, reviews etc. is not borne out by the actual position. He states that he had no access to any such information from the RBI about security irregularities wether in the State Bank of India or in any other bank. In a categorical statement, Mr Jankiraman, who retire from RBI recently, has said, "it would not be fair to accuse the nominee directors of inaction in respect of information to which they had no access at all the relevant time".

Source: Financial Express, New Delhi; *The Observer of Business and Politics,* New Delhi; *The Hindu,* New Delhi and *The Hindustan Times,* New Delhi.

HIGHLIGHTS JPC REPORT

- Finance minister Manmohan Singh : Held responsible for lapses of his ministry, banks and FIs.
- Rural development minister Rameshwar Thakur : As minister of state for finance, delayed to forward crucial note on Hashad Mehta by one month.
- Health minister B Shankaranand : As petroleum and natural gas minister, mocked at OIDB rules and made disproportionate investments in

Cantina and Syndicate Bank.

* Former civil aviation minister Madhavrao Scindia : Delayed seeking explanation from Vayudoot's irregular investments.
* Former RBI governor S Venkitaramanan : "Not unaffected" by the all pervasive malaise.
* Former RBI deputy governors, Amitava Ghosh and R Janakiraman : showed insufficient concern at bouncing of SGL forms.
* Chief officer DBOD, RBI, N D Parameswaran : Responsible for lapses of DBOD.
* BSE : Market leader in irregularities.
* Finance ministry : Failed to observe financial sector rules.
* Industrial houses, RIL and UB group : Colluded with banks in misues of funds.
* Railway ministry : Invested funds flouting rules.
* Department of Public Enterprises : Failed to superise guidelines on PSU's investment.
* SBI : Officers robbed it of its status and its top management needs to be proceeded against for dereliction of duty.
* Department of Company Affairs : Failed to inspect PSU account books.
* Eight PSUs, RCTC, ONGC, IRFC, Kribhco, Iffco, Air India, Vayudoot and PFC : Misused public funds.
* Broker Bhupen Dalal, AD Narottam and T B Ruia: Misused their position on the boards of Bank of Karad and Metropolitan Cooperative Bank to enter into irregular securities deals.

Source: Economic Times, December 22, 1993.

SECURITIES SCAM : JANAKIRAMAN PANEL FINAL REPORT, MAY, 1993

The Janakiraman Committee investigating the multi crore securities scandal has pinpointed "gross problem exposure" of banks at Rs. 4,024.45 crore apart from depreciation and losses suffered by several banks in ready forward transactions aggregating Rs. 12,85,549 crore from April 1, 1991 to May 23, 1993.

Summary of Recommendations

The diversion of funds of brokers through securities transactions has been largely engineered through the process of ready forward security transactions. Since there is no permanent purchase or transfer of investments in such cases, there is no real need to effect the actual transfer of scrips or to deposit SGL transfer forms with the PDO.

In most cases these transactions have been supported by BRs or by SGL transfer forms not intended to be deposited with the PDO. Often the BRs and the SGL transfer forms do not appear to be supported by underlying securities.

The ready forward transaction in substance is a financing transaction and not a security transaction and therefore is possible only when one leg of the transaction is at a rate which is at variance with the market rate.

The committee recommends that until adequate safeguards are devised all ready forward securities transactions be barred.

A key factor in the perpetration of the irregularities has been the system of bank receipts (BRs). The issue of BRs should be an exception rather than the rule. To achieve this end, the committee has made the following recommendations:

There must be a central depository for all securities has been the system of bank normally deals. At present, the PDO is a depository only for Government securities.

In its first report the committee has made a recommendation that a central depository should be created for other securities like PSU bonds, units, etc.

The committee has noted that following upon its recommendations a committee was constituted under the chairmanship of S.S. Nadkarni, Industrial Development Bank of India (IDBI) and that committee has submitted its report.

Its recommendation for setting up of a central depository has been accepted and is in the process of implementation.

There should be no delay in recording the transfer in the PDO and in communicating objection memos to the banks concerned.

These and other recommendations regarding the functioning of the PDOs were made in the first report of the committee. The committee has noted that action in this behalf has already been taken by the RBI.

Steps should be taken to ensure that PSUs and other institutions speedily issue scrips in exchange for "allotment letters" so that physical delivery of the scrips can be facilitated, where such scrips are not deposited in the central depository.

Irregularities have also been facilitated because banks have not strictly adhered to IBA guidelines for issue of BRs and because proper controls have not been maintained in this regard.

The committee would therefore recommend that:

BR rules formulated by IBA and enclosed with its letter dated May 6, 1991 addressed to the chief executives of all member banks be strictly enforced.

Like cheques, BRs should have a validity period of 30 days and if not redeemed within that time, the BR should be deemed to be dishonoured and the fact of dishonour should immediately be notified to RBI for penal action.

Similarly, a BR should normally be redeemed only by actual delivery of securities and not by cancellation of the transaction or by set-off against another transaction.

It a bank is not able to redeem its BR by actual delivery, it should obtain the prior approval of RBI for settlement in any other manner and RBI should take penal action if it is not satisfied regarding the circumstances in which delivery cannot be effected.

There should be proper systems in each bank for the custody of unused BR forms and for control on their utilisation and the existence and operation of these controls must be reviewed periodically by internal audit, bank supervisors and external auditors.

An equally important factor which has allowed the irregularities to develop has been the fact the brokers have acted on their own account and banks have provided facilities for this purpose. The committee would make the following recommendations in this regard:

Only "approved" persons should be allowed to operate at bank brokers. This approval must be given by an independent authority like RBI, Securities and Exchange Board of India (SEBI) or a similar body and there must be well-defined criteria for the grant for approval.

All brokers should remain registered with this body which must have the power to refuse registration or cancel registration, if already granted, to a broker who is guilty of professional misconduct.

There must be a clear distinction between brokers and traders and persons who are registered as approved brokers should be prohibited from trading in securities on their own account either by themselves or through associated concerns. Such a distinction already exists in many stock exchanges abroad between brokers and jobbers.

Registered brokers and their associated concerns must be debarred from carrying on other activities, particularly as share brokers, merchant bankers, etc.

Source: Hindustan Times May, 8, 1993.

31

TRANSPORT AND COMMUNICATION

31.1 TRANSPORT

31.1.1 Railway Budget 1994-95

Following are the highlights of the railway budget presented on Feburary 24, 1994 by Railway Minister C.K. Jaffar Sharief.

Freight Charges

* Freight traffic is telescope in nature that is, the freight rate per kilometre decreases as the distance increases. Keeping in view the rising cost of operation, it is proposed to modify the taper for freight tariff so that the decrease is more gradual than at present.
* The existing classificationes of the following commodities are proposed to be revised upwards, both for wagon loads and train loads (wherever applicable);

  (i) Coal from class 130 D to class 130 for train loads and from class 135 D to class 135 for wagon loads.
  (ii) Iron-ore, limestone and dolomite–by one step.
  (iii) Cement, HSD oil, oil cake, stone NOC, gypsum, other ores (excluding iron ore), soda ash, manganese ore, molasses, sugger mills (not khandsari molasses) and sand–by two steps.

* It is proposed to do away with the existing sub-classifications of iron or steel divisons. A, B and C, all of which are now proposed to be charged at class 230 for train loads and class 250 for wagon loads.
* It is also proposed to set up classification in regard to grains and pulse for other than public distribution system, from class 80 to class 95 in train loads and from class 85 to 100 in wagon loads. With a view to avoid undue burden on the common man, it is not proposed to change the classification for grains and pulses meant for public distribution system.
* At present a rebate of 6 per cent on freight is allowed for cement and chemical manures loades in open wagons. It is proposed to enhance this rebate to 10 per cent.
* It is proposed to reduce the minimum distance for charge in respect of freight traffic from 100 km to 75 km.
* The distance blocks for charge beyond 2400 km are at present 50 km.

It is proposed to reduce the same to 25 km.

* The railways have been exempting certain essential commodities from freight increases in the past. I propose to continue the exemptions given in the past in respect of these commodities, namely: salt for human consumption; kerosene; livestock, oilseeds; liquid petroleum gas; edible oils; fodder; gur, shakkar and jaggery; fruits and vegetables; tea; organic manures; and chemical manures.

Passenger Fares

Proposals in regard to passenger fares are as under:

For distances beyond 100 km, marginal increases, ranging from Re. 1 at 101 km to Rs. 5 at 601 km and beyond are proposed. Thus, bulk of the ordinary second class passengers, belonging to the poorer sections of the society, who travel up to 100 km, will not be affected.

* Second class mail/express fares for distances 51 to 65 km, 101 to 110 km, 116 to 125 and 151 to 155 km are proposed to be marginally reduced, as a measure of rationalisation. A modest increae from a minimum of Rs. 1 to a maximum of Rs. 20 has been proposed in the fares for various other distances.
* Sleeper class fares will continue to be 25 per cent higher than the second class fares, as at present.
* Fares for AC first class, first class, AC sleeper and AC chair car are proposed to be raised by 6 per cent.
* Fares for AC 3-tier will be charged at 25 per cent higher than the fares of AC chair car, as at present.
* Fares for Rajdhani including August Kranti Rajdhani and Shatabdi Express trains are also propose to be suitably revised.

  The fares for second class monthly season ticket up to a distance of 90 km are proposed to be increased by Re. 1 to Rs 9 only, depending upon the distance. Thus, about 90 per cent of the monthly season ticket holders, who travel up to 90km, will have to pay extra up to a maximum of Rs.9 per month. For distances beyond 90 km, the increases in the monthly season ticket fares would range from Rs. 11 to Rs. 40.
* The quarterly season tickets will continue to be charged at 2.5 times the monthly season ticket fares.
* First class season tickets will continue to be charged at four times the second class season ticket fares.
* The fees now levied for computerised reservations are proposed to be made applicable for manual reservations also.

The above proposals will be made effective from 1-4-1994 and are expected to yield in additional revenue of Rs. 997 cr in the year 1954-95.

31.1.2 Civil Aviation

The civil aviation sector has two functional divisions: operational, and infrastructural. On the operational side, Indian Airlines, Vayudoot and private air taxis provide domestic air services, and Air India provides international air services. Pawan Hans provides helicopter services to ONGC in its offshore operations and to inaccessible area and difficult terrains. Infrastructural facilities are provided by the International Airports Authority of India (IAAI) and the National Airports Authority (NAA).

The total revenue of Indian Airlines increased by 27.3 per cent in 1991-92 and by 6.2 per cent in 1992-93, while expenses increased by 36.7 per cent in 1991-92 and 5.2 per cent in 1992-93. The net loss at Rs. 195.2 crore in 1992-93 was marginally less than that in 1991-92. The load factor in 1992-93 was 70.9 per cent compared to 69.8 per cent in 1991-92.

The financial performance of the domestic carrier during the current year is very poor. The net loss at the end of April-December 1993 was Rs. 226.9 crore, thus marking a 111.84 per cent increase in losses over the corresponding period of the previous year. Revenues were 5.7 per cent lower but expenses were 14.46 per cent highr than in the corresponding period last year. The load factor has further deteriorated to 65.9 per cent from 71.4 per cent.

The losses incurred by Vayudoot Limited during 1991-92 and 1992-93 were Rs. 30.6 crore and Rs. 24.2 crore respectively. During April-December 1993 the loss incurred was Rs. 16.4 crore as against Rs. 17.2 crore during April -December 1992.

Pawan Hans Limited (PHL) basically provides helicopter support service to the oil sector. The total member of flying hours during 1992-93 was about 17,000 and the revenue earnings an net profit during the year were Rs. 123.6 crore and Rs. 27.5 crore respectively. The flying hours during April-December 1993 were 14013 and revenue and net profit were Rs. 96.41 crore and Rs. 26.11 crore respectively.

The number of passengers carried by taxi operator has increased from 15,000 passengers in 1990 to 4.12 lakh in 1992.

There is a marked shift of traffic from the Indian airlines to the private air taxis.

Air India is among the top ten profit making airlines in the world. The net profit of Air India at Rs. 333.14 crore in 1992-93 was 128.4 per cent higher than in 1991-92. However, the net profit during April-December 1993 at Rs. 164.93 crore was 39.1 per cent lower than that during April-December 1992. During 1992-93 revenue increased by 24.6 per cent while expenditure rose by 16.8 per cent. During April-December 1993, the revenues have decreased marginally by 0.15 per cent and expenditure increased by 5.99 per cent.

The share of Air India in the international traffic originated from India has come down from 42 per cent in 1981 to 35 per cent in 1990-91 and 26 per cent in 1992-93. This represents a significant erosion of market share. Air India's load factor at 57.8 per cent during international airlines.

International Airports Authority of India (IAAI) manages, operates and develops the five international airports at Bombay, Calcutta, Delhi, Madras and Trivandrum.

31.1.3 Roads and Road Transport

The total road network in the country increased from 16.9 lakh kms in 1985 to 20.4 lakhs kms at the end of 1990-91, half of which is made up of unsurfaced roads. The National Highways network of 3400 kms at the end of 1992-93 constitutes less than two per cent of the total road network but carries nearly 40 per cent of the total road traffic.

TABLE 31.1: Performance of the Railways

			April-December*		Change over previous year	
	1991-92	1992-93*	1992	1993	1992-93	1993-94@
1	2	3	4	5	6	7
Total revenue earning freight traffic (million tonnes)	337.98	350.04	254.63	258.62	3.6	1.6
(i) Coal	146.43	157.72	113.87	121.40	7.7	6.6
(ii) Raw Materials for steel plants (excl.coal)	29.56	32.76	24.47	23.88	10.8	-2.4
(iii) Pig iron and finished steel from steel plants	11.44	12.04	8.79	8.67	5.2	-1.4
(iv) Iron ore for export	12.76	10.48	7.76	7.71	-17.9	-0.6
(v) Cement	30.51	30.21	21.80	22.86	-1.0	4.9
(vi) Foodgrains	27.38	27.30	19.38	18.75	-0.3	-3.3
(vii) Fertilizers	18.59	18.93	14.48	12.81	1.8	-11.5
(viii) POL	25.63	26.41	19.73	19.02	3.0	-3.6
(ix) Balance (other goods)	35.68	34.19	24.35	23.52	-4.2	-3.4
Net tonne kilometres (million)	250.24	251.49	184.82	183.39	0.5	-0.5
Net tonne kilometres per wagon per day (broad gauge)**	1439.00	1458.00	1383.00	1402.00	1.3	1.4
Passenger traffic originating (million)**	4048.62	3749.37	1836.00	1776.00	-7.4	-3.3
Passenger kilometres (billion)**	314.56	300.10	156.00	147.00	-4.6	-5.9

*Provisonal. @April-December. **April-September

Source: Economic Survey 1993-94, Ministry of Finance, Government of India, New Delhi, 1994, Chapter 8.

Road transport accounts for about 80 per cent of passenger traffic and 60 per cent of freight traffic. This is in sharp contrast to the optimal modal distribution of freight traffic between railways and roads in the ratio of 72:28. The share of Public Sector in road transport had diminished to 33 per cent in 1989-90 compared to 45 per cent in 1980-81. Road freight transport is almost entirely owned and operated by the private sector.

The State Road Transport Undertakings operate a fleet of nearly 1.2 lakh buses employing about 9 lakh workers. The undertakings with a few exceptions face serious financial constraints. Major reasons for the losses have been the social commitment to operate even on uneconomic routes and absence of cost-based fare structure. Over-manning, poor management and widespread inefficiencies have also affected a majority of undertakings.

The number of goods vehicle registered at the end of March 1993 was 16 lakh.

31.1.4 Shipping

Indian vessels carried about 35 per cent of the total sea-borne cargo during 1992-93 against 36 per cent during 1991-92. The share of Indian vessels in POL was 57.3 per cent in 1992-93; in bulk carries 23.3 per cent; and in liner traffic 15 per cent. Long-term targets for Indian share in bulk carrier and liner traffic are 50 and 40 per cent respectively. The fleet strength at the end of December 1993 was 443 vessels of 6.27 million Gross Resigtered Tonnes (GRT) against 441 vessels of 6.29 million GRT in December 1992. Overseas trade during 1992-93 was 122.30 million tonnes against 111.80 million during 1991-92.

Shipping Corporation of India (SCI) showed a better financial performance although its gross tonnage came down to 2.91 million GRT (46.1 per cent of the fleet) by December 1993 from 3.02 million GRT (about 50 per cent of fleet) at the beginning of the Eighth Plan. SCI's gross internal resources rose to Rs. 263 crore in 1992-93 against Rs. 235 crore in the previous year. Its net profit after tax at Rs.143.18 crore in 1992-93 registered an increase of 31.5 per cent over the previous year. During April-September 1993 the net profit after tax has been provisionally estimated at Rs. 78.33 crore which is about 66 per cent higher than the level achieved during the corresponding period of last year.

SCI To Acquire New Ships

The public sector Shipping Corporation of India (SCI), which has doubled its profits to about Rs. 109 crore in 1991-92, has drawn up an ambitious plan to expand and modernise its fleet. Under this, the SCI proposes to acquire 79 vessels at an overall cost of around Rs. 5,000 crore over the next four years. Giving an overview of the corporation's performance and future plans, SCI's Chairman-cum-Managing Director P.P. Radhakrishnan told newsmen in New Delhi on Feb. 12 that the SCI was exploring the possibility of alternative sources of finance for the ship acquisition programme, including an equity issue, so as to curtail the dependence on the Government.

The SCI, it may be recalled, is one of the public sector undertakings where disinvestment has taken place. During the current fiscal year, 18.5 per cent of SCI shares have been disinvested. The disinvested shares are owned by and large by 22 financial institutions and mutual funds. As for the size and timing of the proposed equity issue, Capt Radhakrishnan said this would be guided by the market opportunities over the next few months. In the current fiscal year, the SCI has placed orders for three celluar container ships and two product tankers. The investment on these is of the order of Rs. 650 crore. In addition, two ships have been acquired and reconditioned at a cost of Rs. 25 crore.

According to Mr.Radhakrishnan, the SCI is also closely examining several other projects including acquisition of double hull crude oil tankers. These ships would be utilised to replace some of the existing ships as well as to meet the enhanced demand of transportation of crude oil into the country. Dwelling on the corporation's financial performance, the SCI chairman said that during 1991-92 the revenue level have gone up by about Rs. 230 crore, representing a 20 per cent rise over the preceding year's level. The corporation's gross profit shot up by Rs. 114 crore to touch the level of Rs. 330 crore, a good deal of which is said to have been brought about by a tight control on cost. Mr Rakhakrishnan said that the SCI has paid dividends to the tune of Rs. 41.3 crore in the last 13 months. The SCI during the year also cleared off the arrears pertaining to the early 1980s when the shipping sector was in deep recession. The total amount paid by the SCI to the Government during the 13 month period is put at Rs. 153.1 crore.

Source: The Hindustan Times, New Delhi.

31.1.5 Ports

During 1992-93 the cargo-handling capacity at major ports was 166.61 million tonnes registering a growth rate of 5.7 per cent over last year. This compares well with 4.5 per cent growth achieved during the second half of 1980s. During April-December 1993 the major ports handled 130.23 million tonnes compared with a target of 123.7 million tonnes, which was 6.8 per cent higher than the level achieved during the correspondig period of last year. Major increased in traffic were observe in respect of iron ore (19.9 per cent) and vegetable oil (30 per cent). Containerised cargo maintained the trend of growth and registered in increase of 24 per cent during April-December 1993 over the corresponding period of last year.

TABLE 31.2: Trends in the Traffic at Major Ports

			April-December*		Change over previous year	
	1991-92	1992-93*	1992	1993	1992-93	1993-94@
1	2	3	4	5	6	7
1. POL	69.30	73.70	54.99	56.83	6.3	3.3
2. Iron Ore	32.10	29.79	20.25	24.27	-7.2	19.9
3. Fertilisers & raw materials	7.11	7.38	6.26	5.53	3.8	-11.7

(Contd.)

TABLE 31.2 *(Contd,)*

1	2	3	4	5	6	7
4. Foodgrains	1.25	2.24	1.25	1.14	79.2	-8.8
5. Coal	22.47	24.37	18.14	19.45	8.5	7.2
6. Vegetable oil	0.39	0.24	0.20	0.26	-38.5	30.0
7. Other liquids	4.25	4.16	3.11	2.34	-2.1	-24.8
8. Containerised cargo	7.63	8.98	6.42	7.96	17.7	24.0
9. Others	12.10	15.75	11.29	12.45	30.2	10.3
Total	156.60	166.61	121.91	130.23	5.7	6.8

* Provisional. @ April-December.

Source: Extracts from Chapter 8 of the *Economic Survey 1993-94.*

31.2 THE COMMUNICATION

31.2.1 The Post

India has the largest network of post offices in the world. By the end of March 1993, the national postal network had over 1.5 lakh post offices in the country.

Speed post traffic is growig at a rate of 38 per cent. Durng 192-93, the domestic revenue was Rs. 32 crore and the traffic generated was 73 lakh articles.

Postal Life Insurance (PLI) consists of over 1.5 lakh policies with an assured sum of Rs. 576.6 crore.

The Post Office Savings Bank operates through the wide network of post offices of which 89 per cent are located in rural areas. The gross collection during 1992-93 through Savings Accounts were Rs. 1149 crore and net collection were Rs. 1149 crore.

The Postal Department has been able to bring down the deficit from Rs. 214 crore in 1991-92 to Rs. 92 crore in 1992-93. Establishment expenses account for 80 per cent of the total expenditure.

Source: Economic Survey 1993-94.

31.2.2 Telecommunication

India has a network comprising of over 17790 Exchanges with a capacity of 84.2 lakh lines an 71.4 lakh working telephones as on November 30, 1993. The network has been expanding at the rate of 15 to 17 per cent per annum for the last two years.

During the eighties, the number of telephone connections grew at 8.3 per cent annually. The number of new telephone connections provided in 1992-93 was 9.87 lakh direct exchange lines (DELs) 34.3 per cent more than in 1991-92. The four Metros accounted for 24.2 per cent of the increase. The number of people waiting for new connections on March 31, 1993 was 28.46 lakh,

24.3 per cent higher than a year earlier. The demand for telecommunication services has so far been ahead of the availability. The Eighth Plan endeavours at reducing the waiting period by installing additional switching capacity of 93 lakh lines in order to provide 75 lakh new telephone connections.

The increase in telex switching capacity during 1992-93 was 3274 lines, 38.73 per cent higher than in 1991-92. 331 telex connections were added during 1992-93, as compared to 1779 during 1991-92. Demand for telex connections, is going down because of increased use of FAX.

During 1992-93, 107.35 lakh conductor kilometers (LCKMS) of cables were laid, 17.6 per cent more than 1991-92.

The Telecommunication Department has embarked upon a programme of providing public telephones in village panchayats. During 1992-93, 30072 villages were provided with telephone facilities which was 38 per cent more than the level achieved in the previous year.

Source: Extracts from the Chapter of *Economic Survey 1993-94.*

Telephone Lines during 8th Plan

The Department of Telecommunication will invest Rs. 40,000 crore to install around 7 million telephone lines in the country during the Eighth Five Year Plan. This was announced by Union Communication Minister Sukh Ram at a press briefing held in Bombay on Aug.26. As per the Eighth Five Year Plan, the telecommunication department will attempt to increase the telephone density to 14 per thousand at the all-India level and to 1.85 per thousand in the rural areas. The telephone density, presently, is 6.4 per thousand at the all-India level and less than one per thousand in the rural areas. In the current year, around 2 million lines will be installed out of which one million lines will be of the latest Digital Switcing System (DSS). It is further decided to purchase one million lines of latest technology to be introduced in all the big cities and state capitals. Facilities like Data Transmission, fax will be stressed in the next year.

Mr. Sukh Ram announced that, according to revised telecom policy, priority will be given to the educated unemployed, especially from the economically backward in the allotment of PCOs (public call offices). A target to set up 4,00,000 PCOs has been fixed. A local committee will be set up to decide the allotment in each Secondary Switching Area (SSA). It has been decided to reduce the security deposit from Rs. 10,000 to Rs. 5,000 which can be paid on instalment basis by the owner of the PCO.

Source: The Observer of Business and Politics, New Delhi.

32

WOMEN AND CHILDREN

32.1 WOMEN

32.1.1 Census Study on Women

There has been a remarkable increase in the number of women getting out of the four walls of the household and becoming workers in both cities and villages. At the same time, there has been a sizable drop in the participation of males in the country's workforce during the last decade. The women have apparently edged out males in factories, household industry, agricultural fields with the change in the scenario being more pronounced in States other than Goa, Punjab, West Bengal and Gujarat.

Another significant change in the scene of economic activity in most of the States has been a sizable "shift" of workers in rural areas from agriculture and cultivation (primary sector) and manufacturing sector to get absorbed in services sector including domestic services. But most of the female workers are engaged in areas where wages are regarded to be relatively lower than other fields of economic activity (called primary sector).

The number of "unpaid" workers was more among women than in the case of male workers in both the cities and villages where they were engaged as farm labour. The reasons for such a bias against women workers are yet to be worked out.

During 1981-91, there was an increase of 2.68 per cent in the women's participation in the total country's workforce – while at the end of 1981, women workers were 25.89 per cent, they constituted 28.57 in the workforce at the end of 1991. The increase has been sharper in States like Uttar Pradesh, Tamil Nadu, Himachal Pradesh, Rajasthan, Karnataka and Mizoram.

But this trend was not unfirm and there were several States where the share of women in the workforce has declined during the last decade. It was more so in Arunachal Pradesh, Sikkim, Punjab. It was the sharpest decline of 8.8 per cent in Arunachal Pradesh, but it was surprisingly a drop of nearly two per cent in the case of a forward-looking and prosperous State like Punjab.

There are also States where the number of male workers has gone up. this included Kerala and West Bengal. The number of male engaged as cultivatior declined in almost all the States, except Nagaland and Sikkim. But their figure has gone up as agriculture labour, in Goa, Gujarat, Madhya Pradesh, Tripura and West Bengal. But the number of women as cultivators has gone up much faster. While the proportion of males as cultivators went up by 11.7 per cent at the end of 1991, the increase in the case of women as cultivators jacked by 45.23 per cent. The census document noted that the increase in the workforce during the decade was much more than the growth in the population of women in the country during that period – which meant a real increase in the share of women in the workforce as cultivators.

In the field of agriculture labour, the number of males went up from 34.67 million in 1981 to 45.48 million at the end of the decade—which means a net increase of 31.18 per cent. The number of women in this field of economic activity was again slightly higher—from 20.76 million to 28.27 million by 1991 (an increase of 36.15 per cent). The number of agriculture labour in general, increased in most of these but it went down in Madhya Pradesh, West Bengal and Tripura. While in M.P., agriculture labour formed 23.51 per cent of the workforce, in Rajasthan it was 10 per cent less.

The number of people engaged in household industry has declined from 7.61 million in 1981 to 6.74 million, despite a growth in population. It was more so in the case of male workers—of 18.78 per cent, as compard to an increase of women in the sector. But in Orissa and West Bengal, the number of both male and female workers in household industry went up during that period. In the other industrial sector, the number of workers in general went up by 58.24 million. Those engaged in "main" activity, like cultivation, agriculture labour, forestry, mining, manufacturing process, trade and commerce, showed an increase of 26.39 per cent in the case of males and 22.81 per cent in respect of women.

A "shift" in the pattern of work is there, while in 1981, 69.41 per cent people were engaged in the primary sector those working in that sector at the end of 1991 was 67.37 per cent. The details also showed that the number of agriculture labourers and workers in mining has gone up.

Source: Paper 2 of 1992 Census Commissioner, Government of India, New Delhi, 1994.

32.1.2 The National Commissioner for Women on Dowry and Sati Penalties

The Commission has received all the major laws concerning women and suggested amendements to the Dowry Prohibition Act, (DPA) Commission of Sati (prevention) Act, 1987 and the Section 198 of the CrPC regarding bigamous marriages. The Delhi Bill on Eve-Teasing, it has suggested, should be made a national law.

Since the special laws on dowry and sati have proved "ineffective," it has suggested dowry-taking and abetment as well as "sati murder" and glorification of the act be moved into the IPC.

The Commission has categorically stated that sati should be labelled. "sati murder" and the person attempting sati sentenced to death or life imprisonment.

Among the experts who assisted the Commission in reviewing the laws were Justice Chinnappa Reddy, retired judge of the Supreme Court, eminent lawyer Vasudha Dhagamwar and former Secretary of the Law Ministry, Dr. Rama Devi.

The Commission has recommended that Section 2, 3, 4, 7, 8 and 8A of the

DPA are to be incorporated into the IPC, CrPC and the Indian Evidence Act.

Since cruelty and violence against women has acquired serious dimensions, the Commission has recommended that Section 498 A of IPC be amended and the punishment increased from three to seven years. A new Section, 498 B, has been suggested and under it dowry offence becomes "cognisable and non-bailable" with punishment and fine of Rs. 15,000.

Necessary amendments have also been suggested in Section 39 of the CrPC so that there is greater public involvement in giving information on dowry and sati offences.

To bring sati offence into mainstream of criminal law, the Commission has said that new Section 303 A (sati murder) and 303 B (glorification of sati murder) should be inserted in the IPC. For glorification of sati murder, under Section 303 B, imprisonment of a year to seven years and a fine of not less than Rs 5000 but going up to Rs. 30,000 have been proposed.

Sati will be a cognisable, non-bailable offence. After inclusion of various provisions in the criminal laws, it has been suggested that the Act be called the Commission of Sati Murder (prevention) Additional Provisions Act.

With bigamy on the increase, the expert committee has accepted the recommendation of Hyderabad-based social activist Roda Mistry that welfare organisations, legal aid cells and public spirited persons can file a case of bigamy on behalf of a woman who is deserted by her husband. To ensure justice for the deserted woman, amendment of Section 198 of the CrPC has been suggested.

32.2 CHILDREN

32.2.1 Nutritional Status of Children

The nutritional status of children has been accepted as the most sensitive indicator of socio-economic and human development of nations. Nutrition in the key to individual social and economic development of a nation. Four major form of malnutrition in the developing world are: Protein energy malnutrition, anacomia vitamin A deficiency and iodine deficiency disorders.

Protein energy malnutrition manifests itself in growth faltering, wasting, stunting or both. Children can recover their weight, but most of the stunting is irreversible. Children born with low birthweight (i.e. below 2.5 kg) are born malnourished. This adversely affects the growth of the child, and deprives children of their right to holistic development. Malnutrition is most prevalent in the vulnerable young child when the synergistic relationship between malnutrition and disease can result in mortality. In India, significant strides have been made in malnutrition reduction through a spectrum of policies and programmes, resulting in reduction of severe malnutrition by approximately 6 per cent between 1975 and 1990. However, 43 per cent children continue to be moderately malnourished.

The other forms of malnutrition are caused due to deficiency of micro nutrients like iron, vitamin A and iodine also known as the "Hidden Hunger" since such deficiencies are not so easily apparent. The main nutritional cause of anaemia is iron and iron/folate deficiency, dur to low iron intake or poor iron absorption from cereal based diets. Blood loss from malaria and hookworm also contribute to anaemia. Nutritional anaemia causes impairment of child growth and development, both physically and intellectually, as well as increased morbidity and mortality rates.

The manifestations of iodine deficiency are many and varied, and are known collectively as 'Iodine Deficiency Disorders (IDD)'. IDD affects the development of children at all stages from foetal life to adulthood. It is associated with impairment of mental and intellectual functions in children and adults, and in severe cases with deafness and mutism, neuro-muscular disorders, increased abortion and still-birth rates, and perinatal and infant mortality.

Nutritional blindness, which affects over seven million children in India per year, results mainly from the deficiency of Viatamin A. In its severest form it often results in lack of vision and it has been estimated that around 60,000 children become blind every year.

The nutritional status of an individual, including any of the four forms of malnutrition is an outcome of complex biological and social processes. Improved nutrition requires (a) adequate household food security, (b) healthy environment and control of infections and (c) adequate maternal and child care.

32.2.2 The National Nutrition Policy, 1993 April

The National Nutrition Policy aims to articulate nutrition considerations in major policy spheres of the Government. It further aims to identify vulnerable groups, who require immediate intevention to improve their nutritional status.

The Strategy

The strategy to implement the National Nutrition Policy includes nutrition intervention for specialy vulnerable groups through

* fortification of essential foods
* control of micro-nutrient deficiency
* improvement of dietary pattern through production and demonstration
* land reforms
* health and family welfare
* communication
* community participation
* popularization of low-cost nutritious food
* food security
* public distribution system
* prevention of food adulteration
* nutrition surveillance
* equal remuneration
* status of women
* research

Implementation

The National Nutrition Policy will be implemented by Department of Women & Child Development, Government of India by the constitution of Special Working Groups in departments of Agriculture, Rural Development, Health, Education, Food and Women & Child Development. The Special Working Groups will analyze and design sectoral proposals and programmes in the context of the policy.

An Inter-Ministerial Coordination Committee shall function in the Ministry of Human Resource Development to overseas and review the implementation of nutrition measures. A National Nutrition Council constituted in the Planning Commission will coordinate, review and give directions at the national level. Special working groups will be set up at state level in the various departments responsible for sectoral schemes relevant to nutrition.

The Food and Nutrition Board with its 67 centres and field units will disseminate information and monitor the quality and performance of nutritional programmes in the country.

Source: Hindustan Times, April 21 and September 1, 1993.

32.2.3 Infant Mortality

The Government has decided to upgrade existing facilities in 90 identified poor performing districts in the country categorised by high birth and infant mortality rates and low level of institutional delivery. Eighty-three of these districts were located in Uttar Pradesh, Madhya Pradesh, Bihar and Rajasthan.

To reduce the high maternal mortality rate, increase institutional deliveries and provide care to high risk pregnancies, the Government had decided to utilise the entire assistance likely to be available under the World Bank Social Safety Net Programme over a period of five years on upgradation of facilities.

Concurrently, 11 area projects were also being implemented in 15 States and in Delhi at a cost of Rs. 1,190,18 crore, with financial assistance from the World Bank. United Nations Fund for Population Activities and other agencies.

These projects had contributed substantially to the strengthening of health and family welfare infrastructure in the states. A total of 13,630 sub-centres and training institutions had been constructed and equipped under projects up to October, 1993. In addition, 3.43 lakh medical and para-medical functionaries had been trained.

The daunting fact that while India accounted for 2.4 per cent of the world land area, it supported 16 per cent of the world population.

The absolute addition to the population in 1981-91 was 163 million — almost equal to the population added in three decades during 1931-41, 1941-51 and 1951-61.

An allocation of Rs. 1,270 crore has been provided for family welfare programmes in 1993-94. The report noted that the programme has succeeded in reducing birth rate from 41.7 per thousand in 1951-61 to 29 per thousand in 1991. The total fertility rate has gone down from 5.97 to 3.8 and the infant mortality rate from 146 to 79 during the same period.

The couple protection rate has gone up from 10.4 per cent in 1970-71 to 43.4 per cent by March, 1993.

Listing the policy initiatives taken recently to impart new dynamism to the family welfare programme, the report mentions the action plan which identifies 90 poor performing districts with a birth rate of 39 and above for special focus.

It noted that the Rs. 1,125.58 crore child survival and safe motherhood programme was being implemented over a period of seven years with assistance from UNICEF and the World Bank. A total of 154 districts have been taken up since 1992, under the child survival component while 51 districts were covered during this period under the Safe Motherhood Component.

The sanction of Rs. 302 crore World Bank aid for leprosy eradication in India, the ban by 23 States on salt other than iodised salt to check iodine deficiency disorders and a 90 per cent drop in the prevalence rate of leprosy in the 40 districts covered by Multi Drug Therapy (MDT) for five years or more are some of the highlights of the health and family welfare sector during this period.

The other special features include the setting up of an expert committee to draft a national population policy, a 16.6 per cent increase in acceptors of family planning methods over the last year and a 25 per cent drop in infant mortality rate over the decade since 1982.

There were five lakh deaths in the country annually on account of tuberculosis. While the Central plan outlay was enhanced each year (Rs. 50 crore have been provided in 1994-95) the cost of drugs alone for ensuring coverage of the sputum positive cases would amount of Rs. 150 crore per year.

Project proposal has been made for obtaining World Bank financial assistance based on Short Term Course chemotherapy for Sputum Positive cases.

Source: Annual Report, 1993-94, Ministry of Health and Family Planning Government of India, New Delhi, 1994, as reported in *Hindustan Times,* March 29, 1994.

32.2.4 Child Labour

Prevalence of child labour in spite of constitutional and legal deterrents, is a scourge on our society. Policies and programmes relating to child-survival and development have been accorded high priority in the Eighth Plan. It is recognised that successful implementation of programmes of poverty alleviation reforms in existing social and economic structures, institutional changes and female education will by raising the standards of living of the underprivileged sections of society have a favourable impact on child survival and development. But specific programmes and services directed at children would also be necessary. The National Child Labour Policy formulated in 1987 envisaged *inter alia,* a project-based plan of action aimed at rehabilitation of children withdrawn from employment through provision of welfare inputs like non-formal education vocational training, health care and suplementary nutrition. Nine National Child Labour Projects have been set up in areas of concentration of child labour. Special schools form a major component of the project through which welfare inputs are provided to such children; 124 schools covering 6900 children have been set up. Ten States/UTs and two project areas have been identified for complete elimination of child labour. Special attention has been given to rigorous implementation of Child Labour Policy of 1987. Some of the important initiatives taken in this ragard include review of the working of the existing laws by the statutory Child Labour Advisory Committee; and the Child Labour Technical Advisory Committee: strengthening flow of external assistance to the NGOs to undertake programmes for the benefit of children, and efforts for enlisting the employers' cooperation in industries where child labour is prevalent towards its elimination. Further, a scheme has been launched in 11 most populous cities for the welfare of street children for providing integrated community based non-institutional basic services for their care protection and development.

Source: Economic Survey, 1993-94.

32.2.5 Integrated Child Development Services

Since 1975, the Integrated Child Development Services (ICDS) programme has been the chief vehicle for improving the healthy physical, psychological and social growth of children in India. The heart of the ICDS system is a network of *anganwadis,* which literally are "courtyard" child-care centers. Open four hours a day, these centers are the mechanism for reaching mothers and their children. They offer pre-school education for children ages 3 to 6 and special food supplements for children and for pregnant and breastfeeding women. In addition, *anganwadis* are focal points for delivery of other village-level services such as immunization, growth monitoring, health referrals, women's literacy and skills training for adolescent girls. Each center serves about 1,000 people in rural and urban areas and 700 in less populated tribal areas. The anganwadi centers are staffed by an Anganwadi worker (AWW).

The programme now reaches over 250,000 poor villages and urban slums. It is financed by the Government of India and individual states. Bilateral and multilateral donors have also provided assistance in various components of the programme. In 1983, the U.S. Agency for International Development (AID) funded a project to strengthen services for infants and toddlers, focusing on reaching pregnant women and mothers of children below the age of three years. Evaluations conducted by ICDS had, shown that often pregnant women and mothers of infants were not able to go to the anganwadi to use the services available to them.

The AID project was developed to test new approaches to strengthening ICDs services. The project operated within regular ICDS guidelines, infrastructure and budget, but it featured innovations in three areas: training, health and nutrition education and management information. The project included a health and nutrition education package. Working with an Indian market research firm to study local feeding and health-related practices, researchers identified a number of common practices that could be changed. For example, while women usually breastfeed their children, they often delay the introduction of solid foods. This is based on their belief that babies could not or should not eat such food. Pregnant women often ate less rather than more. They believed that extra food would produce larger babies and result in more difficult deliveries. Materials and messages were developed for women advising them to eat more during pregnancy and to give their babies other foods starting at 4 to 6 months.

During the project, severe malnutrition fell by 25 per cent in Panchmahals, in spite of a drought and by 53 per cent in Chandrapur. Vitamin A and iron/folic acid tablets are now distributed at anganwadi centers and health centers. Vitamin A deficiency and anemia have been greatly reduced. More mothers now participate in ICDS activities and are receiving pre and post-natal care. Based on findings from the AID project showing that pregnant women benefit from early supplementary feeding for women as soon as pregnancy is confirmed, rather than during the third trimester.

Source: Mothers and Children.

33

DIVERSE ISSUES

33.1 ARCHAEOLOGICAL EXCAVATIONS

An 11th century bathing ghat and an apsidal shrine close to the Pallava architectural marvel–the shore Temple structures at Mamallappuram-about 50 km from Madras have been excavated by the Archaeological Survey of India (ASI).

These significant discoveries were made by ASI, Madras circle, who have taken up nearly 20 major conservation works including temples, churches and forts.

The 11th century bathing ghat, running north-south almost 120 metres long, is parallel to the sea.

"Surprisingly the water in the bathing ghat is sweet", says superintending archaeologist, Dr. B. Narasimhaiah of the Madras circle.

Archaeologists got some indications of the existence of the ghat in June 1992 and work on excavating it began in right earnest in May 1993, he said.

A couple of years ago the archaeologists had found an 'apsidal shrine' which definitely belonged to an earlier period than the Shore Temple and was probably constructed first by the Pallavas, according to Dr. Narasimhaiah.

The shrine, though shaped like a Buddhist Vihara, was definitely a Hindu structure dedicated to Lord Shiva, he said.

During excavation, a pillar was found which appeared to be a victory pillar and a miniature shrine depicting Ananthasayanam Vishnu, according to the ASI offical. These discoveries have lead archaeologists to believe that there may be more such structures still hidden and only after their exposure could a full picture emerge.

While conserving the Gingee Fort in South Arcot district of Tamil Nadu, built during Vijayanagaram period in 14-15th century, exposition of some ancient structures were also being carried out side-by-side. In royal enclosure inside the fort, the archaeologists found just two structures standing, while lot of ruins were found besides it.

"At that time we did not know the purpose of these structures. It was thought that it could be a horse stable, Later, it was found workers employed in a king's resting house, because after piecing together it was seen that they enclosed the resting house", he said.

The resting house had been built for the king when he came to give audience to the people. Adjacent to the resting house was a structure which appeared to be a *Kalayan Mandapam*, but it was not so. It is actually a bathing pool and a Hawa Mahal".

Dr. Narasimhaiah said during the excavation archaeologists traced the water system and its flow from the terrace on people bathing below in the pool.

When the conservation and exposure work was in progress, archaeologists also discovered a 'probable' *nrithya mandapam* also, just near the resting house of the king. The audience hall of the king had been exposed now and works were on to expose other structures fully, Dr. Narasimhaiah said.

The superintending archaeologist said there were plants to take up excavation of a megalithic site in Adhichanallur in Tirunelvelli district, early next year.

The Director-General of Archaeology had already given his approval for the project. (Three years ago a similar megalithic site was excavated in Chermankadu in Kerala).

"We do not know much about megalithic people of Tirunelveli" he said, adding that once excavation beings, some of the findings would be able to throw some light.

On some other projects, Dr. Narasimaiah said in Salem district, reconstruction of a 'Sugriveshwara temple' near Sarkarperiyapalayam had been taken up. The foundation of this 13-14 century Panday structure was dismantled and after strenghening of the foundation, it was being reconstructed.

In a similar work, a 13th century Chola period Shiva temple in Kulathur in Pudukottai district, which had completely collapsed was rebuilt last year.

Exposure work of another Shiva Temple of Chola period in Nangupatti in Pudukottai district, which had also collapsed, had been taken up. The exposure revealed three *praharas*, where it was believed only one existed. 'We may even find a fourth one', he said.

The conservation and exposure work at the Bakel Fort in Wynad district of Kerala, which had been built by Nayakas around 14-15th century and even occupied for some time by Tipu Sultan, had been taken up, he said.

The conservation work was done as far as possible without changing the original structure. "We do not even use any new material". If plastering work was to be done, the ancient plaster used in the monument was analysed thoroughly and a similar plaster was prepared and used.

He said a huge beam of the Kalyana Mandapa was found broken in a couple of places at the Talakantswara Temple in Vellore.

"We searched for a suitable material and found 'I' girders which were used inside the beam without disturbing the panel. While the girder took the load of the beam, from outside it actually appeared that the beam itself had taken the load", the ASI official said.

In case where ASI was forced to use a non-original material, an indication was given. Supposing a structure had collapsed, in order to reconstruct it, both original and new materials were used judiciously, he said.

Dr. Narasimhaiah said a Chola period temple at Ariyur in Pudukottai district was taken up this year.

The ancient temple had suffered much damage, both natural and man-made. There was the problem of growth of vegetation on the structure and outside it, water logging inside. Water had even seeped down the foundation. There were signs of vandalism also as people had taken away some stones.

Much work had been taken up in Pudukottai district mainly because the area had been neglected, he said.

Source: *Hindustan Times,* December 28, 1993.

33.2 ARCHIVES EXHIBITION, DECEMBER 1993

The exhibition highlights the Voice of Indian Unity which was seen in the desire for autonomy as reflected in the political process, the first large scale elections held in 1937 giving provincial autonomy in eleven British India provinces.

The period of 1929-1939 has been mirrored through original records contemporary photographs, rare and proscibed book and private papers as well as newspaper clippings found in the National Archives of India.

The first section 'Towards the Government of India Act 1935' starts from the Lahore Session (December 1929) where the Indian National Congress demanded 'Purna Swaraj' for India. Dr. Saifuddin Kitchlew and Jawaharlal Nehru emphasise that the people of India were indivisible and they would not submit to imperialist domination and design. Neither the failure of the Round Table Conference nor the anti-Indian provisions of the Government of India Act 1935 slugged the spirits of the nationalists and the mass movement of the people marched towards "Purna Swaraj" through Provincial Legislature.

There is a photograph of Dr. Saifuddin Kitchlew, chairman of the reception committee of the Lahore Session of the Congress and a very relevant quotation from his speech 'Hindu, Muslim differences are only transitory, ephemoral and skin deep... Let our people understand that so long as some of us indulge in dividing India politically on a religious basis there can be no peace in the county".

Besides excerpts from the speech of Nehru who was President of Lahore Congress and other photographs of the session there is also the Pledge of Independence adopted by the Lahore Congress 1929, and first taken on Jan. 26, 1930.

Both Dr Kitchlew's speech and Jawaharlal Nehru's presidential addresses are perhaps the only originals available.

There is a photograph of Gandhiji at the Second Round Table Conference, London.

There is a copy of 'Karachi Ki Congress', a book in Hindi edited by Mr Jitmal Luniya in 1931 prescribed by the British Government.

There is a cartoon on the new Constitution for India.

There is a very rare photograph in this section showing Khan Abdul Ghaffar Khan translating Gandhiji's speech at an election meeting in North West Frontier Province.

"Self government can only be a success when, after long years of training, education and willing cooperation, a people incorruptible and resolute to administer impartial justice can be considered fit to govern themselves. The history of India proves conclusively that she cannot satisfy any of these conditions."

This is the view of Lieutenant-Colonel Sir William A. Wayland, MP, a British Conservative in 'Save India for The Empire', Daily Mail, 1934, India Blue Book, in the section 'Why I Oppose Surrender In India' by 14 well known Conservatives.

Excerpts from the Book have been put on display at the National Archives of India at an exhibition 'Archives and the Voice of Indian Unity in 1937'.

It is interesting to read what some of the other Conservatives had to say regarding India's independence.

Mr Randolph S. Churchill said, "I believe that British rule in India has been a blessing, not a curse, to the inhabitants; that peace and prosparity can only be preserved for India by continuance of British rule, that the British empire is the greatest stabilising and civilising institution in the world today, and that its dissolution would be a disaster for the whole world, I believe that our trade with India is vital for the welfare of Britain, and that trade can only prosper so long as the Pax Britannica is maintained."

"I believe that the abdication of British rule would be fatal to India, to Britain, to the Empire and to the world."

The Right Hon. Viscount Wolmer, P. C., M. P.. said, "India is not yet fit self-government. Ninety-two per cent of her 350,000,000 inhabitants are liter-ate heathens whom England has rescued from chaos, carnage, famine and pestilence. To hand them over to a minute fraction of high caste reactionaries would not be democracy but a gross betrayal of England's trust".

Lord Amphill G. C.I.E., G.C.S.I. wrote, "We have made India what she is today and we have a right to be in India to protect our own vital interests. We have made it our exalted duty to protect the people of India from the disastrous evils of civil war and anarchy and it would mean disgrace and ruin to England to abandon that duty".

Field Marshal Sir Claude W. Jacob, G.C.B.., G.C.S.I. wrote, "The way in which municipal government and the District Boards have been carried out in India during the past 50 years, the great increase in bribery and corruption, the danger to the safety of the British Army in India and to the defence of India when all communications such as railways, roads, telegraphs and so forth are handed over to the Indian ministers, these are a few of the many reasons."

Major-General Sir Alfred Knox K.C.B., C.M.G., M.P., wrote, "India, diverse in races and creed and united only by Britain, is not ready for democracy. The Government proposals are an attempt to placate talkative politicians at the expenses of the working masses, who want impartial rule; if carried out they will reduce India to chaos and Lancashire to starvation".

Mr Brendan Bracken, M.P., wrote, "During the last 30 years parliamentary constitutions were adopted by a number of Asiatic countries. Followed chaos, corruption and anarchy. In those countries the people hailed as saviour the leader who feed them of a system of government alien to Eastern conditions. In fact, Asiatics were as glad to be rid of parliamentary institutions as our forefathers were to receive them".

"Disregarding this ruinous record of parliamentary government in the East, an allience of sentiment and prematurely senile English politicians, together with a coterie of ambitious, but utterly unrepresentative India are endevouring to spread a litter of parliaments over the subcontinent of India. If their singularly ill-contrived schemes are not resolutely opposed. India will be plunged into a state of carnage and anarchy worse than that which existed before our rule began in India".

The exhibition also has what Indian leader M. N. Roy had to say when war clouds gathered before the outbreak of World War II. In a clipping of *Amrita Bazar Patrika,* he said, "There are many among us who are wistfully waiting for the day when England will be involved in another World War, and it is even fondly hoped that she will be defeated. There are others who expect that in such a predicament England will be obliged to concede to the demands of India for securing her support."... "These are all vain hopes and idle speculations and they only betray a lack of confidence in our power to fight imperialists effectively and win."

Source: Hindustan Times, December 21, 1993.

33.3 CONSTITUTIONAL AMENDMENT BILLS, 1993

Following is the text of the Constitution Amendment Bills presented by the Joint Select Committee after amendments in its report to both Houses of Parliament.

A Bill further to amend the Constitution of India. Be it enacted by Parliament in the Forty-fourth Year of the Republic of India as follows:

1. (i) This Act may be called the Constitution (Eightieth Amendment) Act, 1993.
   (ii) It shall come into force on such date as the Central Government may, by notification in the Official Gazette, appoint.

In Part III of the Constitution, under the heading "Right to Freedom of Religion" and before article 25, the following article shall be inserted, namely:
24A. The State shall:

(a) have equal respect for all religions; and
(b) not profess, practise or propagate any religion.

In Part III of the Constitution, after article 28 and before the heading "Cultural and Educational Rights", the following article shall be inserted, namely:

28A.(a) Parliament or the legislature of a State may, by law, provide that any association or body of individuals be banned, if it, by words, either spoken or written, or by sings or by visible representations or otherwise, promotes, or attempts to promote, on ground of religion, disharmony or feelings of enmity, hatred or ill will between different religious groups.

(b) The law referred to in clause (a) may make provisions for the forfeiture of property, movable or immovable, of the banned association or body of individuals and other incidental or consequential provisions".

After article 102 of the Constitution, the following article shall be inserted, namely:

"102A. (1) A person shall be disqualified for being chosen as a member of either House of Parliament if, after such persone makes and subscribes the oath or affirmation in accordance with the form set out for the purpose in the Third Schedule for election to Parliament, he or any other person with the consent.

(i) makes an appeal to vote or refrain from voting for any person on the ground of his religion or uses, or appeals to, religious symbols; or

(ii) promotes, or attempts to promote, on ground of religion, disharmony or feelings or enmity, hatred or ill-will between different religious groups for the furtherance of the prospects of his election or for prejudicially affecting the election of any other person.

(2) Notwithstanding anything in this Constitution, Parliament may, by law, provide that the question of disqualification under clause (1) shall be determined by such authority and in such manner as may be specified in such law".

After article 191 of the Constitution, the following article shall be inserted, namley:

191A. (1) A person shall be disqualified for being chosen as a member of the Legislative Assembly or Legislative Council of a State if, after such person makes and subscribed the oath or affirmation in accordance with the form set out for the purpose in the Third Schedule for election to the legislature of a State, he or any other person with his consent.

(i) makes an appeal to vote or refrain from voting for any person on the ground of his religion or uses, or appeals to, religious symbols; or

(ii) promotes, or attempts to promote, on ground of religion, disharmony or feelings of enmity, hatred or ill-will between different religious groups.

For the furtherance of the prospects of his election or for prejudicially affecting the election of any other person.

(2) Notwithstanding anything in this.

The Representation of the People (Amendment) Bill, 1993 (As reported by the Joint Committee)

This Act may be called the Representation of the People (Amendment) Act, 1993.

In section 29A of the Representation of the People Act, 1951 (hereinafter referred to as the Principal Act), 43 of 1951.

(i) in sub-section (7), for the existing proviso, the following proviso shall be substituted, namely:

"Provided that no association of body shall be registered as a political party under this sub-section, if.

(a) the association or body bears a religious name; or

(b) the memorandum or rules and regulations of such association or body do not conform to the provisions of sub-section (5);"

(ii) for sub-section (8), the following sub-section shall be substituted, namely:

Notwithstanding anything contained in any other provision of this Act or in any other law for the time being in force, an appeal shall lie to the Supreme Court from any decision of the Commission under this section.

Provided that every appeal under this section shall be preferred within a period of thirty days from the date of the decision of the Commission:

Provided further that the Supreme Court may entertain an appeal after the expiry of the said period of thirty days if it is satisfied that the association or body and sufficient cause for not preferring the appeal within such period".

In Part IVA of the principal Act, after section 29A, the following section shall be inserted, namely: "29B. (1) Where,

(a) any political party bears a religious name; or
(b) the memorandum or rules and regulations of the political party no longer conform to the provisions of sub-section (5) of section 29A; or.
(c) the political party promotes, or attempts to promote, on ground of religion, disharmony or feelings of eminity, hatred or ill-will between different religious groups.

its registration as a political party under Section 29A shall be liable to be cancelled by an order of the High Court within whose jurisdiction the main office of that political party is situated.

(2) On receipt of a complaint that there is sufficient cause for cancelling the registration of a political party under sub-section (1), the High Court may call upon the political party affected by notice in writing to show cause, within thirty days from the date of the service of such notice, why the registration of the political party should not be cancelled.
Provided that where the High Court is not satisfied that there is sufficient cause for cancelling the registration of the political party, it may summarily reject the complaint.
(3) After considering the cause, if any, shown by the political party,*** the High Court may, after holding such inquiry as it may deem fit and after calling for such information as it may consider necessary from the political party,*** decide whether or not there is sufficient cause for cancelling the registration and make such order as it may deem fit either dismissing the complaint or cancelling the registration of the political party.
(4) No complaint under sub-section (2) shall lie to the High Court on the ground specified in clause (a) of sub-section (1), if the political party changes its religious name within a period of ninety days from the commencement of the Representation of the People (Amendment) Act, 1993.
(5) Notwithstanding anything contained in any other law for the time being in force, an appeal shall lie to the Supreme Court from any order of the High Court under this section :
Provided that every appeal under this section shall be preferred within a peiod of thirty days from the date of the order of the High Court:

Provided further that the Supreme Court may entertain an appeal after the expiry of the said period of thirty days if it is satisfied that the political party had sufficient cause for not preferring the appeal withing such period".

33.4 HUMAN RIGHTS BILL

33.4.1 Human Rights Bill

The Lok Sabha on December 18, 1993 passed the Protection of Human Rights Bill (1993) which provides for the setting up of a National Human Rights Commission, similier Commissions in the States and human rights courts to meet the growing concern for human rights in the country and abroad.

The Bill passed unanimously was brought forward to replace the Presidential Ordinance promulgated in September for similar objectives. The National Human Rights Commission has since started functioning.

Provisions of the Bill would be applicable to the Armed Forces and the State of Jammu and Kashmir.

Home Minister S.B. Chavan affirmed that he had studied well all aspects of the issue – and the legislation formulated would thwart the designs of some countries that sought to malign India in the United Nations and other international fora.

The Human Rights Commissions will have powers to go into instances of negligence on the part of public service personnel in preventing violations.

The Home Minister told the House that it would not be mandatory for the State Governments to constitute State Human Rights Commissions.

He said representations had been given on the Commission to various communities. After the other backward classes were identified and notified, they would be given proper representation on the Human Rights Commissions.

The Commission would, if necessary, publish interim reports. Annual reports along with the action taken by the Government would be presented in Parliament. The Government would give due consideration to its recommendations, Mr Chavan assured.

Before bringing the legislation in Parliament, wide ranging discussions were held on the subject at various levels such as the Chief Ministers' conference on human rights, seminars organised in various parts of the country and meetings held with leaders of various political parties.

Taking into account the views expressed in these discussions, the Human Rights Commission Bill (1993) was introduced in the Lok Sabha on May14. The Bill was referred by the Speaker to the Standing Committee of Parliament on Home Affairs.

Source: Hindustan Times, December 19, 1993.

33.4.2 Indian Participation in World Conference on Human Rights

Increasing importance being attached to the question of promotion and protection of human rights manifested in the World Conference on Human Rights in Vienna from 14 to 22 June 1993. India was active both in the preparatory phase of the Conference and at the Conference. The Conference was preceded by four meetins of the Preparatory Committee and three regional meetings including the Asian regional meeting in Bankok. A high level Indian delegation, led by Finance Minister, Dr. Manmohan Singh, participated in the World Conference.

Pakistan's attempt to introduce a country-specific resolution against India on the situation in Jammu & Kashmir, coupled with sustained propaganda on human rights violations in Jammu & Kashmir, dominated the meeting of the Commission on Human Rights in Geneva and the Third Committee in New York. Kashmir was raised by Pakistan in all possible forums, including the Security Council, but on account of the efforts made by India, at headquarters as well as in Missions abroad, no resolution was tabled. A vast majority of the States urged direct dialogue between India and Pakistan and refused to take sides on the issue. Pakistan also raised the Kashmir issue in meetings of other UN bodies and agencies including ECOSOC, UNESCO, ILO and UNDP.

The unanimous adoption of a resolution on terrorism as an obstacle to human righ at the 48th UNGA, co-sponsored by India, was another achievement of Indian diplomacy during the year. The resolution uequivocally condemned act, methods and practice of terrorism as activities aimed at the destruction of human rights and fundamental freedoms and democracy, threatening territorial integrity and security of States and destablishing legitimately constituted governments. It called upon all States to take effective measures and prevent, combat and eliminate terrorism. Pakistan's efforts to amend the resolution to exclude the struggle for self-determination from terrorism found no support in the Committee. Earlier, the Commission on Human Rights and the Sub-Commission on the Prevention of Discrimination and Protection of Minorities also adopted resolutions against Terrorism. The resolutions reflect growing awareness of terrorism as a violation of human rights.

India succeeded in shelving a proposal made by Liechtenstein for self-determination through autonomy because of its implications on multi-ethnic societies such as India.

India also played a prominent role in the negotiations on the mandate of the post of the High Commissioner for Human Rights and ensured that this mandate would not be intrusive, but would respect and the UN Charter and the sovereignty, territorial integrity and domestic jurisdiction of States.

India acceded to the Convention on the Rights of the Child and the Convention on Elimination of Discrimination against Women during 1993.

33.5 PER CAPITA INCOME OF STATES

	State	Per Capita Income (Rs.)
1.	Punjab	9643
2.	Haryana	8690
3.	Maharashtra	8180
4.	Gujarat	6425
5.	Andhra Pradesh	5570
6.	Karnataka	5555
7.	West Bengal	5383

(Contd.)

	Stale	Per Capita Income (Rs.)
8.	Himachal Pradesh	5355
9.	Tamil Nadu	5078
10.	Kerala	4618
11.	Rajashtan	4361
12.	Assam	4230
13.	Madhya Pradesh	4077
14.	Orissa	4068
15.	J.& K.	4051
16.	Uttar Pradesh	4012
17.	Bihar	2904

Source: Economic Times, January 5, 1994.

33.6 SPORTS

National Sports Policy : An Appraisal

The National Association of Physical Education & Sports Science, in collaboration with the Kortball Federation of India 1993 organised a one-day Seminar on "National Sports Policy – An Appraisal" in New Delhi. Shri M.C. Gupta, President, Korfball Federation of India and Member Secretary, Tenth Finance Commission, in his presidential address, suggested an innovative approach to produce more than a million sportsmen in India is different disciplines in the next few years. He also suggested that every middle/high school and college should be earmarked for one game or sport such as Football, Hockey, Cricket, Volleyball, Korfball etc., though having facilities for any other sports if possible. Even with just ten schools dedicated to one game in a district, and with only 25 reasonably good players in each school, every district would have 250 or more players of reasonable standard. With more than 400 districts in the country, each game could have more than one lakh players. Shri Gupta further emphasized that promotion of sports in India was not so much a question of arranging finances but of managing our affairs in the desired manner. Sustained and sincere efforts were required for sports promotion. Talking of constraint of resources, he pleaded for a larger role by voluntary and non-governmental organisations and utilization of sports funds raised in educational institutions.

Prof. Upendra Baxi, Vice-Chancellor, University of Delhi, in his inaugural address, stressed upon the need for inviting social and natural scientists in sports seminars so as to promote the application of social and natural science techniques for the promotion of Sports in India. He was of the opinion that separating the world of academics from the world of sports resulted in demoralization of sports participants. He called upon the Seminar to evolve a Citizen's Resolution on National Sports Policy.

Delivering the keynote address Shri M.M. Rajendran, Secretary, Parliamentary Affairs and former Secretary, Youth Affairs and Sports emphasized the need to broad-basing of sports, and broad-basing of human resources in the form of sports trainers and teachers. In his valedictory address

Shri Bhagwat, Secretary, Youth Affairs and Sports and Director General, Sports Authority of India, assured the participants that the recommendations and suggestions made at the seminar would be duly considered by the Government of India and Sports Authority of India.

Shri O.P. Bhatia, Executive Director, Sports Authority of India opined that an inter-disciplinary approach to talent scouting was called for. Dr.D.K. Kansal, Co-Chairman of the Seminar and Principal of Indira Gandhi Institute of Physical Education & Sports Sciences referred to the absence of prescribed textbooks of physical education for school children and non-existence for any degree course in sports coaching. He also stressed that in order to produce competent teachers there was a need to provide appropriate infrastructure facilities to all the institutions of physical education and sports sciences in the country.

After detailed deliberations the following recommendations were made:

(i) Middle/High schools should be earmarked for one premier game or sports to facilitate production of large base for selection of good teasm and to improve district level, state level and national level competitions;

(ii) There should be a provision of higher education and research in physical education in Indian universities;

(iii) The Department of Sports and Youth Affairs should provide encouragement to authors for producing books on physical education, sports and games;

(iv) There is a need to have uniform course material/syllabi for Bachelor's degree in Physical Education and Sports. The University Grants Commission or the Association of Indian Universities were called upon to take up this tasks;

(v) Guidelines may be formulated for quality control at the production centre of physical education teachers and sports coaches in the country;

(vi) A three year Bachelor Degree in coaching should be started in the Indian universities;

(vii) There is an immediate need to improve scientific criteria of sports talent search and training of selected sportsmen;

(viii) There is a need of effective testing of physical fitness of the students of physical education at the universities in India.

Over 100 deleglates from all over India participated in the seminar.

Source: University News, May 24, 1993.

34

SIGNIFICANT NATIONAL EVENTS

April

1 Left Front – J.D. Alliance sweeps Tripura Assembly Elections.
7 Reserve Bank of India liberalises credit policy.
8 C.B.I. raids V.H.P', R.S.S., Shiv Sena and Bajrang Dal offices in four States of Himachal Pradesh, Madhya Pradesh, Rajasthan and U.P. and Union Territory Delhi (New State).
13 The Union Government challenges Madhya Pradesh High Court's judgment on B.J.P. Government, in the Supreme Court. The High Court had quashed the Presidental Order of December 15, 1992 imposing the Central rule in Madhya Pradesh after Ayodhya episode of December 6, 1992.
16 Supreme Court of India stays judgment of Madhya Pradesh High Court on the B.J.P. government.
18 B.J.P releases whitepaper on Ayodhya.
19 I.A. Boeing crash near Aurangabad kills 55.
Government hikes telecom rates.

May

4 The Finance Minister Manmohan Singh raises the exemption limit for the personal income tax payers from Rs. 28,000 to Rs. 30,000.
11 Three Indian women namely Santosh Yadaw, Konga Bhutia and Dicky Dolma Climb the World's highest summit, Everest.
The first Impeachment Motion in the Parliament since its inception, against justice V. Ramaswami falls through – 196 opposition MPs voting in favour of removing justice Ramaswami on grounds of misbehaviour and 205 MPs mainly from the Congress abstaining from voting. No vote against the motion.
15 Field Marshal K.M. Carriapa, the first Indian Commander-in-chief of free India passes away at the age of 94.
16 Four Indian women, Radha Devi, Dipoo Sharma, Suman Katiyal and Savita Matoliya scale mount Everest.

June

4 The Supreme Court strikes down ban on Bajrang Dal and R.S.S. but

confirms in the case of V.H.P. These organisations were banned by the government after the demolition of Babri Masjid structure in Ayodhya on December 6, 1992.

July

9 The Union Commerce Ministry Pranab Mukherjee resigns following his failure to fulfil the Constitutional obligation of securaing election to either House of Parliament within six months of his induction into the Cabinet.

28 The Central Government headed by Prime Minister P.V. Narasimharao survives the no-confidence motion by a margin of 14 votes.

August

2 The Election Commissioner (EC) postponed all bye-election to the Lok Sabha and State Assemblies as well as the biennial election to the Rajya Sabha and State Legislative Councils on account of the tussle between the EC and the Government over the powers and justification of E C.

September

1 Government revises interest rates on certain small savings accounts and instruments.

3 Cabinet approves the proposal to permit the nationalised banks to raise equity capital from the market.

October

6 Hundred per cent tax relief for donations to Chief Minister's Earthquake Relief Fund, Maharashtra.

15 Government of India lifts ban on trade with South Africa.

November

4 Government releases the status report on India's external debt.

21 The Joint Parliamentary Committee on Scam releases its report and indicts a few ministers and officials.

December

24 Finance Minister Manmohan Singh submits his resignation to the Prime Minister soon after the release of the Joint Parliamentary Committee's report on December 21.

31 Prime Minister rejects the resignation of the Finance Minister.

January

2 Noted music director Rahual Dev Burman (R.D. Burman), composer of over 400 songs for Hindi films passed away following a massive heart attack at the age of 54.

9 Sri Chandrasekharendra Saraswathi, the 100 year old Paramacharya of Kanchi passed away.

16 National games start at Shiva Chhatrapati Stadium, Pune.

27 Increase in retail price of sugar for supply through the Public Distribution System by 75 paisa per kg (from Rs. 8.30 per kg. to Rs. 9.05 per kg.

30 Kapil Dev equalls Sir Richard Hadlee's 431 wicket record, at Bangalore stadium in a Test Match against Sri Lanka.

February

1 Increase in price of wheat and rice by 21 to 23 per cent.

2 Petrol and Diesal prices up by Re.1 and .75 paise per litre respectively.

5 11th World Book Fair opens at Pragati Maidan, New Delhi.

8 Kapil Dev sets world record of 432 wickets in Test cricket by taking one wicket in the final test against Sri Lanka at Ahmedabad.

14 Shri V.P. Singh is elected J.D. President.

18 Gujarat Chief Minister Chiman Bhai Patel dies of heart attack at Ahmedabad.

24 Railway Minister C.K. Jaffer Sharief presents railway budget for 1994-95 Hike in railway fares and freight.

28 Finance Minister Manmohan Singh presents the 1994-1955 budget.

March

1 Strike by newspapers employees and Delhities miss their papers; this was the first occasion in the history of the country that the Delhities missed budget specials.

11 The Supreme Court upholds the dismissal of the BJP government in Madhya Pradesh, Rajasthan and Himachal Pradesh in the wake of the Ayodhya incidents of December 6, 1992.

12 R.S.S. chief Balasaheb Deoras nominates Prof. Rajendra Singh, as his successor (Sanghchalak).

18 Supreme Court quashes governments order of December 10, 1992, declaring the Jamate-e-Islami Hindi (JEIH), as an unlawful association.

30 Opposition stages walk out in the Lok Sabha over GATT pact.

Government announces changes in Exam Policy.

Parent's Forum moves Delhi High Court on the difficult class XII Maths Paper of the C.B.S.E, Delhi.

CICIL LIST

CONCEPTS IN COMMUNICATION, INFORMATICS & LIBRARIANSHIP

(CICIL)

General Editor: **S.P. AGRAWAL**

CICIL-1 Development of Library Services in India: Social Science Information/**S.P. Agrawal** Rs. 150

CICIL-2 Development of Documentation in India: Social Science Information/**S.P. Agrawal** Rs. 250

CICIL-3 UNESCO and Social Sciences: Retrospect and Prospect/**S.P. Agrawal** and **J.C. Aggarwal** Rs. 250

CICIL-4 INDIANA : A Bibliography of Bibliographical Sources/**M.K. Jain** Rs. 200

CICIL-5 Dimensions of Library and Information Science: Kaula Festschrift/**V. Venkatappaiah** (Eds.) Rs. 600

CICIL-6 Book Numbers: Some Indian Methods/**M.P. Satija** and **S.P. Agrawal** Rs. 100

CICIL-7 National Policy for University Libraries in India: Problems and Perspectives /**N.B. Inamdar** and **L.S. Ramaiah** (Ed.) Rs. 250

CICIL-8 Media Utilisation for the Development of Women and Children/**B.S. Thakur** and **Binod C. Agrawal** Rs. 150

CICIL-9 Terrorism: An Annotated Bibliography/**Susheela Bhan** (Ed.) Rs. 275

CICIL-10 Transnational Library Relations: The Indo-American Experience/**M.B. Konnur** Rs. 175

CICIL-11 Geography of Marketing and Commercial Activities in India (Documentation on Research Information)/**R.S. Dixit** Rs. 130

CICIL-12 Information India 1988: Global View/**S.P. Agrawal** and **J.C. Aggarwal** Rs. 200

CICIL-13 Women's Education in India: Historical Review, Present Status and Perspective Plan/**S.P. Agrawal** and **J.C. Aggarwal** Rs. 360

CICIL-14 Cultural Communication in India: Role and Impact of Phonograms/**J.M. Ojha** Rs. 220

CICIL-15 Second Historical Survey of Educational Development in India: Select Documents 1985-1989/**S.P. Agrawal** and **J.C. Aggarwal** Rs. 490

CICIL-16 Documentation Encyclopaedia of UNESCO and Education/**J.C. Aggarwal** and **S.P. Agrawal** Rs. 800 (set of 2 parts)

CICIL-17 Attitude Towards Information: A Study of Post-Graduate Teachers and Researchers in Social Sciences/**N.G. Satish** (in press)

CICIL-18 Librarianship and Bureaucratic Organisation: A Study in the Sociology of Library Profession in India/**P.K. Jayaswal** Rs. 175

CICIL-19 Literature Search/**K.A. Isaac** Rs. 150

CICIL-20 Child Education in India: Index to Scholarly Writings in Indian Educational Journals and Newspapers since independence/**S.P. Agrawal** and **Naresh Kanta** Rs. 100

CICIL-21 Lok Sabha and Vidhan Sabha Elections in India 1989 & 1990: Process and Results with Comparative Study of Manifestos/**S.P. Agrawal** and **J.C. Aggarwal** Rs. 250

CICIL-22 Islamic Studies in India: A Survey of Human, Institutional and Documentary Sources/**Mohamed Taher** Rs. 180

CICIL-23 Panchayati Raj: An Annotated Bibliography/**N.B. Inamdar, N.G. Satish** and **Anil Takalkar** 290

CICIL-24 Information India 1989-90: Global View/**S.P. Agrawal** and **J.C. Aggarwal** Rs. 500

CICIL-25 First Handbook of Psychological and Social Instruments/**Udai Pareek** and **T. Venkateswara Rao** Rs. 500

CICIL-26 Educational and Social Uplift of Backward Classes: At What Cost and How? Mandal Commission and After/**S.P. Agrawal** and **J.C. Aggarwal** Rs. 275

CICIL-27 Mass Media and New Horizons: Impact of TV & Video an Urban Milieu/**H.R. Trivedi** Rs. 180

CICIL-28 Indian Writings on Education : An Indicator to Indian Educational Journals Grouped by Subject Deseriptors 1979 to 1986 (in two parts) **S.P. Agarwal** Rs. 900 (per set)

CICIL-29 Nation in Crisis/**S.P. Agrawal** and **J.C. Aggarwal** Rs. 200

CICIL-30 Information India 1990-91: Global View/**S.P. Agrawal** and **J.C. Aggarwal** Rs. 500

CICIL-31 Development of University Libraries in India after Independence/**O.P. Gupta** Rs. 270

CICIL-32 Handbook on Child : With Historical Background/**Pramila Pandit Barooah** Rs. 320

CICIL-33 Weaker Section in Indian Society : Undiscovered Past, Uncertain Present and Unpredictable Future : Index to Writings in Indian Scholarly Journals and 10 National Newspapers Classified under 1500 Descriptors 1886-1990/**S.P. Agrawal** and **Rajeev Kumar Sharma** Rs. 600

CICIL-34 Communication Informatics and Librarianship in India : An Introductory Guide to Publications Based on a Survey of Libraries in Capital City of India/**S.P. Agrawal** and **Pushpa Rani Sharma** Rs. 720

CICIL-35 Problems of Collection Development in Special Libraries/**M.S. Sridhar** Rs. 225

CICIL-36 National Information Resources for Social Sciences in India : Mobilisation, Dispersal and International Enhancement/**S.P. Agrawal** Rs. 225

CICIL-37 Modern History of Punjab : A Look Back into Ancient Peaceful Punjab Focusing Confrontation and Failures Leading to Present Punjab Problem, and a Peep Ahead : Relevant Select Documents/**J.C. Aggarwal** and **S.P. Agrawal** Rs. 400

CICIL-38 India Information Sources : Economics and Business/**Kyllikki Ruokonen** and **Manohar Lal** Rs.

CICIL-39 Educational Planning in India : With a Slant to Educational Financing and Administration, Vol. 1, Reports of Committees and Commissions, Five Year Plans, Statistical Tables/**J.C. Aggarwal** and **S.P. Agrawal** Rs. 650

CICIL-40 Integrated Library System : Two Case Studies : Latin America and India **Maria Luiza Rigo Pasquarelli, Rosaly Favero Krzyanowski, Ines Maria M. Imperatriz** and **S.P. Agrawal** Rs. 160

CICIL-41 Social Science Information in India: Effort towards Bibliographical Control/**S.D. Vyas** Rs. 300

CICIL-42 Higher Education in India Since Independence: U.G.C. and Its Approach **O.P. Gupta** Rs. 360

CICIL-43 Government and Politics in India: A Bibliographical Study of Contemporary Scenario Chronicling Rajiv Gandhi Era/**S.P. Agrawal** and **Rajeev Kumar Sharma** Rs. 500

CICIL-44 Second Handbook of Psychological and Social Instruments/**D.M. Pestonjee** Rs. 300

CICIL-45 Development/Digression Diary of India; 3D Companion Volume to Information India: 1990-91/**S.P. Agrawal** Rs. 200

CICIL-46 Development/Digression Diary of India; 3D Companion Volume to Information India: 1991-92/**S.P. Agrawal** Rs. 300

CICIL-47 Information India 1991-92: Global View/**S.P. Agrawal** and **J.C. Aggarwal** Rs. 500

CICIL-48 Committees and Commissions in India 1974, A Concept's Project, Compiled by a team of professionals guided/ **Virender Kumar** (Vol. 12) Rs. 450

CICIL-49 Committees and Commissions in India 1975, A Concept's Project, Compiled by a team of professionals guided/**Virender Kumar** (Vol. 13) Rs. 450

CICIL-50 Committees and Commissions in India 1976, A Concept's Project, Compiled by a team of professionals guided/**Virender Kumar** (Vol. 14) Rs. 450

CICIL-51 Committees and Commissions in India 1977, A Concept's Project, Compiled by a team of professionals guided/**Virender Kumar** (Vol. 15) (in four parts) Rs. 450 each

CICIL-52 Committees and Commissions in India 1978, A Concept's Project, Compiled by a team of professionals guided/**Virender Kumar** (Vol. 16) (in two parts) Rs. 450 each

CICIL-53 Subject Guide to Communication, Informatics and Librarianship in India (Based on a Survey of Library Holdings in Capital City of India)/**S.P. Agrawal** and **Pushpa Rani Sharma** Rs. 400

CICIL-54 Restructurring of Library and Information Science Curriculum/**A. Tejomurty** Rs. 250

CICIL-55 Committees and Commissions in India 1979, A Concept's Project, Compiled by a team of professionals guided/**Virender Kumar** (Vol. 17) (in two parts) Rs. 450 each

CICIL-56 Committees and Commissions in India 1980, A Concept's Project, Compiled by a team of professionals guided /**Virender Kumar** (Vol. 18) (in two parts) Rs. 450 each

CICIL-57 Third Historical Survey of Educational Development in India/**S.P. Agrawal** and **J.C. Aggarwal** Rs. 700

CICIL-58 Model Library Legislation/**Velaga Venkatappaiah** Rs. 400

CICIL-59 Indian Library and Information Science Literature (1990-91)/**Sewa Singh** Rs. 525

CICIL-60 Librarianship and Library Science in India/**Mohamed Taher** and **Donald Gordon Davis, Jr.** Rs. 350

CICIL-61 Comprehensive Glossary for Library & Information Science/**O.P. Gupta** Rs.300

CICIL-62 Information India 1992-93:/**S.P. Agrawal** and **J. C. Aggarwal** Rs. 500

CICIL-63 Automation of Libraries and Information Science/**R.K. Shukla** Rs. 250

CICIL-64 Modern History of Jammu and Kashmir **J.C. Aggarwal** and **S.P. Agrawal** Rs. 1500 (per set of 2 vols.)

CICIL-65 Library and Information Science: Emerging Trends:/**Sister M. Esperanza,** A. C. Rs. 250

CICIL-66 Mental Retardation in India (A Bibliography)/**S. Venkatesan** and **V.G.D. Vepuri** Rs. 275

CICIL-67 Information India 1993-94: Global View/**S.P. Agrawal** and **J.C. Aggarwal** Rs. 500

CICIL-68 Information Behaviour of Scientists and Engineers:/**M.S. Sridhar** Rs. 500

CICIL-69 Uttarakhand: Past, Present and Future/**J.C. Aggarwal** and **S.P. Agrawal** Rs. 750

CICIL-70 National Information System in Education: A Comparative Study/**S. L. Verma** Rs. 650

CICIL-71 Not Published by us.

CICIL-72 Not Published by us.

CICIL-73 Second Historical Survey of Women's Education in India/**S.P. Agrawal** and **J.C. Aggarwal** Rs. 600

CICIL-74 Library and Information Science: Parameters and Perspectives/**R.G. Prasher** (Ed.) 2 Vols. Set Rs. 1500

CICIL-75 Third Handbook of Psychological and Social Instruments/**D.M. Pestonjee** (in two volumes) Rs. 1100 per set

CICIL-76 Information India: Global Views 1994-95 & 1995-96/**S.P. Agrawal** and **J.C. Aggarwal** Rs. 500